REMEMBERING THE RENAISSANCE

BRILL'S STUDIES IN INTELLECTUAL HISTORY

General Editor

A.J. VANDERJAGT, University of Groningen

Editorial Board
M. COLISH, Oberlin College
J.I. ISRAEL, University College, London
J.D. NORTH, University of Groningen
H.A. OBERMAN, University of Arizona, Tucson
R.H. POPKIN, Washington University, St. Louis-UCLA

VOLUME 85

REMEMBERING THE RENAISSANCE

Humanist Narratives of the Sack of Rome

BY

KENNETH GOUWENS

BRILL

LEIDEN · BOSTON · KÖLN

1998

This book is printed on acid-free paper.

Library of Congress Cataloging-in-Publication Data

Gouwens, Kenneth.
    Remembering the Renaissance : humanist narratives of the sack of
Rome / by Kenneth Gouwens.
        p. cm. — (Brill's studies in intellectual history ; v. 85)
    Includes bibliographical references and indexes.
    ISBN 9004109692 (cloth : alk paper)
    1. Rome (Italy)—History—Siege, 1527. 2. Humanists—Italy—Rome.
3. Humanism in literature. 4. Papacy—History—1447-1565.
5. Renaissance—Italy—Rome.   I. Title.   II. Series.
DG812.12.G68 1998
945'.63207—dc21
                                                  98-2822
                                                   CIP

Die Deutsche Bibliothek - CIP-Einheitsaufnahme

Gouwens, Kenneth:
Remembering the Renaissance : humanist narratives of the sack of
Rome / by Kenneth Gouwens. – Leiden ; Boston : Köln : Brill, 1998
   (Brill's studies in intellectual history ; Vol. 85)
   ISBN 90–04–10969–2

ISSN 0920-8607
ISBN 90 04 10969 2

PRINTED IN THE NETHERLANDS

For Lewis Spitz and Ronald Witt

CONTENTS

ACKNOWLEDGMENTS

In the course of researching and writing this book, I have received generous financial support, including a Paleography Institute Fellowship from the Center for Reformation Research in St. Louis (1986), an Italian Government Fulbright Fellowship (1987-88), Harris and Weter Fellowships from the Department of History at Stanford University (1987, 1989), a travel grant from Stanford's Institute for International Studies (1990), a graduate scholarship from the Northern California chapter of Phi Beta Kappa (1990), and a Short-Term Fellowship from the Newberry Library (1993). From the University of South Carolina I have received three Research and Productive Scholarship Grants (1992, 1994, 1996) that enabled me to return to Italy briefly at critical junctures. A Southern Regional Education Board Travel Grant (1992) helped to finance the first of those trips, and a grant from the American Philosophical Society (1994) enabled me to remain in Rome long enough to complete the transcriptions that appear in the appendices to this volume. I am grateful as well for stipends to attend an NEH Institute, "Culture in Crisis: Italy, 1494-1527," led by Albert Ascoli (1993); an NEH/Folger weekend seminar on "Shakespeare and the Arts of Memory," led by Stephen Greenblatt (1994); and a Folger Institute Spring seminar on "Encounters with Antiquity," led by Donald Kelley (1995). I also wish to thank the personnel of the archives and libraries in which I have researched this volume, especially Leonard Boyle, the prefect-emeritus of the Vatican Library, whose efficiency, patience, and generosity helped to make that marvelous institution welcoming to junior scholars.

Portions of Chapters Two and Five appeared in earlier versions in *Renaissance Quarterly* and in *The Sixteenth Century Journal.* I am grateful to the editors of those journals for permission to include material from the articles in this text. I also wish to thank the Vatican Library for granting me permission to include two plates of pages from BAV MS Vat. Lat. 3436.

While the task of writing tends to be a solitary enterprise, I am deeply indebted to the many scholars whose advice and insights have helped to shape my thinking about the culture of Renaissance Rome.

Among these I should mention Albert Ascoli, Amittai Aviram, Paula
Findlen, Katherine Gill, Katherine Hoffman, Frances Jamerson,
John Martin, Thomas Mayer, Maureen Miller, Nelson Minnich,
Lawrence Rhu, Ingrid Rowland, and Barbara Watts. Four outstand-
ing Latinists, Anthony D'Elia, Gregory Guderian, Brian Roots, and
Jan Ziolkowski, offered many helpful suggestions as I set about revis-
ing my transcriptions and translations.

Melissa Meriam Bullard, Thomas V. Cohen, Julia Haig Gaisser,
John Najemy, and Randolph Starn read and critiqued chapters at
various stages of revision. John Headley, Sheryl Reiss, Anne Reynolds, Diana Robin, Charles Stinger, Ronald Witt, and Price Zimmermann all read intermediate drafts of the entire manuscript and
offered invaluable criticisms and suggestions. Paul Grendler gave a
meticulous reading to the penultimate draft, and his recommenda-
tions have made the book both more precise and less arcane. I am
grateful to my editor, Theo Joppe, for his enthusiasm and efficiency.
The responsibility for the remaining errors is, of course, my own.

I am indebted to four family members who have profoundly
shaped my thinking and values. My maternal grandfather, John
Robert Moore, set an example of scholarly dedication and of the
pleasures of the life of the mind that has remained an inspiration to
me. My parents, Robert and Joyce Gouwens, nurtured my interest in
history and supported my career decisions despite their seeming im-
practicality. My wife, Joan Meznar, has been wonderfully supportive
and encouraging. She read drafts of all the chapters, urged the timely
completion and submission of the manuscript, and tolerated grace-
fully her husband's tendency to disrupt circadian rhythms when fin-
ishing sections of the manuscript.

I am grateful, finally, to my teachers. Judith Brown, whose courses
introduced me to the questions and methods of social history, directed the dissertation and encouraged creative approaches to my
chosen subject. Teachers in Stanford's Graduate Program in Humanities, including Martin Esslin, Alban Forcione, John Freccero,
and Lawrence Ryan, helped me to appreciate the importance of
grounding innovative literary theories in an understanding of sources
and contexts. John D'Amico, who spent the 1985-86 year at the
Stanford Humanities Center, introduced me to the catalogues of the
Vatican Library just weeks before his death in the autumn of 1987.
Beyond the substantial contributions of his scholarship, he added
immeasurably to my thinking about Renaissance Rome through our

conversations, and he helped to affirm my belief in the continuing vitality of intellectual history even as that field was temporarily out of favor in American universities. Reginald Foster provided the advanced training in Latin without which this book could not have been researched. Shortly after arriving in Rome in 1987, with linguistic skills insufficient to the task before me, I asked him for permission to take part in his classes at the Gregoriana. He nodded and smiled indulgently as one who had heard it all before. All those who have been so fortunate as to study with Reginald know well both the rigor of his methods and the selflessness with which he devotes himself to his students.

While a freshman at Duke University, I took a survey course taught by Ronald G. Witt that introduced me not just to intellectual and cultural history, but also to the skills of close reading of documents and of building scholarly arguments. At Stanford, I worked initially under the direction of Lewis W. Spitz, whose graduate colloquia on Renaissance Humanism and the Reformation provided an erudite, expansive, and congenial initiation into the profession that I hoped to enter. In their teaching and scholarship, Professors Witt and Spitz have illuminated and demonstrated how humanistic study can be a pursuit infused with moral purpose, addressing issues of meaning that, for all their historical specificity, continue to have profound significance and repercussions in our own time. They both set a remarkably high standard of dedication and generosity to their students. With gratitude and with great pleasure, I dedicate this book to them.

KG
Villa I Tatti, Florence
October, 1997

ABBREVIATIONS

ASV	=	Archivio Segreto Vaticano, Vatican City
BAV	=	Biblioteca Apostolica Vaticana, Vatican City
Cors.	=	Biblioteca Corsiniana, Rome
CWE	=	*The Collected Works of Erasmus.* Ed. Peter G. Bietenholz et al. Toronto and Buffalo: University of Toronto Press, 1974
DBI	=	*Dizionario biografico degli Italiani*
EE	=	Desiderius Erasmus, *Opus Epistolarum Des. Erasmi Roterodami* ed. P. S. Allen (Oxford: Oxford University Press, 1906-58)
Epistolae	=	Jacopo Sadoleto, *Epistolae quotquot extant proprio nomine scriptae nunc primum duplo auctiores in lucem editae,* ed. Vincenzo Costanzi. 5 vols. (Rome, 1760-67)
Hoff.	=	Pietro Alcionio, "Oratio habita in Senatu Romano praelectis literis a Carolo V. post Urbis direptionem scriptis" [i.e., "Declamatio in literas Caesaris"], in Christophus Godofredus Hoffmannus, *Nova Scriptorum ac Monumentorum Partim Rarissimorum, Partim Ineditorum Collectio . . .* (Leipzig, 1731), I: 550-88
Isol.	=	Archivio Isolani, Bologna
Iter	=	Kristeller, Paul Oskar, *Iter Italicum: A Finding List of Uncatalogued or Incompletely Catalogued Humanistic Manuscripts of the Renaissance in Italian and Other Libraries.* 6 vols. to date. Leiden, 1963
LP	=	*Lettere di Principi,* 1 (Venice, 1570)
LP 2	=	*Lettere di Principi,* 2 (Venice, 1581)
Ricc.	=	Biblioteca Riccardiana, Florence
Valeriano, *DLI*	=	Pierio Valeriano, *Joannis Pierii Valeriani ... De litteratorum infelicitate, libri duo* (Venice, 1[6]20)

Valeriano,
PSB   =   Pierio   Valeriano,   *Pro   sacerdotum
                  barbis* (Rome, 1531)

A NOTE ON THE TRANSCRIPTIONS AND TRANSLATIONS

This volume includes numerous transcriptions from manuscripts, including some from unfinished drafts. It employs the following conventions:

1. Pointed brackets enclose editorial conjectures.

2. Square brackets enclose superfluous material in the text.

3. Punctuation and capitalization have been standardized.

4 The following orthographical conventions are employed:
   a. The usage of the letters "u" and "v" has been standardized in accordance with modern practice.
   b. The letter "j" has been modified to "i" in accordance with modern practice.
   c. Diphthongs are represented as two letters.
   d. In all other respects, the orthography of the documents has been left intact. Variants that appear frequently in Alcionio's orations include, for example, *tera* (for *terra*), *omneis* (for *omnes*), *literae* (for *litterae*), *imo* (for *immo*), *caussa* (for *causa*), and on occasion *Barbonius* (as a disparaging pun on *Borbonius*).

5. Footnotes in the appendices have been kept to a minimum.
Editorial conjectures that are unexceptional (e.g., supplying letters that are missing because of damage to the paper) appear in pointed brackets without further annotation. Abbreviations, where their sense is clear, have been expanded without brackets or annotation. Notes are used when the text is either illegible or grammatically misleading, or where a word has been supplied that cannot be established with certainty as the correct reading. In addition, they are used to indicate possible allusions to classical sources, as well as to present marginalia that the author did not integrate into the text.

6. Where the readings differ in minor ways from those in my earlier articles, the present readings should be taken as superseding the older ones.

7. All ordinal numbers have been spelled out, as have cardinal numbers under ten, except in the page numbering and in the dates.

Unless otherwise indicated, all translations are my own.

PRELUDE: 6 MAY 1527

Around four in the morning on 6 May 1527, an Imperial army under the command of Charles of Bourbon began its attack on the city
of Rome.[1] His armor draped in a white coat for visibility, Bourbon
circulated among his men—mostly Spanish and German Imperial
troops, augmented with some French and Italian soldiers—urging
them onward. At first they directed their attack against the city walls
that enclosed the Vatican and Borgo districts on the west side of the
Tiber River, concentrating their efforts upon a low point in the south
wall near the Porta San Spirito. The defenders repelled the initial
assaults, but within an hour an unusually dense fog rolled in, rendering useless the cannons of the nearby papal fortress, the Castel Sant'
Angelo. Early in the fighting, an arquebus shot mortally wounded
the Duke of Bourbon as he was urging his men to scale the walls at
the Porta Torrione. But his troops persevered, and around six a.m.
they breached the defenses in three places just as the fog—which
many would later interpret as divinely sent—began to lift.

There followed an immediate breakdown of discipline among the
defenders. Most sought to flee either by bridge or by boat across the
Tiber to the intact center of the city. Renzo da Ceri, the commander
who had been responsible for organizing the Romans' defense, responded to the incursion with mingled bewilderment and terror, and
he himself ultimately fled into the papal fortress. When Pope Clement VII, at prayer in his private chapel in the Vatican, heard the
commotion of the approaching troops, he and several others—including the humanist Paolo Giovio and the Cardinal Alessandro Farnese (the future Pope Paul III)—fled along the Alexandrine corridor
to the Castel Sant' Angelo. From its confines, crowded with around a
thousand refugees, the pontiff could look out upon the destruction
below, helpless to halt it.

Next, the Imperialists set upon Trastevere, the district lying to the
south of the Vatican on the west side of the Tiber. Soon they broke

---

[1] The brief summary in this preface draws primarily upon the account in Pastor's
History of the Popes, vol. 9, modified by observations in Hook's *The Sack of Rome, 1527*,
and by the addition of details from primary sources cited in subsequent chapters of
the present study.

through the defenses at the Porta Settimiana and continued their conquest. That evening they made their way across the Ponte Sisto and into the central districts of Rome, shouting triumphantly as they went. The disoriented populace offered little resistance, and by the following morning, with the exception of the Castel Sant' Angelo and a handful of private palaces, all Rome had fallen to the Imperialists.

Thereafter, the plight of the Romans only became more desperate. The death of Bourbon had left the contingents of the Imperial army without a common commander who could put a stop to the sacking of the city. If out of righteous zeal German Lutheran troops desecrated relics, Spanish Catholic soldiers proved no less eager to strip precious metals and stones from the statues and tombs of saints and of popes. Even the German and Spanish churches in Rome did not escape the plundering. Often Romans were captured, tortured, and ransomed by one contingent of soldiers only to endure similar treatment from another. Those who lacked the resources to pay at once might be killed on the spot, or else enslaved until a ransom could be extorted from their relatives.

Eyewitnesses expressed shock particularly at the barbaric treatment of members of the clergy. The humanist Pietro Alcionio, who watched the initial weeks of carnage from the Castel Sant' Angelo, wrote that "we have seen practiced upon priests tortures from which a victorious Carthaginian or Turk indisputably would have abstained." Neither age nor sex nor political affiliation conferred immunity from abuse. Thus the pro-Imperial Cardinal Piccolomini, who had imagined himself safe because of his friendship with the emperor, was dragged through the streets amidst kicks and blows. The Archbishop of Corfù, Cristoforo Marcello, fared less well: when he could not pay the exorbitant ransom demanded of him, his captors tortured him to death for their amusement. Small wonder, then, that an eyewitness to Rome's destruction could conclude that this was the worst sacking of a city ever, a sight uglier even than hell itself.[2]

---

[2] Petrus de Franciscis, cited in Marino Sanuto, *I diarii di Marino Sanuto*, vol. 45 (Venice, 1896), 219: "Il sacco è stato de quelli che mai più se dice esserne stato uno simile, nè quello di Genoa è da comparar ad una minima parte di questo. ... Tutta questa città è in tanta tribulatione che veramente vostra magnificentia pò considerar, che per universal dicto, l'inferno è più bella cosa da veder." The letter is dated from Rome, 10 May 1527.

Beyond the cruelties and depredations that the Romans endured at the hands of their captors, they soon suffered a visitation of the plague, which began in mid-May and spread rapidly. A heat wave and a drought ensued, exacerbating the food shortage, and those surviving in the city resorted to eating draft-animals or whatever vermin they could trap. With the exception of mid-summer, when they withdrew to the nearby hill-towns, most of the imperial troops occupied Rome until the following February, living off the carcass of the city. Although Clement VII capitulated on 5 June, he remained in the papal fortress for six more months, under direct Imperial guard. Only on 7 December, aided by the pro-Imperial Cardinal Pompeo Colonna—his longtime rival, but nonetheless the person best positioned to assist him—did the pontiff escape from the Eternal City, to which he would not return until the next autumn.

The Sack of Rome resulted most immediately from the pope's decision the previous year to break an alliance with the Holy Roman Emperor Charles V in favor of joining in the pro-French League of Cognac: an act of disloyalty that had spurred the emperor to send Bourbon and his men toward Rome. The event served as the *coup de grâce* for Clement VII's foreign policy, which had taken as its chief aim preventing either Spain or France from gaining dominance over the Italian peninsula. But beyond its political significance, the Sack raised troubling questions about Rome's cultural role. Previously, Roman humanists acting as papal spokesmen had constructed a discourse dignifying Renaissance Rome, which they described as the rightful heir both of papal prerogatives and of the *imperium* of classical Rome. In that discourse, the humanists lauded the city as the cultural exemplar of Europe and heralded a new golden age that the papacy would initiate. The Sack, however, compelled them to rewrite this narrative to take into account the city's destruction and to accommodate its diminished possibilities. What now could they write about the future of the papacy? In the aftermath of catastrophe, how would they reconceive the cultural significance of Renaissance Rome?

CHAPTER ONE

THE SACK OF ROME AND THE THEME OF CULTURAL DISCONTINUITY

i. *Introduction*

The Sack of Rome had unmatched significance for contemporaries, and it triggered momentous cultural and intellectual transformations. It stands apart from the many other brutal conquests of the time, such as the sack of Prato fifteen years earlier, because Rome held a place of special prominence in the Renaissance imagination.[1] This prominence was owed in part to the city's geographical position on the ruins of the ancient city of Rome, which provided an ever-present visual reminder of its classical role as *caput mundi*.[2] Just as important for contemporary observers, it stood at the center of Western Christendom: a position to which it had been restored in 1443, when Pope Eugenius IV returned the papacy to the Eternal City.[3] In the ensuing decades, the Renaissance popes strove to rebuild the physical city and to enhance both the theoretical claim of the papacy to universal *imperium* and its actual political and ecclesiastical sway, which the recent schism had eroded.

Modern historians, who have tended to confirm contemporaries' assessment of Rome's centrality in Renaissance European culture, have similarly viewed the events of 1527 as marking a critical turning point. The nineteenth-century German scholar Ferdinand Gregorovius chose the Imperial conquest of 1527 as the *terminus ad quem* for his monumental eight-volume history of Rome in the Middle Ages,

---

[1] Eric Cochrane, *Italy, 1530-1630* (London and New York, 1988), 9-10, also draws attention to this contrast.

[2] On Renaissance Roman antiquarianism and archaeology, see the sources cited in Philip Jacks, *The Antiquarian and the Myth of Antiquity: The Origins of Rome in Renaissance Thought* (Cambridge, 1993); and *idem*, "The *Simulachrum* of Fabio Calvo: A View of Roman Architecture *all'antica* in 1527," *Art Bulletin* 72 (1990): 453-81.

[3] Charles L. Stinger, *The Renaissance in Rome* (Bloomington, 1985), 5-6, chose this date, rather than Martin V's return to Rome in 1420, as the beginning of the Roman Renaissance. Not until 1443, Stinger argued, did Roman humanism begin to develop a distinct identity centered on the theme of the *instauratio Ecclesiae Romanae*.

claiming that in this year the decadent "feminine" [sic] culture of the papal court finally collapsed from exhaustion and was forced to begin serious reform.[4] More tellingly, in his classic *History of the Popes*, Ludwig von Pastor detailed the scholarly and artistic diaspora that the Sack caused. While offering a more sanguine assessment of Roman culture before 1527 than had Gregorovius, he too concluded that the Sack "marked, in fact, the end of the Renaissance, the end of the Rome of Julius II and Leo X."[5] Subsequent scholarship on Julian and Leonine Rome has only reinforced the assumption that the decades before 1527 merit special attention.

The persistence of "High Renaissance" Rome in the collective memory attests not just to the indisputable splendor of its cultural production, but also to the success of the papacy's own efforts at self-promotion. In particular, curial humanists—professional rhetoricians whom the papal court employed—systematically dignified and magnified the papal image with their literary praises. Using the idioms of Ciceronian and Vergilian Latin, these humanists constructed a shared narrative that emphasized the papacy's role as heir both to the classical *imperium* of ancient Rome and to the Church's ecclesiastical prerogatives and history.[6] In so doing, they helped to invent the construct of Renaissance Rome as the cultural exemplar of Europe, a construct so vivid that it has captured the imaginations of nearly all subsequent generations.

Although elements of this narrative appeared in Roman humanists' discourse as early as the 1440s, they did not fully articulate it until the early sixteenth century. The cornucopian patronage of cardinals and of several popes—most notably Alexander VI (1492-1503), Julius II (1503-13) and Leo X (1513-21)—brought to Rome leading artists, musicians, and intellectuals from throughout Italy and Europe.[7] For example, at various points in those three decades, Ra-

---

[4] Ferdinand Gregorovius, *History of the City of Rome in the Middle Ages*, trans. Annie Hamilton, vol. 8, pt. 2 (London, 1902). For Gregorovius' profoundly unsympathetic view of pre-1527 Renaissance Roman culture, see vol. 8, pt. 1, chap. 4.

[5] Ludwig von Pastor, *The History of the Popes from the Close of the Middle Ages*, trans. Ralph Francis Kerr, vol. 10, third ed. (London, 1923), 332-63; 442-47. Quotation from 443.

[6] John F. D'Amico, *Renaissance Humanism in Papal Rome: Humanists and Churchmen on the Eve of the Reformation* (Baltimore, 1983), chap. 5 (115-43), provides the best treatment of Ciceronianism in Renaissance Rome.

[7] On the development of Roman humanism under Julius II and Leo X, see, *inter alia*, the above studies by D'Amico and Stinger; John W. O'Malley, *Praise and Blame in Renaissance Rome: Rhetoric, Doctrine, and Reform in the Sacred Orators of the Papal Court,*

phael, Michelangelo, Josquin des Prez, and the Latin scholars Pietro
Bembo and Jacopo Sadoleto all worked in Rome and took part in
shaping its culture. In these and other capable hands, the claims for
the papacy became extravagant: humanists praised Pope Julius II, for
example, with comparisons not only to his uncle Pope Sixtus IV, but
also to Moses, Julius Caesar, and Jesus Christ. In a similar fashion
they dignified Renaissance Rome itself with classical and Christian
parallels and described it as the center of contemporary culture.
Through its political leadership and cultural patronage, the humanists claimed, the papacy would soon initiate a new golden age.[8]

While this official narrative may sound contrived, humanists an-
chored it firmly in their convictions about the role of Renaissance
Rome in Christian history, convictions reinforced by the Christian
prophetic tradition that flourished in early Cinquecento Rome.[9] In
humanists' rhetoric, the classical topos of the incipient golden age
resonated and commingled with Biblical prophecies that anticipated
the imminent arrival of an "angelic pastor" who would lead Christendom into the new age. To be sure, the conceptual vocabulary that
humanists forged from the materials in their chosen sources served
their own professional interests by affirming publicly the centrality of
humanism to the definition of curial culture; but the seriousness of
purpose with which Roman humanists worked to integrate the classical and the Christian is attested also by hundreds of manuscript
pages evidently not intended for public consumption, in which they
sought to make the unstable combination of pagan and Christian
elements cohere.[10]

---

c.1450-1521 (Durham, North Carolina, 1979); Domenico Gnoli, *La Roma di Leon X*
(Milan, 1938); Ingrid D. Rowland, "Some Panegyrics to Agostino Chigi," *Journal of
the Warburg and Courtauld Institutes* 47 (1984): 194-99; *eadem*, "'Render unto Caesar the
Things Which are Caesar's': Humanism and the Arts in the Patronage of Agostino
Chigi," *Renaissance Quarterly* 39 (1986): 673-730; Loren Partridge and Randolph Starn,
A Renaissance Likeness: Art and Culture in Raphael's Julius II (Berkeley and Los Angeles,
1980); and Bonner Mitchell, *Rome in the High Renaissance: The Age of Leo X* (Norman,
1973). See also the excellent survey by Vincenzo De Caprio, "Roma," in *Letteratura
italiana—Storia e geographia*, vol. 2: "L'età moderna," ed. Alberto Asor Rosa (Turin,
1987), 327-472; and, on Leonine Rome, T. C. Price Zimmermann, *Paolo Giovio: The
Historian and the Crisis of Sixteenth-Century Italy* (Princeton, 1995), 20-41 (chaps. 3 and 4).
    [8] Stinger, *Renaissance in Rome, passim*, and esp. 296-99 on the theme of the golden
age.
    [9] Marjorie Reeves, ed., *Prophetic Rome in the High Renaissance Period* (Oxford, 1992);
John W. O'Malley, *Giles of Viterbo on Church and Reform* (Leiden, 1968).
    [10] For a provocative assessment of such tensions, see William J. Bouwsma, "The
Two Faces of Humanism: Stoicism and Augustinianism in Renaissance Thought," in

The dominant discourse that the humanists constructed remained fundamentally intact until the Sack of Rome. In the decade 1517-1527, events did widen the cleft between the ideological claims of Roman humanism and the realities of the papacy's political and cultural role. Leo X's exhaustion of papal revenues, the consolidation of Habsburg power in the north, and the spread of the Lutheran heresy all threatened to diminish Rome's economic, political, and religious sway. Such challenges, however, did not compel Roman humanists to rethink assumptions. Pope Adrian VI (1522-23), whom they lambasted as an enemy of the muses, reigned only briefly, and following the election in 1523 of Giulio de' Medici as Pope Clement VII, they once again burnished the image of the papacy and lauded Rome's cultural preëminence much as they had in the preceding decades.[11]

While modern scholars have traced and analyzed the formation and efflorescence of this Roman humanist discourse, the impact of the Sack of Rome upon it has remained largely unstudied. In *Renaissance Humanism in Papal Rome*, John D'Amico argued that the Sack ended the confidence and creativity of a Roman humanist culture whose decline had started even before the death of Pope Leo X in 1521.[12] Documentation of that assertion, however, lay beyond the scope of his research, which emphasized the period before 1520. Similarly, for Charles Stinger, the Sack changed fundamentally the character of humanistic culture—a culture that had reached its apogee long before, under Julius II and Leo X; Stinger too, however, gave only cursory treatment to post-1527 sources.[13] By contrast, some authoritative examinations of Rome's history following the

Itinerarium Italicum, ed. Heiko A. Oberman with Thomas A. Brady, Jr. (Leiden, 1975): 3-60.

[11] Pastor, *History of the Popes*, vol. 10, 333-43, provides a positive assessment of Clement's efforts to maintain Rome's role as a center of humanistic studies. See esp. 334-35 on orations celebrating the return of the golden age under Clement VII. André Chastel, *The Sack of Rome, 1527*, trans. Beth Archer (Princeton, 1983), interprets Adrian VI's pontificate as a demoralizing interlude rather than as a cultural watershed.

[12] D'Amico, *Renaissance Humanism*, 109: "While the sack of Rome completed the destruction of Roman humanism, the seeds of its internal decay were evident almost a decade earlier when a certain sterility and inbreeding began to characterize the Roman academies."

[13] Stinger, *Renaissance in Rome*, 11-13; on the cultural impact of the Sack of Rome, see esp. 320-32. Thomas Frenz, *Die Kanzlei der Päpste der Hochrenaissance (1471-1572)* (Tübingen, 1986) provides the most thorough examination of curial personnel in Renaissance Rome. Frenz, however, focuses upon institutional history and takes 1527 as the terminus of his study.

Sack have tended to downplay the event's importance. In his survey of Renaissance Rome, Peter Partner has emphasized Rome's rapid economic and cultural recovery after 1527.[14] For Partner, the Sack created only a temporary gap in Roman social history rather than marking a turning point. He argues, moreover, that the culture of Paul III's court (1534-1549) "was directly continuous with that of his Medici predecessors...."[15] Paolo Prodi, meanwhile, has shown that despite the Sack, the papacy in later decades of the sixteenth century actually increased its political and institutional control over the Papal States and the city of Rome.[16] Other economic and institutional historians, such as Jean Delumeau and Pio Pecchiai, have similarly played down the Sack.[17]

By contrast, André Chastel and Vincenzo De Caprio, the two authors who have dealt most directly and extensively with humanist writings following May of 1527, have offered support to the view that this year marks a critical turning point in the history of Renaissance Rome. In an art historical study that drew as well upon literary sources, André Chastel limned an impressionistic, suggestive picture of the truncation of a vibrant culture which he (unlike D'Amico or Stinger) believed still flourished in the mid-1520s.[18] While Chastel often misrepresented his literary sources, his book has the considerable virtue of actually examining the impact of the Sack, rather than simply making assumptions about it. De Caprio, finally, has outlined the effect of the Sack upon professional opportunities available to Roman humanists and has also examined Italian vernacular poetry written in response to it.[19] Most recently, his collection entitled *La*

---

[14] Peter Partner, *Renaissance Rome, 1500-1559: A Portrait of a Society* (Berkeley and Los Angeles, 1976), especially 32-33.

[15] Partner, *Renaissance Rome*, 35-37. Partner, 32-33, does note the diaspora of artists and scholars following the Sack, but ultimately judges the Sack "as much a cultural bonus for Italy as a cultural disaster for Rome."

[16] Paolo Prodi, *Il sovrano pontefice. Un corpo e due anime: la monarchia papale nella prima età moderna* (Bologna, 1982).

[17] Jean Delumeau, *Vie économique et sociale de Rome dans la seconde moitié du XVIᵉ siècle* (Paris, 1957); Pio Pecchiai, *Roma nel Cinquecento* (Bologna, 1948).

[18] Chastel, *Sack of Rome*, esp. chap. 5, "The 'Clementine' Style." I view Chastel's assessment of the flourishing of Roman culture prior to the Sack as highly problematic, and especially so for the period 1525-27.

[19] Vincenzo De Caprio, "Intellettuali e mercato del lavoro nella Roma medicea," *Studi romani* 29 (1981): 26-46; *idem*, "L'area umanistica romana (1513-1527)," *Studi romani* 29 (1981): 321-35; *idem*, "'Hor qui mi fa mestier lingua di ferro.' Note sull'immaginario poetico," in Alberto Asor Rosa, ed., *Il Sacco di Roma del 1527 e l'immaginario collettivo* (Rome, 1986), 19-41.

tradizione e il trauma includes a study of "The Sack and Francesco Guicciardini" and an important synthetic introductory chapter. In that introduction, he argues that the Sack rendered critical the tensions in Roman humanism between its classicizing impulse and its religious purpose.[20] As we shall see, the Latin writings in which Roman humanist ideology received its fullest articulation—writings to which De Caprio has yet to give systematic attention—allow us to confirm and elaborate upon his hypothesis that the Sack marked the end of a particular type of "curial" humanism.

The following chapters analyze the efforts of four Roman humanists to comprehend the implications of the Sack of Rome. Their writings exemplify the variety of ways that the catastrophe prompted them to reconsider the role of papal Rome as cultural arbiter as well as their own identities as members of a localized community of scholars with common professional interests. In so doing, these writings also help us to address three broader questions: First, in what ways did the Sack of Rome transform the perspectives—and even the memories—of Roman humanists? Second, to what extent is it useful to conceive of the Sack as a watershed in Roman Renaissance history?[21] Finally, what does this incident, as a test-case, suggest about the significance of traumatic events as historical and historiographical markers?

Focusing on individual writers, we can address these questions by setting each author's distinct subjective experience in the context of his particular position within the group of Roman humanists.[22] The juxtaposition of these case studies facilitates a more meaningful analysis of human experience and its literary representations than would be possible in an aggregate treatment of Roman humanists. The following chapters therefore focus upon four individuals who

---

[20] Vincenzo De Caprio, *La tradizione e il trauma: idee del Rinascimento romano* (Manziana: Vechiarelli, 1991), esp. 42-47. The treatment of Francesco Guicciardini (297-357) includes analysis of the *Accusatoria*, *Consolatoria*, and *Storia d'Italia*. For other thoughtful recent assessments of the significance of the Sack, see Manfredo Tafuri, "*Roma coda mundi*. Il Sacco del 1527: fratture e continuità," in his *Ricerca del Rinascimento: Principi, Città, Architetti* (Turin, 1992), 223-53; and Massimo Firpo, *Il Sacco di Roma del 1527. Tra profezia, propaganda politica e riforma religiosa* (Cagliari, 1990).

[21] Establishing such definitive boundaries in one's conception of the past is, of course, a problematic enterprise. See the cautions expressed in Randolph Starn, "Historians and 'Crisis,'" *Past and Present* 52 (August, 1971): 3-22.

[22] The masculine pronoun suffices here since not only the four humanists central to the present study but seemingly the entire learned culture of Roman humanist sodalities consisted exclusively of men. See below, 15-19.

were active in Clement VII's patronage network prior to 1527: Pietro Alcionio, Pietro Corsi, Jacopo Sadoleto, and Pierio Valeriano, all of whom sought in their writings to comprehend the significance of the Sack of Rome.[23] Before the event, all four had been affiliated with the group of humanists clustered around Angelo Colocci and Johann Küritz, who hosted many of their social and literary gatherings.[24] After the Sack, these four figures wrote about the event and its significance in classicized Latin, and each employed a different one of four major genres that Renaissance humanists had appropriated from Roman antiquity and revived: oratory, poetry, letters, and dialogue.

If the employment of these scholars in the curia created a professional bond among them, their private gatherings provided a forum both for learned debate and for literary playfulness. This social setting, more than the professional one, allowed them to exchange and elaborate upon the creative ideas that underlay the theoretical innovations of Medicean Rome.[25] While Alcionio, Corsi, Sadoleto, and Valeriano were not equally immersed in the social world of humanist symposia, all four shared in the activities at different points in the early 1520s. After the disaster of 1527, which scattered this community of scholars, their career paths diverged, and their writings articulated four distinct interpretations of its cultural significance.

Before turning to these interpretations, however, let us first survey the pre-Sack, Roman milieu in which these four authors participated. In part, one must understand this milieu as a development in Italian Renaissance humanism, a "movement" that dates back at least to Petrarch. Yet owing to the unique ideological requirements and social structure of the Renaissance papal *curia*, which provided employ-

---

[23] Alcionio's orations on the Sack of Rome date from its earliest months; Corsi's *Romae urbis excidium*, probably from late November, 1527; the letters of Sadoleto on which I focus, from mid-1527 until late 1529; and Valeriano's *De litteratorum infelicitate*, evidently left unfinished, was set in Rome in early 1529.

[24] On the professional commonalities of Roman humanists, see esp. D'Amico, *Renaissance Humanism*. On the activities of the Colocci/ Küritz sodality, see Gnoli, *La Roma di Leon X*; Phyllis Pray Bober, "The *Coryciana* and the Nymph Corycia," *Journal of the Warburg and Courtauld Institutes* 40 (1977): 223-39; Federico Ubaldini, *Vita di Mons. Angelo Colocci: Edizione del testo originale italiano (Barb. Lat. 4882)*, ed. V. Fanelli (Vatican City, 1969); and Julia Haig Gaisser, "The Rise and Fall of Goritz's Feasts," *Renaissance Quarterly* 48:1 (Spring, 1995): 41-57.

[25] Ingrid D. Rowland has made this argument in numerous papers at conferences, including the American Historical Association annual meeting (New York, 1990) and the Renaissance Society of America annual conference (Stanford, 1992).

ment for many humanists as bureaucrats and scribes, Roman humanism developed a character all its own.

ii. *Roman Humanism in the Context of Renaissance Humanism*

The construction of a comprehensive definition of the term "humanism," one of the more intractable problems of Renaissance historiography, certainly lies well beyond the scope of the present study.[26] Nonetheless, since this study takes humanist narratives as its subject, let us begin with Paul Oskar Kristeller's influential definition of "humanism," only then turning to specific strains of thought within the humanist tradition that are particularly germane for understanding the culture of early Cinquecento Rome. According to Kristeller, although Renaissance humanism was a "broad cultural and literary movement" with "important philosophical implications and consequences," no common philosophical doctrine united humanists, excepting "a belief in the value of man and the humanities and in the revival of ancient learning."[27] Humanism was not a philosophical system, but instead a "cultural and educational program."[28] "Humanists" were those who pursued the *studia humanitatis*—grammar, rhetoric, history, poetry, and moral philosophy—training in each of which included the study of Greek, and especially Latin, classical texts. According to Kristeller, they tended to be professional rhetoricians, serving either as teachers of the humanities or as secretaries to princes or civic governments. Some humanist interests, Kristeller acknowledged, did not exclusively concern the classical tradition: humanists shared an emphasis on the dignity of man and on the importance of individual experience, and they valued highly the written expression of that experience.[29] Yet it was the forms and models of classical authors, and particularly of Cicero, that furnished them with

---

[26] The bibliography on this topic is vast. See, for example, Wallace K. Ferguson, *The Renaissance in Historical Thought: Five Centuries of Interpretation* (New York, 1948); Vito R. Giustiniani, "Homo, Humanus, and the Meanings of 'Humanism,'" *Journal of the History of Ideas* 46 (1985): 167-95; and especially Paul Oskar Kristeller, "The Humanist Movement," in *Renaissance Thought: The Classic, Scholastic, and Humanist Strains* (New York, 1961), 3-23.

[27] Kristeller, "Humanist Movement," 22.

[28] For this and the points which follow, see esp. Kristeller, "Humanist Movement," 10.

[29] Kristeller, "Humanist Movement," 20-21.

a vocabulary for expressing these concerns. Cicero's rhetorical works provided both a theory of composition and models for imitation, and his own efforts to combine rhetoric with philosophy drew the attention of many Renaissance authors.[30]

This strict definition of humanism is a useful starting point, but its very strictness is problematic. William Bouwsma has argued that "since this [i.e., Kristeller's] approach depends on the identification of a kind of lowest common denominator for humanism, it may also have the unintended effect of reducing our perception of its rich variety and thus of limiting our grasp of its historical significance."[31] In Bouwsma's estimation, "humanism was a single movement in much the sense that a battlefield is a definable piece of ground."[32]

Rather than attempting any general redefinition of "Renaissance Humanism," the present study emphasizes the ways that Cinquecento Roman humanists perpetuated and elaborated upon three characteristic features of Petrarchan humanism. First of all, Petrarch's interest in the recovery of the classical Latin language laid the groundwork for Roman humanists' oft–excessive Ciceronianism, their obsession with employing only the strict vocabulary and syntax

---

[30] Kristeller, "Humanist Movement," 19. On Cicero in the Renaissance, see esp. Hans Baron, "Cicero and the Roman Civic Spirit in the Middle Ages and Early Renaissance," *Bulletin of the John Rylands Library* 22 (1938): 72-97; idem, *The Crisis of the Early Italian Renaissance*, rev. ed. (Princeton, 1966).

[31] Bouwsma, "Two Faces," 3. On the other hand, as Kristeller has observed ("Humanist Movement," 20), "Any particular statement gleaned from the work of a humanist may be countered by contrary assertions in the writings of contemporary authors or even of the same author."

[32] Bouwsma, "Two Faces," 3. In part because of the strictness of Kristeller's definition, many of the leading scholars of humanism who emphasize one of its philosophical dimensions, be it political, moral, or religious, have found it necessary to elaborate upon that definition. For example, on civic humanist political thought, see Baron, *Crisis*, and Eugenio Garin, *Italian Humanism: Philosophy and the Civic Life in the Renaissance*, trans. Peter Munz (New York, 1965); on the humanist use of eloquence to direct people toward the good, see Hanna H. Gray, "Renaissance Humanism: The Pursuit of Eloquence," *Journal of the History of Ideas* 24 (1963): 497-514; and on humanist religious thought, see Charles Trinkaus, *"In Our Image and Likeness: Humanity and Divinity in Italian Humanist Thought,"* 2 vols. (Chicago and London, 1970). The recent publication of an authoritative three-volume collection of essays by leading scholars on the subject of Renaissance humanism has by no means put an end to controversy: Albert Rabil, Jr., ed., *Renaissance Humanism: Foundations, Forms, and Legacy*, 3 vols. (Philadelphia, 1988). See Bouwsma's trenchant review of this collection in *Church History* 59 (1990): 65-70. For a rethinking of the broader analytic categories in which the debates about Renaissance humanism have long been embedded, see Randolph Starn, "Who's Afraid of the Renaissance?" in John Van Engen, ed., *The Past and Future of Medieval Studies* (Notre Dame: University of Notre Dame Press, 1994): 129-47.

of Cicero in their prose writings. Second, Petrarch's use of the literature and thought of both classical and early Christian antiquity to
revivify Trecento culture anticipated and inspired Roman efforts to
appropriate antique images and rhetoric to invest Renaissance Roman culture with special status. In poetry no less than in prose,
Petrarch moved beyond his models to make an artistic statement
uniquely his own.[33] If Cinquecento Roman humanists were less creative than he, like Petrarch they transcended their sources and models. Still, the tensions between classical and Christian language, topoi,
and assumptions, which Petrarch had left unresolved, continued to
bedevil Roman humanists, despite the herculean efforts of individuals such as the prominent Augustinian theologian, Giles of Viterbo,
to harmonize them.[34] Finally, one finds in Petrarch's writings a sense
that he believed that he stood at the dawn of a new age, an attitude
that helps explain the assurance with which he trumpeted the importance of his own work and, indeed, of himself.[35] Early Cinquecento
Roman humanists followed suit, heralding a rosy future for European Christendom under papal leadership and for themselves as
spokesmen for a revived papacy that would usher in the new age.

The articulation of Roman variants of the three "Petrarchan"
themes took place over the course of several decades of papal encouragement of humanism and the arts. In fact, while a distinct Roman humanist ideology received expression as early as the 1440s, it
did not reach its point of fullest development until the early years of
the Cinquecento. To be sure, this development owed much to a
growing awareness on the part of Renaissance popes of the intrinsic
value of humanistic studies. For example, Pius II (1458-64) not only

---

[33]   E.g., Robert M. Durling, "Petrarch's 'Giovene donna sotto un verde Lauro,'"
MLN 86 (1971): 1-20; *idem*, "The Ascent of Mt. Ventoux and the Crisis of Allegory,"
Italian Quarterly 18:69 (Summer, 1974): 7-28; John Freccero, "The Fig Tree and the
Laurel: Petrarch's Poetics," *Diacritics* 5 (1975): 34-40. Among historians' accounts of
Petrarch, see esp. Charles Trinkaus, *The Poet as Philosopher: Petrarch and the Formation of
Renaissance Consciousness* (New Haven, 1979).

[34]   On the tension of classical and Christian elements in Petrarch, see Trinkaus,
Poet as Philosopher. On Quattrocento efforts to make Plato "safe" for Christian readers,
see James Hankins, *Plato in the Italian Renaissance*, 2 vols. (Leiden, 1989); and on Giles
of Viterbo, see Ingrid Rowland, "Abacus and Humanism," *Renaissance Quarterly* 48:4
(Winter, 1995): 695-727.

[35]   Theodor E. Mommsen, "Petrarch's Conception of the 'Dark Ages,'" *Speculum*
17 (1942): 226-42, provides the classic analysis of this theme. He cites (242) Joa-
chimsen's earlier formulation, "If there is one thing that unites the men of the Renaissance, it is the notion of belonging to a new time."

supported classical and patristic scholarship but also applied his own learning to the task of writing a commentary on his times in elegant Latin, and he enjoyed a considerable reputation as a man of letters.[36] Julius II (1503-13), however, manifested a particular awareness of the propagandistic value of humanist rhetoric. Described by contemporaries as "choleric," "audacious," and especially as "*terribile*," he brought to the papacy exceptional political acumen and at least as great ambitions.[37]

From the time of his election, which was effected through open simony, Julius invested heavily in both the reality and the imagery of papal power.[38] As a practical political move, he sought to retake by military conquest portions of the papal states alienated by Alexander VI—a policy that won for the papacy a degree of local political autonomy—and to drive the "barbarian" French from the Italian peninsula.[39] Working closely with his banker, Agostino Chigi, Julius also shored up sources of papal revenue, most notably by enforcing a papal monopoly on the supply of alum, a chemical necessary for the process of dyeing wool cloth.[40] In ecclesiastical politics, meanwhile, he strengthened papal authority by convoking the Fifth Lateran Council, which countered the schismatic Council of Pisa (1511-13) and reasserted the pope's ecclesiastical prerogatives.[41] At the same time, Julius recognized the political usefulness of projecting visual

---

[36] On the humanism of Pius II, see R.J. Mitchell, *The Laurels and the Tiara: Pope Pius II, 1405-1464* (Garden City, 1962); and G. Paparelli, *Enea Silvio Piccolomini: L'Umanesimo sul soglio di Pietro*, 2nd ed. (Ravenna, 1978).

[37] Partridge and Starn, *Renaissance Likeness*, 4-6.

[38] Felix Gilbert, *The Pope, His Banker, and Venice* (Cambridge, Mass., 1980), 76-77 and 138, n.48, notes contemporary accusations of simony and argues that Agostino Chigi played a key role in bankrolling Giuliano della Rovere's election as Julius II. Concerning Chigi's relationship with Julius II, see also Rowland, "Render unto Caesar"; and *eadem*, "A Summer Outing in 1510: Religion and Economics in the Papal War with Ferrara," *Viator* 18 (1987): 347-59. For a dissenting view, see Christine Shaw, *Julius II: The Warrior Pope* (Oxford, 1993), chap. 7. Shaw argues that the pope did not regard himself as a second Julius Caesar, and she claims that his policies were firmly grounded in Italian political realities rather than in grandiose imperial ambitions. But need the two have been mutually exclusive?

[39] Pastor, *History of the Popes*, vol. 6, *passim*.

[40] Gilbert, *The Pope, His Banker, and Venice*, esp. 85-91. Gilbert writes (85) "His [Julius's] concern with the maintenance of the alum monopoly was not a unique case. On various occasions economic rights and claims emerged as motives for his foreign policy."

[41] Nelson H. Minnich, S.J., "Concepts of Reform Proposed at the Fifth Lateran Council," *Archivum historiae pontificiae* 7 (1969): 163-251; *idem*, "Prophecy and the Fifth Lateran Council (1512-1517)," in Reeves, ed., *Prophetic Rome*, 63-87.

images of his grandeur and accomplishments. Under his direction, Bramante began construction of the Belvedere and of the new St. Peter's basilica; Michelangelo painted the Sistine Chapel ceiling and worked on Julius's ostentatious tomb; and Raphael began painting frescoes in the Vatican *stanze*. These projects served not only to adorn the city, but also to enhance the reputation of their sponsor. Often the art carried distinct subtexts, casting Julius in the role of Moses or as a second Julius Caesar.[42] Finally, Julius made use of the medium of public spectacle, as in his triumphal entry into Rome on Palm Sunday of 1507.[43] The imagery of the event itself, and of the commemorative medal issued shortly thereafter, linked the pope explicitly both with Julius Caesar and with Christ, the two authorities from whom his *imperium* was, at least in theory, jointly derived.

The literary production of Roman humanists, who helped to formulate and broadcast the Julian ideology, complemented the visual rhetoric of the art. Combining classical and Christian motifs, humanists lauded Julius as the *princeps* exercising supreme power over the church's *imperium*.[44] In his oration at the Fifth Lateran Council, the apostolic protonotary Cristoforo Marcello asserted this theme, praising Julius's deeds, including his military exploits, above those of all other popes.[45] Other humanists, such as Marco Girolamo Vida and Johannes Michael Nagonius, lauded Julius's military accomplishments with Latin poetry.[46] Nagonius, for example, boasted that the pope had exceeded Julius Caesar both in glory and in promise. Following papal conquests in Italy, he claimed, Julius II would lead a crusade and retake the city of Jerusalem.[47]

Thus, by the first decades of the Cinquecento, the humanist spokesmen for the papacy elaborated upon a discourse at least as old as the Trecento so that they could effectively convey a distinct set of

[42] Stinger, *Renaissance in Rome*, 216-21 and, for further bibliography, 382. On Julius II's building projects, see esp. Arnaldo Bruschi, *Bramante architetto* (Bari, 1969). On Raphael's paintings in the Vatican, see the essential article by John Shearman, "The Vatican Stanze: Functions and Decoration", in George Holmes, ed., *Art and Politics in Renaissance Italy: British Academy Lectures* (Oxford, 1993), 185-240.

[43] Partridge and Starn, *Renaissance Likeness*, 57-58, 63; Stinger, *Renaissance in Rome*, 236-38.

[44] Stinger, *Renaissance in Rome*, 238-46.

[45] Stinger, *Renaissance in Rome*, 238-39; Minnich, "Concepts of Reform," 181-83. On Marcello's untimely death in 1527, see below, chapter 5.

[46] Stinger, *Renaissance in Rome*, 109, 242.

[47] Stinger, *Renaissance in Rome*, 106-23, details the Roman humanist topos of the need for a crusade against the Turk.

ideological claims on behalf of papal Rome. Where Petrarch had expressed concern for purging the Latin language of medieval "corruptions," Cinquecento curial humanists utilized the often-restrictive idiom of Ciceronian Latin for their formal prose writings.[48] Where Petrarch had employed classical and late-antique literary models for self-expression, later Roman humanists more rigidly adhered to classical notions of literary decorum, and their self-expression took on special meaning in the context of their efforts to dignify the Renaissance papacy. Finally, where Petrarch had portrayed himself as a privileged observer announcing the dawning of a new historical era, the curial humanists of High Renaissance Rome confidently asserted their own centrality as heralds of a golden age that the papacy would soon initiate.

If Roman humanist intellectuals thus articulated an ideology on behalf of the papacy, they were not just mouthpieces for the ideas of others.[49] Rather, as we shall see, the active part that they took in creating the narrative about papal Rome went well beyond their official bureaucratic responsibilities. Both in compositions for presentation at social gatherings and in private writings evidently never intended for publication, they embellished the image of the Renaissance papacy with rhetorical elements distinctly their own. These embellishments, although they tended to laud the pope, were often too abstruse to serve any political function at all. Instead, they were aimed at the amusement of others "in the know." Consequently, although the shared narrative centered on the papacy, it took shape within a discursive field that extended beyond the confines of official

---

[48] D'Amico, *Renaissance Humanism*, chap. 5 ("The Idiom of Roman Humanism"), 115-43.

[49] Arthur Field, *The Origins of the Platonic Academy of Florence* (Princeton, 1988), 47, makes a similar argument about the intellectual creativity of Ficino and Landino in Laurentian Florence: "Theirs was no ideology produced for them by the Medici party, where they would become disseminators of ready-made truths; rather, striking chords and hitting on predisposed spirits, to be sure, they themselves, in large part, created the ideology of the Medici party." Unlike Field, however, I do not wish to imply any linkage of the term "ideology" with a particular social class engaged in dialectical struggle. Instead, following Peter Novick, I use "ideology" to mean "an overarching, and at-least-tacitly-coherent outlook on the world." Peter Novick, *That Noble Dream: The "Objectivity Question" and the American Historical Profession* (Cambridge, 1988), 61. According to Novick (62), in the social and political realms, ideology consists of "three elements: (1) a picture of the way that the world is; (2) a picture of the way the world ought to be; (3) a set of propositions about the relationship between the first and the second." This comprehensive definition of ideology helps us to avoid the limitations and pitfalls of Marxist or Althusserian applications of the term.

policy. The common factor of employment in the papal court gave
humanists professional coherence that reinforced the harmony: for
their collective reliance upon papal and curial patronage necessarily
fostered uniformity in thought and expression.[50] Yet the social coherence of Roman humanism extended beyond the professional sphere
to private social gatherings, both formal and informal. Among these
gatherings, the most notable were those of the overlapping sodalities
of Angelo Colocci and Johann Küritz.[51] Colocci, who had studied
with Giovanni Pontano in Naples, came in the late 1490s to Rome,
where he bought several curial offices.[52] Although Colocci himself
wrote little—mostly short poems, and an unfinished magnum opus
on weights and measures—he was an avid collector both of classical
archaeological remains and of manuscripts. Most important, the
gatherings that he hosted in his villa, located on property that had
once been part of Sallust's gardens, provided an opportunity for the
interchange of ideas among luminaries such as the papal secretaries
Sadoleto and Bembo, the artist Raphael, and the theologian Giles of
Viterbo.

Küritz, originally from Luxembourg, had been trained in canon
and civil law. Like Colocci, in the 1490s he migrated to Rome,
where he initially found employment as a registrar of supplications
under Alexander VI. In the following decades, he accumulated several other posts, the highest being that of apostolic protonotary.[53]
With the revenue from these positions he purchased a villa (located
between the Campidoglio and Trajan's forum) where he hosted
learned gatherings at which he sponsored artistic and literary
endeavors.[54] Küritz's patronage of arts and letters centered on the

---

[50] See in particular D'Amico, *Renaissance Humanism*, 212-37, on ways that Roman
humanists' social position helped shape and limit their views on Church reform.

[51] Bober, "The *Coryciana*"; D'Amico, *Renaissance Humanism*, 107-112; Domenico
Gnoli, "Orti letterari nella Roma di Leon X," in *La Roma di Leon X*, 136-63; Ubaldini, *Vita di Mons. Angelo Colocci*. Ubaldini, "Appendix iv," 114-15, provides a listing of
members of Küritz's sodality.

[52] D'Amico, *Renaissance Humanism*, 107-108, provides a brief summary of Colocci's
career and interests. See also Ingrid D. Rowland, "Raphael, Angelo Colocci, and the
Genesis of the Architectural Orders," *Art Bulletin* 76 (1994): 81-104. On the purchase
of church offices, see Barbara McClung Hallman, *Italian Cardinals, Reform, and the
Church as Property, 1492–1563* (Berkeley and Los Angeles, 1985).

[53] Protonotaries served directly under the cardinal vice-chancellor in the papal
chancery. On the administrative posts that humanists often held in the papal curia,
see D'Amico, *Renaissance Humanism*, 19-27, with extensive bibliography, 248-51.

[54] On Küritz, see Théophile Simar, *Christophe de Longueil, humaniste (1488-1522)*

cult of Anne, his patron saint. Beginning in 1512, he financed the decoration of an altar to St. Anne in the church of Sant' Agostino in Rome, commissioning for it a fresco of the prophet Isaiah, by Raphael, and a sculpture of St. Anne with the Virgin Mary and the Christ Child, by Andrea Sansovino.[55] Each year on 26 July, the Feast of St. Anne, Küritz and his humanist friends gathered at this altar, to which they affixed poems celebrating the occasion. The festivities extended to Küritz's *vigna*, where humanists read poems aloud and posted them on trees.[56]

Since the conversations at the symposia of the Colocci and Küritz sodalities went unrecorded, modern scholars can only speculate on the extent to which such informal discussion facilitated the ideological harmony of Renaissance Roman culture.[57] Very likely a meeting of these humanists constituted what Erving Goffman has called a "focused gathering"—that is, "a set of people who relate to one another through the medium of a common activity."[58] One finds in these gatherings variants of three of the themes central to official expressions of curial ideology: 1) the use of literary forms drawn from classical antiquity; 2) the synthesis of images drawn from classical and Christian antiquity to give new meaning to the present; and 3) the humanists' sense of their own special significance as an intellectual elite heralding the new golden age.

One can see these themes, for example, in the humanist poetry connected with the "sleeping nymph" fountain in Colocci's garden.[59] This statue of a naïad, or water nymph, was installed above an inscription believed to be antique: "I, the nymph of this place, the

---

(Louvain, 1911), 194-203; Bober, "The *Coryciana*"; D'Amico, *Renaissance Humanism*, 108-109; and Gaisser, "Goritz's Feasts."

[55] Virginia Anne Bonito, "The Saint Anne Altar in Sant' Agostino: A New Discovery," *The Burlington Magazine* 122 (1980): 805-12; *eadem*, "The Saint Anne Altar in Sant' Agostino: Restoration and Interpretation," *The Burlington Magazine* 124 (1982): 268-76. D'Amico, *Renaissance Humanism*, 108, wrongly identifies the prophet in Raphael's fresco as Elijah.

[56] Bober, "The *Coryciana*," 228.

[57] On the significance of informal conversation in the Renaissance, and on the need for modern scholars to take it into account sufficiently, see Edgar Wind, *Pagan Mysteries in the Renaissance*, rev. ed. (New York, 1968), 15.

[58] Lawrence W. Levine, *Highbrow/Lowbrow: The Emergence of Cultural Hierarchy in America* (Cambridge, Mass., 1988), 56, provides this pithy summation of Goffman's concept, which Levine applies to the American theater at the beginning of the nineteenth century.

[59] Bober, "The *Coryciana*"; Elisabeth B. MacDougall, "The Sleeping Nymph: Origins of a Humanist Fountain Type," *Art Bulletin* 57 (1975): 357-65.

sacred guard of the fountain, rest while I hear the murmuring of the alluring water. Whoever of you touches the hollowed-out marble channels, be reluctant to interrupt my sleep. Whether you drink or are washed, be silent."[60] Humanists adorned this naïad with Latin poems written in Augustan elegiac style. These poems had profound philosophical significance, in that the naïad symbolized the "presence of the Muses who presided over the newly reborn academies of learning and the reborn art of poetry."[61] More specifically, humanists linked her with the nymphs of Corycium Antrum, an enchanted cave on Mount Parnassus, which the ancient writer Pausanias had identified as a source of poetic inspiration.[62] Yet for Renaissance humanists, steeped in the writings of neoplatonists such as Porphyry, this water deity could have a further significance, representing not only the force of water but also the transmigration of souls.[63] For the members of the Colocci/Küritz academies, then, the nymph was also a "fitting image for the repose and refreshment of the soul which is a foretaste of salvation."[64] The poetry sponsored by Küritz evidenced a similar synthesis of classical and Christian elements, the pagan mystery of the nymph becoming conflated in this setting with the cult of St. Anne.[65] For example, a poem by Pierio Valeriano addressed to Sansovino's sculpture (i.e., of St. Anne, the Virgin, and the Christ

---

[60] Bober, "The *Coryciana*," 224: "HUIUS NYMPHA LOCI, SACRA CUSTODIA FONTIS./ DORMIO, DUM BLANDAE SENTIO MURMUR AQUAE./ PARCE MEUM, QUISQUIS TANGIS CAVA MARMORA, SOMNUM RUMPERE. SIVE BIBAS SIVE LAVERE TACE." Bober suggests that the earlier Roman Academy headed by Pomponio Leto (d.1497) may have been responsible for the composition of this inscription. Küritz's garden contained a similar fountain, also featuring this water nymph, with a shortened version of the same inscription: "NYMPHIS LOCI/ BIBE LAVA/ TACE/ CORITIUS." (Bober, "The *Coryciana*," 226). According to both Bober and MacDougall, the immediate model for both fountains was a similar one constructed in the Belvedere in 1512 and adorned with the longer version of the inscription.

[61] MacDougall, "Sleeping Nymph," 363.

[62] Bober, "The *Coryciana*," 225. Of course, this association also lends significance to Küritz's Latinized name, "Corycius."

[63] Bober, "The *Coryciana*," 233.

[64] Bober, "The *Coryciana*," 238.

[65] Gaisser, "Goritz's Feasts," 44, draws a provocative contrast between the activities of the Küritz and Colocci gatherings: "Most of Colocci's sodality (including Colocci himself) belonged also to Goritz's [i.e., Küritz's], but the two groups were different in kind: Colocci's was patriotic and antiquarian, while Goritz's was religious and literary." On the two sodalities, see also the important new work of Anne Reynolds, *Renaissance Humanism at the Court of Clement VII: Francesco Berni's* Dialogue against Poets, *an Edition and Translation with Contextual Studies* (New York and London, 1997).

Child) explicitly connected the two themes, punning on the double meaning of the Latin word "nympha" as both "nymph" and "young girl."[66]

Not all of the poetic endeavors of Roman humanists were so pious or edifying. Indeed, these scholars produced an abundance of fairly inane boilerplate praises of one another's eloquence and character.[67] At the same time, in satirical verses (some acknowledged and others anonymously posted), they ridiculed one another, both for literary incompetence and for moral turpitude. For example, a masked man delivered to Pietro Corsi verses that caricatured him as a *rusticus* ("country bumpkin") who authored clumsy and tedious poetry.[68] When Küritz canceled the St. Anne's Day festivities in 1525, Giovanni Battista Sanga traduced him as a Lutheran, a drunkard, a philanderer, and a syphilitic. As an outrageous flourish, Sanga even suggested that Küritz had jettisoned the veneration of St. Anne in favor of honoring a slut (*meretricula*) named Anna, who served as a patron saint of sorts for his sexual exploits.[69] Roman humanists frequently disparaged one another with accusations of practicing homosexuality and bestiality. Thus, anonymous verses accused Paolo Giovio of keeping a *Cynaedus*, or passive homosexual partner; and an even more scurrilous poem faulted Pietro Corsi for his voracious and unconventional carnal indulgences.[70]

If such criticisms may at times have provoked tensions among Roman humanists, they served in subtler ways to further a sense of collective identity. After all, most of the slurs—like the poetic forms in which they were expressed—were part of the common classical heritage that the humanists sought to revive.[71] Moreover, the homo-

---

[66] Bober, "The *Coryciana*," 228, n.30.

[67] e.g., in BAV MS Vat. Lat. 5227, I, fol. 52v, Marcantonio Casanova lauded Pietro Corsi as "Ille, ille optimus omnium sodales,/ ille, ille optimus omnium poeta."

[68] The poetry delivered to Corsi by the masked man is copied into BAV MS Vat. Lat. 3436 and is reproduced in G. F. Lancellotti, *Poesie italiane e latini di mons. A. Colocci* (Jesi, 1772), 166-70.

[69] Reynolds, *Renaissance Humanism*, 91-92, reproduces the poem from BAV MS Vat. Lat. 2836, fols. 122-23, and provides an English translation. The poem strikes this reader as drenched in irony.

[70] The poems, to date unedited (perhaps mercifully so), appear in BAV MS Vat. Lat. 5225, t. 4, fols. 903v-904v. Petrucci, "Corsi," 581, identifies the poem's "Curtius" (e.g., "stolidum poetam et mentulatum Petrum Curtium") as Pietro Corsi.

[71] Paula Findlen, "Humanism, Politics and Pornography in Renaissance Italy," in Lynn Hunt, ed., *The Invention of Pornography: Obscenity and the Origins of Modernity, 1500-1800* (New York, 1993), 49-108, 345-58. As Findlen observes (79), "In attempting to

erotic discourse in which they participated was itself a unifying factor, regardless of any given humanist's sexual proclivities.[72] However
hostile the expression of affect might be, it was still a form of cathexis
between individuals who, whatever their sexual practices, shared in
an exclusively male, agonistic intellectual environment in which skill
at classical Latin was of central importance.[73] Thus, while the verbal
sparring was at times vitriolic, the medium and, at least to some
extent, even the message itself were conducive to a sense of connectedness among the Roman humanists.[74]

The sodalities of Angelo Colocci and Johann Küritz reinforced the
social and ideological harmony of Roman humanism. In the more
formal compositions for their gatherings, humanists joined in promoting the "official" papal theme of the golden age that Rome
would soon experience.[75] One poem attached to the Saint Anne al-

---

create a culture modeled on antiquity, humanists had to come to terms with all of its
values and practices, however antithetical those might be to the goals of a Christian
society."

[72] It is worth noting that the stereotyping of poets as homosexuals was a common-
place. Thus, in the words of the satirist Ariosto, "The vulgar laugh when they hear of
someone who possesses a vein of poetry, and then they say 'it is a great peril to turn
your back if you sleep next to him.'" (Ariosto, *Satires*, 6:31-33, cited in Findlen,
"Humanism, Politics and Pornography," 83). The degree to which the discourse did
in fact correspond to sexual practice is a nettlesome issue that may be intractable. I
am inclined to agree with Paula Findlen's observation that, in humanist culture,
"homosocial bonds were often imperceptible from homosexual relationships, and the
playful relationship between textuality and sexuality was not simply noted but celebrated." (Findlen, "Humanism, Politics and Pornography," 85) On the prevalence
of homosexual practice in early sixteenth-century Italy, see Michael Rocke, *Forbidden
Friendships: Homosexuality and Male Culture in Renaissance Florence* (New York, 1996), 227-
35.

[73] Because of the uniquely male constituency of the papal curia, Roman humanism was even more exclusively androcentric and androcratic than Florentine or Venetian humanism. On education in Renaissance Latin as conducive to homosocial
bonding, see Walter Ong, S.J., "Latin Language Study as a Renaissance Puberty
Rite," in *idem, Rhetoric, Romance, and Technology: Studies in the Interaction of Expression and
Culture* (Ithaca, [1971]), 113-41. See also *idem, Fighting for Life: Contest, Sexuality, and
Consciousness* (Ithaca, 1981), esp. chap. 4, "Academic and Intellectual Arenas."

[74] Reynolds, *Renaissance Humanism*, provides detailed examinations of several rival-
ries which certainly transcended the bounds of civility (e.g., Aretino vs. Berni). By
1525, Giles of Viterbo, at least, had come to find the verbal jousting at Küritz's
parties too hostile to be enjoyable (see Gaisser, "Goritz's Feasts"). Gaisser, Reynolds,
and I agree in identifying a decline of optimism in many Roman humanist writings of
the early- to mid-1520s. I would argue that the change was more of degree than of
kind, perhaps partly in response to the increasingly strained economic and political
situation of the papacy in those years.

[75] Predictably, they tended to be less specific about the role of the papacy in
bringing about that change.

tar, for example, invoked the saints above it to "look favorably and
let Rome again govern the reins of things and let it be once again the
accustomed theatre of the world."[76] Furthermore, the activities of the
academies enhanced Roman humanists' sense of collective identity.
Where publicly they were heralds of the new golden age that the
papacy would help initiate, privately they were initiates in mysteries
that would remain unheralded, hidden knowledge available only to
the learned few who could comprehend it and benefit from it.[77]
Moreover, in these informal writings, which used classical Latin
models and forms, they synthesized classical and Christian motifs
much as they did in compositions for the papacy. If academy rhetoric
necessarily focused less on the role of the papacy in initiating the
golden age than did orations written in hopes of papal patronage, it
similarly attributed special importance both to Renaissance Rome
and to its humanist intellectuals.

Beyond their official duties within the papal curia and their involvement in the sodalities, humanists also took part in the complex
ceremonial and festive life of the Eternal City. Because of Rome's
centrality to Christendom, it offered more opportunities than did
other Italian centers for humanistic contributions to ceremonial
events, whether in the form of orations, poems, or iconographical
programs.[78] Such occasions for public display showcased humanists'
talents. Thus, they were among those offering sermons before the
popes; they delivered orations to cardinals entering conclaves; they
delivered funeral orations; and they took part in such pageantry as
Alexander VI's celebration of the Jubilee Year (1500), Julius II's triumphal entry into Rome (1507), and Leo X's coronation rites
(1513).[79] Not all such occasions lent themselves to expressions of

---

[76] Bonito, "Restoration and Interpretation," 276. I reproduce her translation (the
Latin poem, by Delius Hieronymus Alexandrinus, appears on 276, n.27, of the article). Bonito argues that the Hebrew inscription on the scroll that Isaiah holds in
Raphael's fresco for this altar also anticipates a return of the golden age. She attributes its composition to Giles of Viterbo.

[77] Bober, "The *Coryciana*," 238, writes that the nymphs "and their sacred fountains
fulfilled in Christianized context the promise of apotheosis first held out by Plato to
an intellectual elite."

[78] For this insight I am indebted to Charles Stinger. On ceremonial life in Medicean Rome and Florence, see the important study by Anthony M. Cummings, *The
Politicized Muse: Music for Medici Festivals, 1512–1537* (Princeton, 1992).

[79] On sacred oratory *coram papa*, see O'Malley, *Praise and Blame*. On funeral oratory, see McManamon, "The Ideal Renaissance Pope: Funeral Oratory from the

papal ideology, inasmuch as purpose and context placed constraints upon content. For example, the Masters of the Sacred Palace, the pope's official theologians, sought to ensure that orations delivered before the popes during the liturgy adhered to strict standards of decorum. Focusing upon the solemnity being observed, such presentations were not supposed to celebrate the papacy's military or diplomatic successes. Still, they provided a setting in which humanists could position themselves near the center of the revival of Rome's cultural and intellectual life.[80]

Public processions, by contrast, could blazon papal claims and ambitions. The *possesso*, the ceremonial procession of a pope-elect from the Piazza San Pietro to the Lateran, included a series of traditional rituals, such as the tossing of coins to the crowd at designated points. In the coronation of Leo X, however, the focus had shifted decisively to the procession itself, in which music, elaborate costumes, and decorative triumphal arches replete with art and inscriptions gave graphic expression to Roman humanist ideology, associating Leo both with Biblical precedents such as the "Lion of Judah" and with classical gods and goddesses such as Apollo and Athena. The new pontiff, the arches proclaimed, would initiate a golden age that would flourish particularly in Rome. Thus, in their programs for ceremonies, as in their formal writings, humanists expressed their shared ideology and, by implication, reinforced their own role as spokesmen whose harmonious voices defined and dignified the Renaissance papacy.[81]

The harmony of pre-Sack Roman humanism did not, however, preclude dissent. Some humanists authored pasquinades—satirical poems affixed anonymously to a public statue known as "Pasquino"—

Papal Court," *Archivum Historiae pontificiae* 14 (1976): 9-70; and idem, *Funeral Oratory and the Cultural Ideals of Italian Humanism* (Chapel Hill, 1989). On pageantry and public ceremony, see Stinger, *Renaissance in Rome*, e.g., 46-59 and 236-46.

[80] O'Malley, *Praise and Blame*, 17-35.

[81] Stinger, *Renaissance in Rome*, 54-57. If Leo X himself designed the pageantry of his *possesso* in collaboration with the papal Master of Ceremonies, Paris de Grassis, humanists such as Tommaso "Fedra" Inghirami built their careers upon their production of such spectacles for Renaissance cardinals and popes. See Stinger, *ibid.*, 59, on Inghirami's program for the 1514 *Festa di Agone* for Pope Leo. The reference to the Lion of Judah recalls prophetic imagery from the New Testament, *Revelation* 5:5, rendered in the NRSV as follows: "Then one of the elders said to me, 'Do not weep. See, the Lion of the tribe of Judah, the Root of David, has conquered, so that he can open the scroll and its seven seals.'"

THE SACK OF ROME

in which they expressed scathing criticisms of popes, cardinals, and other important personages, criticisms that must qualify any picture of unity and deference.[82] Adrian VI (1522-23), whose conservative fiscal policy created difficulties for those dependent upon papal patronage, drew especially virulent criticism. One pasquinade composed shortly following his election, but before his arrival in Italy, alleged that the *"mal barberotto"* who had circumcised Adrian had accidentally castrated him.[83] More frequently, humanists attacked Adrian's proverbial stinginess: a later pasquinade claimed that he had been so tight-fisted in order that more precious metal might await him under the earth upon burial.[84] Adrian may well have been the most roundly abused in humanist pasquinades, but no Renaissance pope escaped criticism: Alexander VI for lechery, Julius II for rapacity, Leo X for timidity and gluttony, and Clement VII for heavy taxation, political vacillation, and general incompetence.[85]

Pasquinades offered more a vent for social criticism and resentment than a tool for change or political organization. Certainly authority figures were not immune to Pasquino's sting; but however much any given target might take umbrage, the criticisms did not fundamentally threaten either the social order or the formal ideology that helped to legitimate it.[86] Still, pasquinades and other surreptitious criticisms of papal policy indicated weaknesses in the fabric of Roman humanism. The engagement of early Cinquecento popes in both European and local politics created particular problems. Military adventurism, even if undertaken to secure papal autonomy,

---

[82] Valerio Marucci, Antonio Marzo, and Angelo Romano, eds., *Pasquinate romane del Cinquecento*, 2 vols. (Rome, 1988). See also Anne Reynolds, "The Classical Continuum in Roman Humanism: The Festival of Pasquino, the *Robigalia*, and Satire," *Bibliothèque d'Humanisme et Renaissance* 49 (1987): 289-307; *eadem*, "Cardinal Oliviero Carafa and the Early Cinquecento Tradition of the Feast of Pasquino," *Journal of Neo-Latin Studies* 34A (1985): 178-209; and, for a brief overview, Partner, *Renaissance Rome*, 201-204.

[83] Marucci et al., *Pasquinate romane*, 1:311-12 (#314).

[84] Harvard University, Houghton Library Ms. Lat. 358. Citation provided by Prof. Ingrid D. Rowland, University of Chicago.

[85] See, for example, Marucci et al., *Pasquinate romane*, 1:368-69 (#375), which lambastes Clement VII.

[86] Of course, if the criticism failed to be entirely anonymous, its author could be held privately accountable, as in the well-known incident in which Gian Matteo Giberti, the papal datary, purportedly dispatched a goon to impress upon the satirist Pietro Aretino the merits of leaving Rome in a timely fashion.

tended to raise old, nettlesome questions about the proper temporal role of the Roman See.[87] Julius II's wars in northern Italy, for example, drew criticism not only from humanists elsewhere, as in Erasmus's anonymously published *Julius Exclusus*, but also in Sistine Chapel composer Loyset Compère's *Sola caret monstris*. This motet, which survives in a Sistine manuscript, used the Scriptural passage in which the brothers of Joseph convince their father that Joseph has been eaten by wild animals (*Genesis* 37:31-35) as an excuse to characterize Julius as the "wild beast," and to note that in present circumstances, "Joseph is sold down the river once more."[88] In the 1520s, Clement VII's vacillation between pro-French and pro-Imperial policies would again draw humanists' criticisms of papal meddling in temporal affairs.[89]

More important, the unsettled internal politics of early Cinquecento Rome gave rise to tensions among humanists. Old Roman noble families such as the Caetani, Colonna, and Orsini resisted papal efforts to assert local authority; in 1511 and 1526, the Colonna even led open revolts against the papacy.[90] In addition, the alliances of some of these old baronial families with foreign powers—most notably, the Colonna with the Spanish and the Orsini with the French—gave strong local resonance to the popes' foreign policies.[91] When the dual loyalties of Roman baronial cardinals to family alliances and to the pope came into conflict, their humanist employees could get caught in the middle.[92]

Until the Sack of Rome, however, such political tensions usually remained submerged under the harmonious surface of curial humanism. Above all, the institutional and social structure of the curia

---

[87] On the late medieval background of this predicament, see Denys Hay, *The Church in Italy in the Fifteenth Century* (Cambridge, 1977); and Daniel Waley, *The Papal State in the Thirteenth Century* (London, 1961).

[88] Capella Sistina ms. 42, fols. 78v-80. Citation provided by Prof. Rowland.

[89] Marucci et al., *Pasquinate Romane, passim.*

[90] Partner, *Renaissance Rome*, 150-51; Stinger, *Renaissance in Rome*, 27.

[90] Partner, *Renaissance Rome*, 150-51; Stinger, *Renaissance in Rome*, 27.

[91] Judith Hook, "Clement VII, the Colonna and Charles V: A Study of the Political Instability of Italy in the Second and Third Decades of the Sixteenth Century," *European Studies Review* 2 (1972): 281-99; and *eadem, The Sack of Rome, 1527* (London, 1972), esp. chap. 1.

[92] In an extreme case, such as that of Pietro Aretino, a literary client's vituperation of political figures in Rome might even draw a violent response. See Danilo Romei, "*Pas vobis, brigate*: una frottola ritrovata di Pietro Aretino," *Rassegna della letteratura italiana* 90 (1986): 429-73; and Reynolds, *Renaissance Humanism*, 133-38.

helped keep strains in check. Humanists, as beneficiaries of the curia, had a strong professional disincentive to do more than just talk about change and reform. Unsurprisingly, the orations at the Fifth Lateran Council included much reformist rhetoric, yet engendered few substantive policy changes.[93] Iconographical programs for public ceremony tended to celebrate the status quo rather than to subvert it. Private gatherings, finally, involved humanists in a rarefied world largely of their own creation, providing further common experience that reinforced their sense of interconnectedness.

If an exceptional degree of uniformity in experience and role thus fostered harmony among Roman humanists, this harmony was not without its detrimental aspects. John D'Amico argued that the excessive inbreeding of Roman humanists, particularly in the last decade before 1527, inclined them toward intellectual sterility:

> While the assembling of so many men who were interested in similar ideas had its obvious value, it also tended to enforce a uniformity which had an ultimately deleterious effect on the vitality of Roman humanism by making it inbred; the same men met at the same places to discuss the same questions within the same general strictures and with the same results.[94]

Recent research by scholars such as Anne Reynolds and Ingrid Rowland indicates that this criticism is both overdrawn and misleading: there remained, in fact, quite a lot of vitality in humanist thinking in Leonine and early Clementine Rome: indeed, perhaps too much, in that some humanists paid little heed to the boundaries of orthodoxy, civility, or both.[95] But D'Amico's unflattering assessment is nonetheless suggestive, inasmuch as it highlights the tendency toward self-validation within the interpretive community that Roman humanists collectively comprised.[96] As Steven Shapin has recently argued, while the tendency of communities of "experts" to trust one another's authority and findings may be necessary for any scholarly enterprise to

---

[93] D'Amico, *Renaissance Humanism*, 212-37; Hallman, *Italian Cardinals*; Minnich, "Concept of Reform."

[94] D'Amico, *Renaissance Humanism*, 109.

[95] Rowland, "Abacus and Humanism"; Reynolds, *Renaissance Humanism*.

[96] On interpretive communities and the tendency toward self-validation, see Thomas Kuhn, *The Structure of Scientific Revolutions* (Chicago, 1962; rev. ed, 1970); Toulmin, *Human Understanding*, vol. 1 (Princeton, 1972) and *idem, Cosmopolis: The Hidden Agenda of Modernity* (Chicago, 1990); and Stanley Fish, *Is there a Text in this Class?: The Authority of Interpretive Communities* (Cambridge, Mass., 1980).

move forward, that very interdependence has its epistemological pitfalls.[97] Relying too much upon one another's "authoritative" conceptions of Rome and its mission, curial humanists were inclined not to
appreciate adequately the significance of developments elsewhere in
Europe for the roles both of papal Rome and of its humanist advocates. In the 1520s, while humanist rhetoric continued to laud the
papacy as Europe's cultural arbiter, the gap between the assumptions
embedded in that narrative and the actual course of events became
increasingly difficult to bridge. Two factors in particular—the growth
of northern European territorial states and the spread of the Lutheran heresy—posed serious challenges to Rome's role in European
politics and culture. While the nation-states of France and Spain
dwarfed the political and economic resources of the papacy, Luther
and his followers struck at it most directly, calling into question the
rights and claims of the papal See.

   These same factors challenged the role of Roman humanists themselves. Northern European courts came to employ humanists as
spokesmen for their policies and as representatives of their elegant
taste and cultural sophistication. In Rome, meanwhile, the failure of
Leo X, Adrian VI, or Clement VII to match Julius II's exceptional
abilities for financing lavish expenditure led to an inevitable contrac-
tion in patronage.[98] In addition, the spread of Protestantism was di-
minishing the effectiveness of humanists as papal spokesmen: as
learned discourse in Europe increasingly centered on questions of
Christian theology and righteousness, the classicist element within
Roman humanism—its conscious forging of links with the language
and culture of ancient Rome—could only diminish papal Rome in
the eyes of its critics.[99]

---

[97] Steven Shapin, *A Social History of Truth: Civility and Science in Seventeenth-Century
England* (Chicago, 1994), esp. chap. 1: "The Great Civility: Trust, Truth, and Moral
Order," 3-41. See also Mario Biagioli, "Galileo's System of Patronage," *History of
Science* 28 (1990): 1-62; and Paula Findlen, *Possessing Nature: Museums, Collecting and
Scientific Culture in Early Modern Italy* (Berkeley and Los Angeles, 1994).

[98] The decline in revenue from Protestant areas in the north must have contrib-
uted to this problem at least by the time of Clement VII. On Pope Clement's precari-
ous financial situation and his efforts to remedy it, see Melissa Meriam Bullard,
Filippo Strozzi and the Medici: Favor and Finance in Sixteenth-Century Florence and Rome
(Cambridge, 1980); and *eadem, Lorenzo il Magnifico: Image and Anxiety, Politics and Finance*
(Florence, 1994), esp. chap. 8 (215-33), "The Power of Middlemen."

[99] e.g., Erasmus, *Ciceronianus* (1528), attacked the classicizing of Christian ceremony in Roman humanist sermons. On this subject, see John O'Malley, *Praise and
Blame*; Silvana Seidel Menchi, "Alcuni atteggiamenti della cultura italiana di fronte a

Two decades later, under Paul III (1534-49), the papacy would recognize its need for theologically trained advocates who emphasized doctrinal orthodoxy: employing humanistic skills, perhaps, but in strictly delimited contexts, and bolstering church authority less with grand classical analogies than with rigorous textual-critical proof.[100] In the early 1520s, however, Roman humanists underplayed the import of these incipient changes for their own social and intellectual world. Lacking any serious internal challenges to harmony and well-insulated from developments in the north, they avoided addressing such issues in any substantive way, occupying themselves instead with ever more recondite academic questions.

The pathological nature of Roman humanists' insularity became evident at least by 1519 in the reception they accorded the Flemish scholar Christophe de Longueil.[101] At the start, all went well for Longueil, a skilled Ciceronian stylist, who rose rapidly in the curial bureaucracy, in part because of his friendship with the papal secretaries Pietro Bembo and Jacopo Sadoleto.[102] In January of 1519, Longueil was approved for honorary Roman citizenship: a distinction rich in symbolic significance if not in actual privileges. Thus far, only native Italians had been so honored. Before Longueil could formally receive citizenship, however, his nomination drew the criticism of Roman humanists jealous of his success. Making use of the fact that, a decade earlier, Longueil had written a panegyric of St. Louis that praised the Franks as the true heirs of classical Roman culture, they insisted that he defend himself against a charge of *lèse majesté*. On 16 June, even though Longueil had already left Rome, a group of humanists assembled on the Capitoline hill in the presence of Pope

Erasmo (1520-1536)," in *Eresia e riforma nell' Italia del Cinquecento. Miscellanea I*, ed. Luigi Firpo and Giorgio Spini (Florence, 1974), 71-133, at 106-107, n.169; and Kenneth Gouwens, "Ciceronianism and Collective Identity: Defining the Boundaries of the Roman Academy, 1525," *Journal of Medieval and Renaissance Studies* 23:2 (Spring, 1993): 173-95.

[100] This change can be usefully interpreted in the context of Stephen Toulmin's conception of "ecological niches." Because of changes in the intellectual ecology of early sixteenth-century Rome, humanists lost their distinctive role as papal spokesmen. See Stephen Toulmin, *Human Understanding*, esp. 300-318; and, for a more accessible explication and application of the theory, see *idem, Cosmopolis*, esp. 180-92; and 208-209, on the need for an "ecology of institutions."

[101] On Longueil, see especially Simar, *Christophe de Longueil*, 62-74. D'Amico, *Renaissance Humanism*, 110-11, offers a useful analysis of the significance of the episode.

[102] For this and the details which follow, see Simar, *Christophe de Longueil*, 62-74.

Leo X to hear Celso Mellini assail the absent Flemish scholar with an
impassioned attack that culminated in a *prosopopoeia* calling to witness
the shades of Cato, Cicero, and Livy, among others, against this
barbarian who dared presume himself worthy of the Roman
name.[103]

The Longueil episode would merit little attention had not the Roman humanists expended such extraordinary energy in its resolution.
In fact, Baldesar Castiglione, who was among those present for the
ceremonial "trial" on the Capitoline, even suggested (doubtless with
considerable exaggeration) that emotions at the event ran so high
that had Longueil been in attendance, he would have been killed on
the spot.[104] Longueil, for his part, composed an elaborate defense
against the charge of *Romanitas laesa*. Submitted in Rome by a third
party on 9 August 1519, this defense, which scrupulously avoided
using any phrase not found in Cicero, ultimately led the judges to
find in Longueil's favor.[105]

Taken as a whole, the Longueil affair demeans both the protago-
nists and the social world of Roman humanism over whose privileges
they were fighting: a world preoccupied with its own petty honors
and agonistic games instead of focused upon the profoundly significant changes taking place outside its immediate confines. In the decade preceding the Sack of Rome, curial humanists were disinclined
to heed the growing threats to Roman cultural hegemony and to
their own rarefied world. While calls for a crusade against the Turks
and polemics against Luther and his followers indicated their awareness of such threats, the shared narrative of Roman humanism remained fundamentally intact. Not until 1527 would events force
them to confront the reduced possibilities of Renaissance Rome.[106]

---

[103] Simar, *Christophe de Longueil*, 66-70, notes that Longueil's humanist supporters
included Sadoleto, Lelio Massimo, [F.M.] Molza, and Girolamo Negri. His declared
enemies included Celso and Pietro Mellini, Tommaso Pighinuzzi da Pietrasanta, and
Lorenzo Grana. Both Angelo Colocci and Johann Küritz were in attendance at the
Capitoline meeting.

[104] Letter of Castiglione to Isabella d'Este (Rome, 16 June 1519), reproduced in
Domenico Gnoli, "Un giudizio di Lesa Romanità sotto Leone X," *Nuova antologia* 115
(1891): 251-76 & 691-716, at 715.

[105] Simar, *Christophe de Longueil*, 74.

[106] For provocative accounts of intellectuals' disillusionment following political re-
verses, see Christopher Hill, *The Experience of Defeat: Milton and Some Contemporaries*
(Harmondsworth, 1984); and Toulmin, *Cosmopolis*, 45-87. The way that Roman hu-

iii. *Remembering the Renaissance after the Sack of Rome*

A dearth of contemporary sources complicates our assessment of the initial impact of the events of 1527 upon Roman humanism. Some, such as Paolo Bombace and Cristoforo Marcello, met their deaths in Rome at the hands of the invaders. Others, including Johann Küritz, died elsewhere shortly thereafter as a result of injuries suffered during the siege and occupation. Few of the surviving members of the Colocci/Küritz sodalities, mostly dispersed throughout Italy, wrote much about the Sack of Rome and its significance.[107] Therefore, the writings of Alcionio, Corsi, Sadoleto, and Valeriano are all the more valuable. While each author chose a different genre for narrating the Sack of Rome, all four approached the subject with a common set of tools and categories for reëvaluating Renaissance Rome and for reconceiving their own life-stories so as to accommodate the events of 1527. After the Sack, their career paths diverged, and their writings suggest the range of Roman humanists' responses. The lens of current research on narrative, trauma, and memory allows us to see how these authors rendered an otherwise overwhelming event manageable by constructing a narrative that incorporated it into a stable system of meaning. When taken together, these writings also exemplify the interplay between sociopolitical and cultural change.

Pietro Alcionio blamed the Sack partly on the pope. Though he had long relied on Clement's patronage and was among those taking refuge in the papal fortress during the fighting, soon afterward he sought the protection and support of the pope's arch-rival, the pro-Imperial Cardinal Pompeo Colonna. In four orations written in 1527-28, Alcionio combined criticism of Clement's political mistakes

---

manists had built their expectations for papal Rome in part upon scriptural prophecy can only have exacerbated the sense of disillusionment and disorientation. On this theme see Chastel, *Sack of Rome*; Reeves, ed., *Prophetic Rome*; and Massimo Firpo, *Il Sacco di Roma*. For a useful general treatment of the phenomenon, see Leon Festinger, Henry W. Riecken, and Stanley Schachter, *When Prophecy Fails* (Minneapolis, 1956).

[107] Several other Roman humanist accounts do, however, survive, most notably Giovio's "Ischian" dialogue, analyzed briefly in Zimmermann, *Paolo Giovio*, 86-105. I am presently preparing an article on this dialogue. See also Rosanna Alhaique Pettinelli, "*Amicos expertus varios parumque fidos*: Lilio Gregorio Giraldi e il Sacco di Roma," chap. 3 in her *Tra antico e moderno: Roma nel primo Rinascimento* (Rome, 1991), 51-62; and the sources cited in De Caprio, *La tradizione*.

with qualified optimism about Roman culture's potential for recovery.

Pietro Corsi, who continued to seek papal patronage after the Sack, exonerated the papacy and Roman culture from any responsibility for it. Earlier, he had written eclogues hailing Pope Julius II as initiator of the golden age. Now, in a long poem lamenting Rome's destruction, he dignified Clement VII and described the pontiff's ill fortune as undeserved. If new social realities circumscribed what Corsi could convincingly claim on behalf of the papacy, he nonetheless remained among its staunchest advocates.

Jacopo Sadoleto made the sharpest break with Roman humanist ideals. As Pope Clement's domestic secretary, he had occupied a position near the center of curial culture. In mid-April of 1527, however—less than one month before the Sack—Sadoleto left Italy for his diocese in France, not returning until 1536, and then only as part of a reform commission. Sadoleto's correspondence suggests the influence of the Sack upon his gradual move from a position of centrality in the papal court to that of a comparative "outsider" who stood as its critic and who defined his ecclesiastical responsibilities differently.

Pierio Valeriano, whose quest for patronage elsewhere in Italy removed him from Rome's political polarities, initially questioned whether moral failings had brought about the disaster, but later avoided assigning responsibility. In a dialogue surveying the misfortunes of several decades of humanists, he concluded that the golden age had already passed well before 1527. He described a remnant of humanists who retained a degree of collective identity despite the decimation of their already-declining culture. But his narrative—like those of Alcionio, Corsi, and Sadoleto—provided closure to a period of Renaissance Roman history that he saw as definitively having ended.

Placed in their specific social contexts, these narratives of the Sack of Rome attest to the cultural repercussions of conquest and of the collapse of a regime. Of course, their meanings are far from transparent: in each case, the author employs a classical genre and filters personal expression through layers of literary convention. Nonetheless, we cannot simply dismiss them as rhetorical constructs devoid of affective content, especially given the magnitude and immediacy of the experiences they describe. In writing about a traumatic event that affected them directly, Alcionio and Corsi struggled to render comprehensible not only the Sack in general but their own personal suffering in particular. Sadoleto, by contrast, had to confront what psychologists have termed "survivor guilt," which complicated his efforts to explain both to himself and to others why he had been spared. Valeriano, who wrote at the greatest chronological remove from the Sack, maintained an ironic distance from the event and better placed it in perspective. Yet even for him, narrating the Sack of Rome served in part as a form of life-writing, giving coherence and meaning to changes in his own career in the years after 1527.

Taken together, these narratives evidence the fragmentation of the humanist consensus that their authors had once helped to build. The discourse of Roman humanists would not be entirely transformed by the Sack: indeed, the literary tropes and philosophical categories of classical Latin writings would continue to provide much of their conceptual vocabulary. Still, the memory of the Sack would endure, tempering any renewed optimism with an awareness of the precariousness of the cultural position of papal Rome and of its humanist spokesmen. Against this backdrop, they took stock of their own lives. As they reminisced about Rome before the Sack, they deployed the remembered elements in new narratives that rendered meaningful both the catastrophe and its particular impact upon them.

That humanists' remembering of Rome was itself a creative act should not surprise, given recent psychological findings on the malleability and tenuousness of memories. Rather than being inscribed on writers' minds as on computer hard-disks, our recollections of past events become constellated within fields of meaning that are far less stable. Half a century ago, the psychologist Frederick Bartlett characterized memory as an "effort after meaning," in which we map out perceptions into patterns organized around visual images.[108] Recent research by Ulric Neisser and others has confirmed richly Bartlett's hypothesis that recalled information tends to conform to interpretation rather than the reverse.[109] Thus, in the act of remembering, we tell new stories in which the remembered elements are juxtaposed with one another differently, with different meanings. Furthermore,

---

[108] Frederick C. Bartlett, *Remembering: A Study in Experimental and Social Psychology* (Cambridge, 1932).

[109] See especially the recent elaborations upon Bartlett's work in Ulric Neisser and Robyn Fivush, eds., *The Remembering Self: Construction and Accuracy in the Self-Narrative* (Cambridge, 1994).

recent work on "recovered" memories of childhood traumas has suggested the difficulties of being sure of our own experiences: for, in the mind's eye, vivid recollections of graphic scenes that we have only imagined or heard described can become indistinguishable from memories of actual experiences. Both kinds of information are stored and recalled in the same manner, with the same kind of image.[110] Through their intensity of imagery and explicitness of detail, idealized accounts can become counter-narratives that rival or even displace the recollection of what actually happened. Thus humanists' narratives of the Sack of Rome may tell us as much about the authors and their search for meaning as they do about the event itself.

Finally, humanists' narratives of the Sack of Rome have had a profound historiographical impact. When reflecting in their writings upon the Renaissance in Rome before 1527, they treated it as a completed era of cultural efflorescence rather than as an ongoing project in which they could still participate. In so doing, ironically, the Roman humanists themselves first gave theoretical closure to the period that we today persist in calling the High Renaissance.

---

[110] On the forensic complexities of establishing the validity of "memories" of childhood trauma, see for example Elizabeth Loftus, *The Myth of Repressed Memory: False Memories and Allegations of Sexual Abuse* (New York, 1994); and Lenore Terr, *Unchained Memories: True Stories of Traumatic Memories, Lost and Found* (New York, 1994). One could argue that Ronald Reagan's infamous "movie memories" are perhaps only an extreme example of the kind of confusion endemic to memory in general.

CHAPTER TWO

PIETRO ALCIONIO'S ORATIONS ON THE SACK OF ROME

When the Vatican was besieged during the Sack of Rome, and Pope Clement VII fled into the Castel Sant' Angelo, others scrambled to do likewise. Some, such as Paolo Bombace, failed to reach the fortress and were cut down by the invading troops, but Pietro Alcionio, despite being wounded by an arquebus shot as he fled, ultimately did find refuge there.[1] When the siege was first lifted, however, Alcionio—who had enjoyed Medicean patronage since 1522—defected and went over to the protection of the pope's arch-rival, whose fortunes had just improved dramatically: Cardinal Pompeo Colonna, the prominent imperialist whom Clement had excommunicated and stripped of his rank the previous November. Unfortunately Alcionio did not live to profit much from his promising new allegiance: not long after the Imperial army left Rome in February of 1528, he died of an illness in Colonna's palace.[2] In the last year of his life, however, Alcionio wrote four orations that allow us to trace his efforts to establish a fixed meaning for the Sack of Rome, even as sociopolitical instability and turbulence forced him repeatedly to reevaluate that meaning.[3] Since the orations spanned his move to the protection of

---

[1] Valeriano, *DLI*, 63: "Fortunarum mox direptionem Columnensi sacrilegio passus, mox Hispanorum Germanorumque incursionibus occupata Roma, dum vitae consulturus suae Pontificem Clementem in Arcem Aeliam confugientem subsequeretur, instantibus a tergo grassatoribus sulfurea glande brachium traiectus est."

[2] *Ibid.*: "Ubi primum obsidio soluta est, rebelli in Principem animo, qui hominem fovendum susceperat, ad Pom<peium> Columnam Cardinalem transfugit, apud quem pauculos commoratus menses vitam morbo finivit, atque utinam de pietate nostra melius sensisset, ne vitae finem, quod indignissimum est homine litterato, infidelitatis labe contaminasset." I date Alcionio's death to mid-February 1528 at the earliest, rather than the conventionally given 1527, based in part upon the internal evidence of the oration "De urbe servata," analyzed below.

[3] Cors. MS 33 E 26 (formerly Fondo Rossi 289) contains a polished copy of Alcionio's "Declamatio in literas Caesaris," along with its dedicatory letter to the poet Antonio Tebaldeo and a separate transcription (fols. 4r-5v) of the letter of Charles V to the Romans, to which the declamation responds. The letter to Tebaldeo indicates that the oration had been delivered before an assembly on the Capitoline. Alcionio assures Tebaldeo (fol. 5v), who had not been present, that the delivered version was as candid as the written one (see below, n. 105). Later copies of this

Pompeo Colonna, they also illuminate why he severed one patron-
client bond and how he began to forge another: a change by no
means unprecedented among Italian humanists, but one that was
intrinsically problematic because it meant violating the loyalty expected of clients in the *fides* relationship.[4] In his dialogue *De litteratorum
infelicitate*, the curial humanist Pierio Valeriano, who had been in
Florence during the Sack, would censure Alcionio for deserting
Clement and for showing "a spirit rebellious toward the prince who
had undertaken to support [him]."[5] In fact, Valeriano's interlocutor
criticizes Alcionio specifically for transgressing the conventions of the

oration are found in Ricc. Ms. 2022, 189r-207v; and in Isol. Ms. F.6.1. None is in
Alcionio's hand. A printed edition appears in Hoff., I, 550-88. The MS Raccolta
Serassi 67 R4 (3) (18th cent., now lost) of the Biblioteca Civile Angelo Mai in Berga-
mo would appear from its description in Kristeller, *Iter*, V, 487, to have included yet
another copy of this oration, its dedicatory letter to Tebaldeo, and the letter of
Charles V to which the oration responds. Another manuscript, inaccessible because
sold to an anonymous private collector by H. P. Kraus, would appear from its catalogue description to contain yet another copy, in three Italic hands, from Venice
c.1540. Despite the cataloguer's claim that the manuscript contains "two orations
against the Emperor Charles V," the description of content, date, and dedication
leads me to suspect that the manuscript contains only the known declamation.
    The other orations are only known to have survived in single manuscript copies in
the Vatican Library. BAV MS Vat. Lat. 3436, 23r-55r contain drafts of writings of
Alcionio, including all three of the other orations that deal with the Sack of Rome:
23r-34r, "Petri Alcyonii pro S.P.Q.R. oratio de republica reddenda atque e custodia
liberando Clemente VII Pontifice Maximo ad Carolum Caesarem Designatum"; 35r-
40r, untitled, beginning "Inter maximos dolores"; and 42r-45v, "Petri Alcyonii oratio
pro S.P.Q.R. ad Pompeium Columnam de urbe servata," with a dedicatory letter
(fol. 41v) to Oberto Strozzi. There are three quires of paper (less one unnumbered
page, which has been excised), fols. 22-34, 35-45, and 46-55. All are in the same
hand in rough-draft form. Mario Rosa, "Alcionio (Alcyonius), Pietro," in *DBI* 2
(1960): 77-80, at 80, follows Pierre de Nolhac's incorrect pagination of the oration to
Pompeo Colonna as continuing through fol. 54. In fact, fols. 46-54 contain other
writings of Alcionio. Of the orations in BAV ms. Vat. Lat. 3436, only one has been
published: a severely flawed transcription of the oration "De urbe servata," taken
from this manuscript, appears as an appendix to Aida Consorti, *Il Cardinale Pompeo
Colonna*, 2nd ed. (Rome, 1909), 190-98. I am grateful to Nelson Minnich for bringing
this rare augmented edition to my attention. Representing all three genres of classical
oratory, Alcionio's orations suggest the range of rhetorical options open to a Renaissance humanist orator interpreting a major historical event for a contemporary audience. On the significance of the three *genera* (deliberative, judicial, and epideictic) as
models for Renaissance rhetoric, see John W. O'Malley, *Praise and Blame in Renaissance
Rome: Rhetoric, Doctrine, and Reform in the Sacred Orators of the Papal Court, c.1450–1521*
(Durham, North Carolina, 1979), esp. 39-41.
    [4] On the rhetoric of the patronage bond and its inherent contradictions, see Diana
Robin, *Filelfo in Milan: Writings, 1451-1477* (Princeton, 1991), esp. 13-17. For a less
sympathetic account of clients' motivations, see Lauro Martines, *The Social World of the
Florentine Humanists, 1390-1460* (Princeton, 1963).
    [5] Valeriano, *DLI*, 63. For the Latin text, see note 2 above.

patron-client bond: "would that he had thought better about our obligation (*nostra pietate*), so that he might not have defiled the end of his life with the stain of treachery (*infidelitatis*)—a thing most unworthy of a scholar!"[6]

Closer examination of Alcionio's predicament will suggest a more nuanced interpretation. Reliant upon a Maecenas who could no longer guarantee support, and surrounded by colleagues who rejected him socially, Alcionio had little practical reason to honor his *fides* relationship with Clement. Still, in the discourse of patronage, he would be cast as a traitor for failing to do so.[7] The charge of *infidelitas* may also have had a deeper resonance in the case of Alcionio: for in his orations, he would move beyond the traditional language of deference, violating the sense of decorum that humanists so valued, to challenge Clement rhetorically in a way that foreshadowed his defection. This rhetorical change, like Alcionio's subsequent ideological marginalization of the papacy, is particularly revealing when interpreted in the context of the catastrophe's impact upon his role as a humanist spokesman for Roman culture.

In order to appreciate fully the significance of Alcionio's transformation, however, we must view it against the backdrop of his previous career and expressed values. Alcionio's efforts to imitate the ideal of the perfect orator—the ultimate exemplar and arbiter both of literary style and of appropriate behavior—repeatedly fell flat. In Venice, Florence, and finally Rome, his unwillingness—or perhaps even inability—to adhere to humanist conceptions of literary and social decorum militated against his acceptance among humanist colleagues. To be sure, many of these other humanists despised him, and they did all they could to thwart his efforts to create an imposing self. But if Alcionio did not have anything approaching exclusive control over his image, an outspokenness beyond what was considered appropriate to his station contributed substantially to the low regard in which he was held. It is precisely this outspokenness, ironically, that would allow his individual voice to come across so forcefully in his orations on the Sack of Rome.

---

[6] *Ibid.*
[7] Robin, *Filelfo*, esp. chap. 1.

i. *Obscure Origins and Uneven Success*

Alcionio was probably born in the 1490s somewhere near Venice.[8] If
his contemporaries had difficulty ascertaining his provenance, he
himself did little to clarify the issue. Paolo Giovio said of him that
"although he suppressed the names of his two cities, [he] confessed
himself a hybrid...."[9] Girolamo Negri noted that Alcionio claimed
different origins on different occasions, perhaps hoping to incite the
most famous cities of Italy to quarrel over which one could take
credit for him.[10] The first surviving mention of him dates from 1516,
in a letter from John Watson to Erasmus detailing Watson's encounters with literati in Venice the previous year.[11] While a student of
Marcus Musurus at the Scuola di San Marco, Alcionio was also affiliated with the circle of Aldo Manuzio. Although he practiced medicine, too, the study and imitation of classical authors was evidently
his primary aspiration.[12] When, following the death of Musurus in

---

[8] The best brief summary of Alcionio's life and works is Mario Rosa, "Alcionio."
For further detail, see [A. Zeno], "Articolo I," *Giornale de' letterati d'Italia*, I,3 (Venice,
1710): 1-42; Pierre Bayle, *Dictionaire historique et critique, par Mr. P.B. Cinquième edition,
revue, corrigée et augmentée.* I (A-B), (Amsterdam, 1740), 143-145; G. M. Mazzuchelli, *Gli
scrittori d'Italia* I, i (Brescia, 1753), 376-383. Less useful are Jean Le Clerc, *Bibliotheque
Choisie, Pour Servir de Suite a la Bibliothèque Universelle* (Amsterdam, 1707 or 1708), XIV,
118-134; Jean Pierre Niceron, *Mémoires pour servir à l'histoire des hommes illustres dans la
République des lettres avec un catalogue raisonné de leurs ouvrages* (Paris, 1729-1745), VI, 150-
166; and G. Fattini, "Alcionio, Pietro," in *Enciclopedia italiana di scienze, lettere ed arti*
(Rome, 1950), II, 251. Zeno, 4-5, limits the year of Alcionio's birth to the last decade
of the fifteenth century on the basis of Alcionio's portrayal of himself as in puberty at
the time in which his dialogue *De exsilio* is set (i.e., 1512) and on circumstantial
evidence in Leoni's letter to Erasmus (see below). Rosa, "Alcionio," 77, bases his
estimate of 1487 upon a calculation from Alcionio's supposed date of death: Alcionio,
he says, "Nacque... nel 1487 (se morì appena quarantenne, come affermano concordi
i biografi, nel 1527)." I suspect this claim is based wrongly upon Zeno, 11, who says
Alcionio was "non ancor giunto all'anno quarantesimo dell'età sua" when he died.
But the only source Zeno cites (note b, p. 10) is Valeriano's *DLI*, which does not
specify Alcionio's age.
[9] Paolo Giovio, *An Italian Portrait Gallery*, tr. Florence Alden Gragg (Boston, 1935),
152. On Giovio's dislike of Alcionio, see below. Giovio does not specify the cities to
which he refers.
[10] BAV ms. Vat. Lat. 5892, 228v.
[11] Erasmus, *EE* (2:315) letter 450, lines 29-30: "...qui (i.e., Ambrogio Leoni) me
fecit plurimi tua causa: quomodo fecerunt Petrus Halcionius, meo iudicio egregie
facundus, et alii complures." A further piece of evidence from 1516 is a Greek epi-
gram at the beginning (fol.A[VI]v.) of *Ioannis Baptistae Egnatii... in Dioscoridem... anno-
tamenta...* (Venice), cited in Rosa, "Alcionio," 77.
[12] In his commentary on Book XV, letter 29 of Cicero's letters to Atticus, Paolo
Manuzio mentions Alcionio's practice of medicine. *In epistolas Ciceronis ad Atticum, Pauli*

1517, the Venetian Senate announced a contest to choose a successor in the public lectureship in Greek, Manuzio's friend Ambrogio Leoni described the competition to Erasmus, identifying Alcionio as a leading candidate. "He has reproduced several orations of Isocrates and Demosthenes in such pure Ciceronian style," Leoni wrote, "that you might think you were reading our Arpinate himself, and has turned many of Aristotle's pieces so lucidly that Latium could proudly say 'Lo, Aristotle now belongs to us.'"[13]

Despite Alcionio's failure to obtain Musurus's appointment, his career continued to progress: in 1521, his translations of Aristotle were published in Venice, with the privileges of Pope Leo X and of the Venetian Senate.[14] By July of 1522, he had moved to Florence, where the Florentine Signoria engaged him as a teacher of Greek.[15] Later that year, the Aldine press published his best-known work, the *Medices Legatus: de exsilio*, which Alcionio dedicated to Nikolaus von Schönberg, Archbishop of Capua and close friend of Cardinal Giulio de' Medici.[16] By late 1523, he augmented his teaching income with a

Manutii commentarius... (Venice, 1547), 446r. Various pasquinades and slurs in other sources also describe Alcionio as a doctor.

[13] *EE* lett. 854: lines 55-56. *CWE* 6 (1982): 60n dates the decree to June of 1518. The quotation follows *CWE* 6 (1982): 59. In his response to this letter, dated 15 October [1518], Erasmus says that he intends to write to Alcionio and that he desires to see his editions of Aristotle (*EE* lett. 868: lines 56-61; 3:403). The promised letter to Alcionio is not known to have been written. Although Alcionio published his collection of translations of Aristotle in 1521, neither the Isocrates nor the Demosthenes is known to have been published, nor does either appear to survive in manuscript form.

[14] On the appointment of Vettore Fausto to succeed Musurus, see James Bruce Ross, "Venetian Schools and Teachers, Fourteenth to Early Sixteenth Century: A Survey and a Study of Giovanni Battista Egnazio," *Renaissance Quarterly* 29 (1976): 521-66, at 544-45. Zeno, 7-8, speculates that perhaps disgust over this loss led Alcionio to leave Venice in 1522. Aristotle, *De generatione et interitu...* trans. Pietro Alcionio (Venice, 1521).

[15] G. Hugo Tucker, "Exile Exiled: Petrus Alcyonius (1487–1527?) in a Travelling–Chest," *Journal of the Institute of Romance Studies* 2 (1993): 83-103, at 94, cites the Signoria's official letter of commendation (5 July 1522), which provides a *terminus ad quem* for his appointment to the Greek lectureship. As of mid-March, however, he was evidently still in Venice. See the letter from Longueil to Grimaldi, cited below, notes 18 and 19.

[16] Pietro Alcionio, *Medices legatus: de exsilio* [Venice, 1522]. This dialogue, set in 1512 in the Medici palace in Rome, has as interlocutors Giulio de' Medici, Giovanni de' Medici, and the latter's nephew Lorenzo, and took its name from Giovanni's service as a legate for Pope Julius II. Its theme gains further resonance from Giulio de' Medici's service as papal legate in 1521. In parts of the dialogue, Alcionio both lauded the Medici at length and expressed an ethnocentric pro-Italian, pro-Roman position that foreshadows later developments in his ideology. See Tucker, "Exile

stipend from Cardinal Giulio himself to translate Galen's *De partibus animalium*.[17]

Already in early 1522, however, before Alcionio had left Venice, his work had come under direct attack, when the prominent Spanish humanist Juan Ginés de Sepúlveda—a figure not generally noted for his tolerant disposition—published his own version of the same ten books of Aristotle's *De animalibus* that Alcionio had just translated, as well as a tract devoted expressly to highlighting Alcionio's errors in translation.[18] Christophe de Longueil, who had earlier entertained Alcionio in Padua, expressed mild amusement at his acquaintance's predicament, and wrote to Ottaviano Grimaldi in Venice, suggesting that he might enjoy telling Alcionio himself so as to be able to see the reaction.[19] Alcionio tried to reduce the circulation of the *Errata* by purchasing as many copies as he could and destroying them; still, the damage was done, and in his *Elogia* (1546), Paolo Giovio gleefully emphasized the shortcomings of Alcionio's translations, the positive reception of Sepúlveda's *Errata* in the scholarly community, and the expense to which Alcionio had been forced to go to burn the books.[20] Probably because of the 1523 publication of Niccolò Leonico Tomeo's influential translation of these same ten books of the *De*

Exiled," 98-100. Tucker provides the most thorough and provocative analysis to date of the *De exsilio*.

[17] *LP*, 99v (Negri to Michiel, 1 Sept. 1523).

[18] J.G. Sepúlveda, *Libri Aristotelis, quos vulgo latini, parvos naturales appellant; Errata P. Alcyonii in interpretatione Aristotelis, a Ioanne Genesio Sepúlveda Cordubensi collecta* [Bologna, 1522]. The letter of 23 March 1522 from Longueil to Grimaldi provides a *terminus ad quem* for the publication of the latter text (*Lucubrationes*, 386-87): "Misi ad te nuper nescio quid de quodam Hispano homine, qui P. Alcyonii in faciendo Aristotele Latino errata Bononiae colligeret."

[19] Longueil, *Lucubrationes*, 387: "Hoc, si tibi videbitur, Alcyonio significabis, aut per alios certe denuntiandum ei curabis. Sed si bene te novi, ipse tu denuntiabis, ut hominis ad tantae contumeliae nuntium, vultum videas: quod unum sane spectaculum tibi magnopere invideo."

[20] *LP*, 99v (Negri to Michiel, 1 Sept. 1523): "Uno Spagnuolo, non però lo Stunica, ha tolto la gatta con l'Alcionio, ha raccolto tutti gli errori delle tradottioni dell'Alcionio, & ne ha stampato un libretto in Bologna. L'Alcionio ha comprato tutti quei libri, ma lo Spagnuolo li vuol far ristampare." On unsuccessful searches for copies of this extremely rare volume, see Angel Losada, *Juan Gines de Sepúlveda: A Traves de su "Epistolario" y Nuevos Documentos* (Madrid, 1973), 388-89. Giovio, *Gli elogi*, ed. Renzo Meregazzi (Rome, 1972), 133: "Quum aliqua ex Aristotele perperam insolenterque vertisset, in eum Sepúlveda, vir hispanus, egregie de literis meritus, edito volumine peracuta iacula contorsit, non hercle indigna tanti philosophi vulneribus, si vindictae nomine merita poena mulctaretur, tanto quidem eruditorum applausu, ut Alcyonius, ignominiae dolore misere consternatus, hispani hostis libros in tabernis ut concremaret gravi pretio coëmere cogeretur."

animalibus, Alcionio's collection of translations—like Sepúlveda's attack upon it—has fallen into obscurity.[21] But the terms and assumptions of the dispute reveal something of how hostile peer review and Alcionio's own violations of decorum combined to frustrate his efforts to create and promote a coherent, imposing self.

Alcionio's dedicatory letters for the translations of Aristotle could scarcely have done much to endear him to the reader. For instance, in the guise of thanking Girolamo Negri for support and encouragement, Alcionio asserted that he himself alone was the first to have rendered the "real" Aristotle accessible to a Latinate audience, an accomplishment which would (he claims) impress the philosopher himself, were he alive.[22] Set alongside such grandiosity, ·the Spanish humanist's withering attack is almost refreshing. To devastating effect, Sepúlveda itemized passages where Alcionio's ornate Latin badly misconstrued the sense of the Greek. More important than particular errors, however, was an underlying methodological flaw: namely, Alcionio's misunderstanding of the guidelines for imitation that Cicero and Quintilian had set down. In particular, Alcionio indiscriminately blurred generic boundaries, assuming that "to the extent that one is more eloquent, he is the more to be proposed for imitation in *every* kind of writing."[23] Sepúlveda pounced eagerly upon this fundamental stylistic error, recalling Quintilian's instruction that each subject matter had its own standard of decorum and, therefore, required the use of a particular literary style.[24]

If Alcionio's flawed sense of literary decorum thus hampered his ability to translate effectively, his efforts at *imitatio* of the character of

---

[21] Rosa, "Alcionio," 78. Tomeo's edition was published by the same house as Alcionio's (Vitali).

[22] Aristotle, *De generatione,* trans. Alcionio: "Nos quidem in commentario, quo multas ex veteribus Medicis observationes complexi sumus, contra hominis accusationem doctissimum Philosophum defendimus, atque eidem ipsi ita adesse studuimus, & quae obiicerentur diluere, ut certo sciamus illum non vulgareis gratias nobis habiturum esse, quod nostra tandem opera aliquando desierit animos hominum confictis sensibus puerilibusque deliramentis confundere, & fabulosissimis commentis implicare."

[23] Sepúlveda, *Errata:* "Nec enim quo quisque eloquentior est, eo magis in omni scribendi genere est proponendus ad imitandum." Emphasis mine in English translation.

[24] *Ibid.:* "quo quid pot<est> ineptius excogitari. cum stilus oratorius ab historico charactere tam longe distet, ut plerasque historiae virtutes oratori vitandas esse Fabius idem praecipiat. Et Cicero nec Thucydidem nec Xenophontem utiles esse oratori dictaverit.... quae si recte praecipiuntur, viderit Alcyonius, quam bene historicus et oratorius stilus cum temperato dicendi genere conveniat, quo philosophos usos fuisse constat. Sua etenim cuique (ut idem ait) proposita Lex, suus cuique decor est."

the perfect orator appear to have failed on similar grounds—a com-
plementary shortcoming that would correspondingly injure his reputation. With his arrival in Florence in 1523, Alcionio's problems with
other scholars only became more pronounced. On 17 March, Girolamo Negri noted that certain Florentines, including Filippo Strozzi,
criticized Alcionio and even wrote against him: a situation which
Cardinal Giulio de' Medici merely found amusing.[25] Still, Cardinal
Giulio was more sympathetic than the others. Thus, in noting that
the cardinal had decided to come to Rome for Easter to avoid the
plague ravaging Florence, Negri speculated that Alcionio might ac-
company him since, without the cardinal present, the Florentines
would be more contumelious toward their then-unprotected rival.[26]

That same year, Cardinal Giulio awarded a large stipend, for the
translation of Alexander of Aphrodisias's commentary on Aristotle's
Metaphysics, to none other than Sepúlveda, who was then in Rome.[27]
Anxious about competition from his nemesis, whose translations had
been well-received in the scholarly community, Alcionio proceeded
to write letters "full of venom" to Medici favorites, asking that they
not speak well of the Spanish humanist to Cardinal Giulio.[28] These
found the whole affair comical, however, and goaded Alcionio by
protesting that they would seem either spiteful or ignorant were they
to criticize Sepúlveda, since the Cardinal de' Medici held him in
such high esteem. The cardinal, meanwhile, found the two humanists' backbiting entertaining, and he continued to employ both.[29]

---

[25] *LP*, [95r] (Negri to Michiel, 17 March 1523): "In Fiorenza l'hanno, come si
dice, annasato, et ho inteso, che'l Cardinal de' Medici si piglia spasso di certi Fiorentini, che lo travagliano, etiam in literis; tra gli altri un Filippo Strozzi assai in-
gegnoso. Credo non starà saldo, perche sapete il naso de' Fiorentini, & la importunità
loro." (fol. 95 is incorrectly numbered "93")

[26] *Ibid.*, 95v (Negri to Michiel, 17 March 1523): "La peste lavora in Fiorenza
terribilmente, & per questo dicesi il Cardinal de' Medici verrà quì [Rome] per Pas-
qua, & forse verrà con esso l'Alcionio, perche non essendovi il Cardinale, quei fiorentini lo tratteriano troppo male."

[27] *Ibid.*, 99v (Negri to Michiel, 1 Sept. 1523): "Il detto Spagnuolo è quì [Rome], &
ha havuto dal Cardinal de' Medici ducati dugento, per tradurre Alessandro sopra la
Metafisica...."

[28] *Ibid.*: "...[Alcionio] si dispera, che costui [Sepúlveda] habbia credito, & scrive di
quì a i favoriti de Medici lettere piene di veneno; pregandoli, che non lo vogliano
favorire appresso il Cardinale."

[29] *Ibid.*: "Di che essi prendono grande spasso, & gli rispondono, che non fanno che
si fare, perche la dottrina di costui lo ha tanto posto innanzi al Cardinale, che essi
pareriano ò maligni, ò ignoranti a volerlo disfavorire. Della qual cosa l'Alcionio più
s'avampa, & il Cardinale, che sà la cosa, ne piglia gran solazzo."

When Giulio de' Medici became Pope Clement VII that November, many humanists hoped for a restoration of the lavish patronage that they had enjoyed under his cousin, Leo X.[30] Negri speculated that Alcionio would immediately come to Rome, even though it would mean proximity to Sepúlveda, whom he said Alcionio dreaded "as the sparrow fears the hawk."[31] In fact, as soon as Alcionio heard of Clement's election, he asked permission to leave his obligations in Florence at once. The Signoria, however, denied the request on the grounds that it had not yet found a suitable replacement for him.[32] Impatient with the delay, Alcionio left town in secret and on 5 December he arrived in Rome, certain that great things lay in his future.[33]

From the outset of Clement's pontificate, however, Alcionio sought support from a papacy that had been bankrupted by the profligate Leo X and little enriched even by the tightfisted Adrian VI.[34] Howsoever humanists might desire it, a return to the level of patronage they had enjoyed under Leo X was simply not possible in the 1520s, when papal revenues fell ever shorter of expenditures.[35] Already by the time of Alcionio's arrival in Rome, opportunities were sufficiently competitive that Negri felt it would be difficult for Alcionio to match his earlier status. In fact, he even speculated that Alcionio might be forced by circumstances to return to Florence, if the Signoria would deign to take him back.[36]

---

[30]   e.g., see *LP*, 101r (Negri to Michiel, 18 Nov. 1523): "Le buone lettere, già quasi fugate dalla Barbarie preterita, sperano d'esser restituite. Est enim genuinum Mediceae familiae decus, fovere Musas."

[31] *LP*, 101r: "Credo che l'Alcionio correrà al romore, benche questo Spagnuolo quì lo spaventa, come lo sparvier la quaglia."

[32] *LP*, 102r (Negri to Michiel, 8 Dec. 1523): "Messer Pietro Alcionio, subito che intese la creatione del Pontefice, dimandò licentia, & publicè & privatim, di venirsene in Roma. La Signoria di Fiorenza non gliela volle dare, dicendo, che non haveva ancora proveduto di un'altro in luogo suo."

[33] *Ibid.*: "Egli impatiens morae appostò due feste, che non si leggeva, &, nemine salutato, se ne partì. Et così già tre giorni arrivò qui con infinita speranza di cose grandi."

[34] There is as yet no thorough examination of papal finances in the early sixteenth century. Mèlissa Meriam Bullard, *Filippo Strozzi and the Medici: Favor and Finance in Sixteenth-Century Florence and Rome* (Cambridge, 1980), esp. 119-72, provides a graphic portrait of the monetary problems of Clement VII. See also *eadem, Lorenzo il Magnifico: Image and Anxiety, Politics and Finance* (Florence: Olschki, 1994), esp. chap. 8 (215-33), "The Power of Middlemen," which includes further bibliography as well as a close study of economic policies implemented by Francesco del Nero on behalf of Clement VII.

[35] Bullard, *Filippo Strozzi*, esp. 124, 128-29, and 145.

[36] *LP*, 102r.

Once in Rome, Alcionio took part in the humanist sodality of
Angelo Colocci and Johann Küritz: Giovio includes him in a list of
participants in this circle, and a 1524 letter of Erasmus links him in
passing with Küritz and Sadoleto.[37] Yet his position in the sodality
seems to have been marginal. Meanwhile, Alcionio wrote to Francesco del Nero, then the vice-depositor for the Florentine Signoria,
trying to obtain the remainder of the sum owed him for his service
there in 1522–23.[38] In this letter, in which he invoked the authority
of Clement VII on his behalf, he nonetheless reminded del Nero of
his neediness and said that he wrote on his own account out of
necessity.[39] The following year, his status may have improved somewhat, in that he was honored by being asked to present an oration
before Pope Clement on Pentecost Sunday. If Girolamo Negri's account of the episode contains even a grain of truth, however, the
presentation failed miserably to increase the orator's esteem.[40] While
Alcionio used Ciceronian language and syntax to a fault in this oration, referring to Christian ceremonies as "*ludos sacros*" and to the
apostles as the "*duodecemviri*," Negri's letter attacked him for not being
Ciceronian enough in his manner of presentation, which violated
classical standards of decorum and appropriateness.[41] In fact, Negri
contrasted Alcionio's mode of holding forth with that enjoined by the
interlocutor "Crassus" in Cicero's *De oratore*, who had stated modestly, "I should say nothing obscure, nothing worthy of your waiting
in suspense, nothing either unheard-of to you, nor new to anyone."
Alcionio, on the other hand, went beyond the pale on the topos of

---

[37] Federico Ubaldini, *Vita di Mons. Angelo Colocci: Edizione del testo originale Italiano*
(Vatican City, 1969), 114; Erasmus, *EE* 1479, 167-170 (Erasmus to Haio Herman,
31 August 1524): "Haec morosis censoribus et malignis arrosoribus responsa sunto;
quorum odium te crebra contentione nolim exacerbare. Benevolorum catalogum
libenter legi. Inter quos nullius nomen agnosco, praeterquam Sadoleti, Alcyonii, et
Coricii." Herman, originally from Friesland, was at this time in Padua.

[38] The autograph copy of the letter, dated 1 April 1524, is preserved in the
Bibliothèque Nationale de Paris, MS Ital. 2033, 5r-6v. I am grateful to April Shelford
for obtaining for me a photocopy of this letter. On Francesco del Nero's service as
vice-depositor in Florence, see Bullard, *Filippo Strozzi*, 119-150, esp. 134-35.

[39] BN (Paris) MS Ital. 2033, 5r-5v: "son povero, et son necessitato aiutarmi del
mio."

[40] BAV MS Vat. Lat. 5892, 225r-28v, is a copy of the letter of Girolamo Negri
(dated 22 June 1525) recording the incident, which took place on 4 June. For further
analysis of Negri's letter and the events it describes, see Kenneth Gouwens, "Ciceronianism and Collective Identity: Defining the Boundaries of the Roman Academy, 1525," *The Journal of Medieval and Renaissance Studies*, 23 (1992-93): 173-95.

[41] e.g., Cicero, *De oratore*, 3210.

novelty, saying, "From me, you should await nothing generally known, nothing snatched from the crossroads. I will announce new things, and things heard in no centuries before."[42] Similarly, Negri contrasts the advice of Cicero's "Crassus", that one should modestly and timidly enter upon the task of speaking, with the performance of Alcionio, who "persisted to the end with that impudence with which he began."[43]

It was, then, in his thoroughgoing violation of any sense of decorum—in manner no less than in vocabulary—that Alcionio strayed from classical models. "Good gods," Negri exclaimed, "who could adequately put into words the farcical gesticulations of Alcionio, the baseness, the rusticity?"[44] Alcionio's speaking voice, too, was ill-suited to its task, sounding at times like the crowing of roosters and at times like an ass braying. To the end, he maintained an inappropriate tone, apparently assuming that his audience was delighting in his sparkling wit rather than laughing at his excesses.[45] While Clement VII once again appeared as his amused protector, Alcionio's fellow literati—many, perhaps, envying the honor bestowed upon him by his selection to deliver the oration—responded to the spectacle of its failure with malevolent glee.

Besides criticisms of Alcionio's specific performances such as those which Sepúlveda and Negri voiced, we find overwhelming documentation in other sources of his disagreeable temperament and vainglorious boasting—characteristics that would repeatedly help to undermine his efforts to project the image of the ideal orator. Lilio Gregorio Giraldi, in his dialogue on contemporary poets, had one interlocutor describe Alcionio as "biting and abusive, and no more modest than prudent."[46] Giraldi admitted that Alcionio was a good Latin-

---

[42] BAV MS Vat. Lat. 5892, 225v: "Nova et inaudita se allaturum pollicitus est, contrario more quam usus est apud Ciceronem Crassus. Sic enim ille: 'Nihil dicam reconditum, nihil expectatione vestra dignum, nihil aut inauditum vobis aut cuiquam novum.' Contra is: 'Nihil a me expectes vulgatum, nihil arreptum ex triviis. Nova afferam, et nullis ante seculis audita.'"

[43] Ibid., 227r and v.

[44] Ibid., 227v: "Dii boni! Quis Alcyonii mimicas gesticulationes, turpitudinem, rusticitatem, oratione consequi possit?"

[45] Ibid. "Alcyonius vero ea qua coepit imp[r]udentia ad calcem orationis perseveravit. Hac una re mirabilis, quod cum videret neminem qui <non> aperte rideret, non commovebatur, non ab ineptiis temperabat. Credo sic interpretabatur, nos dulcedine et suavitate orationis suae oblectatos ridere."

[46] Lilio Gregorio Giraldi, De poetis nostrorum temporum, ed. Karl Wotke (Berlin, 1894), 39: "Diversae naturae est Petrus Alcyonius Venetus, mordax et maledicus nec pudens magis quam prudens..." Alcionio is here contrasted with Pierio Valeriano.

ist; the problem was that his claims exceeded his abilities.[47] Giraldi had another interlocutor dismiss the subject, saying, "Enough about this worthless fellow, who has declared war on all good men and needs to be restrained with whips and a cudgel...."[48] In the *De littera-torum infelicitate*, Pierio Valeriano corroborated this picture of a hostile and vain man. As the interlocutor *Cathanaeus* noted, Alcionio's satiri-cal disparagement of all the literati had aroused against him "the hatred of all men, learned and ignorant alike."[49] His excessive pride had denied him the possibility of being considered among the fore-most of scholars.[50]

Paolo Giovio's *elogium* of Alcionio tempered grudging praise for his literary skill with intense criticism of personal qualities that were det-rimental to Alcionio's career. An "excellent literary style," says Giovio, "brought [Alcionio] no honor, since it was sullied by a char-acter utterly mean and vulgar, without a trace of the gentleman."[51] Giovio limned a portrait of a man of unequaled swinishness, who gorged himself at others' tables (and expense) to the point of nau-sea.[52] Alcionio's crudeness was enough of a standing joke among his colleagues that Negri teased a Venetian friend, "I expect your letters [to be written] more often and with more diligence than in the past, unless you want me to mark you down as *Alcionico*."[53]

In fairness to Alcionio, one should note that boorishness is, at least in part, in the eye of the beholder. Giovio's assessment of him as a half-breed ("*Hybridam*") possessed of a character that was "utterly mean and vulgar, without a trace of the gentleman" ("*nulla ex parte*

---

[47] *Ibid.*: "huius tamen oratio, si saperet, magis Arpinatem lecythum redolet. Qůae-dam Alcyonii iambica ipse legi digna laude, tum lyricos quosdam sane castos et eruditos...."

[48] *Ibid.*: "'Mitte', inquit Iulius, 'de hoc nebulone plura, qui bellum bonis omnibus indixit flagris et fuste coercendus...."

[49] Valeriano, *DLI*, 63: "Verum is eo primum infelicitatis incommodo flagellatus est, quod dum de litteratis omnibus male sentit, dicacissima omnes obtrectatione lacerebat, unde omnium tam doctorum, quam imperitorum in se odium concitarat."

[50] *Ibid.*, 62-63: "Non displicuisset mihi Alcyonius, excepit Cathanaeus, si quantum stylo profecerat, amicorum consilium de rebus adhibere voluisset, qui nisi ipsimet sibi tantum arrogasset, futurus omnino fuerat e primoribus; multam enim Graecis, Lati-nisque litteris operam impenderat, & disciplinis variis oblectatus erat."

[51] Giovio, *Gli elogi*, 133: "ad praecellentem scribendi facultatem pervenit." "Sed hic partus honos non erat in conspectu, quum nulla ex parte ingenuis sed plane plebeis et sordidis moribus foedaretur."

[52] *Ibid.*

[53] *LP*, 100v (1 Sept. 1523): "Aspetto vostre lettere più spesso, & con più diligentia, che per il passato, se non volete, ch'io vi dia in nota per Alcionico."

ingenuis sed plane plebeis et sordidis moribus") carries with it at least a trace of class prejudice.[54] Similarly, the diction of Girolamo Negri's letter on the Pentecost oration implies social disdain for Alcionio, who displayed his "*rusticitas*," and who spoke with a "*vox illiberalis*," a "voice unworthy of a free man."[55] In a vernacular tailed sonnet, Francesco Berni expressed similar criticisms of Alcionio.[56] In the poem, when Alcionio's beast of burden, a she-mule, prophesies to him in the manner of Balaam's ass, the "*poeta laureato*" fails to catch the meaning because he is preoccupied with fine points of the animal's grammar.[57] Beyond mocking Alcionio's literary acumen, the poem also ridicules his social standing: unable to afford either a horse or a concubine, Alcionio (says Berni) has taken to using the she-mule as his "mount" in place of both.[58] One may conclude, then, that Alcionio's inability to gain respectable standing in the Roman Academy was to some extent beyond his control: for like his mule, he lacked proper breeding.

But another, more tangible constraint upon Alcionio's chances for success in Rome was that criticisms of his scholarship had preceded him there (as had, perhaps not coincidentally, Sepúlveda). Already in March of 1523, Negri had written from Rome that "the Dialogue [i.e., the *De exsilio*] of Alcionio is greatly torn apart by these Academicians, and there are some who write against him, who have constrained me not to make known their names."[59] One of these figures was probably Giovio, who had taken umbrage upon hearing that Alcionio was writing history, an undertaking to which Giovio felt he had exclusive rights.[60] According to Negri, however, Alcionio had not in fact been writing any histories; Giovio had been misled (said

---

54 Giovio, *Gli elogi*, 133.

55 BAV MS Vat. Lat. 5892, 227v.

56 Francesco Berni, *Opere burlesche di M. Francesco Berni, con annotazioni e con un saggio delle sue lettere piacevoli* (Milan, 1806), Sonnet XV, 112-13.

57 *Ibid.*, 112: "Ma il matto da catene,/ Pensando al paracimeno duale,/ Non intese il pronostico fatale...."

58 *Ibid.*: "Una mula sbiadata, damaschina,/ Vestita d'alto e basso ricamato,/ Che l'Alcionio Poeta laureato/ Ebbe in commenda a vita masculina:/ Che gli scusa cavallo e concubina,/ Sì ben altrui la lingua dà per lato...."

59 *LP*, 93r (Negri to Michiel, 17 March 1523): "Il Dialogo dell'Alcionio è molto lacerato da questi Academici, et sono alcuni, che gli scrivono contra, i quali m'hanno astretto congiuramento a non publicare i nomi loro."

60 *LP*, 99v (Negri to Michiel, 1 Sept. 1523): "Harei salutato il Giovio.... È in rotta con l'Alcionio, perche gli è stato detto, che l'Alcionio scrive historia, la quale impresa egli non vuol cedere ad alcuno."

Negri) just so that he could be set upon Alcionio.[61] Throughout the
period 1523-1526, despite his connections with Clement VII, Alcionio appears to have published little if anything, and he clearly did
not succeed in gaining an estimable reputation. And yet, two of the
orations on the Sack of Rome, which circulated too late to salvage
his career, would elicit the grudging respect of at least one of his
detractors—none other than Paolo Giovio—who would praise them
in his *Elogia* as "*splendissimi.*"[62]

ii. *Discourses of Vulnerability*

Alcionio's orations on the Sack of Rome must be read against the
intellectual backdrop of pre-1527 Roman humanist discourse. As detailed in Chapter One, by the late Quattrocento, humanist scholars
had come to see the papacy as an ally of their new classically–based
culture and increasingly placed their rhetorical skills in its service.
Linking Renaissance Rome to classical Rome, they fashioned a rhetoric that dignified the city's historic role as cultural exemplar of Europe and infused that identity with religious motifs suitable to the
papacy. Giving the Renaissance popes credit for the revival of
Rome's greatness, they heralded the beginning of a golden age in
church and society. Curial humanists served effectively as papal
spokesmen, articulating a distinct discourse that buttressed and dignified the actions and goals of their foremost patron. The Sack of
Rome, however, issued in the imprisonment of that patron, the temporary disintegration of the patronage network upon which they had
relied for support, and the shattering of hopes for the dawning of a
new age. Consequently, curial humanists such as Alcionio needed to
rethink their conceptions of Roman culture and their understandings
of their own relationship to that culture.

Alcionio's four orations, which speak to these disruptions with
both force and eloquence, span the three genres of classical oratory
that were revived in the Renaissance. The first two, addressed to
Clement VII and to Charles V, respectively, represent the *genus deli-*

---

[61] *LP*, 100r (Negri to Michiel, 1 Sept. 1523): "Altra historia non scrive l'Alcionio,
che questa oratione, benche al Giovio altramente sia stato dato ad intendere, per
attacargli insieme."
[62] Giovio, *Gli elogi*, 133.

berativum, in which the orator strives to persuade the listener to take a particular action. The third, which adheres to the *genus iudiciale,* indicts Charles V before an ad hoc "jury" of Romans. The fourth, a panegyric to Pompeo Colonna, belongs to the *genus demonstrativum* (epideictic), in which the orator uses a rhetoric of praise and/or blame to arouse sentiments suitable to a given ceremonial occasion.[63] Taken together, these orations reveal Alcionio's reshaping of Roman humanist discourse to accommodate different rhetorical contexts and sharply changed political circumstances. In the first, evidently written during the most violent phase of the Sack and occupation of Rome, Alcionio departs from the language of cliental deference in a way that anticipates his subsequent departure from the protection of Pope Clement. In the last, the panegyric to Colonna, Alcionio's rhetoric— like the political situation in Rome following the departure of Imperial troops in February of 1528—returns to a more conventional mode and gains a new equilibrium. Recasting Roman humanist formulae to accommodate Rome's diminished political role and the papacy's temporary incapacity, Alcionio boldly affirms the city's continuing symbolic significance and the special role of his new patron as exemplar of *Romanitas.*

a) *"Among the Greatest Anguishes"*

Alcionio wrote the first oration, beginning *"Inter maximos dolores,"* during the initial weeks of the occupation, while he—like his patron, Pope Clement—was virtually a prisoner in the Castel Sant' Angelo.[64] Addressed to the pope, whose political influence outside the papal fortress was severely limited, the oration nonetheless exhorts him to assert his prerogatives to deny the request of two chaplains of Charles of Bourbon to sanction the transfer of Bourbon's body from

---

[63] O'Malley, *Praise and Blame,* esp. chap. 2.

[64] BAV MS Vat. Lat. 3436, 35r-40r. While this oration contains no date, its subject matter and a key passage (39v) indicate that Alcionio was among those in the Vatican during the siege and that the oration was at least set in Castel Sant' Angelo: "Reliquum est, o Clemens, ut te admoneam te nulla ratione me iudicare debere tam iratum caussae Borbonii esse ob privatas quas accepi iniurias (id quod isti sacrificuli aiunt), quoniam existimav<i> fortunas quas Hostes compilarunt, domestica ornamenta quae eripuerunt et tot gravia, pene mortifera quae inflixerunt vulnera, cu<m> te publicamque domum defenderem, nihil me unquam movere posse, quotienscunque animum refero (id quod semper facio), ad publicas et miserabiles civium clades et gravissimum ac luctuosissimum totius urbis exitium, quo<d> infinitis lacrimis ex hac mole prospeximus."

Rome to Milan to be reburied.[65] Instead of being placed upon the
high altar in the church of San Giacomo, Alcionio inveighs, Bourbon
should have been left behind on the battlefield to be consumed by
scavenging animals. At the time, however, no one could prevent
Bourbon from receiving last rites, since the soldiers were striking so
much terror into the conquered that none dared to speak out or take
action.[66]

Alcionio confesses that he, too, would have remained silent, despite the injuries he had received, had not these priests' request provoked him to risk his own life so that he might defend the honor and
majesty of God.[67] In this capacity, he urges Clement to "order a dash
made to that place where the carcass of Barbon [sic] has been set
down, that it may indeed be dug up, not so that it may be trans-
ported to Milan . . . , but that having been dragged through the city
with a hook imbedded in it, it should be flung into the Tiber."[68] This
classical Roman solution he bolsters with elegant rhetoric concerning
the significance of burial and the foulness of Bourbon's body, so great
that it will corrupt any substance with which it comes into contact.[69]

The public offenses for which Bourbon was responsible—the murder of priests, the scattering of martyrs' bones, and the violation of
the will of God—have provoked Alcionio to write, he says.[70] Beyond
recounting Bourbon's crimes, he focuses upon the Constable's designs on the person of the pope. From the outset, Bourbon had
sought "the final death of the republic, and also that you [Clement],
along with all [your] possessions, might serve as spoils of war for the
most-cruel enemy."[71] Bourbon had offered conditions of peace not

---

[65] On Pope Clement VII's political positioning during these weeks, see Judith
Hook, *The Sack of Rome, 1527* (London, 1972), esp. 207-210. On the desperation of
the pope's situation, see Luigi Guicciardini, *The Sack of Rome*, trans. and ed. James H.
McGregor (New York, 1993), 115-16.

[66] BAV MS Vat. Lat. 3436, 35r and v: "Accedebat etiam crudelis militum qui
operam illi in bello navarant importunitas. Hi enim adhuc armati et praeda ac victoria feroces, tantum terroris multis nostri ordinis hominibus incutiebant ut nihil paulo
liberius vel agere, vel dicere auderent...."

[67] *Ibid.*, 35v.

[68] *Ibid.*: "imo vero quam primum iubeas eo advolandum ubi Barbonii cadaver
situm est ut illud quidem effodiatur, non ut Mediolanum transvehatur, id quod isti
petunt, sed per Urbem unco impacto tractum in Tiberim proiiciatur."

[69] *Ibid.*

[70] *Ibid.*, 39v.

[71] *Ibid.*, 36r: "Neque rectum neque fas est credere, o Clemens, illum sacrorum
hostem et religionum omnium praedonem, transgressum Appeninum cum tanta la-

out of a sincere desire for an end to the fighting, but rather as a delaying tactic and as a means of lulling Clement into a false sense of security.[72] A desire to see Clement undergo a misfortune similar to his own had motivated Bourbon: "Undoubtedly [he] always sought . . . that just as he himself was without a fatherland, and had oppressed France with a prolonged attack of military force, so you, Clement, might be without a fatherland, liberty, and even life . . . ."[73]

In describing Pope Clement's role, Alcionio is ostensibly circumspect. With examples drawn from ecclesiastical history and, to a lesser extent, from the classical past, he implicitly reaffirms Clement's inheritance both of papal prerogatives and of local political control over Rome. He notes that, with respect to the disinterment and transportation of corpses, the Caesars in their wisdom had left authority in the hands of provincial rulers.[74] Moreover, he invokes the topos of the refusal of burial to an enemy as a means of posthumous punishment: for example, he observes that Sulla had ordered that the bones of Marius be scattered. Alcionio's argument strains particularly hard when he cites Creon's punishment of Antigone as a precedent to be followed: a moral not commonly derived from the ending of Sophocles's tragedy, for fairly obvious reasons.[75]

Alongside his traditional secular *imperium*, Clement possesses sacred authority that gives him inalienable jurisdiction over Bourbon insofar as the latter has committed crimes against the faith.[76] Alcionio calls to mind instances when past popes either denied, or

tronum multitudine, aliud quaesisse nisi id quod evenit, hoc est extremum reipublicae fatum atque etiam ut cum omnibus fortunis crudelissimo hosti esse praedae."

[72] *Ibid.*: "Quae autem latae sunt pacis conditiones propterea latae videri possunt, ut, interposita in consultando mora, tuis minus rebus consuleres; tum etiam ut, aliqua primum lenitatis specie quaesita, nihil tam atrox et crudele esset quod ad internicionem nostram non aggrederetur—non ut salus urbis integra permaneret ac dignitas tua inviolata constaret...."

[73] *Ibid.*, 36r and v: "Dux nimirum ille semper hoc quaesivit, ut quemadmodum ipse patria careret et Galliam diuturna armorum tempestate pressisset, ita tu, o Clemens, patria libertate atque adeo vita, careres . . . ." For Alcionio's description of Bourbon's loss of his estate, see 37v.

[74] *Ibid.*, 35v-36r.

[75] *Ibid.*, 38v: "Fabulas hic non consectabor de Polynece quem Creontis iussu omnes insepultum relinquere debebant ut hostem regis, cuius tamen imperium Antigone soror haud verita illum sepeliit; idcirco viva sub tera condita est." While this is by no means the only misrepresentation of historical precedent in the oration, it is probably the most egregious, since in the end Sophocles' Creon explicitly acknowledges that he was wrong to push Antigone for burying her brother's corpse.

[76] Beyond the crimes of his troops, Bourbon is accused (36v) of intercepting payments intended for shrines.

placed constraints upon, the burial of conquered opponents, including Alexander IV's treatment of the tyrant Ezzelino III da Romano (d.1259), and Martin V's stipulation that the mercenary captain Braccio da Montone (d.1424) not be interred within the Roman city limits.[77] Here, Alcionio's use of evidence becomes irreparably muddled: for example, he claims that Clement IV exposed Conradin's body as food for wild animals; yet it was Charles of Anjou, not Clement, who in 1268 had ordered the beheading of Conradin.[78] His intended point, however, is clear: historic precedents should remind Clement of the dignity and power of the papacy as an instrument of divine punishment.[79]

But Alcionio's vision of what Pope Clement has allowed himself to become belies this picture of papal power. He holds out hope that Clement will yet live up to his responsibilities, and he counsels him to "make use of the favor of the immortal gods who, even if you are a captive and a person of shattered fortune, all things having been ruined, nonetheless wish that the unimpaired power of passing judgment concerning sacred matters be left to you."[80] Yet the oration insinuates that Clement thus far has failed to give any indication of the forceful, responsible leadership that the situation demands. Alcionio's criticisms emerge indirectly when he suggests that enforcing justice will "put to the test those things which have been spread around about your pontificate by the conversations of very judicious people."[81] By itemizing these rumors, Alcionio voices obliquely some devastating criticisms of his own: that up to the present time Clement's pontificate has been "disastrous for the liberty of Italy, fatal to the health of the city, lamentable for the dignity of religion, and both offensive and pestiferous to the universal church of God . . . ."[82] The good fortune which embraced Clement as a private citizen has not

---

[77] *Ibid.*, 38v-39r.

[78] Perhaps Alcionio conflates the execution of Conradin, mentioned in Dante, *Purg.* 20:67-68, with the exposure of Manfred's remains, described in *Purg.* 3:124-32. Alcionio also includes a spurious account of Innocent IV's alleged exhumation of the German Emperor Frederick II (whom, Alcionio claims, Manfred had smothered).

[79] BAV MS Vat. Lat. 3436, 39r.

[80] *Ibid.*, 37r: "Utere igitur beneficio daeorum immortalium, o Clemens, qui, etsi rebus omnibus eversis captivus afflictaque fortuna es, tamen integram tibi potestatem adhuc relictam volunt de rebus sacris statuendi . . . ."

[81] *Ibid.*, 39v: "Ita enim probabis quae sermonibus prudentissimorum hominum de Pontificatu tuo divulgata sunt . . . ."

[82] *Ibid.*: "illum hactenus fuisse libertati Italiae calamitosum, Urbis saluti funestum, dignitati religionis luctuosum et universae Dei ecclesiae tetrum ac pestiferum . . . ."

continued for him in his current official role.[83] Still, should Clement take forceful action in the case of the disposition of Bourbon's body, "all good men . . . will judge that you [Clement] are undeserving that the voices of distressed citizens should burst out *any more* against your name."[84]

Alcionio then proceeds with even more direct criticism of the pope's erratic and inconstant policy-making, always characterizing the fault as either in the past or potentially superable:

> if you are not at the same time both the author and overturner of your own laws, if you repudiate those bad counselors with whose insane judgment and perverse advice you have run your pontificate, if you administer the grain supply in such a way that neither you nor your own people are perceived as reducing it to profit and booty—then you will have reclaimed from silence, and from the most adverse circumstances of fate, the now languishing and nearly extinct memory of famous and learned men.[85]

Beyond these indirectly phrased but pointed criticisms, Alcionio interprets the Sack as a divine chastisement intended to rebuke Clement for his ill-advised and inappropriate military adventurism:

> as I incline to believe, [God] wanted you to be vexed with imprisonment, with the loss of most-valued possessions and with such great evils, in order that you might know that liberality and innocence, not arms, would have been a most faithful protection for you. For with the support of those virtues, you would have had at least no barbarians as enemies . . . , and if you ever would have, in the end you would have been an object for reverence to them. But by your reliance upon arms, you provoked the most-monstrous barbarians, to whom you were, ultimately, an object of plunder and of ridicule.[86]

---

[83] *Ibid.*: "eorum caussam Fortunam sustinere, quae quidem non eadem te principem quae privatum complexa est."

[84] *Ibid.*: "Omnes praeterea boni te indignum existimabunt in cuius nomen voces afflictorum civium amplius erumpant . . . ." (emphasis mine in translation)

[85] *Ibid.*: "si tuarum legum idem non auctor fueris ac eversor, si malos suasores insano quorum arbitrio et perversis consiliis Pontificatum gessisti repudiaveris, si rem frumentariam ita curaveris ut nec tu nec tui illam ad lucrum et praedam intellegantur revocare, languescentem ac prope demortuam illustrium ac doctorum virorum memoriam a silentio et iniquissima fati conditione adserueris . . . ."

[86] *Ibid.*, 40r: "qui <i.e., Deus>, ut mea fert opinio, carcere orbitate rerum carissimarum tantisque malis te conflictari voluit ut certo scires liberalitatem ac innocentiam fidissimam tui custodiam futuram fuisse, non arma. Illarum enim virtutum praesidio nullos saltem barbaros (ut de aliis sileam), hostes habuisses, et si quando habuisses illis tandem venerationi fuisses. Armorum fiducia immanissimos barbaros lacessisti, quibus tandem praedae ac ludibrio fuisti."

By contrast, proper behavior on Clement's part will result in his having "God as an avenger and certainly a zealous deliverer."[87] Alcionio strains to close the oration on a positive note, expressing hope that Clement will take charge of restoring Rome and defending the priesthood. But such goads to action appear unrealistic and pathetic when viewed in light of the pope's habitual indecisiveness and political fickleness, and they accord ill with the tone of the remainder of the oration.[88] Most important, in his criticisms, Alcionio uses Ciceronian elegance to attack his patron, Clement. This departure from the deference appropriate to his position—a deference recently codified by another papal servant, Baldesar Castiglione—anticipates his subsequent shedding of the client's role.[89]

b) *"On the Need to Restore the Republic"*

In the second oration, an appeal to the Holy Roman Emperor Charles V to restore Rome and to free Pope Clement from imprisonment, Alcionio further articulates his interpretation of "curialist" values. Although the oration is undated, its contents indicate that it was written after 24 June 1527, when Clement first heard of the birth of Charles V's son, Philip.[90] Most likely it was completed before 10 July 1527, when the remnants of the Imperial army left sweltering, plague-stricken Rome for the summer, and probably also the time when Alcionio left Castel Sant' Angelo.[91] In the oration, he casts

---

[87] *Ibid.*: "Miserabilis haec tua fortuna vindicem et acrem omnino adsertorem Deum habebit . . . ."

[88] Of the many contemporary criticisms of Clement VII's indecisiveness and changeability, see, inter alia, L. Guicciardini, *Sack of Rome*; Girolamo Balbi, *De Pace inter christianos principes ineunda*, chap. 13 (BAV MS Vat. Lat. 8122, esp. 13v-14v); and the famous assessment of Clement's character in Francesco Guicciardini, *Storia d'Italia*, ed. Silvana Seidel Menchi (Turin, 1971), Book 20.

[89] Castiglione's *Il Cortegiano* provides a nearly contemporaneous guide to the the place of deference in decorous behavior toward one's patron.

[90] BAV MS Vat. Lat. 3436, 24r, notes the setting of Clement's ransom at 400,000 ducats: an event that took place on 6 June. References to intolerable heat, plague, and mass-starvation (27v) help confirm that the oration was written well after the initial assault of 6 May. Most importantly, 32v refers to the recent birth of a son to Charles. Pastor, *History of the Popes*, IX, 433, notes that news of Prince Philip's birth reached Clement on 24 June.

[91] BAV MS Vat. Lat. 3436, 26r, treats the ransoming and recapture of prisoners as ongoing. Throughout, Alcionio assumes the continuing presence of the army. Hook, *Sack of Rome*, 213, notes that with the exception of 2,000 troops, who remained to guard the pope and Castel Sant'Angelo, the rest of the Imperial army left the city

himself as a legate sent to Charles to present the Romans' case.[92]

Since the oration is intended to elicit sympathy and assistance, Alcionio is careful from its outset to dissociate the actions of the Imperial army in Rome from Charles's intentions. The peace treaty to which Pope Clement and the Imperial Viceroy Lannoy had agreed in March ought to have protected the city from any Imperial troops, including those under the command of Bourbon. To stir Charles V to action, Alcionio then proceeds to set before the Emperor's eyes a systematic account of the villainy of his troops in the Sack and occupation. Owing to the death of Bourbon in the first assault, there was no sure commander to restrain the soldiers' depredations, which Alcionio describes in graphic detail. If he expresses concern about the torturing of priests, he makes clear that the fate of non-clerical Romans has been little better: in order to facilitate the extraction of exorbitant ransoms, the soldiers have forced parents to watch their young children, pierced through with spits, being basted with melted fat as they are roasted alive.[93] No rank or category of people has been exempt from the savagery.[94]

In closing, Alcionio directly links emperor to pope, stating that their names are jointly embedded in the Roman people's memory.[95] He affirms Clement's personal services to Charles, but notes particularly the pope's forbearing to use the powers that could have prevented the present hardships:

> certainly so great a mass of calamities would by no means have befallen us if he [Clement] had had a mind hostile toward you, if he had alienated from you the surrendered subjects of your empire, if he had incited Christian kings against you, if he had armed free peoples and territories, if he had deprived you of the highest office—if, finally, he

---

on 10 July. On the timing of Alcionio's move to the protection of Pompeo Colonna, see Valeriano, *DLI*, 63.

[92] While I have found no solid evidence that the oration was actually delivered to Charles, Alcionio later claims in the "Declamatio" that it had been (Hoff., 574): "Cur etiam Caesar, *me causam Pontificis captivi agentem*, in Hispania libenter audivit?" Whatever the accuracy of this claim, the contents of the oration do bear striking and curious resemblance to the instructions (dated 10 July 1527) that Cardinal Salviati, then resident in France, gave to Giacopo Girolami for an embassy to Charles V. See Pastor, *History of the Popes*, 9:434-35, who remarks that the instructions "do not exactly give evidence of Salviati's diplomatic talent." I am presently preparing an article comparing the two documents in detail.

[93] BAV MS Vat. Lat. 3436, 26r and v.

[94] *Ibid.*

[95] *Ibid.*, 32r.

had execrated you publicly, and had with dreadful curses expelled the execrated one from the community of Christians.[96]

Clement's willingness to forego use of these powers, Alcionio notes, sets him apart from other popes, who certainly would have exercised them.[97] But beyond considering the personal qualities of this particular pope, Charles should uphold the papacy's dignity and authority, which transcend the shortcomings of individual pontiffs:

> For as human beings the Supreme Pontiffs can err, be deceived, be cheated, and certainly give offense no differently than the [fallen] condition of men requires;   but when they take on the role of Christ, . . . nothing in the earthly abode is more admirable, majestic, holy,   or divine . . . .[98]

Past popes, then, enlisted the support of emperors so that the latter would be "not only defenders of such great divine might and majesty, but also its advocates and supporters."[99] Alcionio provides an extended prosopopoeia in which Charles is to imagine his predecessors as emperor, including Charlemagne, speaking to him of the manifold historical reasons he should defend papal prerogatives. Finally, he points to Charles's personal stake in liberating this particular pope: "You should think of this thing: that you have been designated a 'Caesar' in such a way that you be called 'Augustus' by a free pope, not by a captive one. But you ought not to wait for another pope as the bestower of your great fortune rather than this one, who is in your confidence and in your power . . . ."[100]

If this oration provides a strong vindication of papal authority in

[96] *Ibid.*, 29r and v: "At nimirum tanta calamitatum moles in nos minime decubuisset si hostili animo in te fuisset, si imperii tui dedititios a te abalienasset, si reges Christianos in te concitasset, si liberos populos et provincias armasset, si summo honore te spoliasset, si denique publice te devovisset dirisque detestationibus exsecratum e Christianorum communione exterminasset."

[97] *Ibid.*, 29v.

[98] *Ibid.*, 31v: "Pontifices enim Maximi, ut homines, possunt errare decipi falli et omnino haud secus offendere quam hominum conditio postulat; ut personam Christi sustinent, nihil plane est quod a nobis non debeatur, quandoquidem in terris nihil illis est admirabilius, nihil augustius, nihil sanctius, nihil divinius, nihil etiam omni religione munitius."

[99] *Ibid.*: "Veteres igitur Pontifices sibi Caesares adsciverunt, quo tanti sui numinis tantaeque maiestatis non modo propugnatores essent, verum etiam advocati et adstipulatores."

[100] *Ibid.*, 33v: "Tum etiam illud cogita: sic te Caesarem designatum ut a Pontifice libero, non captivo, Augustus appelleris. Nec vero tu alium Pontificem auctorem tantae tuae felicitatis exspectare debes quam hunc qui in fide ac potestate tua est . . . ."

keeping with the Roman humanist tradition, it also offers some hope
for the city's restoration: Alcionio gives a rather optimistic account of
the preparations of Clement's allies in Italy and abroad to come to
Rome's rescue.[101] The elements of confidence, however, have necessarily become attenuated. Alcionio is constrained in his claims by the
need to plead for the Emperor's support: it is unquestionable who
has the upper hand. The protestations of Rome's ruin, employed to
gain Charles's sympathy, also have the effect of further documenting
the pope's political impotence. Most significant, Alcionio calls into
question the theme of *Roma caput mundi* that had dominated previous
Roman humanist discourse.[102] To be sure, he asserts the necessity of
Rome's continuation in this role: "the sun could more easily fall from
the firmament than . . . mortals do without Rome and our universal
republic not have its capital there, where the foundations were laid,
strengthened by the blood of the saints whom they call martyrs
. . . ."[103] Yet the unthinkable has in fact occurred, and consequently,

> that city, o Caesar, which used to rejoice in the commerce of foreign-
> ers on account of the suitability of its location and the character and
> principles of its citizens, to boast of asylum for those who had suffered
> calamities, and to be richly ornamented with a concourse of pilgrims,
> and which, distinguished both by the splendor of kings and by the
> visitation of foreign peoples, was easily the first city over all others,
> [now] lacks its population, is afflicted with famine and a shortage of
> grain supply, and *clings to no vestige of its former esteem and beauty.*[104]

That this change had taken place was undeniable, and it had irrevo-
cable consequences for future perceptions both of Pope Clement and
of Roman culture.

c) *"A Declamation Against Caesar's Letter"*

---

[101] *Ibid.*, 30v.

[102] The best detailed account of the theme of *Roma caput mundi* appears in Stinger,
Renaissance in Rome, esp. chaps. 5 and 6.

[103] BAV MS Vat. Lat. 3436, 30v: "Qua quidem in re non intellegere visi sunt
facilius (ut ita dicam) solem e mundo excidere posse quam mortales Roma carere et
rempublicam nostram perpetuam ibi sedem non habere ubi fundamenta iacta sunt
sanguine divorum quos martyras vocant compacta . . . ."

[104] *Ibid.*, 28r: "Itaque Urbs illa, o Caesar, quae tum propter loci opportunitatem,
tum etiam propter civium naturam et institutum advenarum commercio gaudebat,
calamitosorum profugio gloriabatur, peregrinorum celebritate florebat et regum
splendore illustris et exterarum gentium adventu aliarum omnium facile princeps
erat, suo populo caret ac fame premitur, inopia rei frumentariae nullum pristinae
dignitatis et pulcritudinis vestigium retinet . . . ." (Emphasis mine in the translation.)

The third text, the *"Declamatio in literas Caesaris,"* evidences a major
transformation in Alcionio's narrative of Rome. Ostensibly a response to a letter Charles V sent to the Romans on 26 July 1527, it
appears to have been delivered by Alcionio before an assembly on
the Capitoline at some point between 7 December 1527, when the
pope escaped from Castel Sant' Angelo, and mid-February 1528,
when the Imperial troops finally left Rome for the second time.[105]
Unlike the earlier appeal to Charles, this declamation aims to sway
the Romans to be united in their negative judgment of the Emperor,
whose glib and self-justifying letter confirms his evident failure to
sympathize with the Romans, let alone to help them. In the letter,
Charles says that his troops had endeavored to settle an honorable
peace with the pope despite the latter's repeated bad faith, and he
blames the Sack on his officers' inability to control their men. He
claims, however, that he was not consulted, and that he would have
preferred to shed his own blood rather than to have seen this fate
befall Rome.[106]

Alcionio's declamation rebuts Charles's letter line by line, and
sometimes word by word. He notes that Charles had seemed receptive to the embassy sent him in mid-July 1527, which had included
presentation of Alcionio's oration "On the Need to Restore the Republic."[107] But rather than relieving the miseries of the Romans by
actions, he had merely sent smooth-tongued envoys whose deeds had
not corresponded to their reassurances. Such show of flashy words,
whether on the part of envoys or of Caesar himself, cannot excuse
the deeds of his men.[108] If Bourbon approved the attack on Rome, he
did so only "in the name of Caesar, and with clear authorization."[109]

---

[105] This dating is tentative. References to the cardinals given over as hostages in
early December provides the *terminus a quo*; present-tense references to continuing
troop actions within Rome provide a likely, although not certain, *terminus ad quem*. I
follow the text in Hoff., with the exception of the dedicatory letter and the letter of
Charles V, of which he prints neither. I follow the Corsiniana MS for both. In the
dedicatory letter to Antonio Tebaldeo, Alcionio refers to his public performance of
the oration (Cors. MS 33 E 26, 5v): "Dolebam equidem, Antoni, quod e doctis viris,
qui adhuc per Barbarorum furorem in Urbe supersunt, tu qui doctissimus es, solus
contioni meae Capitolinae non interfuisses"; *ibid.*, "atque in eadem pronuntianda
scias non minore me usum libertate, quam in scribenda."

[106] *Ibid.*, 4v-5r.

[107] Hoff., 574: "Cur etiam Caesar, *me causam Pontificis captivi agentem*, in Hispania
libenter audivit?" Again, one should note the close resemblance between that oration
and the main points of Salviati's instructions to Girolami. See above, n. 92.

[108] *Ibid.*, 551-52.

Far from feeling sorrow over Rome's plight, as he alleges in his letter, Charles had taken advantage of Pope Clement's weakness to extract concessions, including control over the strategic port cities of Ostia and Civitavecchia. In addition, Charles had allowed Clement to remain prisoner until the latter was able to pay the sum demanded of him by his captors. Such actions render implausible Charles's protestations that he had not intended the Sack.[110]

Pope Clement, meanwhile, is portrayed as a well-intentioned figure who has been duped. The oration makes little mention of Clement's political missteps, since acknowledging them would distract attention from Charles's failings. The trusting pope has fallen into the trap set by the "barbarians" Lannoy and Bourbon, who took advantage of Clement's honorable behavior.[111] The pontiff's political maneuverings have issued in disaster not because he has dabbled in affairs improper to a Roman pontiff—the charge Alcionio leveled at Clement in the first oration—but because of his innocence and political naïveté in dealing with opportunistic advocates of *Realpolitik*.

The link between the pope and the Roman citizenry has become more tenuous than in the two earlier orations. Gone are the references to the pope as the head of the Roman people. A direct connection between pontiff and people remains, since Charles's offenses against Clement have also resulted in the devastation of the populace. Yet the pope is no longer their leader and spokesman: instead, he is just a prominent victim sharing the same lot. Addressed to the leaders of the city, this oration deals not with the ecclesiastical weapons in Clement's control, but instead with the formulation of a response to Charles that is "fitting for a Roman" and in keeping with the authority of Rome's leading citizens.[112] Consequently, most of the oration is concerned with the impact of the emperor's policy upon the Romans.

Charles's letter commences, notes Alcionio, by addressing them as "*illustres*" and "*magnifici*." The first of these titles, however, can only make sense now as tragicomic reversal. Although "nothing on Earth

---

[109] *Ibid.*: "<Borbonius> qui nomine eiusdem Caesaris, certaque auctoritate in Nos invadere probabat . . . ."

[110] *Ibid.*, 576-77.

[111] *Ibid.*, 577: "O miserandam Pontificis Romani conditionem! Cum immanissimis Barbaris optima fide egisti. Illi singulari perfidia Te afflixerunt . . . ."

[112] *Ibid.*, 552: "... quod vel hominem Romanum deceat, vel huiusce Ordinis auctoritate dignum iudicetur."

has ever been more illustrious than the Roman name, nothing more esteemed, nothing more acceptable to every race of mortals," after the Sack "*illustres*" can no longer refer to the Roman people, who have been robbed, killed, or scattered, but only to the occupying soldiers:[113]

> Caesar's brigands are truly *illustres* and resplendent, inasmuch as they have snatched away every furnishing, every womanly ornament, every apparatus fashioned of expensive materials, and all household goods. Furthermore, not having been contented with these things, they even robbed the saints' holy shrines of votive gifts, with which they now have decorated shields, breastplates and helmets. And they have been equipped in such a way that when they march through Rome shining, it seems proper that they thus be called "*illustres*."[114]

Alcionio plays upon Charles's use of "*magnifici*" in a similar fashion to reëmphasize the inversion of Rome's fortunes. Should Charles be looking back upon earlier times, the appellation would be fitting; but since he knows Rome's present situation, "I think we are being mocked. For we have been despoiled of those possessions which are absolutely necessary for attesting to [our] magnificence."[115] Unable to restore this magnificence to buildings and to public display, the Romans will consequently be unable to receive Charles "magnificently" for his official coronation.[116] The reversal of the city's role could not be more pronounced. Despite having been "the head of the world, the refuge of Christians, [and] the haven of all peoples," Rome is "in flames, is being destroyed, and is polluted by murder."[117]

---

[113] *Ibid.*: "Nihil enim in terris unquam nomine Romano fuit illustrius, nihil acceptius, nihil omni mortalium generi gratius."

[114] *Ibid.*, 553: "At Caesariani latrones vere illustres & splendidi, quippe qui omnem supellectilem, omnem mundum muliebrem, omnem rerum pretiosarum apparatum, omnia domestica ornamenta eripuerunt; atque his non contenti, sacras etiam Divorum aedes donis spoliarunt, quibus nunc clypeos, loricas, galeas, decorarunt; atque ita armati, ut per Urbem illustres incedunt, ita Illustres appellandi videntur."

[115] *Ibid.* The theme of the necessity for ecclesiastical sanction of Charles's power, so prominent in the earlier oration "De republica reddenda," makes only brief appearances, e.g., 553.

[116] *Ibid.*: "Quocirca nec ipse mirabitur, cum huc venerit, ut Imperii insignibus honestetur, si nec suo hospitio ullam dignam domum invenerit, nec in se excipiendo quidquam magnifice a nobis agi viderit." In the event, in February 1530 Charles was crowned by Clement VII in Bologna rather than in Rome.

[117] *Ibid.*, 556: "Videmus has sedes sanctitatis, amplitudinis, mentis, consilii publici, caput orbis, aram Christianorum, portum omnium gentium, inflammari, exscindi, funestari." See Cicero, *Pro Milone* 90.

Significantly, in this oration Alcionio has modified Roman humanist themes in a way that parallels his own social repositioning. Previously, curial humanists had defined themselves collectively in part by a discourse in which the *imperium* of classical Rome was closely intertwined with the papacy and with church prerogatives. Now, following his break with Clement VII and his circle, Alcionio no longer identifies with them or the scholarly community, but instead with the Roman citizenry. Now, he places his rhetorical skills in the service of the *Respublica Romana* and articulates a humanist conception of *Romanitas* that is no longer curialist, but predominantly civic.[118]

d) *"On the Deliverance of the City"*

The fourth oration, *"Pro S.P.Q.R. ad Pompeium Columnam de urbe servata,"* evidences a further shift in Alcionio's perspective on the Sack.[119] Written at some point after mid-February 1528, it describes an external situation of restored calm. When the Imperial troops, who had left Rome during the plague, had returned in the autumn to renew their depredations, Pompeo Colonna had played a vital role in restoring order: as Alcionio describes it, he "dashed to pieces the audacity and ruthlessness of those who returned by force of arms into Rome, from which they had gone out by force of law."[120] Apparently a statue was to be erected in honor of Colonna for this service.[121]

---

[118] Throughout (e.g., Hoff., 556: "Expectabamus quidem Romani . . . ."), Alcionio uses the second-person plural to identify himself with the collectivity of the Romans. Near the beginning, he casts himself as advisor to Rome's civic leaders on the formulation of policy (p. 552): "Sed tamen, ne vanus fuisse tantus labor Primorum Civitatis, in nobis convocandis, & frustra suscepta de mea sententia expectatio videatur; dicam omnino, quid censeam, P<atribus> C<onscriptis> istis litteris respondendum. Qua in re illas per capita primum nobiscum recognoscere necesse est; ut facilius Principes Civitatis in rescribendo nostrae causae satisfacere possint."

[119] BAV MS Vat. Lat. 3436, 42r-45v.

[120] *Ibid.*, 45v: "Hoc igitur factum tum beneficio gratum, tum fama gloriosum erit, cum praesertim audaciam atque importunitatem illorum etiam fregeris qui armis in Urbem redierunt, e qua legibus excesserant." On the basis of this concluding sentence, and other contents of the oration, I date it to shortly after the final exit of the Imperial troops from Rome, which began 13 February 1528 (Hook, *Sack of Rome*, 227-28). The earlier exodus of troops took place in July of 1527.

[121] BAV MS Vat. Lat. 3436, 42r: "Maxime optabat S.P.Q.R. ut tibi pro patria servata urbanisque rebus compositis tum, o Pompei, gratias agerem cum statuam decretam poneret, cuius quidem honorem multo illustriorem fore sperabat, si eodem tempore orationem eam adiungeret quae laetitiam suam et grati animi voluntatem declararet."

The oration, dedicated to Pompeo Colonna's friend Oberto Strozzi, takes as its theme the greatness of Colonna's service in rescuing
Rome.[122] Through a combination of well-placed bribes, threats, and
a certain amount of yielding and patience, depending on the individuals involved, Colonna has managed to get the returning Imperial
forces under control, with the consequence that "once the armed
troops had been led away from Rome, which had not been entirely
destroyed, citizens were loosed from the danger of death, and the
pope himself was liberated from custody with his majesty intact."[123]
These good deeds redound to the credit not only of Pompeo but also
of his illustrious family.[124]

Again Alcionio graphically recounts offenses of the invading
troops, who have barbarously abused even Rome's "best citizens"
(*optimorum civium*).[125] Once again, he expresses outrage about the ill
treatment of ecclesiastical figures. He tells too of how the hostages
demanded from the pope had been marched to the gallows and
threatened with death in order to extort money from them.[126] He
does not recount such events, however, to emphasize the guilt of any
particular perpetrator of the Sack. At no point does the name of

---

[122] Colonna's behavior and motives appear in a similarly sympathetic light in
Consorti, *Il Cardinale Pompeo Colonna.* Judith Hook, "Clement VII, the Colonna and
Charles V: A Study of the Political Instability of Italy in the Second and Third
Decades of the Sixteenth Century," *European History Review,* 2 (1972): 281-99, provides
a useful (if overstated) corrective. The dedicatory letter (41v), addressed to Oberto
Strozzi, praises both Strozzi and Colonna profusely, strategically noting the bond
between them and implying that Strozzi should bring the oration to Colonna's attention. Strozzi became host of the *Accademia dei Vignaiuoli,* a circle of poets that emerged
in the late 1520s or early 1530s. See Richard S. Samuels, "Benedetto Varchi, the
Accademia degli Infiammati, and the Origins of the Italian Academic Movement," *Renaissance Quarterly* 29 (1976): 599-634, esp. 606.

[123] BAV MS Vat. Lat. 3436, 42v: "Tu vero alios minis et armorum terrore
fregisti, alios muneribus epulis et largitionibus benevolos tibi reddidisti, alios obsequio
et patientia quae mater est felicitatis, mitigasti ita ut, ab Urbe non omnino incensa
armatis abductis, cives mortis periculo soluti sint et ipse Pontifex Maximus custodia
liberatus incolumi maiestate fuerit."

[124] *Ibid.,* 42v-43r: "Et certe summa haec tua ad benemerendum de salute patriae
alacritas atque etiam insignis ac memorabilis in sacerdotibus conservandis industria,
et industriae adiuncta felicitas, et memoria perfuncti periculi et praedicatione amplissimi beneficii et laude officii praesentis et testimonio praeteriti temporis in dies
magis atque magis efflorescet domesticaque vestrae familiae ornamenta ita amplificabit ut, quae alii gesserunt pro dignitate et gloria reipublicae, vel certiora a te
confirmata habebuntur vel admirabiliora tam illustrium patriae commodorum accessione exsistent."

[125] *Ibid.,* 44v.

[126] *Ibid.*

Emperor Charles V appear. Neither, in fact, does that of Bourbon, although Alcionio refers to him in passing as a brigand who had already been a traitor and parricide to his own fatherland and who now wished to destroy another's.[127] Instead, the itemization of atrocities serves primarily to bring into sharper relief Pompeo Colonna's exceptional service to Rome.

Alcionio implies Pompeo's suitability for the papacy by comparing him favorably with his Colonnese kinsman Martin V (pope, 1417-31). For if the people of Rome had been indebted to Martin on account of his service to the *respublica*, now, Alcionio tells Colonna, they are "both much more indebted to you and rejoice to be so indebted."[128] When Martin V had dwelt across the Alps among barbarians, he had done so safely, as a friend; Pompeo, on the other hand, had to act against barbarians who had invaded Rome, subsequently pillaging and destroying it.[129] Martin V had preserved intact the freedom of bishops and priests; Pompeo, by contrast, helped to free and to restore the spirits of captive ones who had been tortured.[130] Whereas Martin V had propped up a tottering republic, Pompeo raised up a collapsed and ruined one.[131] Finally, whereas Martin V "in a turbulent republic laid claim to the pontifical authority for his own glory," Pompeo "rescued the pontifical authority from near-destruction, enriched the rescued authority with honor, and adorned it with praise."[132]

Alcionio further bolsters Colonna's reputation with classical parallels. He likens Colonna to Camillus, the "second founder of Rome after Romulus": "Both of you, certainly formerly exiles, and similarly magnanimous and full of goodwill, and fitted by nature for every proper duty, gave safety and life to those who desired that each [of

---

[127] *Ibid.*, 43v: "Gallis (duce Gallo hoste latrone et paricida Patriae suae ut alienae eversor esset) . . . ."

[128] *Ibid.*, 43r: "Multum quidem antea optimo illi Pontifici Martino Quinto eidemque in omni virtute principi, debebamus ob praestantissima illius in rempublicam merita, sed iustae nunc et necessariae sunt caussae cur multo plus tibi et debeamus et debere gaudeamus."

[129] *Ibid.*

[130] *Ibid.*

[131] *Ibid.*: "Ille enim labantem ac prope cadentem rempublicam fulxit et sustinuit, tu collapsam et prostratam excitasti ac erexisti."

[132] *Ibid.*: "Ille in turbulenta republica pontificiam auctoritatem in suum decus asseruit, tu afflicta et funditus deleta republica pontificiam auctoritatem a propinquo interitu vindicasti, vindicatam honore auxisti, laude ornasti."

these things] had been torn away from you."[133] Yet Colonna's service
is even greater than that of illustrious classical figures. Whereas once
Caesar had conquered Pompey without the mercy he customarily
showed the defeated, now Caesar has at last been overcome by another Roman "Pompey."[134] Colonna's treatment of Clement VII has
been even more forgiving than Caesar's treatment of Marcellus:

> after the disfavors and suspicions had been recounted, he handed over
> M. Marcellus to the Senate and the republic; you, however—with no
> mention made of offenses or injuries or suspicions—wished that past
> times had been torn out of all memory, as if you would have had no
> feeling ever of them.[135]

In his analysis of Pope Clement's position, Alcionio reinforces his
earlier vindication of the office of the papacy. The atrocities which
have particularly called for Pompeo's swift action include not only
attacks on the pope's character, but actual threats to his life.[136] Colonna receives praise from all for his restoration of Clement to his
former position, since in so doing he has made the papacy secure in
Rome.[137] As in the oration concerning Bourbon's body, however,
Alcionio combines this defense of the dignity of the papacy with
criticism of pontifical dabbling in military affairs. A reference to earlier princes "offering their resources to restrain the madnesses of
vainglorious popes" suggests the limitations which Alcionio saw as
appropriate for the temporal exploits of the papacy.[138] In dealing
with the interaction of Clement and Pompeo, Alcionio emphasizes
the pope's debt to the Cardinal: all can see that "twice you [Pompeo]
have thus merited well from Pope Clement . . . , once when you
conferred the highest authority upon him when he was a private
citizen, and a second time when you restored the same authority

---

[133] *Ibid.*, 44r: "Camillus ille, Romani nominis lumen et rite secundus ab Romulo
Urbis conditor appellatus, ut omnino eadem te laus liberatae ac restitutae patriae
sequeretur, qua illum floruisse constat. Ambo enim antea exsules iidemque magnanimi et beneficae voluntatis pleni ad omneque rectum officium nati, salutem et
vitam iis dedistis qui vobis ereptam volebant . . . ."

[134] *Ibid.*, 45v.

[135] *Ibid.*: "ille, commemoratis offensionibus et suspicionibus, M. Marcellum Senatui reipublicaeque concessit; tu autem, nulla offensionum aut iniuriarum aut suspicionum mentione facta, praeterita tempora ex omni memoria aeque evulsa esse
voluisti ac illorum sensum nullum unquam habuisses."

[136] *Ibid.*, 44v.

[137] *Ibid.*, 45r.

[138] *Ibid.*, 42r: "cum nostri generis dynastis qui opes suas libenter ad comprimendas
ambitiosorum Pontificum insanias conferebant."

which had almost been lost."[139] In return for this debt, Colonna supposedly asks only that the pope live up to his responsibilities:

> We have perceived that now you are giving the same pope no other advice (when he was giving thanks to you on account of the benefit bestowed) than that which you gave as advice at another time, when you favored the man in obtaining the papacy: that is, that you were both asking and expecting this alone from him, that he should be a good ruler, that he should devote energy to establishing peace among Christian kings, and that he should be mindful of being the Vicar of Christ.[140]

If references to the theme of papal authority are somewhat circumscribed so that Pompeo Colonna's role can be emphasized, the theme of the dignity and greatness of Rome, so prevalent in pre-1527 Roman humanist writings, continues, albeit in an attenuated form. Pompeo's voice, heard at precisely the right time, has been effective "because the name of the city itself can be enough for its restoration and deliverance."[141] Pompeo's achievement, however, also confirms the role of the people of Rome in this restoration: "very many historians" have written that "Rome must fear all [sorts of] plagues, afflictions, disgraces, and destructions from the barbarians," but that it "cannot be restored and renewed from any deadly event, except by the Romans."[142] The terms in which Pompeo's honor is couched affirm Rome's role as *caput mundi*. He is to be called not only "Father of the Fatherland," but also "Savior of Italy" and even "Liberator of the World."[143] For indeed, the whole world has benefited from his

---

[139] *Ibid.*, 45r: "Iam vero nemo est tam rerum ignarus . . . qui integra veritate adseverare non queat bis te de Clemente Pontifice ita benemeritum, ut tempora illius ferebant: semel cum privato summam potestatem detulisti, iterum cum eandem pene amissam restituisti."

[140] *Ibid.*, 45r and v: "nihil aliud te eidem Pontifici nunc respondere sensimus, cum tibi ob collatum beneficium ageret gratias, quam id quod alias cum in pontificatu adipiscendo homini studebas, respondisti: te hoc solum ab eo et petere et exspectare ut princeps bonus esset, ut in pacem constituendam inter reges Christianos incumberet, ut se vicarium Christi meminisset."

[141] *Ibid.*, 45r: "quia ipsius Urbis nomen satis esse potest ad sui restitutionem et salutem."

[142] *Ibid.*, 44r: "Docuistique nimirum, ea re ita magnifice et praeclare gesta verum esse quod plerique Romanorum rerum scriptores literis prodiderunt, Romae omnia mala, omneis pestes, omneis miserias, omneis labes, omneis ruinas timendas esse a barbaris, verum illam fatali quodam eventu restitui ac renovari non posse nisi ab Romanis."

[143] *Ibid.*, 43v: "Merito igitur et pater patriae et Italiae servator et orbis terae libera-

accomplishment: "we see that the earth was rendered more peaceful and more tranquil after these barbarians had been removed from Rome, which is its head."[144]

Yet if the view of Rome's future in this oration can be said to be in any way optimistic, it is cautiously so. As Rome's leading citizen, Pompeo constitutes the hope of the Roman nobility for the recovery of some degree of dignity and glory, but that hope is outweighed by a pervasive gloom. If Colonna's leadership has produced "not only a settled condition of the republic, but also a good, fortunate, and flourishing one," these terms must be redefined to mean "that which allows us in whatever manner to prolong life or draw in breath." Indeed, Alcionio states that "both we and future generations for many centuries shall see nothing in the city except that which is wretched . . . and pitiable."[145] Despite its praise, the oration presents more a picture of survival than of cultural efflorescence, of dim hope rather than of bright promises for the future. For Rome, as for Alcionio—who would die soon after composing this piece—Colonna's patronage had only limited capacity to restore what had been lost.

iii. *Imitation and Singularity*

Alcionio's reformulation of Roman humanist discourse after the Sack evidences not only his skills as a rhetorician, but also his rethinking, in the crucible of sociopolitical crisis, of long-standing assumptions about Rome and curial culture. In each of the four orations, he employed a classical genre and filtered personal expression through

---

tor vocaris . . . ." These three names have never befallen any one person, even among the Greeks or ancient Romans (43v-44r): "Atque haec tria cognomina nec apud Graecos in sua patria aut regione nec apud veteres Romanos ulli contigisse legimus."

[144] *Ibid.*, 43v: "orbem terae, sublatis his barbaris e Roma, quod illius caput est, pacatiorem et tranquilliorem redditum videmus."

[145] *Ibid.*, 44v-45r: "populique Romani fortunis iam eversis semper cogitans, ea curasti quae efficerent ut in possessionem libertatis propriam Romani generis et nominis pedem ponere inciperemus, et non modo certum reipublicae statum sed bonum etiam, beatum et florentem efficerent. Dixi beatum et florentem, o Pompei, non ignarus tantam vim huius teterrimi et calamitosissimi belli tantumque ardorem animorum et armorum fuisse ut omnia foede prostrata sint, atque etiam nihil nos et multorum seculorum posteros in Urbe visuros nisi erumnosum funestum detestabile luctuosum et miserabile. Sed tamen id nunc beatum et florens appellaverim quod pro temporum ratione non omnino malum est, imo potius quod vitam et spiritum nos quoquo modo aut ducere aut recipere sinit."

layers of literary convention. Nonetheless, we cannot simply dismiss them as rhetorical constructs devoid of affective content. Alcionio's willingness to speak openly in ways that were deleterious to his career, a characteristic for which Valeriano specifically faults him, indicates that we ought not to view Alcionio's writings as opportunistic to the exclusion of sincerity. Thus we should not be surprised that, in the first oration, "Among the greatest anguishes," Alcionio asserted an individualistic position highly critical of the patron to whom the oration was at least ostensibly addressed, and one which foreshadows his subsequent departure from Clementine patronage. In addition, the intensity and immediacy of the experiences that his orations on the Sack of Rome detail may have militated against unfeeling abstraction.

Certainly the conquest of Rome and the humiliation of the pope limited the rhetorical possibilities open to humanists, who perforce worked within the confines of the plausible. In addition, pragmatic considerations, such as the need to obtain a given patron's economic support and political protection, obviously influenced their writings, as Alcionio's rehabilitation and elevation of Pompeo Colonna in the "*De urbe servata*" suggest. Howsoever sincerely his praises of Colonna may have been intended, they built upon Colonna's long-established reputation as a defender of citizens' rights against papal rule of Rome.[146]

But the shared discourse of the papal curia, which Roman humanists had helped to construct in their professional compositions, had been intricately intertwined with their personal convictions, at least as these convictions found expression in private writings and, more generally, in a distinctive style that informed even their leisure activities. Indeed, this intertwining of the professional and the personal had long been closer than mere opportunism would require: for (as argued in chapter 1) formal expressions of curial humanist ideology were grounded substantially in individuals' own beliefs and percep-

---

[146] Colonna twice led revolts against papal rule, in 1511 and 1526 (see Consorti, *Il Cardinale Pompeo Colonna*, 34-36 and 86-89, respectively). Alcionio's defense of a civic conception of *Romanitas* in the "Declamatio" may thus have been tailored somewhat to suit Colonna's reputation as an advocate of the Roman populace. In the "De urbe servata," by contrast, Alcionio praises Colonna by implying his suitability for the papacy (see above). For an interpretation linking the revolt of 1526 with Pompeo Colonna's own desire to become pope, see Hook, "Clement VII, the Colonna and Charles V," and Hook, *Sack of Rome*.

tions, giving voice to them, reinforcing them, and lending them coherence. Consequently, the psychological and social stresses to which
humanists such as Alcionio were exposed in 1527 triggered major
changes not only in their personal convictions but also in their understanding and expression of curialist discourse. The uncontrollable
disaster of the Sack of Rome, coupled with Pope Clement's inability
to protect or provide for his clients, virtually forced the ideological
transformation—and fragmentation—of Roman humanism.

In the cases of those such as Alcionio who actually witnessed the
city's destruction, one should expect a close connection between
ideological change and personal experience. Had Alcionio been absent from the city in May of 1527, and had he written about the Sack
at considerable remove both physically and chronologically—as
would Valeriano—one might imagine him a detached observer.
Since, however, he suffered personally in the catastrophe, even being
injured in it, only with difficulty can one conceive of his experiences
as not informing his contemporaneous writings about it. In fact, as
historical examples suggest and recent systematic study confirms, giving testimony to catastrophic events in written form is a common
means of obtaining mastery over them.[147] Thus, beyond their out-
ward political functions—or, rather, in accordance with them—
Alcionio's orations on the Sack of Rome may have served an inward
therapeutic one, helping him to construct meaning by imposing order upon a world that had seemingly spun out of control.[148]

But if theories concerning the psychological effects of disaster help
us to appreciate the intensity of the connection between Alcionio's
ideological transformation and the traumatic experiences to which he
was exposed, they are nonetheless insufficient to explain why he,
unlike other humanists in the Clementine patronage network, chose

---

[147] Noteworthy examples of literary responses to collective and/or personal traumas include Thucydides' narration of the plague in Athens; Boethius' *Consolation of
Philosophy*; Boccaccio's description (in the Prologue to the *Decameron*) of the effects of
the Black Death in Florence; and, more recently, narratives of the Holocaust. On
writing as a means of gaining mastery over traumatic experiences, see Beverley Raphael, *When Disaster Strikes: How Individuals and Communities Cope with Catastrophe* (New
York, 1986), 94. An Australian psychiatrist, Raphael provides a synthesis of recent
research into the study of disasters, their psychological impact, and the responses they
provoke.

[148] Raphael, *When Disaster Strikes*, 94. Alcionio's orations constitute strong evidence
that Ciceronian Latin could in fact serve humanists as an effective vehicle for personal expression, the form not obstructing such expression as much as has sometimes
been claimed.

to rewrite the discourse, and to rebuild his career, around the figure of Pompeo Colonna. To address this question, we must first examine curial humanists' shared experience of Pope Clement's inability to continue in the role of the good patron.

From the early stages of the Sack of Rome, the pope could not even guarantee his clients' physical safety, let alone reward suitably their literary efforts. While he initially afforded some security for those with him inside the papal fortress, he was unable to curtail the destruction outside and its effects upon his humanist clients there. For example, Johann Küritz, the prominent host of humanist gatherings, was captured and stripped of his wealth by German troops.[149] Other curial humanists, such as the protonotary and Archbishop of Corfù, Cristoforo Marcello, failed to accumulate the ransom demanded of them, and were tortured to death for the entertainment of their captors.[150] Clement's capitulation on 5 June 1527 and the departure of the papal garrison from Castel Sant' Angelo two days later provided decisive confirmation of his political impotence. Now that he was directly held prisoner by Imperial troops, his contacts with the outside world became further constricted, and his ability to influence the affairs of his clients was minimal.[151]

The pope's finances, meanwhile, were in shambles. He had, of course, inherited fiscal problems from his predecessors, but the military campaigns of the mid-1520s had exacerbated them.[152] By early 1527, the financial strains on the papacy, magnified dramatically by expenses of war, cut deeply into sources of patronage. Only six weeks before the Sack, Girolamo Negri speculated that Alcionio and others at the University of Rome would teach that year for free.[153] Follow-

---

[149] Valeriano, *DLI*, 87.

[150] *Ibid.*, 10.

[151] Pastor, *History of the Popes*, 9:424, cites several sources in support of this interpretation, most notably a 21 June letter of Francesco Guicciardini.

[152] Hook, *Sack of Rome*, 69, argues that the "vacillation for which contemporaries blamed Clement VII was in the main caused by a constant financial problem, hand-to-mouth expedients, and a complete failure to achieve a permanent solution to the papacy's economic difficulties." Although this view is bolstered by much circumstantial evidence and the testimony of contemporaries, little systematic work on papal finances in this period has yet been carried out. See, however, Michele Monaco, *La situazione della reverenda Camera Apostolica nell' anno 1525* [Rome, 1960]. The constant underfunding of Imperial, French, and papal troops in northern Italy helps document Hook's statement (*Sack of Rome*, 46-47) that "no state was financially strong enough to support armies of the size . . . deployed in Italian campaigns" in this period.

[153] *LP*, 106r (Negri to Michiel, 25 March 1527): "L'Alcionio legge Demostene la

ing his imprisonment, Clement had to direct all resources at his disposal toward paying the exorbitant ransom demanded of him.[154] Thus, a combination of political weakness and economic destitution would temporarily prevent Clement from adequately supporting artists and writers.[155]

Given this crisis of Clementine patronage, accompanied by the continuing danger posed by the occupying troops, many humanists understandably fled Rome at their earliest opportunity: for example, Paolo Giovio joined Vittoria Colonna on the island of Ischia, Lilio Gregorio Giraldi escaped to Bologna, and Küritz fled north toward his homeland of Luxembourg.[156] For Alcionio, who chose to remain in the city, Cardinal Colonna was in many ways a sensible selection as patron. Long allied with the emperor, Colonna had become increasingly estranged from the pope following Clement's adoption of a pro-French policy in mid-1526, and he had helped lead an attack on the Vatican that autumn.[157] In fact, Colonna may even have colluded with the Imperialists in planning the 1527 attack on

prima Olinthiaca, con molta frequentia d'auditori: ma credo, che & esso, & gli altri quest'anno leggeranno per l'amor di Dio." Ironically, just three weeks before (5 March 1527), Nicolaus Petreius had written to Alcionio from Venice, offering unctuous praises of Alcionio's linguistic skills and, perhaps not coincidentally, asking a favor, namely, that Alcionio bring Petreius to the attention of Nicolaus Maiuranus, another Greek teacher at the University of Rome. The letter has been copied into Biblioteca Comunale Augustea (Perugia) MS G 99, fols. 5r-5v. Petreius writes as follows about Alcionio's place among contemporary literati (fol. 5r): "sententiae nostrae calculum adiecimus, nullam esse bonarum artium laudem qua<n>tumlibet cumulatissimam asseverantes, quam Alcyonius sibi optima ratione vendicet." On the financial constraints facing the papacy in 1526-27, see Pastor, *History of the Popes*, 9:306-87; Hook, *Sack of Rome*; Bullard, *Filippo Strozzi and the Medici*, esp. chap. 6; and *eadem, Lorenzo il Magnifico*, chap. 8.

[154] Hook, *Sack of Rome*, chap. 14, esp. 211: "essentially the pope had been bankrupted by the sack of Rome. Clement did pay the first two instalments of his imperial ransom money; in September 1527 he paid an additional 100,000 ducats, but after 6 December and a payment of 145,000 ducats the imperialists received nothing more" because of Clement's insolvency. Pastor, *History of the Popes*, IX: 463-67, details the pope's continuing financial difficulties in November-December 1527.

[155] This change in the pope's status could, ironically, have had the effect of lessening the distance inherent in the patronage bond: for despite the ideological harmony of patron and client, the socioeconomic inequality of the relationship normally produced tension and instability (Robin, *Filelfo*, chap. 1); but any such lessening of distance would be outweighed by the patron's inability to perform his or her responsibilities effectively.

[156] According to Valeriano, *DLI*, 88, Küritz fell ill in Verona where, unable to complete his intended journey, he soon died.

[157] Hook, "Clement VII, the Colonna and Charles V," esp. 293-96. For a detailed contemporary account of the 1526 assault on the Vatican, see *LP*, 104r-10[5]v (Negri to Michiel, 24 Oct. 1526).

Rome.[158] When he entered Rome on 10 May as an ally of the Emperor and at the head of an army of 8,000 men, Pompeo Colonna was ideally situated to negotiate the release of captured aristocrats and, ultimately, of the pope himself.[159] Thus, while Alcionio's portrayal of Pompeo in the panegyric *"De urbe servata"* conveniently glossed over Colonna's past offenses, it was not entirely mistaken in viewing him as a rescuer of prostrate Rome.[160] Most important for Alcionio, Colonna was a sometime patron of the arts who was exceptionally well positioned now to increase his own power and to reward his adherents.[161]

Such details notwithstanding, Alcionio's decision to pursue Colonna's patronage sets him apart from his curial colleagues. One must ask, therefore, what disposed him to turn his back on the Clementine circle while others remaining in Rome, such as Pietro Corsi, did not. Moreover, if Alcionio was to desert that circle, why did he stay in Rome at all? A partial answer may be found in Alcionio's singularity: in particular, his poor socialization with other humanists in Rome and elsewhere, and his unstinting assertion of the uniqueness of his scholarly abilities. To gain acceptance in the self-validating world of the academy, in addition to establishing a reliable relationship with a given patron, humanists within that patron's network needed to foster positive ties with one another. Alcionio's failure to do so helped to cancel out his successes in obtaining patronage: for humanist contemporaries in Venice, Padua, Florence, and Rome

---

[158] Hook, "Clement VII, the Colonna and Charles V," takes this position, although with less documentation than one might desire.

[159] Hook, *Sack of Rome*, 176-77.

[160] In his "Ischian" dialogue, Giovio took a similar view of Colonna's role. See T. C. Price Zimmermann, *Paolo Giovio: The Historian and the Crisis of Sixteenth-Century Italy* (Princeton, 1995), chap. 7 (86-105).

[161] Better known for military prowess and political machinations than for patronage of the arts, Pompeo Colonna is apparently the dedicatee of very few literary works (e.g., note the scarcity of references to him in P. O. Kristeller's definitive *Iter Italicum* indices of manuscripts). To be sure, Colonna fostered the careers of some scholars, such as Agostino Nifo and Girolamo Balbi (on Balbi, see above, note 88). On the other hand, the counterexample of the poet Marcantonio Casanova does not especially help the case for Colonna being a good and responsible patron. According to Valeriano, *DLI*, 86, after the Sack, Casanova died from hunger and disease on the streets of Rome, where he was unsuccessfully begging for bread: "Quin etiam in eam lapsus est egestatem, ut frustra panem etiam emendicarit, quo non invento fame, tabeque, & omnium rerum incommodis afflictus expiravit." Alcionio, by contrast, appears to have fared somewhat better under Colonna's aegis, in that he at least died indoors.

viewed him as an outsider deserving of ridicule, both for his scholarship and for his character.

If Alcionio's contemporary reception was to some extent beyond
his control, in that it consisted in part of scorn for his humble origins,
it was also owed significantly to his elaborate—and flat-out dishon-
est—self-presentation. Certainly he was not immune to the humanist
tendency to shape a narrative in ways to which one's patrons would
be more receptive, even when this entailed some embellishment or
distortion of fact.[162] Note, for example, his lost oration on the knights
who died in the siege of Rhodes: Girolamo Negri reports Alcionio's
claim in this oration that all the knights were Italian, whereas in fact
not even a tenth of them were: a rhetorical embellishment that Negri
characterizes as "Alcionican."[163]

More significant than such exaggeration, accusations recur that
Alcionio lied about his literary productivity. In his *Dialogue of Contemporary Poets*, Giraldi has an interlocutor suggest excessive self-fashion-
ing on Alcionio's part:

> He is in the habit of boasting openly that he has in hand a tragedy
> concerning the death of Christ, with 'all the traditional meters de-
> ployed perfectly,' as he himself has been accustomed to say. Although I
> don't really believe it myself, nevertheless he managed to get some to
> buy into it.[164]

More seriously still, Giovio argued that Alcionio's *De exsilio* showed
evidence of a style so Ciceronian that it lent credence to the theory
that he had plagiarized parts of it from Cicero's *De gloria* and then
destroyed the only extant copy of the original: "For [many] observed
that in it, as in a varied patchwork, were interwoven brilliant threads
of rich purple, while all the other colors were dim."[165] Paolo Ma-

---

[162] On this tendency see, *inter alia*, Giuseppe Billanovich, *Petrarca letterato*, vol. 1, *Lo
scrittoio del Petrarca* (Rome, 1947); Robin, *Filelfo*, esp. chap. 1; and Lisa Jardine, *Erasmus, Man of Letters: The Construction of Charisma in Print* (Princeton, 1993).

[163] *LP*, 100r: "Aspettiamo dal detto Alcionio una orazione che fa in laude de'
Cavalieri morti nella ossidione di Rodi. Intendo da chi ha veduto il principio, che egli
finge, che tutti sieno Italiani, & comincia dalle lodi d'Italia, sicome Platone delle lodi
d'Atene nel Menesseno. La qual cosa a me pare Alcionica, cum sit, che tra quei
Cavalieri non vi fosse la decima parte di Italiani. Parmi, che saria stato meglio,
volendo pur imitar Platone, lodar l'Europa, & non l'Italia. Sed haec ipse viderit."

[164] Giraldi, *De poetis*, 39: "solet ille vulgo iactare sese tragoediam de Christi nece in
manus habere omnibus, ut ipse dicere solitus est, servatis numeris; id licet ego minus
credam, nonnullos tamen, ut id illi crederent, effecit."

[165] Giovio, trans. Gragg, 152-53. The Latin runs as follows (Meregazzi, ed., *Gli
elogi*, 133): "luculento opere 'De toleranda exilii fortuna' ita eruditionis ac eloquentiae

nuzio accused Alcionio more directly, noting the disappearance of the *De gloria* from a monastic library to which Alcionio had enjoyed privileged access.[166] Finally, Pierio Valeriano reported that in Castel Sant' Angelo during the Sack of Rome in 1527, Alcionio was the last person seen with Pietro Martelli's works, which never surfaced again.[167]

These accusations fail to convince, in part because they all post-date Alcionio's death in 1528. No subsequent scholar has found credible the most damaging charge, that of plagiarizing from and then destroying the sole manuscript of Cicero's *De gloria*.[168] Nonetheless, taken together, such slurs constitute further evidence both of Alcionio's singular temperament and of his overreaching in his attempts to emulate the perfect orator. Just as the orations on the Sack of Rome were penned too late to stand any chance of salvaging Alcionio's career, he appears to have striven after social *savoir-faire* only long after the damage had been done: upon his death, Alcionio would leave behind a draft of an unfinished philosophical tract entitled, poignantly, "The Origin of Disrepute, and What Distinguishes between Abuse and Disparagement."[169] To the end, he appears not to have realized the extent to which the boundaries of *imitatio*—both of character and of literary style—were socially defined, transgressions

famam sustentabat, ut ex libro 'De gloria' Ciceronis, quem nefaria malignitate abo-leverat, multorum iudicio confectum crederetur. In eo enim, tanquam vario centone, praeclara excellentis purpurae fila languentibus caeteris coloribus intertexta nota-batur."

[166] Paulo Manuzio, *In epistolas Ciceronis*, 446r and v: "nemini dubium fuit, quin Petrus Alcyonius, cui monachae medico suo eius tractandae bibliothecae potestatem fecerunt, homo improbus furto averterit. & sane in eius opusculo de ex<s>ilio, as-persa non nulla deprehenduntur, quae non olere Alcyonium auctorem, sed aliquanto praestantiorem artificem videantur."

[167] Valeriano, *DLI*, 76: "Quattuor tamen libros exactissimae interpretationis in Mathematicas disciplinas Braccius eius filius ab interitu vendicarat, vel ipsius auctoris de se testimonio absolutos, atque ii Barbarorum manus effugerant, Braccii ipsius diligentia in Arcem Aeliam asportati. Sed enim in Petri Alcyonii manus cum in-cidissent, ita suppressi sunt, ut nusquam amplius apparuerint."

[168] e.g., Regnier Desmarais, "Dissertation Sur le Traité de Cicéron de Gloria et sur Alcyonius," 467-80 in his translation of *Les Deux Livres de la Divination de Ci-céron*.... new ed. (Paris, "L'an III. de la République Française"), 479-80: "Pour finir, il ne falloit que lire ou qu'avoir lû le dialogue *de exilio*, pour demeurer convaincu de l'innocence de son auteur, & pour soutenir envers & contre tous, que dans les deux parties de son dialogue il n'y a pas une pensée, pas une phrase, car je vais jusques-là, qu'on puisse raisonnablement suspecter de plagiat."

[169] BAV MS Vat. Lat. 3436, 50r-54r: "Origo infamiae, et quid discriminis in-tercedat inter contumeliam et obtrectationem." The panegyric to Colonna is pre-served in BAV MS Vat. Lat. 3436, 42r-45v.

of these limits constituting breaches of decorum that were injurious to one's standing within the *respublica litterarum*. His contemporaries, on the other hand, would continue long after his demise to point to his defects as an imitator of classical models and to invalidate the distinctive image of himself that he had labored to construct for public consumption.

Alcionio's difficulties in social integration, whatever the degree of his responsibility for them, must surely have facilitated his break with the humanist circle centered on Pope Clement. Pietro Corsi, an intimate of Angelo Colocci, continued to associate closely with the surviving members of Colocci's sodality. Similarly, Pierio Valeriano maintained ties with Clementine humanists despite his absence from Rome, and he chose interlocutors for the *De litteratorum infelicitate* from their number. Alcionio, by contrast, having never been fully accepted into that elite (and elitist) circle, had less reason to stay within its boundaries following the decimation of its membership and destruction of its financial base by the Sack. When he left behind his original patron, he had little cause to lament the fact that in so doing he was also severing his connection with a group of humanists who had never fully accepted him as one of their own. Lacking social ties elsewhere, however, he continued—unlike Valeriano and many other curial humanists—to seek his fortune in Rome, albeit outside the Clementine patronage network.[170]

Alcionio's social singularity, finally, may have inclined him to be more traumatized by the catastrophe than were other Roman humanists. Social systems, important generally to one's psychological well-being, are especially so in times of stress. Consequently, those without support networks are most prone to experience intense reactions.[171] Those such as Alcionio, who watched helplessly from the Castel Sant' Angelo as innocent civilians were tortured in the city below, could scarcely have avoided a sense of deracination.[172] To be

---

[170] While Alcionio's choice of Pompeo Colonna as his new patron made political sense, I have found no evidence of previous contact between the two. Alcionio's letter accompanying the panegyric of Colonna, addressed not to Colonna himself but to an intermediary figure, Oberto Strozzi, heightens the impression of remoteness (see above, note 122). I would argue that Alcionio's decision to remain in Rome was motivated less by high hopes of Colonnese patronage than by the lack of other options—a lack in part due to his own tendency to burn bridges behind him.

[171] Raphael, *When Disaster Strikes*, 135-36.

[172] Albert Bandura, "Self-Efficacy Conception of Anxiety," *Anxiety Research*, 1

sure, Alcionio's decision to change patrons and his composition of orations giving shape to recent events did constitute attempts to comprehend threatening circumstances. Still, the writings themselves, despite their idiosyncracies, would not transcend the general climate of gloom—a climate produced in part by a collective sense of powerlessness and by the inability to transform an exceptionally bleak environment.[173]

iv. *Conclusions*

Taken together, Alcionio's orations on the Sack of 1527 bespeak an adaptive response to an event that had exposed Rome's vulnerability. To be sure, the Sack drove home to him just how vulnerable he was as a papal client. Finding himself reliant upon a Maecenas who could no longer adequately protect or support any but his closest advisors, rejected by other curial humanists, and traumatized by injury and the witnessing of disaster, he sought the support of another patron. Yet the Sack had also exposed the precariousness of humanists' hopes that the papacy would continue the *renovatio* and initiate a new golden age. In response to this challenge, Alcionio rewrote the narrative of Renaissance Rome, downplaying curial motifs in favor of civic ones, and acknowledging that the city could not soon return to its former greatness. But if he redefined *Romanitas* as less centered on the papacy, he continued to laud Rome's universal *imperium* and the role as cultural hegemon to which it ought eventually to return.

The example of Alcionio supports the view that the Sack marked a turning point for the culture of Renaissance Rome. Alcionio's hopes for renewal remained within the confines of *Roma Aeterna*, and he continued to articulate those hopes in the theoretically eternal idiom of Ciceronian Latin. Thus some of the ideals and the language of

(1988): 77-98; and esp. Bandura, "Self-Efficacy Mechanism in Human Agency," *American Psychologist* 37:2 (February, 1982): 122-47. While Bandura's findings are highly instructive, they must be applied with caution, particularly since he emphasizes the centrality of *perceived* efficacy rather than one's actual ability to control one's environment.

[173] Bandura, "Self-Efficacy Mechanism," 143-45, addresses collective perceptions of efficacy and their influence upon the taking of constructive action.

Roman humanism would transcend the Sack of Rome.[174] At the same time, however, Alcionio's orations highlight the distance that separated Roman culture at the time of his writing from the glorious period before 1527. By presenting the Sack as a watershed event, in effect he encapsulated the preceding decades as a completed epoch that had irrevocably slipped away. Thus, in the hands of humanists such as Alcionio, the memory of the High Renaissance in Rome first gained closure and became reified as history.

---

[174] It is worth noting that, in Alcionio's hands, Ciceronian Latin proved a far more malleable medium for personal expression than has sometimes been supposed possible (e.g., D'Amico, *Renaissance Humanism*).

CHAPTER THREE

PIETRO CORSI AND THE PERPETUATION OF
CURIALIST IDEOLOGY

While the Castel Sant' Angelo provided a haven during the Sack of
Rome for those who, like Pietro Alcionio, succeeded in reaching it,
the city below offered few places of refuge. Nearly four hundred
people crowded into the palace of Cardinal Andrea della Valle in the
Rione S. Eustachio.[1] Because of della Valle's Imperial connections,
his residence—like those of three other pro-Imperial cardinals, Wil-
lem van Enkevoirt, Alessandro Cesarini, and Giovanni Piccolomini—afforded temporary safety. The respite came at a price: on 8
May, an Italian captain in the Imperial forces, Fabrizio Maramaldo,
extorted over 34,000 ducats in protection money from those in della
Valle's palace. The protection he provided, however, was short-
lived: within a week the German Landsknechts, who were not under
Maramaldo's jurisdiction, laid siege to the palace of Cardinal Piccolomini. When it fell in a mere four hours, the soldiers dragged Piccolomini through the streets to the Borgo. Thus prompted, the Cardinals della Valle, Cesarini, and Enkevoirt fled from their residences
to the Palazzo Colonna which, because of Pompeo Colonna's return
to the city on 10 May, remained secure. Many who had sought their
protection, however, were abandoned to endure imprisonment and
torments at the hands of the German troops.[2]

Among those who had fled into della Valle's palace was Pietro
Corsi, a Roman humanist who had been a staunch papal advocate
since the time of Julius II. When Maramaldo extorted money from
the refugees, Corsi was compelled to pay 50 ducats, but evidently he
lacked the connections to gain access to the Palazzo Colonna when
the della Valle residence fell.[3] After most of the Imperial soldiers left

---

[1] F. Petrucci, "Corsi, Pietro," in *DBI* 29 (1983): 579-81, at 580. Petrucci provides
the most complete and up-to-date survey of Corsi's life and writings.
[2] Pastor, *History of the Popes*, 9:409 & n, 410-12; Petrucci, "Corsi," 580. Cardinal
della Valle and his household paid 7,000 ducats to Maramaldo, and the others who
had taken refuge in the palace paid the remainder.
[3] Petrucci, "Corsi," 580.

Rome for the countryside in mid-July to avoid famine and plague, Corsi escaped to Tivoli for a month, but soon the Imperialists harried that town as well, and Corsi returned to Rome.[4] By early October, the soldiers too had drifted back into the city, where they renewed their depredations.[5] In a letter to Angelo Colocci (20 November), Antonio Tebaldeo reported that both he and Corsi were among those assaulted by the soldiers for trying to enter Colocci's residence.[6] Tebaldeo's letter conveys a sense of the precariousness of life in occupied Rome: for example, the troops recently had been threatening to execute some of their high-ranking ecclesiastical hostages unless Pope Clement were to pay a further exorbitant sum by 27 November.[7]

In the midst of these events, despite being subject to the whims of the occupying forces in a way that Alcionio was not, Corsi set about telling the story of the Sack of Rome in another favorite humanist genre. In dactylic hexameters modeled upon the poetry of Vergil, he composed the *Romae urbis excidium*, which he dedicated to Francis I's mother, Louise of Savoy.[8] Despite its invocation of long-standing

---

[4] Santorre Debenedetti, "Le ansie d'un bibliofilo durante il Sacco di Roma," in *Mélanges offerts à M. Émile Picot* (Paris, 1913): 511-14, includes a transcription (513-14) of a letter from Antonio Tebaldeo to Angelo Colocci (20 November 1527). Writing from Rome, Tebaldeo notes (514) that "M. Pietro Cursio stette un mese a Tivoli, poi sempre è stato in Roma." Judith Hook, *The Sack of Rome, 1527* (London, 1972), 213, notes that with the exception of 2,000 troops, who remained to guard the pope and Castel Sant'Angelo, the rest of the Imperial army left the city on 10 July. On the Imperialist assault upon Tivoli, see Giovio's *Elogium* of Andrea Marone.

[5] Hook, *Sack of Rome*, 214-15.

[6] Debenedetti, "Le Ansie," 513. Tebaldeo writes to Colocci: "Ho ricevuta tandem una vostra, a che vi rispondo che non sapete quanta fatica sia stata il stare in Roma, per la grandissima peste et per le botte che davano li soldati a chi volea andare a vedere le case, come fecero prima a M. Pietro Cursio et ultimamente a me in presentia de le vostre vicine." While Tebaldeo was inspecting the damage to Colocci's library, he says, he was struck by a Spanish captain. Corsi provides a cryptic account of his own mistreatment in *Excidium*, 426, ll.45-65. (Full cite in n. 8 below)

[7] Debenedetti, "Le ansie," 514: "Lo Episcopo di Verona, lo Episcopo de Pistoia, lo Episcopo Sipontino, l'Arcivescovo de Pisa, Iacobo Salviati et Lorenzo Ridolphi sono qui in casa del Cardinale Colonna, in mano de' Thedeschi per obstadesi, et stanno incatenati a dui a dui, che a vederli è una gran miseria; et se a' 27 di questo mese il Papa non paga una certa quantità di dinari, che è grande, li vogliono fare morire in Campo de Fiore...."

[8] An early Roman edition of the poem in the Vatican Library (Racc. I.IV.909, int. 5) bears this title. The poem was republished in Paris in May of 1528. I employ the critical edition of the poem in Léon Dorez, "Le poème de Pietro Corsi sur le sac de Rome," *Mélanges d'Archéologie et d'Histoire de l'Ecole Française de Rome* 16 (1896): 420-436 (hereafter cited as "Corsi, *Excidium*"). In the edition Dorez edits, the poem is entitled, "Ad humani generis servatorem in urbis Romae excidio P. Cursii civis Rom. deploratio."

Roman humanist themes and its vindication of the dignity of the papacy, his poem speaks poignantly to the limited options that confronted curial humanists in the wake of the Sack of Rome, and it contrasts starkly in tone with his writings on behalf of Julius II: writings that had been composed when both Renaissance Rome—and Pietro Corsi as its spokesman—had seemed destined for great things.

i. *Biographical Background*

Unlike Alcionio, Pietro Corsi arrived in the Eternal City without having previously established himself as a published scholar. Aside from the fact that he traced his origins to Carpineto Romano, a small town in the hill country south of Rome on the way to Terracina, we know nothing of his life or career before 1509, when we find him creating a persona exclusively suited to the intellectual and social world of Renaissance Rome. Corsi's earliest known works, three eclogues presented there in 1509-10, attest both in setting and in content to his assimilation into the world of curial humanism. The first, set to music and presented before Julius II on the day of the Assumption (15 August 1509), at the basilica of Santa Maria Maggiore, was performed by six boys and a girl, the children of the pope's kinsman, Bartolomeo della Rovere. Corsi delivered the second in the presence of the pope on All Saints' Day (1 November 1509), and the third on the feast of St. Peter in 1510. All three poems, modeled substantially upon Vergil's eclogues, dignified Pope Julius as the head of the *Respublica Christiana*, the leader who was ushering in the new golden age.[9] In 1511, Corsi further cultivated papal support by writing a poem in honor of the formation on 5

---

[9] Pierre de Nolhac, *La bibliothèque de Fulvio Orsini: contributions à l'histoire des collections d'Italie et à l'étude de la Renaissance* (Paris, 1887), 256. The three orations are found in BAV MS Vat. Lat. 3441, fols. 167r-77v, 193r-204r. To date, none of them has been edited. Corsi strengthened the parallels between the pope and Caesar Augustus by employing the Sapphic meter that Horace used in his odes dignifying the Roman Emperor. Ingrid D. Rowland, "'Render unto Caesar the Things Which are Caesar's': Humanism and the Arts in the Patronage of Agostino Chigi," *Renaissance Quarterly* 39 (1986): 673-730, at 697n, notes the explicit link between the golden age theme and Pope Julius II in these orations and in similar writings by Pacifico Massimi and Fausto Capodiferro. See also Frances A. Yates, *Astraea: The Imperial Theme in the Sixteenth Century* (London, 1975; repr. 1985): 4 & n, which discusses the interpretation of Vergil's Fourth Eclogue as Messianic prophecy—a tradition dating back at least to the emperor Constantine (d.337).

October of the Holy League—an alliance joining Julius II, Ferdinand of Spain, and the Republic of Venice.[10] Once again, Corsi explicitly praised Pope Julius as initiator of the golden age.[11]

If Corsi was thus early established as a client of popes and as an advocate of curialist ideology, he also became an active member of the sodalities of Angelo Colocci and Johann Küritz.[12] The context of some of his own publications indicates this connection: in 1512, he had verses included in the *Suburbanum Augustini Chisii*, a collection in praise of Chigi's villa on the via della Lungara, across the Tiber from the via Giulia; in 1519, he joined Pierio Valeriano and others in writing verses for a volume in memory of Celso Mellini; and in 1524 several of his poems appeared in the *Coryciana*.[13] In 1525, Corsi wrote his *Poema de Civitate Castellana Faliscorum non Veientium oppido*, a hexameter composition addressing another topic of central interest to humanists in Renaissance Rome and Florence: the Etruscans and their association with the founding of ancient Rome.[14] The volume in which the poem appeared was dedicated to the papal datary, Giberti, and Corsi dedicated the poem itself to Celso Mellini's brother, Pietro.

The testimony of humanist colleagues also evidences his position as a curial insider. Valeriano dedicated a book of his *Hieroglyphica* to

---

[10] Petrucci, "Corsi," 579, cites the tract as *Panegyris de federe inter Iulium II pont. max. et Hispanensem regem*. For details on the Holy League, see Pastor, *History of the Popes*, vol. 6, 2nd ed. (St. Louis, 1902), chap. 6, esp. 366-74.

[11] BAV MS Vat. Lat. 5383, fols.137r-39v, contain a manuscript copy of this poem. Already from its outset (fol. 137r), Corsi portrays the golden age as now beginning: "Festa dies noni Qui nunc novus incipit anni/ Iuleos renovat fastos: hinc clarius orbem/ Illustrant solis radii: iactantior hinc est/ Auspiciis Roma alta novis: hinc aurea pubes/ Purpureique patres: et plebs non sordida cultu/ Principis accumulant lucem. non flamina perstant,/ sed variis avium coetus concentibus auras/ Mulcent; et fluvio exultat. Tyberinus amoeno./ Ditior hinc solito templis nitor, altior aris/ Flamma micat, plenaque deis sparguntur acerra *[sic]*/ Quos cylices, divesque tulit Panchaia odores:/ Sic primos decet ire dies, sic secla renasci,/ Iulia, qui celsi referas palatia coeli/ Omnia qui referas ad sacra, et publica vota/ Fama ingens, melior factis, et numine numen,/ Aemula sideribus quisquis tua templa tuetur/ Non opus esse hominum, sed divum moenia credit."

[12] On curialist ideology, see above, chap. 1.

[13] Biblioteca Corsiniana (Rome) Ms. 45 D 4, fols. 20r-20v, reproduces a Corsi poem entitled "In statuas Coritianas epigrammata." In the *Coryciana* (ed. Blosio Palladio, 1524), Corsi's poems appear on D2v, F4r and v, and R4r and v.

[14] Petrucci, "Corsi," 580, lists three later editions of this poem. On the earlier Florentine humanist interest in the Etruscan foundations of Rome, see esp. Hans Baron, *The Crisis of the Early Italian Renaissance*, rev. ed. (Princeton, 1966), esp. 61-78, 418-30.

Corsi, and he dated their friendship from the time of his own arrival in Rome (1509).[15]   The epigrammist Marcantonio Casanova praised Corsi, calling him both "the best fellow of all" and "the best poet of all."[16]   It appears, however, that few of Corsi's colleagues shared this sanguine estimation of his companionship and poetic talents. Giraldi's dialogue on contemporary poets, for example, faults Corsi for his impetuousity and abrasiveness. Corsi, he says, "has been presented with Roman citizenship," but is "contriving certain things every day in a manner more bold than considerate. It is scarcely to be hoped that through age and contact with good friends he will attain to maturity."[17]   In addition, Corsi found himself the victim of anonymous attacks in the form of satirical verses posted publicly, under cover of darkness, by one of his Roman humanist "friends."[18]   In these verses, as indeed throughout his career, he received ridicule for the rusticity of his style.

Thus, we have in Corsi a "rank-and-file" Roman humanist: one who participated actively in the academies and who maintained a close friendship with Angelo Colocci, yet one who evidently never held an important post, and certainly one whose compositions did

---

[15] Pierio Valeriano, *Ioannis Pierii Valeriani Bellunensis, Hieroglyphica, seu de Sacris AEgyptiorum Aliarumque Gentium Literis Commentarii...* (Lyons, 1602), [Book 12,] 115: "Et si minus tibi lucubratio ipsa satisfecerit, ut quae nimium properata non ita omnia complecti potuerit, voluntatem tamen animumque meum existimes, quantum in me fuit, sibi amico tam veteri, tam probo, satis plurimum facere studuisse: non enim recens mea erga doctrinam & ingenium tuum benevolentia firmaque atque constans amicitia, quae ab ipso primum die, quo Romam diu patria cariturus applicui, coepta, mirificum in dies accepit incrementum...." The letter's surface message, in which Valeriano uses the rhetoric of obligation to speak of his indebtedness to Corsi, perhaps sits ill with the fact that the book it accompanies concerns "the donkey." The interaction between the two scholars may have been strengthened by the fact that Valeriano soon served as tutor to the sons of Bartolomeo della Rovere, who performed the first of Corsi's eclogues for Julius II in August of 1509. See chap. 5 below.

[16] BAV MS Vat. Lat. 5227, I, fol. 52v: "Ille, ille optimus omnium sodales,/ ille, ille optimus omnium poeta."

[17] Giraldi, Lilio Gregorio, *De poetis nostrorum temporum*, ed. Karl Wotke (Berlin, 1894), 43: "Petrus Curtius, et ipse ex Marsis, urbe Romana donatus quaedam in dies audacter magis quam parate molitur; vix sperandum est eum aetate et bonorum amicorum consuetudine maturitatem consecuturum." Giraldi's description of Corsi as being "ex Marsis," or "from among the Marsians," confirms his connection with Carpineto Romano.

[18] G.F. Lancellotti, *Poesie italiane e latini di mons. A. Colocci* (Jesi, 1772), 166-70, reproduces these verses. Corsi responded to his critic—whom Petrucci, "Corsi," 580-81, identifies tentatively as Francesco Maria Molza—with verses written in the name of the nymph of Angelo Colocci's fountain.

little to distinguish their author.[19] In his Vergilian poem on the Sack of Rome, Corsi employed a major Latin genre to describe that pivotal historical event, but with neither the creativity nor the vision to move beyond the humanist narrative of the past two decades. Instead, he only managed to invert that narrative's time-worn assumptions and to lament Rome's condition.

ii. *The Romae Urbis Excidium and the Sack of Rome*

The dedicatory letter of Corsi's poem on the Sack of Rome, addressed to Louise of Savoy, beseeches her to secure French intervention on the city's behalf. From its outset, Corsi points to the continuing chaos and terror in Rome: "for seven months already, no kind of outrage, plundering, torture, or sacrilege has been left undone in the city by Caesar's soldiers."[20] After the Duke of Bourbon's death in the initial assault, the lack of a universally recognized commander among the Imperial troops had led to continued unrest and insurrection in their ranks.[21] Furthermore, Charles V's failure to pay the troops provided an excuse for them to continue wringing what they could from the Romans, making the city a perpetual battlefield.[22] As Corsi writes, the Romans must be rescued "from a shameful condition of living and from interminable terrors of death."[23] In fact, were it not for the openness and evident pride with which the occupying army performed its atrocities, Corsi says, he "would certainly not have dared to put this thing into writing at this exceptional time."[24]

---

[19] Petrucci, "Corsi," 579, notes only that Corsi was a canon of Terracina and speculates that he may have become a dependent of Cardinal Niccolò Ridolfi.

[20] Corsi, *Excidium*, 421: "Quum VII iam menses, Princeps clarissima, nullum flagitiorum, rapinarum, suppliciorum, sacrilegiorum genus a Caesarianis esset militibus in urbe Roma praetermissum...."

[21] Corsi, *Excidium*, 422: "Videbam enim calamitates nostras nullo adhuc exitu terminari, quum omni fere temporis puncto, qui in Urbe erant, tumultuarentur, et ut certo duce carentes militaribus seditionibus conflictarentur."

[22] Corsi, *Excidium*, 422: "Perpetuam autem belli sedem ideo Romam se fecisse iactabant, quod a Caesare suo iam annuo essent stipendio fraudati; quod tamen a nobis ut victis repeterent, et quandiu illud non persolveretur, se velle ex fortunis, siquae superessent, ex bonis, ex sanguine demum nostro sibi victum parare."

[23] Corsi, *Excidium*, 423: "caeterosque omnis generis, omnis ordinis mortales a foeda vivendi conditione et ab infinitis mortis terroribus eripiat...."

[24] Corsi, *Excidium*, 423: "Quod sane literis mandare, hoc praecipuo tempore, ausus non fuissem, nisi ipsi qui haec committere non dubitarunt, se tantorum scelerum authores palam fateri, idque in summa laude ponere non erubescerent." In the poem

Corsi tries to persuade Louise to become "savior of the human race on the occasion of the destruction of the city of Rome," imploring her to have her son Francis send his victorious army down from the north to relieve the sufferings of the Romans, a divinely-sanctioned mission that will ensure her reputation for all future generations.[25] Implicitly invoking the French monarch's role as "Most-Christian King," Corsi draws attention to the violation of nuns, the burning of churches, and the "mockery of the bodies of the saints, which have always been honored here with the highest veneration *by your people*."[26] Corsi also connects France and Rome by parataxis at the end of the dedication where, juxtaposing their contrasting fortunes, he bids "farewell to your most-fortunate son and his safe kingdom," writing "from the corpse of Rome."[27] The magnitude of the devastation of the city, according to Corsi, stands out as historically unique:

> it is manifest that [Rome] has been plundered by the Visigoths, occupied by the Herulians, held as property by the Ostrogoths, disfigured by the Vandals, harried by the Lombards, despoiled by the Greeks, assaulted by the Germans, [and] laid waste with fire and the sword by the Saracens; but now it has been struck down by the Caesarian army with every kind of calamity, such that it has exceeded at once the avarice, audacity, treachery, wantonness, and cruelty of all nations and all centuries.[28]

itself (p.429, ll.144-46), however, Corsi notes that he leaves some details unsaid since "it is not now safe to complain of true circumstances and to utter genuine anguishes." (Sed quoniam superant, Genitor, maiora relatis,/ Nec nobis iam vera queri verosque dolores/ Edere iam tutum est....")

25 Corsi, *Excidium*, 421: "AD HUMANI GENERIS SERVATOREM IN URBIS ROMAE EXCIDIO...."; *ibid.*, 422: "filioque tuo Rege post hominum memoriam longe clariss. et religiosiss. susceptam...."; 423: "Eorum autem quae mandata sunt a Civitate legationi, ut tibi nuntiet, haec summa: te filio tuo authorem esse, ut quam primum exercitum, quem victorem in transpadanis habet, huc mittat...." 424: "et homines sperant, et Dii vobis pollicentur, ut non minus fortitudinem, virtutem, magnitudinem animi vestri, quam pietatem, fidem, et constantiam omnis sit posteritas probatura."

26 Corsi, *Excidium*, 422: "quod soleat pro clarissimis suis institutis omnium Christianorum causam tueri, omniumque bonorum dignitatem conservare." *Ibid.*, 423: "te filio tuo authorem esse, ut quam primum exercitum, quem victorem in transpadanis habet, huc mittat, qui divorum corpora, quae summa veneratione semper a vestris hic culta sunt, ab ludibrio vindicet, templa sanctiss. ab incendiis, virgines Deo dicatas ab incestu...." (Emphasis added.)

27 Corsi, *Excidium*, 424: "Vale foeliciss. tuo filio et eius Regno incolumi. Ex Urbis cadavere...."

28 Corsi, *Excidium*, 422-23: "Et eo quidem magis, quod constat eandem Urbem a Visigotis direptam, ab Herulis occupatam, ab Ostrogotis possessam, a Vandalis de-

Neither Turks nor Africans nor any other non-Christian people, Corsi asserts, has ever abused Rome more than has the current occupying force. France, he argues, has a particular historical responsibility to rescue the papacy and the Romans: centuries before, after Gaul had become Christian, it had sought to preserve the safety of Rome and its pontiff.[29] Whereas Alcionio incited Charles V to action by using Charlemagne as an example of how a Holy Roman Emperor should act, Corsi points to Charlemagne's coronation as having established a special relationship between France and Rome:

> we who are of the Roman race seek [military help] especially from you most-religious Gauls because there is a consensus among all men that Charles, that most-holy and most-invincible emperor, consecrated everlasting friendship and concord with our ancestors at the altar of St. Peter.[30]

The prescriptive political appeal of the dedicatory letter contrasts sharply, however, with the absence of similar sentiments in the poem itself, where neither King Francis nor Louise of Savoy, nor even the nation of France, receives mention. To be sure, the poem does have a political subtext. For example, Corsi calls attention at one point to Lautrec, the French commander in Italy, whom he describes as "swooping down on victorious wings."[31] In fact, Lautrec's march south from Piacenza, beginning on 7 November 1527, would ultimately compel Imperial leaders to pay their troops in Rome to leave the city on 16-17 February 1528 and to march to protect Naples.[32] In addition, Corsi notes the naval victories of the Genoese commander Andrea Doria, then employed by the French.[33] As of his writing, however, the threat posed by these leaders had not managed

formatam, a Langobardis vexatam, a Graecis spoliatam, a Germanis oppugnatam, a Sarracenis ferro ignique vastatam; sed nunc a Caesariano exercitu ita omni calamitatum genere afflicta est, ut omnium simul nationum omniumque seculorum avaritiam, audaciam, perfidiam, libidinem, crudelitatem superaverit."

[29] Corsi, *Excidium*, 422.

[30] Corsi, *Excidium*, 424: "hoc a vobis religiosiss. Gallis, nos qui Romani generis sumus, petimus, quum inter omnes constet Carolum sanctiss. illum et invictiss. imperatorem cum maioribus nostris perpetuam amicitiam et concordiam ad maximam divi Petri aram sanxisse."

[31] Corsi, *Excidium*, 433, ll.248-51: "Et licet hinc ultor victricibus advolet alis/ Lutrecus, quo non ductor maturius alter/ Victorem toties, toties evicerit hostem:/ Hinc Venetum pugna, atque mora dux inclytus instet...."

[32] Hook, *Sack of Rome*, 226-31; Pastor, *History of the Popes*, 9: 461, 463 & n.

[33] Corsi, *Excidium*, 433, ll.252-55: "Auria et hinc classe instructa, quem saepe fugantem/ Sternentemque truces vexata per aequora Mauros/ Neptunus, patria et cives videre recepta/ Sublimem curru, et duplici fulgere corona."

to dislodge the Imperial soldiers from Rome: the army "lazily withdrew into the midst of the city, and conducts fierce wars with it [the
city] alone; it is pleased to continue to delay and to knock all Rome
bit by bit from its bottommost foundations, so that neither the physical appearance nor the name of the city should survive."[34] Aside
from a petition to God that He "order that that king, those king-
doms, and the leaders who now maintain your laws are safe and
sound," the poem avoids invocation of France.[35]

Corsi is circumspect, too, in his treatment of Charles V. The sufferings of Rome have resulted in part from its excessive trust of the
Imperialists: "Rome has paid enough penalties because it, credulous,
gave preference to peace over war...."[36] Corsi here refers to Pope
Clement's treaty with the Imperial Viceroy of Naples, Charles de
Lannoy, on 15 March 1527, in accordance with which Clement had
reduced the number of troops he was fielding, thereby making himself vulnerable to Bourbon's attack:

> scarcely after his army had been dismissed, the victor [i.e., Clement],
> lacking military protection, was stormed and conquered by sudden
> force by the troops of Caesar—not, I admit, by the same troops, but by
> Caesar's, the enemy would hardly deny it.[37]

Corsi exonerates only one of the Imperial officers presiding over the
conquest of Rome, Ferrante Gonzaga, who had helped to limit the
plundering in the initial weeks of occupation.[38] Otherwise, he offers a

---

[34] Corsi, *Excidium*, 434, ll.256-60: "Hinc extrema fames, dira hinc discordia glis-
cat!/ Ipse tamen mediam ignavus secessit in urbem,/ Cumque una fera bella gerit:
iuvat usque morari,/ Et Romam ex imis paulatim sedibus omnem/ Vertere, ne facies
urbis nomenve supersit."

[35] Corsi, *Excidium*, 436, ll.323-24: "Illum praecipue Regem, regna illa. Ducesque/
Esse iube incolumés, tua qui nunc iura tuentur." ·

[36] Corsi, *Excidium*, 434, ll.262-63: "Poenarum sat Roma dedit, quod credula bello/
Praevertit pacem, et victis se credidit armis."

[37] Corsi, *Excidium*, 425, ll.11-16: "Nil non Roma mali, nil non perpessa laborum,/
Nil non supplicii, dum qui tua iura, vicesque/ Sustinet, exosus bellum, cum Caesare
pacem/ Hinc init; hinc, misso vix milite, Cacsaris armis,/ Non iisdem (fateor) sed
Caesaris, haud neget hostis,/ Vi victor victus subita, atque oppressus inermis." Hook,
Sack of Rome, 138-40, argues that the confusion over command of Imperial forces in
Italy between Lannoy and Bourbon was part of a conscious policy of Charles V, who
gave conflicting instructions to these two leaders. Unlike Alcionio's *Declamatio* against
Charles V's letter, Corsi's poem does not try to explain or assign responsibility for
this evident confusion of command.

[38] Corsi, *Excidium*, 427, ll.69-75: "Quin reliquis Romam spoliantibus, audiit hoc
te/ Dicentem: Mea non rapere est, sed vincere, praeda./ Regum igitur foecunda
parens te Mantua fratrem/ Principis esse tui merito laetatur, euntem/ Per fratris

uniformly negative image of the victors, who have given themselves over to vices such as drunkenness and gambling:

> The ardor of the soldier must be feared above all at that time when his veins have become swollen with wine, and when the German soldier vomits out here and there scraps of food stuck together with the fruit of Dionysus, or when he has squandered full purses with wicked dice. For all the public squares have been filled with greedy troops of gamblers.[39]

Corsi ironically lauds the prowess of the invaders in this, their area of greatest expertise: "What an outstanding adornment of the foot-soldier, what a thing worthy of victory monuments, either to despoil the rider of his mount or of a golden military collar, or to have returned home heavy-laden with silver and gems!"[40] The gambling has even exacerbated the suffering of the Romans: "He for whom circumstance goes badly in the game, roused by bitter ferocity, attacks the flank of the blameless host with the cruel sword."[41]

Corsi emphasizes the tremendous suffering that the troops have caused, as when fathers have had to buy back "at the cost of robes, gold, houses, [and] estates," the corpses of their children, who had died from "tortures of the kind that all antiquity did not see, nor would posterity suppose [them] true but false."[42] The troops have been ruthless in their cruelty, regardless of the victims' age, sex, or homeland, and nuns and priests have received no preferential treatment.[43] Even plague victims have not escaped persecution:

---

decora alta, et fortia facta parentis/ Aetas nulla tuum, iuvenis fortissime, nomen/ Destruet...." This praise has added resonance, since in early November Ferrante's brother Federico, the Marquis of Mantua, changed allegiance from the Spanish to the French side. See Pastor, *History of the Popes*, vol. 9, 461-62.

[39] Corsi, *Excidium*, 431, ll.183-88: "Sed tum praecipue metuendus militis ardor,/ Cum venae intumuere mero, Germanaque passim/ Cum legio frusta eiectat glomerata Lyaeo,/ Improba seu plenos exhauserit alea fiscos./ Nam fora quaeque avidis ludentum oppleta catervis." The Germans do, however, shudder at some of the offenses (Corsi, *Excidium*, 432, l.207): "facinus Cimber licet impius horret."

[40] Corsi, *Excidium*, 431, ll.192-94: "Egregium hoc peditis decus, haec res digna tropheis,/ Quadrupede aut equitem spoliare, aut torquibus aureis,/ Aut rediisse domum argento, gemmisque gravatum!"

[41] Corsi, *Excidium*, 431, ll.195-96: "Cui male res ludo geritur, rabie incitus acri,/ Hospitis innocui saevo latus impetit ense."

[42] Corsi, *Excidium*, 425, ll.22-27: "Nec modo viva patrum, sed mortua corpora nati,/ Mortua quinetiam natorum corpora patres,/ Mortua tormentis, et qualia tota vetustas/ Nec vidit, nec vera putent, sed ficta minores;/ Veste, auro, laribus, fundis emisse coacti,/ Et quidquid latuit thesauri effundere aviti."

[43] Corsi, *Excidium*, 427, ll.82-90.

Men dragging with difficulty their infected limbs were summoned into foul torments and hung from a beam either by the feet or by that one part of the body which public decency covers (but always with the miserable one's hands bound behind his back), compelled by fire or by the sword, amidst a hastened death, to betray gems and precious vases and gold that they had never possessed.[44]

In addition, the plunderers continued for months to use threats and force to extract food, drink, and shelter from their captive hosts, threatening them with death should they fail to provide on the spot. The bodies of the Romans were similarly subject to the whims of the soldiers, as when Spanish troops entered a church on All Saints' Day (1 November 1527), tore a young girl from her noble mother's arms, and raped her in public.[45] Even tombs have afforded no protection from abuse, and Corsi adorns the soldiers with ironic praise especially for their plundering of sarcophagi: "Surely this is the highest glory of a knight and soldier if to so many spoils even the booty of a tomb be added!"[46]

While the troops have made Rome a living nightmare, the countryside has fared little better. Roads have become impassable, as brigands lie in wait to rob of money and even life any who have managed to escape the city. Meanwhile, orchards, vineyards, and flocks have been devastated, and no one dares tend them.[47] In the universal suffering, "the wild beasts themselves groan, even though they alone enjoy happy leisure on the plains and safely visit lakes and open spaces."[48]

Still, the sufferings of Rome stand out as exceptional. In addition to enduring the depredations of the Imperial troops and the ravages of

---

[44] Corsi, *Excidium*, 427-28, ll.91-97: "Ipsa simul nec tuta lues, aegreque trahentes/ Membra infecta viri foeda in tormenta vocati;/ Eque trabe, aut pedibus pendere, aut corporis acti/ Illa parte, pudor quam publicus occulit unam,/ (Sed manibus semper miseri post terga revinctis)/ Acti igne, aut ferro, gemmas, pretiosaque vasa,/ Aurum nunquam habitum properata in morte fateri." Corsi notes, however, that often before they could enjoy the extorted goods, the tormentors would themselves die of plague, thereby "paying the penalty" for their greed and cruelty (Corsi, *Excidium*, 428, ll.98-99): "Saepeque vix tacto morientis barbarus acre/ Occubuit, poenasque dedit duo fata ferenti."

[45] Corsi, *Excidium*, 431, ll.178-181; and 429, ll.120-27.

[46] Corsi, *Excidium*, 429, ll.142-43: "Scilicet haec equitis, haec gloria militis ingens,/ Accedat si tot spoliis et praeda sepulchri!"

[47] Corsi, *Excidium*, 432, ll.218-226.

[48] Corsi, *Excidium*, 433, ll.227-29: "Sic tamen ut tanto in gemitu credamus et ipsas/ Ingemuisse feras, solae licet otia campis/ Laeta agitent, tutaeque lacus, et aperta frequentent."

the plague, the Romans have also suffered inclement weather and shortages of goods. By late November, when Corsi is writing, anything made of wood has either been burned by the army or broken up and sold to the common people, and most houses no longer have doors or ceilings.[49] Consequently, unusually severe winter storms have found the Romans exposed: "the air sinks down with unremitting showers, [and] the entire sky quakes with frequent thunder.... Early cold waves oppress us.... Neither blankets nor clothes, except those which the enemy overlooked, have been saved by anyone. And under the open sky the soaked earth provides a couch for the naked."[50]

The cold spell is but part of a more general disordering: "The structure of nature and of heaven has been disturbed, and the seasons do not follow their accustomed successions."[51] Corsi characterizes the disturbance as nature's response to the Sack of Rome. Thus, the low visibility that masked the initial Imperial attack on 6 May was an expression of divine revulsion: "Apollo himself ... did not tolerate with a favorable countenance the military destruction of Rome. In fact, he immediately concealed his radiant head with a black cloud and a dense fog."[52] The Anio River, a tributary of the Tiber, similarly "recoiled in horror from these scenes of crimes" and shifted from its usual route: "Certainly it dreaded to be combined with the waters of the Tiber, which it knew carried the sacred body parts of your saints."[53] That autumn, the sun (personified still by Apollo) "did not permit the fruits to turn yellow at the accustomed time, but he postponed the harvest for a month, so that raging fam-

---

[49] Corsi, *Excidium*, 430-31, ll.172-177.

[50] Corsi, *Excidium*, 430, ll.165-66: "ruit imbribus aer/ Assiduis, crebro et tonitru coelum intremit omne;" ll.168-171: "Frigora nos properata premunt, et Phoebus ad aequum/ Phylliriden iam flectit equos, servataque nulli/ Stragula, non vestes, nisi quas neglexerit hostis./ Uda thorum nudis, et sub Iove, terra ministrat...."

[51] Corsi, *Excidium*, 430, ll.164-65: "Naturae, et caeli ratio iam versa, vicesque/ Tempora non servant solitas...."

[52] Corsi, *Excidium*, 435, ll.294-96: "At non ipse Deûm exuvias, neque Cynthius Urbis/ Excidium laeto ore tulit: quin protinus atra/ Nube caput nitidum, densa et caligine texit...." For a prose attribution of the fog to divine providence, see Jean Cave, "Bellum Romanum," 396, in Léon Dorez, ed., "Le sac de Rome (1527). Relation inédite de Jean Cave, Orléanais," *Mélanges d'archéologie et d'histoire de l'Ecole Française de Rome* 16 (1896): 355-419.

[53] Corsi, *Excidium*, 435, ll.300-305: "Flumina et has facies scelerum aversata, suumque/ Occuluere caput, notoque excessit ab alveo/ Ipse Anio, alterius fieri maris advena nixus,/ Aut saltem abiunctus Tyrrheno in marmore condi:/ Scilicet extimuit misceri Tybridis undis,/ Volvere quem sciret Divûm sacra membra tuorum."

ine drove down to the underworld those whom weapons had not been able to kill."[54]

A petition for divine mercy and relief from these ills—rather than any appeal for political help from France—constitutes the organizing principle of the *Romae urbis excidium*. Corsi does not seek an underlying moral or theological explanation for Rome's political troubles. In fact, he suggests that such inquiry would be disrespectful to God: "it is characteristic of pious ones to bear these [calamities] with restraint, and it is not proper to investigate into the causes of such great ills."[55] The Romans, he argues, have endured all the dangers and bloodshed in the service of God.[56] Still, they do not inquire into causes, but instead can only plead that God will finally put an end to the worst torments that they have been enduring.[57] This supplication for divine mercy is the poem's central motif; yet it is offered out of desperation and an expressed concern that God may offer little relief:

> Give back life, Father; you are accustomed to do this, and you alone can do all things. If that is too much, and it should be determined not to spare your Rome, nor to grant forgiveness to Rome asking it and requesting life, at least defend the corpse (should any remain) of the city. And if even that is too much, and it is resolved to knock down the walls themselves, at least spare your temples and those of your people.[58]

Thus, Corsi's *Romae urbis excidium* conveys a sense of hopelessness. Rather than search for meaning in recent disasters—a problematic

---

[54] Corsi, *Excidium*, 435, ll.297-99: "Tempore nec passus solito flavescere fruges,/ Distulit in mensem messem, ut quos perdere tela/ Non poterant, hos saeva fames detruderet orco."

[55] Corsi, *Excidium*, 428, ll.101-103: "Nos tamen his graviora, alti fabricator Olympi,/ Ferre vides; verum moderate haec ferre piorum est,/ Tantorum neque fas causas tentare malorum." In the concluding lines of another poem (unfortunately undated) entitled *De Tiberis inundatione, post direptam a Caesariano milite Romam*, Corsi similarly avoids assigning responsibility to the Romans: "Quod tamen admissum tantum scelus esse putemus,/ Quantum opus ut sociis abluat aequor aquis?// Certe hoc non nostrum crimen: Dii sanguine foeda/ Non alio poterant tergere templa modo." The 16-line poem appears in print in Ianus Gruterus, ed., *Delitiae CC. Italorum poetarum...* ([Frankfurt], 1608), 1:874.

[56] Corsi, *Excidium*, 433, ll.237-40.

[57] Corsi, *Excidium*, 435-36, ll.237-40.

[58] Corsi, *Excidium*, 434, ll.277-82: "Redde animam, es solitus, Pater, et potes omnia solus./ Si nimis hoc, sedeatque tuae non parcere Romae,/ Nec dare poscenti veniam, vitamque roganti,/ Saltem urbis (si quod reliquum) defende cadaver./ Hoc quoque si nimium, statque ipsos sternere muros,/ Parce tuis saltem templis, templisque tuorum."

course, given the flux of political events in late 1527—he chooses
simply to bemoan their consequences for the Romans and to claim
that Rome's fate has been undeserved. The dedicatory letter's political appeal has given way to the poem's essentially apolitical entreaty
for divine mercy.

If the poem is thus only marginally political, it does adhere extensively to earlier Roman humanist themes.[59] As in the eclogues he had
written in praise of Julius II, here too Corsi favors the vocabulary of
classical Latin. He personifies the sun as *Cynthius* (i.e., Apollo), and
describes God the Father as *Iupiter Tonans* (Jove the Thunderer) and
calls Him the "Builder of high Olympus."[60] Often, Corsi employs
words that have differing classical and Christian denotations, the ambiguity of meaning allowing him simultaneously to maintain two distinct patterns of images. For example, throughout the poem, "*templa*"
refers both to pagan shrines and to Christian sanctuaries, and "*divi*"
refers both to classical Roman gods and to Catholic saints.

Following Roman humanist conventions, Corsi uses classical topoi
to describe events in Renaissance Rome. Drawing upon Roman my-
thology, he compares the sufferings and fraternal piety of the young
Porzio brothers during the Sack of Rome —who spelled each other
in the servitude to which one had been consigned—to the proverbial
brotherly love of the Gemini twins, Castor and Pollux, who shared
mortality in the same fashion.[61] Corsi draws as well upon classical
history. After providing a graphic description of an egregious public
rape scene, he asks rhetorically, "O Spaniard, was it proper for
young Latin women to see these things? Are these the thanks that the
Iberian gives to you, brave Scipio?"[62]

The blending of classical and Christian themes is most pronounced in the poem's opening invocation:

> O Highest Father of the Gods, who—once heaven had been left be-
> hind—having put on human form, came down unto earthly dwellings

---

[59] On these three themes and their relationship to Petrarchan humanism, see
chap. 1 above.

[60] e.g., Corsi, *Excidium*, 428, l.101, contains the phrase, "alti fabricator Olympi";
428, l.110, refers to the "fulminations of angry Jupiter" ("irati... fulmina... tonantis");
429, l.132, suggests that the Imperial soldiers are trying to "seize hold of the heavens
and to lay down the law for Jupiter" ("Hoc est posse polos capere, et dare iura
tonanti?").

[61] Corsi, *Excidium*, 425, ll.28-41.

[62] Corsi, *Excidium*, 429, ll.130-31: "Haec decuit spectare nurus, Hispane, Latinas?/
Hasve refert grates tibi, Scipio fortis, Iberus?"

so that You might wash away old guilt, and so that You might take up us [who have been] driven out from starry heaven, [You] the over-thrower of shadowy Avernus, and [the One] Who wanted the sacred temples of the Quirites to be the first and also perpetual seat of Your empire, give rest at last to Rome, and have mercy upon the faltering [city].[63]

Thus, from the classical tradition, Corsi appropriates the images of the "father of the gods," the river Avernus (from Vergil's description of the entrance to hell in *Aeneid* 6.126), and the Quirites (i.e., the citizens of classical Rome); and from the Christian tradition, he draws the image of Christ coming to earth as intercessor to cleanse humans of sinfulness. The notion of *imperium*, conveniently, applies to both: it is the twin spiritual and secular authority to which the Renaissance papacy laid claim.

The fact that the classical allusions might be intended primarily as metaphorical ornaments does not prevent them from creating tensions in the poem. The repeated use of "*Iupiter*" for God the Father, and "*divi*" both for the saints and for classical gods, raises questions about the relationship between God and the saints: to what extent does Corsi wish the analogy with Jupiter and lesser pagan gods to hold? As happened in the case of Pietro Alcionio's Pentecost oration, classicizing could obstruct and convolute the communication of Christian doctrine.[64]

Still, the Christian content of the poem outweighs the classical allusions. Corsi appeals to God repeatedly on the basis of the desecration of sacred objects: "Why should not the scattered and anonymous relics of the saints, despoiled of gold and lying on the ground without honor, touch You? ... Why should all Your altars, deprived of their offerings, not stir [You] to action?"[65] He devotes extensive

---

[63] Corsi, *Excidium*, 424, ll.1-7: "Summe Deûm genitor, coelo qui tecta relicto/ Mortalem indutus faciem terrena subisti,/ Ut veterem ablueres culpam, nosque aethere pulsos/ Stellanti exciperes, tenebrosi eversor Averni:/ Quique tui sedem imperii sacra templa Quiritum,/ Ut primam, sic et voluisti hanc esse perennem!/ Da tandem Romae requiem, et miserere labantis."

[64] On Alcionio's Pentecost oration, see Kenneth Gouwens, "Ciceronianism and Collective Identity: Defining the Boundaries of the Roman Academy, 1525," *Journal of Medieval and Renaissance Studies* 23:2 (Spring, 1993): 173-95.

[65] Corsi, *Excidium*, 435, ll.287-88: "Cur te non tangant sparsae, et sine nomine Divûm/ Relliquiae, spoliatae auro, et sine honore iacentes?" And, ll.292-93: "Cur viduata suis tua cuncta altaria donis/ Non moveant? moveatque sacris erepta supellex?" See also the similar appeal to God on 430, ll.154-57: "Te moveant exusta patrum monumenta sacrorum,/ Qui caeli et superûm terris arcana recludunt;/ Na-

attention to one particular act of desecration, the defacing of an
image of the Virgin Mary:

> Above all, You, to Whom all things are clear, and Who, reposing on
> [Her] chaste bosom, just barely escaped the blow, know that the image
> of your dear Mother, mangled by the Spaniard's sword and unholy
> words, suddenly dripped blood from a savage wound.[66]

Rome, Corsi notes, has responded as piously as has been possible
under the circumstances, offering what gifts it could and preparing
shrines in honor of the portent.[67]

The plea to God that concludes the poem once again unites the
classical and Christian images, highlighting the latter, and noting the
global significance of the blows to Roman *imperium*:

> Bring peace to Italy, and restrain Mars in chains, since enough posses-
> sions have been wasted and enough blood has already been spilled, and
> since your gentle Mother has felt cruel wounds, and since *in Rome nearly
> the entire world has collapsed at once.*[68]

In sum, as in pre-1527 Roman humanist writings—and in stark contrast with Alcionio's nearly-contemporaneous *Declamatio*—classical
pagan topoi continue to commingle with Renaissance Christian images in Corsi's *Romae urbis excidium*.

The last phrase of the above quotation—"in Rome nearly the
entire world has collapsed at once"—evokes central themes of Roman humanism before the Sack: papal Rome as the *caput mundi*, and
the humanists themselves as special heralds of the golden age that the
Renaissance papacy would initiate. Yet Corsi restates the *caput mundi*
theme in a way that transforms its significance. Thus, in the dedica-

---

turae et siquis reserantum occulta potentis/ Tangit honos, moveant mersi nunc Tybridis alveo."

[66] Corsi, *Excidium*, 432, ll.208-12: "Sed tu praecipue nosti, cui cuncta patescunt,/
Quique sinu positus casto, vix vixque ferocem/ Effugisti ictum: charae simulachra
parentis/ Hispani gladio, et verbis foedata nefandis,/ Vulnere et a saevo subitum
manasse cruorem."

[67] Corsi, *Excidium*, 432, ll.213-217: "Attonita urbs monstro, temerata cucurrit ad
ora/ Virginis, invisitque frequens, et vulnere tersit/ Illachrymans, ac dona tulit, sed
qualia ferret/ Urbs toties direpta: Deae tamen aemula templis/ Vicinis delubra pa-
rat, modo strata resurgat."

[68] Corsi, *Excidium*, 436, ll.325-28: "Fer pacem Italiae, et Martem compesce catenis,/ Quando satis rerum, satis et iam sanguinis haustum,/ Alma tua et sensit
crudelia vulnera Mater,/ Quando et in Urbe una totus prope concidit orbis." (Emphasis added.)

tory letter, he refers to Rome as the *caput Italiae*.[69] The change in diction makes sense in the context of the letter's appeal to France, for lauding Rome's international *imperium* would have had implications for the role the French king could be expected to play. Still, such an expression would have been unthinkable in the debate over Longueil back in 1519, when Roman confidence was still near its height.[70]

The poem itself emphasizes that Rome's proper role is as *caput mundi* and as religious center. In speaking near the outset of the poem about the city's capture, he calls Rome the "capital of the world and the celebrated home of the saints."[71] When the Imperial troops attack Rome, they demonstrate their hubris: "[the enemy] boasts that he can climb towards heaven and conquer it," thereby obtaining the title, "Subduer of Olympus."[72] Unmindful of the power of God (or, the gods), this impious foe not only scorns human laws, but "thinks that against him alone the fulminations of angry Jupiter are capable of nothing."[73] The Romans themselves, meanwhile, stand in a special relationship to the divine on account of their city's privileged role. They have borne the recent calamities not only on their own behalf, but also as a form of worshipful self-sacrifice in the honor of God:

> This place, this seat, is the true house of the gods. By fighting in this fatherland we, at any rate, have suffered wounds; we have conquered the enemy by dying on behalf of You and this fatherland....[74]

In describing the calamities, however, Corsi necessarily calls into question the theme of *Roma caput mundi* and the cluster of ideas centered on it. When he asks God to look upon the "mutilated, blood-drained, and disfigured corpse of the city," for example, the portrait he paints of Rome's passivity, helplessness, and desperation under-

---

[69] Corsi, *Excidium*, 422: "... atque etiam Italiae caput Urbem...."

[70] See chap. 1 above.

[71] Corsi, *Excidium*, 425, l.17: "Sic orbis caput ac Divûm domus inclyta capta est...."

[72] Corsi, *Excidium*, 428, ll.111-12: "Scandere quinetiam se coelum, et vincere posse/ Iactitat, et domiti affectat cognomen Olympi."

[73] Corsi, *Excidium*, 428, ll.107-10: "simul impius ille/ Iura hominum, simul ille Deûm contemnit honores,/ Nec rerum putat esse vices, certusque futuri/ In se unum irati nil fulmina posse tonantis."

[74] Corsi, *Excidium*, 434, ll.264-66: "Hic locus, haec sedes, domus haec est certa Deorum./ Nos certe in patria hac pugnando vulnera passi,/ Pro te, pro patria hac moriendo vicimus hostem...."

cuts his assertions of Roman greatness.[75] He asks God not to restore
Rome to its former (and rightful) position, but instead only to free the
city from its continuing torments so that it may make at least a
partial recovery from that which it has suffered:

> [It is] too much to be throttled again with dreadful tortures. Or per-
> haps it is a light matter to the buried to feel the sword again? Behold,
> we wander, mutilated on our shins, feet, [and] faces; behold, we lie as
> scattered ashes and unhonored bones. There is no urn for the ashes,
> nor any burial mound for the bones. But if you graciously call Rome—
> [which is] lacking all form, all sensation and light—back to hoped-for
> life, it will, itself alive, bestow a burial mound for the bones and an urn
> for the ashes.[76]

Its life extinguished, that city which had once been the "goddess of
the lands" has become "last of all things."[77] Corsi does not imagine
Rome returning to its former role, but instead asks only for its release
from its torments.

Contrasting images of Popes Clement VII and Julius II exacerbate
the sense of loss. Corsi laments Clement's misfortunes and notes his
imperium over Rome and over the sacred sphere:

> For indeed, [he] whom alone You put in charge of Rome and of all
> churches, and to whom alone it is permitted here to open or close
> heaven, was captured by force in his fortress [i.e., Castel Sant' An-
> gelo]—a terrible outrage!—by the enemy: his enemy, and equally as
> much Yours [i.e., God's].[78]

---

[75] Corsi, *Excidium*, 435, l.285: "Urbis lacerum, exangue, atque informe cadaver...."
[76] Corsi, *Excidium*, 434, ll.267-274: "Sed nimium, diris iterum cruciatibus angi:/
An leve sit gladios iterum sentire sepultis?/ En crura, enque pedes laceri, laceri ora
vagamur;/ En sparsi cineres, atque ossa inhonora iacemus:/ Nulla urna est cineri,
tumulus non ossibus ullus./ At si forma omni, sensu omni, et luce carentem/ Op-
tatam pius ad vitam revocaveris Urbem,/ Viva dabit cineri tumulum, dabit ossibus
urnam."
[77] Corsi, *Excidium*, 434, ll.275-76: "Da vitam, exstincta est, Pater; et quae maxima
quondam./ Quae Dea terrarum fuerat, nunc ultima rerum est." By contrast, a poem
attributed to Corsi's friend Antonio Tebaldeo inverts the themes of Horace's Sixteenth Epode to portray Corsi's poem as successfully obtaining divine assistance at
last for Rome: "Quos sua non simulachra igni consumpta movebant / sacra, nec
hispana diruta templa manu. // Quos non inçestus, non funera, totque rapinae /
fregerunt Cursi carmina blanda deos. // Vix precibus finem dederat, regnator olympi / Defixit latio lumina amica solo. // ex illo genti Mars est auersus hyberae / seu
tentet terra proelia, siue mari. // Ergo Roma tuo statuam seruata poetae / erige, et
eternos disce timere deos." BAV MS Vat. Lat. 3353, fol. 113.
[78] Corsi, *Excidium*, 428, ll.104-107: "Nanque Urbi et templis quem praeficis omnibus unum,/ Cuique uni fas hic reserare, et claudere coelum,/ Arce sua, horrendum
facinus, vi captus ab hoste,/ Hoste suo, pariterque tuo...."

But Corsi expresses far greater indignation about the Imperial soldiers' treatment of the corpse of Pope Julius II:

> Entry was made even into graves and rich tombs, [and] the diamond ring and emeralds were wrenched off from fingers. Who could take such liberties with you, Julius (not to refer to the tombs that were indiscriminately unsealed), *greatest of the popes* and best father of fathers? [You,] whom the Thracian hero and every region of the earth feared, and *to whom, in your lifetime, every foreign nation ceded control of Italy*, having admitted that the strength of men is inferior to God? [From you] the unpacified Iberian has not feared to despoil the right hand of its signet-ring after you were buried.[79]

This critical passage shows just how far Corsi has moved from the pre-1527 Roman humanist consensus. To be sure, he affirms the secular and spiritual prerogatives of both pontiffs. In both cases, Corsi implies, to attack the pope is to attack God. Yet Corsi identifies Julius, who had died fourteen years before, as the "greatest of the popes," rather than the currently reigning pontiff. Unlike Alcionio, Corsi never blames Pope Clement for incompetence in foreign affairs. His praise of Julius's freeing of Italy from barbarian control, however, contrasts implicitly with Clement's losses, and further points to Julius's pontificate as the high point of the Renaissance papacy. Like Alcionio, Corsi now situates the "golden age" of Renaissance Rome in the past rather than in the imminent future. Unlike Alcionio, however, he writes from the perspective of one remaining within the Clementine patronage network. If Corsi no longer sees himself as a herald of a golden age that the papacy will soon initiate, he nonetheless continues to cast himself as an apologist dignifying and enhancing the image of papal Rome.

Corsi asserts in the dedicatory letter that he writes for his own consolation. Thus, like Alcionio, he may use writing partly as a means of ordering recent events into a coherent narrative so as to gain mastery over them.[80] Most obvious, the hope for assistance from

---

[79] Corsi, *Excidium*, 429, ll.133-141: "In tumulos etiam penetratum, et ditia busta,/ E digitis raptusque adamas, raptique smaragdi./ De te (ne referam passim reserata sepulchra),/ Maxime pontificum, et patrum pater optime Iuli,/ De te cui tantum licuit? quem Tracius haeros,/ Omnis quem tremuit regio, gens extera et omnis/ Cui vivo Italiam cessit, confessa minores/ Esse Deo vires hominum, spoliare sepulti/ Non veritus dextram gemma impacatus Iberus." (Emphasis added.)

[80] Corsi, *Excidium*, 422: "Hoc igitur carmine tam funestum argumentum sum complexus, non ut famam ingenii aliquam, aut pietatis laudem, sed potius, ut nonnullam

the intended recipient, Louise of Savoy, impelled Corsi to write. The assistance for which he hoped doubtless included literary patronage in a time of severely restricted opportunities, but it also meant assistance for Rome in its time of need. Thus, the dedicatory letter refers to his "little book" (*libellus*) as serving not only as reading matter (*lectionis*) but as an embassy (*legationis*).[81] Its explicit appeal for French assistance is politically consistent with the city's needs in November of 1527, when Corsi could plausibly call upon France to make "those criminal brigands pay the penalty for their savageness and most-cruel rapacity."[82]

But the fact that such a poem could be sent with any hope that it might have serious political repercussions points to a fundamental problem of Roman humanism: the tools at Corsi's disposal, while well-suited for ornamenting papal Rome in classical garb, were inappropriate to the task at hand. The poem's appeal to the mercy of Jupiter, for example, clashes with the dedicatory letter's request for help from Louise of Savoy, and the lack of integration of the two themes diminishes the impact of the pleas for French assistance. In keeping with curialist fashion, Corsi has used classical vocabulary and topoi to drive home his message, both in lamenting the destruction of Rome and in dignifying Pope Clement's role as the city's rightful leader whose ill fortune has been undeserved. Like Alcionio, Corsi has located the golden age of Renaissance Rome not in the immediate future, but in the recent past. Thus his vindication of the papacy looks backward, defending the integrity of the office and its former greatness—visible not long before under Julius II—but offering no guideline for the future course of Roman culture. Despite his efforts to dignify the city in the *Romae urbis excidium*—indeed, even through those very efforts—Pietro Corsi has implicitly given closure to the period of the High Renaissance.

---

acerbissimi doloris levationem mihi quaererem." On writing as a means of gaining a sense of personal mastery over catastrophic events, see Beverley Raphael, *When Disaster Strikes: How Individuals and Communities Cope with Catastrophe* (New York, 1986), 94; and chap. 2 above.

[81] Corsi, *Excidium*, 423.

[82] Corsi, *Excidium*, 422: "... ut sceleratos hos latrones poenas dare videamus suae immanitatis, et crudelissimae rapacitatis."

iii. *Later Career and Attachment to Rome*

If the Sack of Rome constituted a watershed in Corsi's perception of the cultural history of the city, it certainly did not mark the end of Roman humanism. Much as before, humanists invested considerable energy in frivolous infighting. Thus, in a letter to one of his patrons, Cardinal Niccolò Ridolfi, Corsi complained of having been attacked with invectives attributed to the cardinal.[83] He summarized the accusations and appealed to Ridolfi to spurn their authors. In Corsi's defense, his friend Giano Vitale actually went to the trouble of writing a poem systematically rebutting all the accusations against him.[84] Although of only marginal historical significance, this sideshow resembles on a smaller scale the controversy over Longueil in 1519: in both incidents, humanists demonstrated an initial playfulness that degenerated into collective self-absorption and even delusions of grandeur.[85] Such delusions amounted to little when they only affected petty infighting within the social world of papal Rome. When Roman humanists strove to comprehend and address major issues of international scope, however, their exaggerated sense of self-importance diminished their ability to enter substantively into those discourses.

Such was the case for Pietro Corsi's next major work, his *Defensio pro Italia ad Erasmum Roteradamum*, which he dedicated to the new pope, Paul III, just six weeks after the latter's elevation.[86] The ostensible occasion for writing, as Corsi portrayed it in the *Defensio*, was a conversation among himself and some humanist friends about Florence's stand against the Imperial army. In that discussion, the Florentine Francesco Marsuppini had brought to Corsi's attention a passage in Erasmus's *Adagia* in which the northern humanist suggested that one comes across a *bellax Italicus*—a warlike Italian— about as rarely as one finds a trustworthy Carthaginian or a learned

---

[83] The letter is contained in fols. 101-109 of BAV MS Vat. Lat. 3436—the volume which contains in earlier leaves Alcionio's orations on the Sack of Rome. Manuscripts containing materials by or related to Corsi include, among others, Vat. Lat. mss. 2835, 3353, 3436, 5225, 5227, 5383, and 7182. The method of the collation of these codices renders problematic the assignment of Corsi's writings to specific years.

[84] Petrucci, "Corsi," 581, describes Vitale's verses in BAV MS Vat. Lat. 5383, fols. 86-90.

[85] On Longueil, see chap. 1 above.

[86] Pietro Corsi, *Petri Cursii civis Ro. Defensio Pro Italia ad Erasmum Roterodamum* (Rome, 1535). According to de Nolhac, *Bibliothèque*, 256, it was this work and the ensuing controversy that kept Corsi's name from being completely forgotten.

Scythian.[87] Stirred by this collective insult, Corsi penned an extensive rebuttal to Erasmus's offhand remark.[88] Detailing the Italian wars since 1494, he vindicated the Italians' military prowess, arguing that their many defeats resulted not from cowardice, but instead from organizational failures and especially from the treachery of their foes.

Like modern historians, Corsi saw clearly the difficulties that local political differentiation caused in the Italian city-states' efforts to unite against the foreigners.[89] Erasmus knew, said Corsi, that

> the wars' injuries, which we have endured for so many years, have come about not so much (that which many suppose) through the lack of unity of the Italian spirits or the changeableness of peoples, as by the variety of those commanding and the dissimilarity of magistracies.[90]

In addition to this problem of particularism, Corsi also emphasized the perfidy of the Italians' opponents which, rather than any shortcoming on the Romans' part, explained the city's easy capture:

---

[87] On the ensuing controversy, see Roberto Valentini, "Erasmo di Rotterdam e Pietro Corsi: a proposito di una polemica fraintesa," *Rendiconti della Classe di Scienze morali, storiche e filologiche*, ser. 6, vol. 12, nos. 11-12 (20 Dec. 1936): 896-922. Erasmus's slur on the Italian temperament appears in his explanation of the adage, "Myconius calvus" ("Mykonian baldpate"), now translated and annotated in *CWE* 32:20 & 344n. Thus Corsi presents the issue (*Defensio*, f.7v): "Franciscus Marsupinus, ciuis Florentinus, senex (ut optimus, sic prudentissimus) qui illi forte sermoni interfuit, nihil a meis laudibus cunctatus, repente e vestigio tua Adagia afferri iussit, voluitque sine mora, Myconii calvi, vulgati sane adagii, non vulgatam tamen tuam interpretationem legerem, In quo Germanorum tu doctissimorum omnium Coryphaeus enodando, sine ulla exceptione militum, equitum, ducum, locorum, armorum, temporum, censorio supercilio, gravitate praetoria, autoritate senatoria, statuis, decernis, pronuncias, Italum bellacem tam inuentu rarum, quam Poenum fidum, quam Scytham eruditum."

[88] Valentini, "Erasmo," 906, describes Corsi's tract as a "protesta calma e moderata." Silvana Seidel Menchi, *Erasmo in Italia, 1520-1580* (Turin, 1987), 63, attributes the "altamente civile, spesso addirittura deferente" tone that Corsi adopts to a desire among some Roman humanists not to push Erasmus and his followers into open opposition to the Catholic Church: "Come capo di un largo movimento d'opinione Erasmo doveva essere risparmiato, per evitare il rischio di spingerlo nel campo opposto."

[89] See, for example, Judith Hook, "Habsburg Imperialism and Italian Particularism: The Case of Charles V and Siena," *European Studies Review* 9 (1979): 283-312; Hook, "The Destruction of the New 'Italia': Venice and the Papacy in Collision," *Italian Studies* 28 (1973): 10-30; and Hook, *Sack of Rome*. Valentini, "Erasmo," 908, testifies to the accuracy of Corsi's military analysis.

[90] Corsi, *Defensio*, fol. 3: "Demum ea me praecipue ratio movit, Quod te, tum longo rerum usu, tum exactissima doctrina, optime omnium scire non ignorabam: bellorum, quas tot annos pertulimus, iniurias, non tam (quod multi putant) Italorum animorum disiunctione, populorumve mobilitate, quam imperantium varietate, potestatumque dissimilitudine contigisse."

you would be mistaken, Erasmus, if you were to attribute to our cowardice that which was a matter of our credulity; or, if you were to attribute to the courage of your men that which was a matter of their treachery.[91]

Relying upon the truce with the Imperial commander, Lannoy, ratified on 29 March, Pope Clement had dismissed the successful *bande nere*, the mercenary soldiers who had earlier served under the *condottiere* Giovanni de' Medici (d.1526), leaving Rome's defense in the hands of a locally raised militia. Had the pope and his allies not been so trusting, "then we would not have lost in one city not only the city of Rome, but even practically the entire Christian world."[92] If this explanation parallels that of the *Romae urbis excidium*, so too does the *Defensio*'s assertion of Rome's rightful role as *caput mundi* and its recent fall from that position:

> The city Rome, which up to this point has been the seat of the Christian religion and of true piety, has been the head of the Christian world. Now, ... [that city] which for so many centuries had been the home of kings, emperors, pontiffs, and heroes, lies wide open to birds' nests, wild animals' lairs, and grazing flocks.[93]

Here, however, Corsi sought not to elicit sympathy or assistance for Rome, but only to affirm the undeservedness of Rome's fate. In the context of the *Defensio pro Italia*, the Sack of Rome constituted one more Italian military failure due to factors other than a lack of martial prowess.

The military issue was by no means Corsi's only concern: for he extended his defense of the Italians into the cultural sphere. Tellingly, he suggested that feelings of cultural superiority had led Erasmus to make excessive claims for the northerners:

> I believe that because you had entered into this opinion, namely, that Latin literature has now been totally carried off from the Italians by you, that you have undertaken to insinuate for posterity that military

---

[91] Corsi, *Defensio*, fols. 19-19v: "Fallereris Erasme, si id nostrae ignaviae dares, quod fuit credulitatis: si id vestrorum fortitudini: quod vestrorum fuit perfidiae."

[92] Corsi, *Defensio*, fol. 19v: "non modo urbem Romam, atque adeo omnem prope Christianum orbem, in una urbe non amisissemus...."

[93] Corsi, *Defensio*, fols. 21r-21v: "Urbs Roma, quae adhuc Christianae religionis, ac verae pietatis est sedes, est christiani orbis caput: nulla nunc prorsus esset, aequata solo funditus iaceret, & quae Regum, Imperatorum, Pontificum, ac Heroum, tot saeculis domicilium fuisset, nunc volucrum tantum nidis, ac ferarum lustris, pascendisque gregibus pateret."

superiority as well has now been carried off from the Italian by your Germans.[94]

In response, Corsi tried to vindicate Italian excellence in all academic disciplines, including philosophy, law, theology, medicine, mathematics, and the fine arts.[95] He warned especially that Erasmus should respect the leading Italian literati despite their lesser scholarly productivity:

> Beware, Erasmus, I beseech you before the gods, lest you should swell up and suppose that all learned Italians are lightweights in comparison with you, for the reason that few, or perhaps none, has published as many books as you.[96]

Corsi then proceeded to list a battalion of Italian scholars who, on account of their literary prowess, merited Erasmus's attention.[97] But if this list defended Italian literary *virtù*, it also served to remind the northern scholar of the sympathy that he should feel with Italian humanists. Rather than attacking Erasmus from the standpoint of Catholic orthodoxy—a course increasingly followed elsewhere in Italy—Corsi emphasized the values and pursuits common to all members of the republic of letters.[98]

When viewed alongside the *Romae urbis excidium*, Corsi's *Defensio* evidences some movement toward a pan-Italian perspective. In the latter work, the Sack of Rome is but one of the military misadventures Corsi examines, and he draws examples of Italian heroes from throughout the peninsula.[99] Still, Roberto Valentini has placed Corsi's attack on Erasmus within the context of Roman humanism:

---

[94] Corsi, *Defensio*, fol. 9r: "credo, quod in certam hanc veneras opinionem, latinas literas Italis abs te iam penitus esse praereptas: rei quoque militaris praestantiam, a tuis iam Germanis Italo praereptam posteritati insinuare es conatus."

[95] Corsi, *Defensio*, fol. 30r.

[96] Corsi, *Defensio*, fol. 30v: "Cave per deos obsecro Erasme ea causa intumescas, omnesque eruditos Italos prae te foenum putes, quod pauci, aut forsan nulli, tot volumi<n>a, quot tu, ediderint." I translate "foenum" (*lit.*, "hay") as "lightweights."

[97] Corsi, *Defensio*, fols. 30v-31v. The list includes many Roman humanists (e.g., Pierio Valeriano), but includes others outside their ranks as well.

[98] Valentini, "Erasmo," 915-16.

[99] Valentini, "Erasmo," 907, summarizes this aspect of Corsi's argument as follows: "Constatata l'integrità della razza, il Corsi ci modella sotto gli occhi il guerriero italiano nel forte rilievo delle sue principali caratteristiche: resistenza alla fatica e alle privazioni, tenacia contro gli ostacoli, intelligenza nell' evitare i pericoli, destrezza nei combattimenti, valore personale, prodigalità della vita: un insieme di doti fisiche e morali sufficienti per innalzare il combattente italiano al di sopra di quelli di ogni altro paese."

"If I judge imprecise the analogy set up by [the modern historian of humanism Giuseppe] Toffanin, 'Corsi is to Erasmus as Mellini to Longueil,' I am nonetheless convinced that Corsi protested against Erasmus in the name of the Roman Academy."[100] According to Valentini, Erasmus became a symbol of anti-Italian sentiment, and Italian scholars sought to win him over to their side.[101] The recent research of Silvana Seidel Menchi on Erasmus in Italy has confirmed this interpretation as specially accurate for the Roman Academy: members of the papal curia tended to support Erasmus against his enemies, and Italian accusations that he was a Lutheran generally originated elsewhere.[102]

Yet another feature marked Corsi's response to Erasmus as distinctly Roman: namely, its irrelevance to topics of major current concern. Seidel Menchi notes the contrast between the solemnity and pedantry of Corsi's *Defensio* and the scantiness of the issue it addressed.[103] "The farcical dimension of the episode," she writes, "did not escape [Corsi's] contemporaries, least of all Erasmus," who described Corsi's tract as *bellax nullo adversario* ("warlike against a nonexistent enemy").[104] Even within Rome, Corsi was subjected to ridicule. Already in 1534, there circulated in Rome a pseudo-Erasmian letter,

---

[100] Valentini, "Erasmo," 904: "Se io considero imprecisa la proporzione stabilita dal Toffanin: «il Corsi sta ad Erasmo come il Mellini al Longolio», sono però convinto che il Corsi protestò contro Erasmo in nome dell'Accademia Romana." Valentini objects to Toffanin's formulation because in Corsi's Latin, "Erasmo nulla trovò da eccepire, nemmeno sull'abbondante retorica."

[101] Valentini, "Erasmo," 904: "E [Corsi] non fu il solo. Perchè Erasmo era divenuto segnacolo di antitalianità: e la spinta, che accomuna gli sforzi di tanti ingegni per portarlo a ricredersi, nasce soltanto da un bisogno di difesa del nome italiano."

[102] Seidel Menchi, *Erasmo in Italia*, 64: "in caso di conflitto la Curia era più propensa a intervenire in favore d'Erasmo che in favore dei suoi avversari...." She also writes (p.64): "Il successo che l'operazione «Erasmo luterano» mancò nella Curia, essa l'ottenne nella sfera extracuriale."

[103] Seidel Menchi, *Erasmo in Italia*, 58-59: "Nata da un puntiglio, la *Defensio pro Italia* riuscì una farsa, sia per il contrasto fra l'esiguità dell'occasione e la solennità paludata della replica, sia per la querula pedanteria con la quale in certi passi il Corsi svolse la sua tesi...." For a somewhat different interpretation, see Luca D'Ascia, *Erasmo e l'Umanesimo romano* (Florence, 1991), esp. 28, which portrays Corsi's *Defensio* as the last gasp of a "campagna dell'umanesimo romano contro Erasmo, aperta dal Casali con la sua *Invectiva* del 1524...."

[104] Seidel Menchi, *Erasmo in Italia*, 59: "La dimensione farsesca dell'episodio non sfuggì ai contemporanei, meno di tutti a Erasmo...." Erasmus's response, now reprinted as epistle #3032 (to Ioannes Choler) in *EE* 11: 172-86, was originally published as *Responsio ad Petri Cursii defensionem, nullo adversario bellacem* (Basel: Froben and Episcopio, 1535). *EE*, 11:172n, dates the letter to August 1535 at the latest, but notes that Erasmus had already drafted part of it by early May.

probably written by Francesco Minizio Calvo, evidently intended to dissuade Corsi from bothering to finish his polemic.[105] Corsi's friend Antonio Tebaldeo, who had praised the *Romae urbis excidium*, also diminished the significance of Corsi's *Defensio*, suggesting in verse that Angelo Colocci's pet cat Ailuros would suffice to terrify the Dutch humanist:

> It's all true what the Samian sage reported,
> That we've all had previous incarnations;
> You, "Erasmouse," were once a mouse, and kept its
> Ugly habit of gnawing; still you're gnawing
> All the legacy left us by our forebears.
> We don't need to call Pietro in against you;
> Let Ailuros come—you'll race to the mouse-holes.[106]

Corsi, meanwhile, went on to answer Erasmus's dismissive response by publishing a lengthy counter-response.[107]

Corsi's perseverance in pursuing this one-sided debate with Erasmus suggests that Toffanin's formulation—"il Corsi sta ad Erasmo come il Mellini al Longolio"—may carry some weight after all. Although Valentini was correct to note the distinctions between the two debates, they did share a fundamental irrelevance to the important religious issues confronting papal Rome. Corsi's *Defensio pro Italia*, like his *Romae urbis excidium*, concerned themes that had long preoccupied Roman humanists, but for precisely that reason it failed to address the pressing questions of the mid-1530's.[108] If the catastrophe of 1527

---

[105] Seidel Menchi, *Erasmo in Italia*, 59.

[106] BAV MS Vat. Lat. 2835, fol. 182: "Credendum est samio seni; putavit/ Qui nos in uarias redire formas./ Erasmus, vitium tibi remansit/ Turpe, rodis adhuc maligne, rodis/ Magnorum monumenta tot virorum/ In te non opus est ciere Petrum/ Elurus veniat, petes latebras." The "Samian Sage" is Pythagoras. The English rendition above of Tebaldeo's hendecasyllabic poem closely follows Ingrid Rowland's verse translation. The pun on "Eras-mus" appears also in an earlier poem of Marcantonio Casanova, found in BAV MS Vat. Lat. 5227 (and reproduced in Seidel Menchi, *Erasmo in Italia*, 371, n.115), entitled "In Erasmum parvulae staturae qui Christo insaniam dedit": "In superos fera bella geris: modo dictus eras mus/ Factus es e parvo tam cito mure gigas."

[107] *Erasmi Roterodami epistola de apologia Petri Cursii. Petri Cursii iudicium de Erasmi epistola* (Rome, 1535). After reproducing the relevant passage from a letter of Erasmus to Gumppenberg [AiV], Corsi wrote over eight folio pages on the controversy to his patron, Ridolfi. Corsi's letter was dated from Rome, 30 August ("*tertio kl. Septembris*").

[108] I incline to believe that the *Defensio* was initially intended for Clement VII, who perhaps died before the completion of the manuscript. Both the prominence of the Florentine Marsuppini and the absence of any explicitly Pauline themes support

had forced Corsi to modify his claims on behalf of papal Rome, he continued to work thereafter within old categories, offering rhetorical defense of the papacy and of Italy in ways that gained nothing either for the papacy, for Italy, or even (with the possible exception of patronage) for himself.

iv. Conclusions: Pietro Corsi and the Sack of Rome

The writings of Pietro Corsi subsequent to May of 1527 demonstrate his reworking of two of the central tenets of the prior curial humanist consensus. Like Alcionio, he provided graphic images of slaughter and devastation that showed how far Rome had fallen from its status as *caput mundi*. Second, he too now located the golden age of Roman culture in the past rather than in the imminent future. The sense of standing on the brink of a new era had been replaced by a sense of loss, a lamentation for a world that had already slipped away.

Despite these changes, however, Corsi remained within the intellectual confines of curial humanism. In the *Romae urbis excidium*, he unquestioningly maintained the universal *imperium* of the papacy, dignifying Pope Clement's role as Rome's rightful leader. Even in the *Defensio pro Italia*, which purported to vindicate the martial prowess and literary skills of all Italians, he viewed his subject from a Roman perspective. In both texts, he concerned himself less with promoting constructive change than with asserting an attenuated version of earlier Roman humanist rhetoric. In contrast with Alcionio, Corsi appears frozen, unable to free himself from the constraints of old assumptions to adapt creatively to sociopolitical change.

Strikingly, despite his personal involvement in the cataclysm, Corsi continued to exhibit those aspects of earlier Roman humanism that were farthest removed from current issues. In his infighting with other humanists in anonymously posted invectives, he still took frivolous attacks on his character with a seriousness evidencing an exaggerated sense of their significance. In the *Romae urbis excidium*, Corsi inadvertently undercut the political purpose expressed in the dedicatory letter when, in the poem itself, he repeatedly called for the mercy of Jupiter and "the gods." The classical rhetorical tools at his

such a conclusion. I am presently preparing an article that will further develop this argument.

disposal were markedly inappropriate for achieving his ostensible aim of obtaining French military assistance. In his hands, moreover, those tools shaped a narrative that could scarcely have been very persuasive even for obtaining Louise's patronage for his muse.

Corsi's preoccupation with the narrowest concerns of earlier Roman humanism comes to the fore in his *Defensio pro Italia*. Although the tract contains realistic political analysis of both Italian disunity and northern treachery, it offers little prescription for constructive change. Both in its pedantic manner of presentation and in its fixation upon a scholarly side issue of scant contemporary relevance, the *Defensio* is reminiscent of the Longueil episode of 1519. In both incidents, humanists engaged in agonistic exchange, exhibiting their erudition in public displays as a means of validating their exaggerated sense of *dignitas*. Meanwhile, they failed to address effectively issues of broader import, such as the spread of the Protestant Reformation.

While Corsi himself may have been unaware of the cultural myopia of Roman humanism, Erasmus recognized it and understood the opportunities lost through such frivolous preoccupations. Just as he dismissed as irrelevant Corsi's attack upon a minor detail of the *Adagia*, so too, in the *Ciceronianus* (1528), he noted how Longueil's talents had been wasted on unworthy subjects: "What benefits Longueil would have bestowed on the Christian religion, or on learning, or on his country, if he had applied to matters of importance the long hours of mental effort he devoted to those stage-performance speeches!"[109] Even when Longueil turned his skills to confronting Luther, his tools were ill-suited to the task: "His passages of vituperation are quite in the Tullian vein, but when he eventually comes to listing the main heads of Luther's errors, he becomes obscure and barely intelligible to Luther's supporters."[110] Unlike Longueil, however, Corsi would not even broach such controversial subjects. His

---

[109] Desiderius Erasmus, "The Ciceronian: A Dialogue on the Ideal Latin Style," trans. Betty I. Knott, in *CWE* 28: 434. In both this and the following quotation, the interlocutor "Bulephorus" is speaking.

[110] Erasmus, "The Ciceronian," 435. Erasmus argues that Longueil is therefore a poor imitator of Cicero (434-35): "A speech cannot be in the Tullian tradition, that is, be of the finest sort, if it does not accord with the times or the people or the subject it is concerned with."

writings following the Sack of Rome exhibit a mind less optimistic than before, but no more open to or comprehending of the significance of changes in the European political and religious theater, either for Renaissance Rome or for his own role as a curial humanist.

Corsi's inability in the *Romae urbis excidium* to cope creatively with the intellectual challenges posed by the Sack might perhaps be explained in part by the psychological impact of the catastrophe. Suffering imprisonment and physical abuse, he found himself in a position of physical powerlessness, a condition conducive to psychological trauma, in which the victim may experience either intensely painful memories, a drastic reduction in affect and adaptability, or an alternation between the two conditions.[111] Such an explanation, however, would not account for Corsi's inability to face up to the significance of Rome's altered position. Instead, one must recall the modest abilities with which he had been gifted and the peculiar institutional ecology in which he had thrived.[112] Paradoxically, the narrow focus that had served him well for over two decades impaired his ability to adjust in the aftermath of disaster, both because of his own limited creativity and because of his single-minded investment in the cultural values of the High Renaissance. As his career had risen with the vitality of Julian Rome, so now it languished amidst the diminished expectations and opportunities of the waning years of Clement's pontificate. Unable to transcend the past, Corsi espoused an outdated vision of Rome and of his own role as a papal spokesman—an approach that was not very useful after the Sack, and one for which there would be an ever-smaller niche in the increasingly polemical

---

[111] David Spiegel, Thurman Hunt, and Harvey E. Dondershine, "Dissociation and Hypnotizability in Posttraumatic Stress Disorder," *American Journal of Psychiatry* 145 (1988): 301-305, point to the third of these possibilities (301): "What may occur in response to trauma is a polarization of experience in which trauma victims alternate between intense, vivid, and painful memories and images associated with the traumatic experience and a kind of pseudonormality in which the victims avoid such memories, using traumatic amnesia, other forms of dissociation, or repression, with a reduction in adaptive capacity and a constriction of the range of affective response." See also Raphael, *When Disaster Strikes*, 78-98, esp. 80-86. On the significance of physical helplessness, see Raphael, *When Disaster Strikes*, 59, 121-22; and David Spiegel, "Hypnosis in the Treatment of Victims of Sexual Abuse," *Psychiatric Clinics of North America* 12 (1989): 295-305.

[112] On the concept of institutional ecology, see Stephen Toulmin, *Cosmopolis: The Hidden Agenda of Modernity* (Chicago, 1990), 208-209, and my application of the concept to Renaissance Rome in chapter 1 above.

climate of the Counter-Reformation.[113] He continued to cling to the memory of Rome as he imagined it to have been, and he sought to perpetuate the culture of the High Renaissance. Already in Corsi's poem on the Sack of Rome, however, the memory of the efflorescence that had preceded the year 1527 had become encapsulated as a completed era, and the Renaissance had passed into history.

---

[113] Here, I follow Elisabeth G. Gleason's identification of Paul III as a "Counter-Reformation" pope. See her ACHA Presidential Address, "Who Was the First Counter-Reformation Pope?," in *The Catholic Historical Review* 81 (1995): 173-84.

CHAPTER FOUR

RENEGOTIATION AND REMEMBRANCE: JACOPO SADOLETO'S LETTERS TO CURIAL FRIENDS, 1527-1529

When Jacopo Sadoleto took leave of his duties in mid–April of 1527 to travel to his diocese of Carpentras in France, his timing could not have been more auspicious. On 31 March, the Constable of Bourbon had renewed his march southward, ignoring the truce that Pope Clement had made with the Imperial viceroy, Charles de Lannoy, just two weeks before.[1] The papacy had slipped into desperate financial straits. Although the Roman citizenry would not turn into a panicky mob until the Sack itself, the mood within the city grew increasingly uneasy as a military crisis loomed. Those in positions of power could scarcely have doubted the gravity of the situation, especially as appeals to Italian allies failed to elicit military support.[2] Shortly before Sadoleto's departure, Girolamo Negri wrote to his friend Marcantonio Michiel in Venice, "This court has now become a chicken yard. Every day makes us more aware of the iniquity of the times and of a desperate situation."[3] But even as Rome's predicament worsened, Sadoleto's own fortunes improved: after a harrowing voyage over both sea and land, he arrived safely in Carpentras on 3 May—a mere three days before the Imperial army sacked Rome.

En route, Sadoleto heard rumors of renewed fighting in Italy, but not until weeks after his arrival in his diocese did certain news of Rome's destruction reach him. Like other humanists who had been active in Pope Clement's court, Sadoleto grappled with the implica-

---

[1] On the complications surrounding this truce, see Judith Hook, *The Sack of Rome, 1527* (London, 1972), esp. chap. 9.

[2] Already in January, Cardinal Alessandro Farnese had suggested to Pope Clement that he leave Rome. Although the pope asserted publicly that the city would not be taken, his decision to post sentries at city gates to keep citizens from fleeing suggests that others were less convinced. See Hook, *Sack of Rome*, 158.

[3] *LP* 2 (Venice, 1581), fols. 72v-73r (Negri to Michiel, 15 April 1527), at 72v: "Questa Corte hormai è divenuta un cortile da galline. Ogni dì siamo più chiari della iniquità de' tempi, & della pessima stagione." I reproduce the translation in Richard M. Douglas, *Jacopo Sadoleto, 1477–1547: Humanist and Reformer* (Cambridge, Mass., 1959), 52 (citation hereafter abbreviated as "Douglas").

tions of the catastrophe. Like Alcionio and Corsi, he needed to re-work the shared narrative that Roman humanists had constructed on behalf of the papacy. How could any of them now envisage a trium-phant papal Rome about to assert its inherited prerogatives by lead-ing Christendom into a new age? Unlike most of his former col-leagues, however, Sadoleto also had to justify—both to them and to himself—his own opportune departure. How came it that he, in par-ticular, had been spared?

In his correspondence during the months following his precipitous departure from Rome, Sadoleto grappled with its implications. In private letters to Roman humanist friends and patrons, he began to renegotiate his relationships with them, to redefine his image of pa-pal Rome, and to rewrite the narrative of his own life. Through a series of labored explanations and self-justifications, he sought to maintain his bonds with the friends he had left behind, despite hav-ing escaped their trauma and no longer being able to draw upon shared present experience as a basis of friendship. Beyond justifying his choices and sustaining friendships, Sadoleto now came to view papal Rome from the vantage point of an outsider. Although when he wrote these letters he did not intend to return to Rome, they mark the first steps in his progression toward 1536, when he would in fact do so—but as an "outside" reformer of the institutionally entrenched abuses that had helped to sustain the bureaucracy and the lavishness of the Roman curia, rather than as an "insider" heavily invested in the system that needed reform.[4] These letters do more, however, than serve as an extension of Sadoleto's dialogues with friends and as a medium for revaluing Renaissance Rome: for they also constitute a form of life–writing, in which he created a coherent narrative that invested with meaning the recent dramatic changes in his own ca-reer. Just as he came to a deeper understanding of the workings of divine providence in the world, so too he developed a strong (if time-ly) sense of God's providential designs for him.

The insider status that Jacopo Sadoleto chose to relinquish in 1527 had been long in the making. Born in 1477, he studied Latin and Greek letters at the University of Ferrara, where his father was a

---

[4] On the extent to which curialists' investment in the status quo militated against such institutional reform, see Barbara McClung Hallman, *Italian Cardinals, Reform, and the Church as Property* (Berkeley and Los Angeles, 1985).

professor of law.[5] Just before the turn of the century, he left Ferrara for Rome, and there he obtained the patronage of the learned Cardinal Oliviero Carafa, through whose agency he obtained in 1506 a canonry at San Lorenzo in Damaso.[6] In his twelve years as a client of Carafa, Sadoleto was already becoming imbued with Roman humanist ideas, as evident in his famous poem (1506) on the newly unearthed Laocoön statue: having returned from the shadows to witness a Rome that was living again, the statue signaled the dawning of a new age.[7]

Following Carafa's death in 1511, Sadoleto briefly enjoyed the patronage of Federigo Fregoso; but his major breakthrough came in 1513 with the election of Leo X, who immediately appointed Sadoleto and Pietro Bembo as domestic secretaries.[8] Although they were limited to drafting papal briefs and bulls, and were not entrusted with secret correspondence to papal nuncios (which Leo stipulated should be conducted in Italian), the appointment did move Sadoleto toward the center of curial power, and also of Roman humanism (Angelo Colocci, for example, also served in Leo's secretariat).[9] During this time, Sadoleto was active in the humanist sodalities centered on Colocci and Johann Küritz, the gatherings of which he would recall wistfully after the Sack.[10] Indeed, in 1518, Sadoleto purchased a villa on the Quirinal where he, too, could host such gatherings—an expenditure made possible by the multiple benefices, canonries, and

---

[5] On the details of Sadoleto's early life, see Antonio Fiordibello's *vita* of him, edited and annotated by Vincenzo Costanzi in Volume Four of his edition of Sadoleto's letters: *Epistolae quotquot extant proprio nomine scriptae nunc primum duplo auctiores in lucem editae*, 5 vols. (Rome, 1760-67), i-cviii. Hereafter, I abbreviate references to this *vita* as "Fiordibello," and to the letters in the edition as "*Epistolae*." Douglas draws extensively upon Fiordibello's account.

[6] Fiordibello, v-viii; Douglas, 7, 10. Douglas views Sadoleto's move from Ferrara to Rome in a negative light, as "exchanging one form of dependency for another" (6). But given the large-scale movement of scholars to Rome, where opportunities abounded, such an explanation seems misleading. On Carafa's role as patron of humanists, see Anne Reynolds, "Cardinal Oliviero Carafa and the Early Cinquecento Tradition of the Feast of Pasquino," *Roma Humanistica: Journal of Neo-Latin Studies* 34A (1985): 178-209.

[7] Douglas, 9-10; Gian Piero Maragoni, *Sadoleto e il Laocoonte: Di un modo di descrivere l'arte* (Parma, 1986), reproduces the poem in a "postfazione" by Marzio Pieri (47-48).

[8] Fiordibello, xi-xiii; in a note (xi-xii), Costanzi provides primary-source documentation of the appointment.

[9] Douglas, 14-16; 246, n.3.

[10] See analysis below of his letter to Colocci in 1529.

pensions that he had persuaded Leo X to shower upon him.[11] In his secretarial capacity, meanwhile, he learned to deploy the official rhetoric of *Roma caput mundi*, evident already in a brief he drafted early in Leo's pontificate, which referred to Rome as the "foremost city in the world, most-abundant in the pursuit of all learned studies."[12]

The accession of Adrian VI to the papacy in 1522 brought a dry spell for Sadoleto as it did for so many who had enjoyed Leonine patronage. In April of 1523, perhaps because Adrian still had no use for his services, Sadoleto departed to his diocese of Carpentras in Provence—a benefice that he had obtained in 1517, but which he now visited for the first time.[13] This absence from Rome was intended, however, as temporary, and when the newly elected Pope Clement VII invited him to return to his secretarial duties that autumn, Sadoleto lost little time in complying.[14] Resuming his post as domestic secretary in January of 1524, Sadoleto found his role significantly expanded from what it had been under Leo, for Pope Clement restored the office's authority over secret despatches to nuncios.[15] Thus, although still not in a position to shape papal policy, he was well-placed to obtain "insider" knowledge of the pope's efforts to

---

[11] On Sadoleto's active role in seeking benefices, see Douglas, 22. According to Douglas, Sadoleto did not directly pursue the diocese of Carpentras, which Leo X conferred upon him on 17 April 1517. Although for years he gave no indication of wishing to reside there — in fact, upon being invested with the diocese, he was promptly "released from the obligation of residence and permitted to appoint a vicar-general in his place" (Douglas, 22) — from the outset he kept tabs on the diocese and looked after its interests from Rome. For details on Sadoleto's *vigna* on the Quirinal, see David R. Coffin, *The Villa in the Life of Renaissance Rome* (Princeton, 1979), 192.

[12] *Epistolae*, 4:24: "in hac enim urbe Orbis principe, & omnium doctrinarum studiis florentissima...."

[13] Fiordibello, xvi-xvii, views this withdrawal in the most positive light: "Post cum ex hac vita Leo excessisset, statim rebus Romanis relictis, Carpentoracte migravit eo consilio, ut populis fidei suae creditis boni & diligentis Episcopi officium praestaret: neque principibus amplius, sed Deo uni, & rectissimis suis studiis inserviret."

[14] On Negri's understanding of Sadoleto's departure from Rome as temporary, and his account of Roman humanists' regrets upon Sadoleto's departure, see *LP* (1570): 114 (Negri to Michiel, 7 April 1523). On Sadoleto's decision to return to Rome, see Fiordibelli, xviii-xix. Douglas, 36, argues that we ought not to see the return to Rome as intended to be temporary: "To hold, as some have, that the Bishop only returned to Rome on condition that he be allowed to go back again to his diocese three years later is to accept the highly questionable argument which Sadoleto used in retrospect in order to justify his precipitous departure in 1527...."

[15] Douglas, 39-40. The other, less prolific domestic secretary serving alongside Sadoleto was Benedetto Accolti.

maintain a balance of power between Spanish and French influences on the Italian peninsula.

The events of the following three years could only have proved disillusioning, as Clement's waffling earned the distrust and outrage, alternately, of the two sides.[16] Following the formation of the League of Cognac (22 May 1526), in which Clement abandoned any semblance of neutrality in favor of an alliance with powers hostile to the Emperor Charles V, the political situation inclined ever more toward crisis.[17] Now Sadoleto's role shifted to that of a single-minded propagandist. It was he who composed the infamous brief to Charles V, dated 23 June 1526, which gives an unyieldingly one-sided reckoning of papal/Imperial relations since the time that Clement had taken office.[18] After the pro-Imperial Colonna faction led an assault on the Vatican that autumn, Sadoleto—whose own room in the Apostolic Palace was among those ransacked—was entrusted with writing a detailed account of the attack to the King of Portugal.[19] Soon thereafter, the situation deteriorated even further. In February of 1527, Imperialist armies led by Georg von Frundsberg and Bourbon joined forces near Piacenza. By the end of March it became clear that Bourbon had no intention of observing the desperate truce that Clement had made earlier that month with the Imperial viceroy, Lannoy.

Although not a maker of policy, Sadoleto was close enough to see the proverbial writing on the wall. When he departed from Rome in mid-April, he did so with papal consent, obtained through the agency of his friend and patron, the datary, Gian Matteo Giberti.[20] The latter remained in Rome, where he would eventually be taken

---

[16] On Clement's notorious indecision, see esp. the character sketch in Francesco Guicciardini, *Storia d'Italia*; Pastor, *History of the Popes*, vols. 9-10; and the sympathetic treatment in Hook, *Sack of Rome*.

[17] Signatories included Francis I, the Doge of Venice, the pope, and Francesco Sforza of Milan.

[18] Pastor, *History of the Popes*, 9:313-16, provides a detailed summary of the argument of the brief.

[19] The brief, dated 18 October 1526, is reproduced in *Epistolae*, 4:174-81.

[20] Sadoleto thanked Giberti for his assistance in this regard in *Epistolae* 1:170-73 (lett. #65). Since Giberti was the key architect of Clement's pro-French policy in 1526-27, Sadoleto was well-placed (as an intimate of the datary) to have "insider" knowledge of just how desperate the political situation had become. Douglas, 52, misreads Sadoleto's subsequent letter to Bini (*Epistolae* 1:177-82; lett. #67) as saying that "the Pope had given him leave for three or four months." Actually, Sadoleto is here considering the possibility of returning to Clement's service for a brief stint of a few months. See analysis of the letter below.

hostage in the aftermath of the Sack; but Sadoleto had made good his escape. From his secure retreat, he proceeded to write letters to Roman humanist friends: letters in which he sought to commiserate with those whose recent miseries he had not shared; letters in which he reconceived the city of Rome, rethinking its historic role as a center of revival; letters, finally, in which he strove to discern the meaning for his own life of his fortuitous escape, attributing it, all too conveniently, not to any insider knowledge of political affairs, but to the inscrutable workings of Divine Providence.

Humanists and the Epistolary Genre

In approaching Sadoleto's letters, one must take into account the tradition of humanist letter-writing that provides their formal context. P. O. Kristeller has emphasized the frequency with which humanists held secretarial positions in which they were entrusted with the official correspondence of cities and of princes. Beyond that professional activity, however—or perhaps in spite of it—Renaissance humanists from Petrarch on refined the art of writing "familiar" letters in which they could express personal sentiments that would have been difficult to communicate within the constraints of the medieval *ars dictaminis* models.[21] Inspired in part by his discovery in 1345 of Cicero's letters to Atticus, Petrarch had assembled collections of his own "familiar" letters, in the process inaugurating a Renaissance epistolary tradition that was still flourishing in the early Cinquecento.[22]

But if the imitation of "familiar" letters from antiquity allowed humanists to move beyond the structural limitations of the *ars dicta-*

---

[21] On the relationship of the *ars dictaminis* to humanism, see Paul O. Kristeller, "The Humanist Movement," in his *Renaissance Thought: The Classic, Scholastic, and Humanist Strains* (New York, 1961), 3-23. On the importance of private letter-writing for the development of humanism, see Ronald G. Witt, "Medieval *Ars Dictaminis* and the Beginnings of Humanism: A New Construction of the Problem," *Renaissance Quarterly* 35 (1982): 1-35. On the ensuing tradition, see Cecil H. Clough, "The Cult of Antiquity: Letters and Letter Collections," in *Cultural Aspects of the Italian Renaissance: Essays in Honour of Paul Oskar Kristeller*, ed. Cecil H. Clough (New York, 1976), 33-67.

[22] G. Billanovich, *Petrarca letterato* (Rome, 1947); John M. Najemy, *Between Friends: Discourses of Power and Desire in the Machiavelli-Vettori Letters of 1513-1515* (Princeton, 1993), 25-30. According to Najemy (26), "Renaissance letter writing, precisely because it felt the imprint of a variety of models and traditions, became a field of freer play and greater experimentation than did certain other kinds of humanist writing."

minis style, this imitation brought with it other constraints which complicated (although they did not altogether obstruct) personal expression.[23] For the "familiar" letter occupies an uncertain space: between traditional models and spontaneous personal expression; between social and individual functions; and, most problematically, between fact and fiction.[24] The first of these polarities, while a necessary concomitant of the imitation of classical models, created special problems for epistolarity, since adherence to the language and conventions of antiquity conflicted directly with the ideal of the letter as a substitute for informal speech.[25] The second polarity, that between the social and individual significances of the letter, further complicates the reading of Renaissance correspondence. The "familiar" letter was perforce an interpersonal document, creating a verbal bridge over physical distance. The influential *Modus epistolandi* of Francesco Negri defined the letter as a substitute for the speech of absent friends.[26] For humanists in particular, letters on Ciceronian models comprised a verbal network for the exchange of philological and philosophical observations and, thereby, for the affirmation of joint participation in scholarly enterprises.[27]

A sense of shared purpose did not, of course, prevent the perpetuation of the hierarchies inherent in humanist networks. Sources such as Horace's verse epistles, in which an experienced man gave advice to a younger man, provided a vocabulary for "mentoring" perceived protégés from afar.[28] Letters allowed, moreover, the expression not just of the affective quality of friendship, but also of its more instrumental aspects, solidifying bonds that were forged and maintained

---

[23] The imitation of models does not, *ipso facto*, prevent personal expression. Since *all* expression adheres to models of one sort or another, we must assess the facility of authors at operating within the constraints of a given genre and discourse.

[24] Efforts to write with *claritas* and *perspicuitas* make these ambiguities all the more poignant. Claudio Guillén, "Notes toward the Study of the Renaissance Letter," in *Renaissance Genres: Essays on Theory, History, and Interpretation*, ed. Barbara Kiefer Lewalski (Cambridge, Mass., 1986), 70-101, at 76, identifies these qualities, along with *brevitas*, as shared values of Renaissance epistolary theorists.

[25] Najemy, *Between Friends*, 33, 37, & 54.

[26] Najemy, *Between Friends*, 43 & esp. 47n., where he cites Negri's definition of the letter: "Epistola est oratio pedestris quae absentes amicos praesentes facit: tam ad voluptatem quam ad utilitatem tum publicam tum privatam." On private letters as revelatory of Renaissance society's notion of friendship, see Najemy, *Between Friends*, 21.

[27] Guillén, "Notes," 91, makes this point, noting the importance of Cicero's *De amicitia* as a guide.

[28] Guillén, "Notes," 78.

between correspondents both for human closeness and for purposes
of advancement.[29] But at the same time, humanists followed the classical authority Demetrius, who asserted that a letter is not just one-
half of a dialogue, but is in fact a gift. It is not merely ordinary
speech to an absent friend, but is itself an exercise of friendship.[30]

Precisely in the ways that it differs from the speech of dialogue, the
letter serves a more private function: for the "gift" to the friend is, in
effect, carried out as a solitary act. According to Guillén, as *écriture*,
the letter involves its author in a "silent, creative process of self-
distancing and self-modeling."[31] Whereas dialogues imply public
space, letters tend to imply solitude, privacy, or even secrecy.[32] The
tension between these social and private aspects constitutes what
Najemy has called the "fundamental paradox of epistolarity": "the
more successfully the letter creates and sustains the illusion of presence, of speech, and of the recovery of the past, the more acutely
does it impose the realization of absence and loss, and of its actual
status as written text."[33] But of course this written text was often
intended for a larger audience than the stated recipient, being meant
to be shared with the correspondent's friends, or even for general
circulation, whether as a self-standing document or as part of a collection.[34] Thus the private and interactive functions of the letter thoroughly commingled.

A blurring of "truth" and fiction, finally, was unavoidable, both
because of the shaping of the letter for its recipient and because of its
autobiographical element. The former was a matter of decorum: according to Renaissance authorities ranging from Petrarch to Erasmus, the language of the letter should be tailored to the addressee.
But this very goal, as Najemy observes, tends to make the writer
adopt a style not his own—in effect, differing from himself—in order
to accommodate the *animus, conditio,* and *affectus* of the recipient.[35] Nor

---

[29] Najemy, *Between Friends,* 21, calls attention to Renaissance Florentines' acute
awareness of this tension, and provides further secondary bibliography.

[30] Guillén, "Notes," 78; Najemy, *Between Friends,* 50, details Poliziano's expression
of the same sentiment.

[31] Guillén, "Notes," 78.

[32] Guillén, "Notes," 100.

[33] Najemy, *Between Friends,* 123.

[34] Guillén, "Notes," 100, refers to the "latent voyeurism" that this "open" quality
of the letter produces.

[35] On Petrarch, see Najemy, *Between Friends,* 28. On Erasmus, see Guillén,
"Notes," 84.

did the autobiographical impulse in letter-writing necessarily lead to intimacy: like more explicitly autobiographical genres, letter-writing could be a form of life-writing in which self-creation took its place alongside (if not entirely displacing) self-revelation.[36] Nowhere was self-creation more pronounced than in letter collections, in which missives originally intended for particular recipients were re-ordered and re-written to convey a deliberate and coherent portrait of their author.

Sadoleto, His Nephew, and the Letter-Book

The key source for Jacopo Sadoleto's letters (1503-1547), the compilation assembled by his nephew and heir, Paolo Sadoleto, in cooperation with Antonio Fiordibello, did not escape such distortions.[37] According to the dedicatory letter to Cardinal Alessandro Farnese (1549), Paolo intended the letter-book to have three functions: 1) to honor the memory of his uncle; 2) to show gratitude toward a patron by its presentation; and 3) to edify students of eloquence. In keeping with the third goal, he included only letters written in Latin, and along with Fiordibello he selected from the "great heap" of Jacopo's letters "only those which seemed to us to have been written rather meticulously."[38] Some letters had remained quite rough, since profes-

---

[36] See the remarks of Guillén, "Notes," 99, on vernacular Renaissance letters, which nonetheless apply here as well; Diana Robin, *Filelfo in Milan* (Princeton, 1991), chap. 1, on the slippage of autobiography into fiction; and the essays in Thomas F. Mayer and D. R. Woolf, eds., *The Rhetorics of Life–Writing in Early Modern Europe: Forms of Biography from Cassandra Fedele to Louis XIV* (Ann Arbor, 1995).

[37] *Epistolarum libri sexdecim. Eiusdem ad Paulum Sadoletum Epistolarum liber unus. Vita Eiusdem autoris per Antonium florebellum* (Lyons: [Gryphius], 1560. I was able to evaluate this volume at the Newberry Library alongside two other early printings with the same title: one, published in 1564 in Cologne (apud haeredes A. Birckmanni); the other is lacking date or place (Newberry call #: Case E5.S1273). Of the three, the Gryphius edition is freest of typographical errors. While Paolo credits Fiordibello with helping him with the task of editing Jacopo Sadoleto's papers, especially with those on religious topics and sacred literature, Paolo alone signs the dedicatory letter, perhaps claiming the letter-book as his own editing alone. See Gryphius ed., esp. p. 2.

An error-laden edition of the letters, including an additional book containing some of Sadoleto's vernacular (Italian) correspondence, is included in *Jacobi Sadoleti Cardinalis et Episcopi Carpentoractensis viri disertissimi, Opera quae exstant omnia*, 4 vols. in 2 (Verona, 1737-38). The edition by Costanzi ("*Epistolae*") contains more accurate renderings of the writings that it includes.

[38] Gryphius ed., 4: "Cum vero orationes quasdam, & magnum praeterea epistolarum acervum invenissemus, eas potius edendas esse iudicavimus: non omnes qui-

sional responsibilities had thwarted Jacopo's long-standing desire to complete and revise them. But if even the selected letters were not perfect literary models, they could nonetheless be useful and pleasing to the reader:

> Even if I do not doubt that his [Jacopo's] correction and (let me put it thus) polishing would have added much charm and elegance, I have not, however, been deterred on that account from publishing: since I seem to myself to hope that the reading of them will be neither displeasing nor useless to students of eloquence.[39]

While effectively providing a *captatio benevolentiae* on his uncle's behalf for any errors remaining in the text, this dedicatory letter leaves unspecified the extent to which Paolo emended his uncle's letters in ways that could affect their meaning. Did his *castigatio* include significant changes in content, especially since he undertook the editing project in part to honor his uncle's "most-holy memory"?[40] Did he select those letters which were particularly conducive to a coherent, positive image of his uncle? In addition, Paolo was limited to those letters in his possession—often drafts rather than finished copies—and many letters must simply not have been obtainable.[41]

Even if Paolo was utterly faithful to Jacopo's purpose and intention, our situating the collection in the tradition of Renaissance humanist letter-books suggests reasons for caution. Two centuries earlier, Petrarch had used his letter collections to depict himself as an *exemplum* of wisdom and morality, enhancing their coherence and exemplarity by painstaking revision, by reordering, and even by adding fictive letters in the midst of ones that had (in one form or another) actually been sent.[42] By the late fifteenth century, many hu-

---

dem, sed eas tantum quae accuratius nobis scriptae esse videbantur."

[39] Gryphius ed., 4: "Sed etsi non dubito, quin illius correctio, & (ut ita dicam) expolitio, multum illis additura fuerit venustatis, atque elegantiae: non propterea tamen sum ab edendo deterritus: cum sperare mihi videar, studiosis eloquentiae hominibus, earum lectionem, neque iniucundam, neque infructuosam fore."

[40] Gryphius ed., 2: "Sed cum officii mei ratio, & illa, quam sanctissimae patrui memoriae debeo, pietas, hoc praeterea a me postulare videretur, ut illius scripta, & lucubrationes, quae penes me essent, ederem...."

[41] In the dedication, Paolo says (Gryphius ed., 2) that he is editing those of his uncle's writings "quae penes me essent." Among the letters absent from the collection are several elegantly constructed missives to Pope Clement VII, which presumably remained in the Vatican, and which Paolo Sadoleto and Fiordibello may simply not have had at their disposal in Carpentras.

[42] See Clough, "Cult of Antiquity," 35-36, for this point and for further bibliography. On the difficulties of distinguishing "real" from "fictional" letters, see also

manists were imitating Petrarch's example by refining their own correspondence for inclusion in such collections. For example, Sadoleto's friend and curial colleague Pietro Bembo spent much of the 1530's polishing his letters for publication.[43] That the humanist letter-book was (as Clough observes) a "literary work in its own right" might seem not to be relevant to Sadoleto, since his nephew rather than he himself did the final editing and selecting. Yet the mentality of the period affected the attitude with which humanists such as Sadoleto approached the art of writing letters. According to Clough, "[a]wareness that one's letters might be collected and published caused the writer to elaborate every letter into a conscious literary creation."[44] Thus, regardless of the disposition of his letters upon his death, Sadoleto must surely have been aware of their significance as documents that, despite having private addressees, might help construct his public persona.

Sadoleto's letters in the months following the Sack of Rome, then, constitute a rich but far from transparent source on how he sought to maintain contact with distant friends and to interpret the significance of his departure from Rome.[45] Taken together, these letters help us to see how Sadoleto renegotiated friendships, how he represented changes in his understanding of his responsibilities to papal Rome and to the Church, and how he rewrote his own "life"—both for himself and for a reading audience—after arriving at his diocese in France.

Guillén, "Notes," esp. 85: "The author of a real letter may be mirroring and shaping through the written word a particular version of himself, a particular moment of an interpersonal relationship, a particular aspect of his future — and of his correspondent's." Conversely, "the fictional letter pretends that it is not fiction and thus imitates the conventions of ordinary correspondence."

[43] Clough, "Cult of Antiquity," 34, 41.

[44] Clough, "Cult of Antiquity," 35.

[45] For the most part, I have followed the texts of the letters in Costanzi's excellent five-volume edition (1760-67), where possible comparing these versions with surviving autograph copies, and including analysis of several letters that remain unedited. The differences consist mostly in minor changes in word order and diction that are not consequential for my argument. While I employ this edition because of its inclusiveness and accuracy, I do so with an awareness that, by adding letters and by re-ordering them all in chronological order, he has disrupted the integrity and possibly the purpose of Paolo Sadoleto's edition of his uncle's letter-book. On the problems such re-ordering creates, see Clough, "Cult of Antiquity," 35, 37.

Unsettling Rumors

The first two surviving letters following Sadoleto's departure from Rome were both dated from Carpentras, 17 May 1527, and written to former curial colleagues: the papal datary Gian Matteo Giberti and the Latinist Lazzaro Bonamico.[46] By its own claim, the letter to Giberti is the very first written following Sadoleto's arrival in Carpentras on 3 May.[47] After attributing his delay in writing (generally a lapse of decorum) to illness, he gives an account of his journey over sea and land.[48] Upon departing Rome, Sadoleto claims, he had supposed that the imperial troops in Italy had been pacified; en route, however, he had heard disturbing rumors of their inclining once again toward fighting. These reports soon ceased, leaving Sadoleto to speculate that they had been false.[49] Still, the possibility of their accuracy leads him in this letter to confront the implications for his role as papal servant—and for his position as humanist client of Giberti— of residing in his diocese, far from his patrons and the Roman curia.

Sadoleto repeatedly stresses his indebtedness to Giberti, through whose agency he obtained leave from Clement for his departure to Carpentras.[50] He asks for Giberti's love and protection, and for assurances of their continuance. For his part, Sadoleto will bear in mind and will communicate to others the extent of his indebtedness to the datary. He sets Giberti in apposition to Clement, both being patrons to whom he maintains emotional attachment and devotes his studies.[51]

---

[46] On Bonamico, a prominent grammarian and Ciceronian Latin stylist, see Rino Avesani, "Bonamico, Lazzaro," *DBI* 11:533-40.

[47] *Epistolae*, 1:170-73 (lett. 64), at 170: "Postquam veni Carpentoracte, has primas exaravi literas...."

[48] *Epistolae*, 1:170-71, include the account of the journey and his resultant illness, as a result of which he is now ideally suited for the *vita contemplativa*: "omnino intelligo, me hac corporis imbecillitate iam non ad aliam rem ullam, quam ad ocium & quietem idoneum esse." He attributes his ill health to city air, from which he is now removed (*Epistolae*, 1:173).

[49] *Epistolae*, 1:171-72.

[50] *Epistolae*, 1:171: "Quod ipsum [i.e., ocium & quietem] videor nunc demum, tuo singulari beneficio, & summa Principis benignitate consecutus." It is perhaps to this that he alludes when he calls Giberti "the counselor of my tranquillity, to which singular benefit another equal will never be found." (*Epistolae*, 1:173: "De te ipso, mi Giberti, aveo plurimum, & ex te cognoscere: quem ego habeo authorem meae tranquillitatis; cui uni beneficio, alterum par nunquam reperietur.")

[51] e.g., *Epistolae*, 1:173: "Quo in genere, quid tibi receperim, quid Pont. Max. fuerim pollicitus, optime in memoria habeo."

But much of the letter suggests his ambivalence about whether his present service to the pope is adequate for the circumstances. On account of his "incredible love" toward Clement, he says, he remains anxious for the pope's welfare.[52] Yet the letter devotes less space to speculating about Clement's well-being than to dramatizing Sadoleto's devotion to his patron: if the pope is in personal danger, "I grieve extremely seriously, both for the sake of him himself, whose safety I have always placed above my own, and also for my own sake."[53] Sadoleto's grief concerning himself would result from pangs of guilt over possibly having left his patron in the lurch:

> For I would seem to myself to have deserted my duty if I were to have abandoned such a master at that time—and that master being the one to whom, in loving, adorning, and cultivating [him] with every piety and all duties, I would never have been able to make satisfaction, either to his own virtue or to my own eagerness.[54]

But Sadoleto leaves less clear just what he proposes to do to remedy the situation. Giberti is the best witness, we are told, of Sadoleto's tormented state of mind when he had left for Carpentras, for the service of God and in the hope of more peaceful circumstances.[55] Now, he feels that he "should gladly leave to others the business of enjoying favorable circumstances," and share in the adversities.[56] But he gives no indication as to how he would do so, other than by praying to God to give peace to the pope and to Italy. Meanwhile, he shall honor God—and his earthly patrons, Giberti and Clement—through his diligence in serving his diocese and in continuing his studies.[57]

The shorter letter to Bonamico, also written on 17 May 1527,

---

[52] *Epistolae*, 1:172: "Sed quoquo modo sese habet res, me meus incredibilis erga Summum Pontificem amor, neutiquam patitur curae & angoris expertem esse."

[53] *Epistolae*, 1:172: "Qui si aliquo est adhuc proprio in periculo ... nae ego perquam doleo graviter, tum eius ipsius causa, cuius ego salutem semper anteposui meae: tum etiam mea."

[54] *Epistolae*, 1:172: "Viderer enim mihi ab officio quasi descivisse, si hoc tempore talem dominum deseruissem: atque eum dominum in quo ego amando, ornando, omni pietate atque omnibus officiis colendo, neque virtuti ipsius unquam, neque meo studio satisfacere potuissem."

[55] *Epistolae*, 1:172.

[56] *Epistolae*, 1:172: "Et nunc in his quoque locis ac terris ea mente sum, ut secundas res ipsius aliis fruendas libentissime relinquam: adversarum non recusem esse particeps."

[57] *Epistolae*, 1:172-73.

reveals far less of Sadoleto's concern.[58] No mention appears of the difficulties encountered during the journey to Carpentras. He describes his work there by invoking the trope of the retreat from *negotium* into scholarly *otium*: while striving to manage his position "dutifully and religiously, for as long as shall be given us by heaven," he will "wallow in books and letters," and will "slake the long-standing and daily thirst for the best arts in those very fonts."[59] The letter serves above all to reaffirm his bonds of friendship with Bonamico and, through him, with other Roman humanists and patrons. Sadoleto here deploys stock formulae, requesting that Bonamico honor a promise to procure some books for him, assuring the recipient of his continuing affection, and using the rhetorical device of *praeteritio* to preclude discussing the possibility that Bonamico might feel otherwise.

What the missive omits, however, speaks volumes. At the outset, Sadoleto notes that he has received no letters from Rome, and asks with seeming innocence for news of friends and familiars there. Giving no indication of anxiety over Rome's precarious situation, he glibly expresses his desire that the news all be good. From the perspective of the now-devoted bishop of Carpentras, "so long as you are safe there, and the affairs of the Supreme Pontiff maintain that condition which we most greatly desire, [there is] nothing [that] does not appear to me to participate abundantly in the hope of a blessed life."[60] No mention is made of the concerns raised in the preceding letter, that things in Rome might well *not* be as he would wish, and that in leaving the pope's side a month before, he might have abandoned his patron at a most inauspicious time.[61] Set alongside the missive to Giberti, this letter jars—reflecting lesser intimacy, surely, but also conveniently omitting mention of the author's hunch that its cheery tone was utterly at odds with his friends' present situation in Rome.

---

[58] *Epistolae*, 1:174-76 (lett. 66).

[59] *Epistolae*, 1:175: "Nam & parvo sat contenti sumus; & in hoc honore pie sancteque administrando, quoad nobis datum divinitus fuerit, Deo ipsi eidem deservire contendemus: & in libris ac literis toti volutabimur: veteremque & diuturnam sitim optimarum artium, nostro tandem arbitrio, in ipsis fontibus explebimus."

[60] *Epistolae*, 1:175: "modo vos isthic salvi, summique Pontificis res eum teneant statum, quem maxime cupimus, nihil mihi ad spem beatae vitae non abunde videtur affore."

[61] Lett. #66 to Bonamico also omits any mention of his own loss of books— strangely so, since he specifically petitions his friend to send books to him.

The News Arrives

Not until June, evidently, did Sadoleto receive written confirmation of the Sack of Rome, from his friend and former subordinate, the humanist secretary Gianfrancesco Bini.[62] In responding to Bini, he describes his insatiable grief over the calamity of Rome and Italy, and the sufferings of friends, about whose well-being he anxiously inquires. The letter's immediate purpose is to assure the client Bini of his erstwhile patron's continuing support. Sadoleto accedes to the request that he write letters of recommendation on Bini's behalf to Benedetto Accolti and to Ercole Gonzaga, both of whom had just been elevated to the cardinalate. In addition, he thinks· to mention the more established cardinals Giovanni Salviati and Jean de Guise as patrons who would surely welcome Bini's services. In any event, Sadoleto assures him, "a good address (*ricapito buono*) will not be lacking to you."[63] But above all, he advises Bini to "return to the services of our lord [i.e., Clement], since he has need of you."[64]

Sadoleto takes pains in this letter to emphasize his own continuing total devotion to the pope, his "sole patron" (*unico padrone*), whose undeserved ill fortunes especially distress Sadoleto. He lauds Clement's character, attesting to the pope's fairness and love of peace.[65] The real culprits who brought about the disaster were certain unnamed bad counselors, who "twisted the very good nature and mind of our lord [i.e., Clement] where they had not been turned on their own."[66] The pope's subsequent misfortunes show not

---

[62] *Epistolae*, 1:177-82 (lett. #67), dated 18 June, is Sadoleto's response to a letter from Bini, which (according to Sadoleto) was dated 1 June. Perhaps because it is in Italian (at least in printed editions), this letter was not included in the sixteenth-century editions of Sadoleto's correspondence. Costanzi does not include the letter to which Sadoleto here responds. On Bini, who later served as papal Domestic Secretary, see *Epistolae* 1:177n; and G. Ballistreri, "Bini (Bino), Giovanni Francesco," in *DBI* 10 (1968): 510-13. Accolti and Gonzaga were elevated to the cardinalate on 3 May 1527.

[63] *Epistolae*, 1:181.

[64] *Epistolae*, 1:180: "Di voi, Bino mio, voi sapete che jure vestro potete fare stima di me, & di quel poco che ho, ch'io non sia per mancarvi mai; ma mi confido, che tornerete a' servitii di N. Signore, perchè ha bisogno di voi, & mi confido, che sarà havuto gran rispetto a Sua Santità...."

[65] *Epistolae*, 1:178.

[66] *Epistolae*, 1:178: "Et io non negherò già, ch'io vedeva le cose drizzate à infortunato essito, per colpa d'alcuni, che l'ottima natura, & mente di N. S. torcevano alcune fiate, dove da se non era volta." Surely this alludes to counselors such as Giberti, the chief advocate of Clement's disastrous pro-French policy, on which see

his guilt, but rather the greatness of the anger of God, "Who has gathered up innocents, too, the better to be recompensed" for more general offenses: the corruption of the age and the "morals of the Court."[67] As for Clement, surely he will recover his dignity, "doing that which his good and religious nature dictates to him, and trusting in his very self."[68]

But on the subject of how he himself should serve the pope, Sadoleto is more conflicted. He emphasizes his commitment to his diocese: "My mind is made up, in life and in death, to serve God in my Church...."[69] Nonetheless, he speculates that, should Clement go to Spain (presumably at the behest of Charles V), perhaps he himself should go there to see if he could be of assistance.[70] But now he takes as his primary responsibility the fulfillment of his duty to God by service in Carpentras. Significantly, he articulates the resolution of the conflict as an easy choice between patrons of infinitely different magnitude:

> And although I am firm and resolved thus [i.e., to serve God in my diocese] still from Him I will have leave for three or four months to go to do this service for my terrestrial patron, from whom I did not part by any means to abandon him, but in order to draw close to the other, greater Master, to Whom he [i.e., Clement] was realizing that I was still more obligated.[71]

Adriano Prosperi, *Tra Evangelismo e Controriforma: G. M. Giberti (1495–1543)* (Rome, 1969), 33-92. On Giberti's patronage of political writings in mid-1520s Rome, see Maria Grazia Blasio, *Cum gratia et privilegio. Programmi editoriali e politica pontificia, Roma 1487–1527* (Rome, 1988), 68-76.

[67] *Epistolae,* 1:178: "Ma il secolo corrotto, & i costumi della Corte hanno tiratosi addosso la sì grande ira di Dio, la quale ha colto anco gli innocenti per ricompensargli di maggior bene."

[68] *Epistolae,* 1:178: "Et non mi diffido che N. S. haverà il modo di ricuperare la obedienza, & la sua dignità, facendo quello, che la sua buona, & religiosa natura gli detta, & credendo a se medesimo."

[69] *Epistolae* 1:179: "L'animo mio è fermato in vita, & in morte servire a Dio nella Chiesa mia...." (full sentence in n. 72 below)

[70] *Epistolae* 1:178-79: "Et se Sua Santità anderà in Ispagna, io mi comincio a deliberar d'andarlo a trovar fin là; & per quanto potrò, opererò quello che sia honore di Sua Santità."

[71] *Epistolae* 1:179: "Et benchè così sia fermo, & deliberato, pur da lui medesimo haverò licentia per tre, o quattro mesi, per andar a far questo officio per il mio terrestre padrone, dal quale io non mi partì giamai per abbandonarlo; ma per trovarmi appresso l'altro S. maggiore, al quale ancora mi conosceva più obbligato." Douglas, 52, misreads this passage as saying that Clement "had given him leave for three or four months" when he left Rome in April. From context, however, the meaning of the passage is quite clear.

By posing the problem thus, as a conflict of obligations in which the proper priority is beyond question, Sadoleto sidesteps entirely the rather obvious point that service to the pope was itself a means of serving God. Moreover, by implying that divine providence has set the course of his life, he is able—perhaps too conveniently—to place the entire issue safely beyond human control.[72] Conspicuously absent from his account, however, is any explicit recognition that returning to Clement's service, however briefly, would be more difficult and dangerous than remaining in his diocese. Small wonder, then, that he found himself unable to write to the pope, or even to follow up on his letter to Giberti.[73] Instead, he asks Bini for news of Giberti and of other friends, contenting himself with praying on behalf of Giberti and of Pope Clement, and with leading all the people of his diocese in doing likewise.[74]

Absence and Identity

Subsequent letters elucidate the negotiations involved in Sadoleto's maintaining contact with friends—whether associates, clients, or patrons—in Rome. In the epistolary exchange between Sadoleto and Girolamo Negri, there arise issues about the bishop's departure that could scarcely have been comfortable for him. On 12 July 1527, from the safety of Venice, whence he had fled following the Sack of Rome, Negri wrote to Sadoleto in Carpentras.[75] Assuming that his friend must already have heard of the destruction of Rome, he writes less to inform, he says, than to commiserate and to seek advice. Negri considers himself to have gotten off lightly: although he has lost his modest possessions and, more important, the fruits of his literary

---

[72] *Epistolae* 1:179: "L'animo mio è fermato in vita, & in morte servire a Dio nella Chiesa mia, ancor ch'io sia indegno servo, & poco meriti la gratia sua; pur tanto più sono obbligato, quanto conosco la man sua onnipotente essere stata sopra di me, che chi sapesse i modi del mio venire, vederia chiaramente non esser stato caso." The only loss by which he is still troubled is that of some of his books (181), a subject upon which he later dilates.

[73] *Epistolae* 1:182: "Io haveva scritto una Epistola i giorni passati a Mons. di Verona, la quale credo non sarà andata bene. Sono acceso di gran volere di scrivere di nuovo, & a lui, & a Nostro Signore, ma non è possibile trovar principio, nè materia conveniente."

[74] *Epistolae* 1:182: "Aspetterò adunque, & pregherò tuttavia Dio per loro, come faccio, & fò fare continuamente in tutta la mia Diocesi."

[75] *Epistolae*, 189-92 (lett. 70).

labors, he expresses gratitude to God for extricating him from the massacre and allowing him to escape to Venice.[76] But Negri's letter is most striking for the way it casts Sadoleto as a prudent counselor whom he petitions for advice. Negri remarks on the exceptional prescience of his friend, "who foresaw past evils and the present ones long before they came about."[77] He recalls specifically Sadoleto's warnings:

> For I remember that you, both at many other times, and moreover just before your departure from Rome, by divine influence foretold to me many things about the impending destruction of Rome, about the laying waste of Italy and the imminent ruin of nearly the entire Christian world.[78]

These prognostications had been accompanied by friendly admonishments that Negri, too, should "yield to the circumstances" and leave Rome for a while—advice that, if followed, would have spared him from witnessing the city's devastation.[79]

Negri notes the common perception that the Romans deserved their fate: "Now there is almost no one who does not keep saying in public that we are paying the penalty for our errors."[80] He obliquely acknowledges that some in Rome did in fact bear some responsibility for its downfall, and he even refers to the Eternal City as the "cesspool of all horrible and shameful things."[81] But while Negri had been caught up in the city's collective punishment, Sadoleto had "very wisely and fortuitously" distanced himself from the criminality:

> For when you saw that your counsels were not sufficiently being judged acceptable by the governors of affairs, shortly before all things were

---

[76] Sadoleto, *Epistolae*, 190.

[77] Sadoleto, *Epistolae*, 190: "qui praeterita mala, atque praesentia, multo ante quam fierent, praevidisti."

[78] Sadoleto, *Epistolae*, 190: "Memini enim te cum saepe alias, tum vero sub tuum ex Urbe discessum multa mihi de impendenti Urbis excidio, de Italiae vastitate, atque imminenti totius fere christiani orbis ruina, divinitus praedixisse, explicatis causis propter quas haec fieri necesse foret...."

[79] Sadoleto, *Epistolae*, 190: "simul etiam me amice monuisse, ut cederem tempori, neque tempestatis iamiam ingruentis vim diutius expectarem. Quibus ego monitis si continuo paruissem, auditor tantum Romanae cladis, non spectator & particeps extitissem."

[80] Sadoleto, *Epistolae*, 190: "Iam nemo est fere, qui non palam dictitet, nos erratorum nostrorum poenas luere."

[81] Sadoleto, *Epistolae*, 191: "Quae si molestissima fuerunt his, qui tantorum malorum causas extiterant, quanto molestiora putes fuisse nobis innocentibus, nisi forte in ea re no<c>entes fuimus, quod Romae hoc est in sentina omnium rerum atrocium & pudendarum deprehensi fuerimus."

upended in military tumult, you departed from Rome in such a way
that propriety, probity, [and] religious observance seemed to have departed along with you.[82]

After the fact, Sadoleto's good judgment and foresight have at last
been widely acknowledged; Rome's loss has been Carpentras's
gain.[83] Negri closes by noting his inability, on account of the general-
ized warfare in Italy, to join Sadoleto in France, and he asks him to
"lessen our grief by means of your letter to me and by some salutary
counsel."[84] Thus, in Negri's reckoning, Sadoleto's timely departure
from Rome has only increased the bishop's standing in his friends'
eyes as a prudent counselor from whose divinely inspired foresight
they ought to have benefited more.

But if Negri could be comfortable with such a formulation, Sadoleto's response, dated 9 September 1527, indicates that he found it
troubling.[85] Struggling to justify his own fortune in the face of his
friend's more immediate sufferings, Sadoleto steers a tortuous course,
emphasizing his own misfortunes while at every point minimizing his
agency. The letter serves to reaffirm their bond of friendship: "May I
not live, my Negri, if I concede to you that you desire me more
avidly than I you."[86] But it contains subtexts that are markedly unsettling. Like Negri, Sadoleto locates the most immediate cause of the
Sack of Rome in poor leadership, but for which "the priesthood,
which has now been thrown down to the injuries and insults of all,
would be remaining in its former reverence."[87] He confirms and
takes farther Negri's point about corrupt morals as the underlying
cause of the catastrophe, which he implies is a chastisement from

---

[82] Sadoleto, *Epistolae*, 191: "Nam quum videres consilia tua non satis probari rerum gubernatoribus, paullo ante quam omnia tumultu bellico miscerentur, sic ab
Urbe recessisti, ut tecum modestia, probitas, religio recessisse videretur."

[83] Sadoleto, *Epistolae*, 191.

[84] Sadoleto, *Epistolae*, 192: "Interea pergratum feceris si dolorem nostrum tuis ad
me literis, & salubri aliquo consilio minues."

[85] Sadoleto, *Epistolae*, 192-97 (lett. 71). The autograph final draft is found in BAV
MS Barb. Lat. 2157, fols. 60-61 (55-56 in arabic hand numeration). In the original,
the date is clearly given as "V. Idus Septembris," which Salomonius renders incorrectly as "III. Idus Septembris," perhaps taking the date as given in the following
letter (*Epistolae*, 198-201; lett. 72) by Girolamo Negri. I follow the original.

[86] Sadoleto, *Epistolae*, 197: "In quo, ne vivam, mi Niger, si tibi concedo, ut tu me
cupidius appetas, quam ego te."

[87] Sadoleto, *Epistolae*, 193: "Quod si hi fecissent, qui maxime debuerunt, ... quod
nunc ad omnium iniurias & contumelias proiectum est, in pristina sua veneratione
maneret sacerdotium."

God, intended for their correction.[88] Much more than Negri,
Sadoleto is at pains to emphasize the virtuous intentions of Pope
Clement, who "wanted to heal the ruined morals."[89] But "when the
matter required force of arms, not a poultice, his nature and mildness
shrank from more violent remedies," with the result that inappropri-
ately applied policies only exacerbated the situation.[90]

At one point, Sadoleto almost censures himself for not being at the
pope's side in adversity:

> Indeed, often, while mulling over in my mind the virtue and probity of
> the Supreme Pontiff, his benevolent spirit even toward me myself, and
> his exceptional kindness, my spirit so burns with [long-standing] love
> that, now and then, I seem to myself to sin, since I am not present for
> him in such great woes as a comforter and companion.[91]

Immediately after this flirtation with self-criticism, however, Sadoleto
turns aside any pangs of guilt over his absence, saying that were it
not for the "holier bonds" (*vinculis sanctioribus*) tying him to his responsibilities in his diocese, where he can at present more effectively
benefit the *Respublica Christiana* than he could at the pope's side, he
would let nothing prevent his going there.[92] Perhaps too conveniently, he concludes that the situation is such that doing so would
serve no purpose.

But what, then, of Sadoleto's timely departure from Rome, which
Negri had attributed to foresight? On this subject, the bishop comes
across as less than comfortable. If he appears to have shown wisdom
in being absent during the Sack, "in no way do I claim this for

---

[88] e.g., Sadoleto, *Epistolae*, 193: "Sed recordaris profecto reliquorum ordinum, mo-
rumque communium labem & confusionem." *Ibid.*, 195: "Cui enim castigatio fuit,
eidem erit Deo salus nostra curae."

[89] Sadoleto, *Epistolae*, 193: "de summo Pontifice non loquor, cuius mihi virtus,
clementia, integritas semper visa est non solum magna, verum etiam admirabilis...."
Ibid., 193-94: "Illud dico quod sentio, Deum hominesque contestans, cupisse optimum Pontificem mederi moribus perditis."

[90] Sadoleto, *Epistolae*, 194: "Sed cum res ferro egeret, non malagmate; ipsius autem natura & lenitas a vehementioribus remediis abhorreret, ut in corporum solet
morbis, sic in corruptis moribus, quae intempestive adhibita est, auxit morbum potius
medicina, quam levavit."

[91] Sadoleto, *Epistolae*, 194: "Mihi quidem saepe summi Pontificis virtutem ac probitatem; benevolum etiam adversus ipsum me animum, egregiamque humanitatem,
mecum reputanti, sic amore animus incenditur, non aliquo novo videlicet, sed illo
veteri & diu ante suscepto, ut interdum mihi peccare videar, quod non praesto sim
tantarum illi miseriarum & consolator, & comes."

[92] Sadoleto, *Epistolae*, 194.

myself," instead recognizing it as an instance of God's kindness toward him.[93] He drives the point home forcefully:

> For certainly, if I saw or presaged anything—if there was in me any-
> thing either of good sense in such a great upheaval of affairs, or of
> provident counsel for the future—it was all from God....[94]

While the recourse to providence befits the Christian themes of the
letter, Sadoleto's rapid deployment of it begs the question of whether
certain more tangible cues might have led him to anticipate Rome's
destruction.

The letter seeks also to resolve the tension between Sadoleto's
fortunate escape and his friends' sufferings in Rome. Near the outset,
Sadoleto acknowledges that "fortune has been kind to me, though
she be the same one who has ruined so many."[95] He notes that
unlike others, he lives in a peaceful region, fulfilling a task for which
he is well-suited. Still, if he does not mourn his own lot, he cannot
help being moved by the hardships of those whom he loves. Addressing this community of interest with sufferers such as Negri leads
Sadoleto to offer some consolation, as his friend had asked him to do.
Here, he interprets the Sack of Rome as a chastisement from God,
Who punishes the sins of His people with an eye to their benefit and
improvement. He urges Negri to join him in taking comfort that the
God who chastises is also the guardian of human salvation. If, then,
material losses shall have been conducive to spiritual growth, "who
would justly mourn? And who would not reckon this to have been a
type of good luck rather than a calamity?"[96]

But Sadoleto himself appears to have taken limited comfort from
this insight, immediately thereafter taking up a subject upon which
he had touched lightly near the outset of the letter: Negri's loss of
writings in the Sack of Rome. He remarks that he is "very troubled

---

[93] Sadoleto, *Epistolae*, 193: "Nam quod ego sapientia quadam videar consequutus,
ut abfuerim in tam acerbis rebus atque temporibus, nequaquam id mihi arrogo, sed
hoc eiusdem Dei erga me beneficium agnosco, gratiasquc ago illi quantas equidem
possum."

[94] Sadoleto, *Epistolae*, 193: "Certe enim si quid ego vidi aut praemonui; si quid in
me aut boni sensus in tanto rerum motu, aut providentis inposterum consilii fuit,
totum id fuit a Deo...."

[95] Sadoleto, *Epistolae*, 194: "Nam me, etsi eadem, quae tam multos pessumdedit,
fortuna afflavit...."

[96] Sadoleto, *Epistolae*, 195: "Quod si multo minore in bono laesi fuimus, ut in eo
quod maximum bonum est, augeamur, quis lugeat iure? neque hanc felicitatem
quandam potius, quam calamitatem fuisse ducat?"

that you lost your work and your vigils of studies."[97] But in an odd
and telling twist, he uses this statement to reintroduce the subject of
his *own* sufferings:

> the same thing happened to me, in an almost incredible event with a
> sadder outcome. For when, after everything else had been plundered,
> my books alone had survived intact from the enemies' injury, had been
> thrown into a ship, and had already arrived at the shore of France, a
> plague fell upon the passengers and upon my household members
> themselves. Troubled by this fear, those at whose shore the ship had
> landed did not allow the cargo to be put out onto the ground. Thus
> they [the books] were carried to foreign and unknown lands; and ex-
> cepting a few volumes which I brought with me when setting out for
> here, those remaining ones of mine—so many efforts that I expended
> especially in seeking everywhere and collecting Greek codices, such
> great expenses of mine, such great troubles—have now once again all
> come to nothing.[98]

Strikingly, Sadoleto uses this anecdote to privilege his own sufferings
over Negri's, and he holds up for imitation his refusal to be bested by
ill fortune:

> By this wound, than which nothing more serious can be inflicted upon
> scholars (I mean, of course, [the wound] of lost vigils and nocturnal
> studies), you—to whom ingenuity and youth are abundant—have been
> struck much more lightly than I, to whom what little bit, I ask, re-
> mains? But nevertheless, not even so am I flagging in spirit; and I am
> your teacher in resuming those same studies more vigorously, so that
> not more seems to have been taken away by injury of fortune than has
> been added through diligence.[99]

---

[97] Sadoleto, *Epistolae*, 195: "Ego te tuos labores, & studiorum vigilias perdidisse,
valde moleste fero...."

[98] Sadoleto, *Epistolae*, 195-96: "quod mihi idem accidit, casu prope mirabili,
eventu tristiore. Cum enim direptis rebus caeteris, libri soli superstites ab hostium
iniuria intacti, in navim coniecti, ad Galliae littus iam pervecti essent: incidit in
vectores, & in ipsos familiares meos pestilentia. Quo metu ii permoti, quorum ad
littora navis appulsa fuerat, onera in terram exponi non permisere. Ita asportati sunt
in alienas & ignotas terras: exceptisque voluminibus paucis, quae deportavi mecum
huc proficiscens, mei reliqui illi tot labores quos impenderamus, Graecis praesertim
tot codicibus conquirendis undique, & colligendis; mei tanti sumptus, meae curae,
omnes iterum iam ad nihilum reciderunt."

[99] Sadoleto, *Epistolae*, 196: "Quid ergo est? hoc vulnere quo nullum gravius studiosis hominibus infligi potest, amissarum scilicet vigiliarum & lucubrationum, tu
levius multo percussus es, cui ingenium & aetas suppeditat, quam ego: cui quantulum
quaeso est reliqui? Sed tamen ne sic quidem deficio animo, tibique au<c>tor sum,
eadem illa studia acrius repetendi, ut non plus detractum fortunae iniuria, quam per
diligentiam additum esse videatur."

Sadoleto even suggests that, on account of losing his books at his advanced age, he exceeds not only Negri, but all others in his victimization: "On account of this, it has been fairly observed that, beyond [its] collective enmities at this time with the Italian people, fortune is waging war specifically against me."[100] But even such exceptional ill-treatment cannot destroy him, "since I understand that God my patron does not fail me," instead favoring him with kindnesses that are no less great for his not having merited them.[101]

Yet if God's patronage is reliable, Sadoleto's own has been conspicuously less so. After stressing his continuing affection for Negri, he makes oblique reference to a favor that he had unsuccessfully tried to obtain for him.[102] Now, he notes, even this outcome may have been for the good, "if indeed it is a lesser ill to be without [something] than to have lost [it]."[103] He assures Negri of his continuing support and goodwill, and he closes by sending greetings through Negri to other friends. Thus his letter would traverse the distance, expressing to one he had known well in Rome, "the noblest city of all" (*Urbi omnium nobilissimae*), the voice of an absent friend— but one whose efforts to draw parallels between Negri's sufferings and his own, could offer only the pretense, rather than the substance, of continued shared experience.[104]

---

[100] Sadoleto, *Epistolae*, 196: "Ex quo sat perspectum est, praeter communes cum genere Italo hoc tempore inimicitias, proprium adversum me bellum gerere fortunam."

[101] Sadoleto, *Epistolae*, 196: "Non me tantum quotidianae illius [i.e., fortunae] iniuriae convellunt, quantum assuefaciunt ferre haec humana fortiter atque constanter: atque eo quidem fortius, quod Deum mihi patronum non deesse intelligo: nullo hoc meo merito, nullis virtutum officiis, fateor. Sed quid refert, si is adest tamen, meque ipse & protegit, & tutatur? cuius quo minus ego illis dignus sum, hoc sunt maiora erga me & praestantiora beneficia."

[102] Sadoleto, *Epistolae*, 197: "Quominus autem, quod summe cupiebam; aliquod illustre ad te commodum atque ornamentum ex nostra amicitia proficisceretur: meministi profecto quae res fuerit impedimento."

[103] Sadoleto, *Epistolae*, 197: "Quod nunc quidem vertit in bonum: si quidem minus malum est carere, quam amisisse."

[104] Remarkably, Negri's response (at least as recorded in the letterbook) appears to treat Sadoleto's letter without irony.

Absence, Identity, and Patronage

Not until 1 September 1527 did Sadoleto at last write to the captive Pope Clement.[105] From the outset, the bishop is at pains to emphasize that he has delayed writing because no reliable messenger to Rome had previously been available.[106] Yet despite the pope's continuing ills, Sadoleto's letter serves primarily to dramatize his own suffering: he writes, he says, "not so much for the sake of soothing your grief as of expressing my own," which has been "so great that the fact that I continued living after my departure from Rome seems to me to have been worse than every kind of death."[107] By contrast, he affirms Clement's great prudence and faith in God, saying, "I know Your Holiness's peace of mind."[108]

In this letter, Sadoleto again attributes the Sack of Rome to the moral corruption that had flourished previously. Indeed, he had foreseen quite clearly that "either the order of public discipline must be changed, or it must plunge headlong to the utmost ruin."[109] Though by no means having wished for the latter result, he suggests that things may after all have turned out for the best:

> if by our sufferings satisfaction is made to the wrath and strictness of God, and if this harshness of punishments is about to open up an approach to good morals and holier principles, [then] perhaps the transaction will not have been made with us with the most unfavorable outcome.[110]

---

[105] ASV Armaria XLV, t.42, fols. 41r-42v (hereafter, Arm. XLV:42), is the original of the letter, in Sadoleto's hand. The letter does not appear in any of the collections of Sadoleto's correspondence, and to my knowledge it has remained unpublished.

[106] ASV Arm. XLV:42, fol. 41r: "Tamen cum haberem certum nuncium, qui in Italiam et Romam esset profecturus, quod antehac mihi scribere cupienti non contigit, statui mei officii esse aliquid litterarum dare ad sanctitatem vestram...."

[107] Arm. XLV:42, fol. 41r: "statui mei officii esse aliquid litterarum dare ad sanctitatem vestram non tam leniendi doloris sui causa, quam mei declarandi quamquam ut dixi, hoc quidem fieri per me nullo modo potest; tantus enim est et fuit: ut quod post meum ex urbe discessum produxi vitae id mihi omni morte deterius fuisse videatur."

[108] Arm. XLV:42, fol. 41r: "sed ego quae a prudentia et religione sanctitatis vestrae quam utranque in ea semper cognovi maximam proficisci potuerunt, ad infestos adversosque casus constanter et moderate tolerandos, omnemque spem et fidem in Deum iaciendam ea arbitror satis fuisse in tantarum concursu calamitatum adhibita. novi enim pacem animi vestrae sanctitatis novi erga Deum egregiam fidem."

[109] Arm. XLV:42, fol. 41r: "At ego semper et sensi et prospexi clarius etiam aliquanto quam ea quae oculis cernuntur, aut mutandum ordinem disciplinae publicae, aut ad extremum interitum praecipitandum esse."

[110] Arm. XLV:42, fol. 41r: "sed si est Dei iracundiae et severitati nostris suppliciis

Surely, he remarks, the goods of virtue and integrity are far preferable to material goods which "are more often harmful to those who possess [them] than to those who lack them, or to those deprived of them."[111] The soldiers have appropriated from the Romans not only their riches, but also the greed and bodily licentiousness that had so besmirched the holy name of the priesthood; but divine wrath and vengeance have moved on to them, as well.[112] Therefore, Sadoleto announces to his patron, "the criminal men whom God could not deter from impiety, nor humanity from cruelty, nor good faith itself from the violation of treaties, are about to pay the price for their savageness."[113] While expressing his wish that these men might become penitent and seek God's mercy, he acknowledges that such an outcome is more to be wished for than to be expected. The matter rests, he recognizes, in the hands of God.[114]

If Sadoleto places the blame for the Sack of Rome upon the abstract qualities of corruption and moral turpitude, and links these in passing with the priesthood, he nonetheless takes care to exonerate Clement from any blame: "I deem that such great harshness of punishment has been inflicted by divine agency not upon Your Holiness, but upon the times."[115] Indeed, these times (ea tempora), rather than any action taken by the pope, had provoked God to take vengeance.[116] When Clement had endeavored to correct the moral corruption, he was "not so much driven away from the best and most salubrious course of action, as impeded" from it, "the treachery of men and a heap of vices overcoming [your] most-holy intent."[117]

satisfactum atque haec poenarum asperitas aditum ad bonos mores et sanctiores leges patefactura est, fortasse nobiscum non erit pessime actum."

[111] Arm. XLV:42, fol. 41r: "illa enim bona profecto quae virtutis et integritatis et in verum Deum perfectae pietatis sunt longe his sunt anteferenda, quae ubi laboraris coacervaris, cum invidia plerunque et infamia possederis. facillime tamen extorquentur e manibus, saepiusque illis sunt noxia qui possident, quam qui eis carent aut qui privati sunt."

[112] Arm. XLV:42, fols. 41r-41v.

[113] Arm. XLV:42, fol. 41v: "itaque nuncio sanctitati vestrae celeriter sceleratos homines, quos nec ab impietate Deus nec a crudelitate humanitas nec a violatione foederum fides ipsa potuit deterrere, daturos poenas immanitatis suae."

[114] Arm. XLV:42, fol. 41v.

[115] Arm. XLV:42, fol. 41r: "sic enim statuo tantam acerbitatem poenae non sanctitati vestrae sed temporibus fuisse divinitus illatam."

[116] Arm. XLV:42, fol. 41r.

[117] Arm. XLV:42, fol. 41r: "Quae cum vestra sanctitas vellet et conaretur corrigere, cuius ego voluntatis optimus sum testis, tamen vincente eius mentem sanctissimam et hominum perfidia et vitiorum mole, ab optimo et saluberrimo consilio, non tam depulsa fuit quam retardata."

Although the "difficulty of the times" has heretofore prevented the pope's success, Clement should nonetheless take the lead in establishing "the true splendor of the priesthood and the true dignity of our power in that True and Highest God," a course which will redound to their benefit and to the ruin of their enemies.[118] Issues of policy mistakes by Clement or his counselors do not receive mention.

The affirmations of connectedness to the pontiff and to Rome in this letter sit uneasily alongside assertions of higher priorities. Sadoleto assures the pope of his devotion and affection, which will remain even should Clement flee Italy or be driven to some distant land. Moreover, he even recommends for papal patronage the messenger, a certain "Gregorius Physicus," whom Sadoleto advocates as if he himself were still active in the Roman court, and through this intermediary he conveys some of his own requests.[119] He affirms his constancy as a papal servant who will continue to commit to Pope Clement's service "a small portion of all the time which has been devoted and consecrated through me to God and the things of God," viewing this as an aspect of his religious responsibilities.[120] Yet he also makes clear that his steadfast loyalty to the pope will not supersede his commitment to his diocese in Carpentras: "fixed in this service and servitude of God, and united to my bride, I have established my life and determined to finish [it] in this undertaking to which I have devoted it."[121] Thus when Sadoleto describes himself near the letter's closing as "suppliant and faithful" (*supplici et fideli*), and asks Clement

---

[118] Arm. XLV:42, fol. 41v: "Sicut tamen et fuit semper, et magis etiam si per difficultatem temporum licuisset, ut esset conata est." *Ibid.*, "Sic dirigamus actus cogitatusque nostros ut verum sacerdotii splendorem veramque magnitudinem mostrae potestatis in ipso vero Summoque Deo statuamus. quo cum si erimus coniuncti non inimici homines nos afflixisse, sed nos illos ad interitum dedisse videbimur, cuius optimis instituti atque consilii sanctitas vestra ut dignitate cunctorum princeps sic in experiundo et agendo prima esse debet."

[119] Arm. XLV:42, fol. 41v: "Valeat quotidie melius atque felicius sanctitas vestra cui et me et harum latorem Gregorium Physicum hominem probum et fidelem eundemque bonorum morum et bonarum partium, quanto animi studio possum diligenter enixeque commendo, ut eius liberalitate aliquod commodum consequatur, cui cum mandaverim non<n>ulla etiam meis verbis sanctitati vestrae exponenda, atque ut preces quasdam pro me porrigat."

[120] Arm. XLV:42, fol. 41v: "non deero nec amori nec observantiae erga illam meae, particulamque totius temporis quod Deo et Dei rebus per me devotum et consecratum est, in sanctitatis vestrae obsequium conferens, non arbitror me abesse ab eius cultu quem posthac solum colere iam decrevi."

[121] Arm. XLV:42, fol. 41v: "quanquam in hoc Dei servitio et famulatu affixus, meaeque sponsae copulatus constitutum habeo et deliberatum, in hoc munere finire vitam cui eam dicavi."

to show his accustomed benevolence toward him, he does so in a way that confirms his own primary attachment to his diocese and that indicates the degree to which he distances himself from his earlier role as papal secretary and curial humanist.[122]

Sadoleto's next letter to Clement, written soon after he had heard of the pope's escape from Castel Sant' Angelo in December of 1527, does little to change this picture.[123] He expresses joy upon receiving the news, a delight mitigated only by uncertainty over Clement's present circumstances. But while still resisting any direct criticism of past papal advisors, he says that now he wishes and prays especially "that the counsels of those be heard who are most suited to the inclinations for tranquillity and dignity and piety."[124] Meanwhile, he praises the pope's outstanding prudence and goodness, and he expresses hope that Clement's pious leadership will spur recovery:

> Now, indeed, now is the time that a safe and salutary path may be selected, and if it will have been properly taken, [then] not only will lost things be recovered, but greater dignity and glory than before may be acquired.[125]

But this sanguine take on the future does not lead Sadoleto to volunteer to return to Clement's side. To be sure, he affirms his loving attachment to the pope, whom he describes as his sole patron and true father. But the only support he offers, other than wishing the pope well, is to state that "in all my prayers, I do not omit room for praying and interceding on behalf of Your Holiness."[126] Since Sadoleto claims in the letter that it was cut short by the imminent departure of the messenger, perhaps we ought not to infer too much

---

[122] Arm. XLV:42, fols. 41v-42.

[123] ASV *Lettere di Principi*, t.4, fol. 311r (mech. numeration; 308 in hand numeration), is a draft of this letter in Sadoleto's hand, dated 30 December 1528 (=1527).

[124] ASV *Lettere di Principi*, t.4 (hereafter, ASV, *LP* 4), fol. 311r: "unum opto et desidero et precor ut eorum consilia audiantur, qui maxime ad tranquillitatis et gravitatis et pietatis studia apti sunt."

[125] *Ibid.*: "nunc enim nunc tempus est ut iter tutum et salutare capiatur, quod si erit rite captum non solum amissa recuperabuntur sed maior quam ante dignitas et maior gloria acquiretur."

[126] *Ibid.*: "neque in omnibus meis precibus praetermitto locum pro vestra sanctitate orandi et deprecandi." In marked contrast to this letter, a missive from Giles of Viterbo to the pope (dated 26 December 1527, from Padua. The original is preserved in ASV, *LP* 4, fol. 297r), which also congratulates Clement on his liberation from captivity, expresses Giles's desire to return to the pope's side: "Poi la nuova felicissima, & precipue poi el breve della sanctità vostra, se io fosse stato sano, non me haverimo tenuto le cathene, chio non fusse subito venuto; ma una febre gia de cinque mesi non me vuole per niente lassare...."

from its omissions. Still, we should note that here he has given no indication of any desire, or even willingness, to return to his earlier position as papal secretary.

A third letter to the pope, dated 17 May 1528, shows Sadoleto's substantial movement toward the role of one who offers counsel from afar.[127] From the outset, he is intent upon assuring Clement of his loyalty. Only illness has delayed him for so long, he says, from the pleasure of writing to the pope, which he now does as a form of continuing their conversations from a distance.[128] Clement is "my most longed-for patron" (*mi patrone desideratissime*), and by returning to his former studies Sadoleto hopes to commemorate for posterity his love and esteem for the pontiff.[129] His efforts thus appear to be directed less to praising Clement than to dramatizing—both for the pope and for others—the extent of his affection for the pope, and to expressing his utmost desire that Clement remain well-disposed toward him.[130] Yet Sadoleto gives no indication even of the possibility of his returning to the pope's service. In a most revealing passage, he draws attention to his attachment to the pope, but does so by noting the extent to which his concern over Clement's misfortunes has disrupted his own recently solidified commitment to his diocese:

> ... nothing is more ardent than my respect [and] extraordinary good-will toward Your Holiness, which has so much influence on me that I myself, who had just resolved to cast off from my very self my own attachments to my business affairs, and had undertaken that one and only charge, i.e., how to make All-Powerful God gracious to my sins, nonetheless have been both upset with the greatest grief by the adverse circumstances of Your Holiness, and restored to some calmness of mind by [your] improved [circumstances], interceding by prayer continually with our Lord and God that he favor all the actions and decisions of Your Holiness.[131]

---

[127] ASV, *Lettere di Principi*, t. 5 (hereafter, ASV, *LP* 5), fols. 169r-70r; original in Sadoleto's hand, addressed on 170v.

[128] ASV, *LP* 5, fol. 169r.

[129] ASV, *LP* 5, fol. 169v.

[130] ASV, *LP* 5, fol. 169v.

[131] ASV, *LP* 5, fol. 169r: "opinor id quod maxime est in promptu nihil esse mea erga sanctitatem vestram observantia nihil incredibili benivolentia ardentius: quae usque adeo <va>let in me et potest, ut ego ipse qui rerum mearum proprios affectus a me metipso abdicare iam institueram unamque et eam solam curam susceperam quo pacto deum omnipotentem meis peccatis propitium facerem, ex vestrae tamen sanctitatis et adversis rebus maximo dolore perturbatus et melioribus ad aliquam animi aequitatem restitutus sim, deum et dominum nostrum assidue deprecans ut sanctitatis vestrae omnia acta consiliaque secundet."

Thus, Sadoleto concentrates again upon his own state of mind, even when describing the pope's misfortunes, and he gives no indication whatsoever that his commitment to the pope's service should entail more than praying on Clement's behalf.

The Sack of Rome appears only implicitly in the letter. We hear of Clement's unspecified "adverse circumstances," as well as of the "many and serious straits and difficulties of all the things which have vexed me and my entire household, [they] whom the storm of these awful times, which has destroyed others, has also struck down."[132] The Sack may also be the unstated but implicit topic of a reference to God having taught his priests, "by the imposition of so great and so serious a penalty," that they must pursue moral reform:

> where the veneration and esteem of a holy and religious life are absent, [God] has openly declared that other resources are of little importance to the stability of good fortune and the preservation of safety and dignity, [and] that he requires different morals [and] different practices from our kind and order.[133]

Through actions that God has taken—actions which Sadoleto leaves unspecified—He has made known His harsh judgment.[134] But these events are not the focus of the letter, which concentrates instead upon Clement's potential role as an agent of reform. Surely, he speculates, there must be some as-yet-untried path for restoring religion and church authority to their former dignity—a course that he hears Clement is already considering. That path, Sadoleto says, is quite clear: once religious matters are not being misdirected to lesser ends, and once all suspicion of profiteering has been eliminated, then the splendor of the venerable priesthood will shine forth to all nations.[135] Should Clement successfully institute reforms, Sadoleto would rejoice exuberantly to see the pontiff whom he has loved above all other people in his life attaining glory in this way.[136]

---

[132] ASV, *LP* 5, fol. 169v: "multas et graves angustias ac difficultates rerum omnium, quae me et meam familiam omnem vexaverunt, quos istorum temporum procella quae caeteros pessundedit etiam afflixit...."

[133] ASV, *LP* 5, fol. 169r: "[Deus] qui cum tanta et tam gravi imposita mulcta, suos sacerdotes edocuit, ubi veneratio absit et sanctae ac religiosae vitae opinio, caeteras opes parvi momenti ad stabilitatem fortunae et conservationem salutis ac dignitatis existere, aperte declaravit alios se mores alia vitae instituta a genere nostro ordineque requirere."

[134] ASV, *LP* 5, fols. 169r and v: "Nam quo plus valent res quam verba, hoc acrior vox dei illa existimanda est, quae est factis declarata non verbis."

[135] ASV, *LP* 5, fol. 169r.

[136] ASV, *LP* 5, fol. 169v.

Sadoleto proceeds to specify the nature of the requisite reforms. Most important, Pope Clement must "give command over churches and ecclesiastical benefices to suitable men."[137] Doing so, however, would pit Clement's good intentions against "the morals and the times," so that "I fear that it is somewhat more difficult than I would wish, and than would be beneficial to the republic."[138] Still, God's judgment, evident in recent events, has made clear His will that such reform take place.[139] Clement must seek protection from God, depending upon His constancy, and placing faith least of all "in these princes of the age, in whom there is no safety."[140] Despite the pontiff's reduced circumstances, Sadoleto invokes the Roman humanist topos of *renovatio*, suggesting that Clement initiate an age which, while new, would approximate by imitation the virtues of the early Church.[141] Thus, if Clement should have become "the reformer of fallen and degenerate times, the restorer of ancient virtue and religion," then:

> it would have been the case that the previous age would have had pontiffs who estimated their position and greatness out of resources, riches, gold and royal treasure, commands, provinces, wicked wars and victories—out of a plenitude and abundance of all things, [and] finally out of the daily cultivation and enjoyment of a very pampered life— and that Clement was the author of a new age, of new times, new institutions, new morals, but nonetheless, the newness of these would draw as near as possible by imitation to that holy and pious antiquity.[142]

---

[137] ASV, *LP* 5, fol. 169r: "cuius rei et rationis caput fuerit ecclesiis et ecclesiasticis beneficiis idoneos homines praeficere."

[138] ASV, *LP* 5, fol. 169r: "Atque hoc ego ita opto precorque cum considero vestrae sanctitatis bonitatem, sapientiam, integritatem facillimum mihi factu videtur esse; cum autem mores et tempora intueor, vereor ne sit aliquanto quo velim et quam reipublicae expediat difficilius."

[139] ASV, *LP* 5, fol. 169r.

[140] ASV, *LP* 5, fol. 169v: "In eo plane ero audax, qui affirmabo et repetam sanctitati vestrae etiam atque etiam, gnarus optime et prudens eorum quae loquor, minime esse habendam his saeculi principibus fidem, in quibus nulla est salus: quorum ab omni spe atque expectatione si ipsa se se dissolverit, et in deo animique sui virtute atque constantia omnem vitae spem omnia praesidia constituerit, vae illa etiam apud eos melius obtinebit statum et gravitatem auctoritatis suae."

[141] On this theme in pre-Sack Roman humanist thought, see esp. Stinger, *Renaissance in Rome*; Minnich, "Concepts of Reform"; and O'Malley, *Praise and Blame*. On scriptural prophecies of a reforming pope that were also current in early Cinquecento Rome, see Reeves, ed., *Prophetic Rome*.

[142] ASV, *LP* 5, fol. 169v: "correctrix temporum lapsorum perditorumque restitutrix antiquae virtutis et religionis ...." "... habuisset prior aetas pontifices qui statum

And yet Sadoleto does not cast himself in any special role in the hoped-for reforms. Only in his continuing efforts at patronage for his own clients in Rome does he remain immediately involved. Thus, he ends the letter by drawing to Clement's attention two individuals well-suited for papal service. Sensing his own changing status, Sadoleto initiates the subject with the conditional phrase, "if the recommendation of others in Your Holiness's ambit has not been blocked off from me...."[143] He then proceeds to give a strong endorsement for the further advancement of papal nuncio Giovanni Antonio Buglio, the Baron of Burgio, who should serve at Clement's side, where his talents can be employed most effectively in affairs of state.[144] Finally, he expresses his desire that his student, Bini, be entrusted with his own former role of handling papal correspondence. But Sadoleto gives no indication that he ought ever to feel any responsibility or willingness to return to that position himself.

The Emergence of a Coherent Narrative

It was, however, in a missive to Angelo Colocci—not to Pope Clement—that Sadoleto definitively moved beyond his earlier identification with the culture of Roman humanism. Only in 1529 did Sadoleto at last write to Colocci, having been spurred by other friends' telling him that Colocci had not forgotten him.[145] This nostalgic letter, with its detailed recollection of the meetings of the Roman academy before the Sack, has frequently been taken as a fully reliable account of that society.[146] Interpreted in the context of Sadoleto's correspondence, however, the letter serves as a capstone of sorts to his ruminations about why he left Rome and about the nature of his

et magnitudinem suam ex opibus ex divitiis ex auro et gaza regia, ex imperiis, ex provinciis, ex perniciosis bellis atque victoriis, ex omnium rerum copia et affluentia, denique ex quotidiano delicatissimae vitae cultu fructuque aestimassent: novi saeculi auctor esset clemens, novorum temporum, novorum institutorum, novorum morum, sed quorum tamen novitas ad sanctam illam et piam antiquitatem imitatione proxime accederet."

[143] ASV, *LP* 5, fol. 169v: "Quod si aliorum etiam mihi apud sanctitatem vestram non interclusa commendatio est...."

[144] Buglio (or, "Puglioni") served repeatedly as papal nuncio to Hungary in the 1520s. See G. Rill and G. Scichilone, "Burgio, Giovanni Antonio Buglio barone di," in *DBI* 15 (1972): 413-17.

[145] The letter, dated only by year, is reproduced in *Epistolae* 1:309-318 (lett. #106).

[146] Douglas, 8-9, is careful to identify the information as Sadoleto's *memories*.

attachments there. With an air of finality, he sets himself apart from
Roman humanistic culture, invoking it only to memorialize a society
that has passed away.

Sadoleto here portrays his departure from Rome in 1527 as a
natural turning-point in his career when he saw the need to shift his
attentions from political service to the care of his own soul: "I was
realizing that now at last, finally, I must turn back to those things
which touch me more closely, and on which my salvation and true
life depend."[147] Awareness of his advancing age spurred a turn inward:

> I had given enough to princes, to friends, and to the Republic. When
> should I give to myself if, reaching by then my fiftieth year, I were not
> to withdraw from those waves into port, and to turn back both my
> attention and my mind from earthly things to heavenly ones?[148]

Once he had conceived of departing from Rome, the prospect of
leaving behind friends, public honor, and high position saddened
him.[149] By retreating into the contemplative life he did not intend to
set aside Christian charity, but instead to shun "the contagion of
turbulent political affairs."[150]

These *res turbulentae* were, however, so compelling as to play a
critical role in his departure. Thus, if he withdrew from the *vita nego-
tiosa* as a personal choice, that withdrawal was also, paradoxically,
beyond his control: "I was constrained to depart from Rome not only
by the chains of my own will, but also by those of necessity...."[151] In
a nearly identical formulation, he describes his continuing absence
from Rome as overdetermined:

> I readily endure my arrangement of living far from Rome, having been
> fettered by chains that are now inescapable, [chains] not only of my

---

[147] *Epistolae*, 1:316: "Dices, quid ergo? quae te ad discedendum causa compulit?
Illa, mi Coloti, quod magna mihi vitae parte in alienis rebus iam acta, ad ea quae me
attingunt propius, & in quibus mea salus & vera vita consistit, mihi aliquando tandem
revertendum intelligebam."

[148] *Epistolae*, 1:316-17: "Dederam satis principibus, dederam satis amicis, dederam
Reipublicae: mihi quando darem? Si iam quinquagesimum attingens annum, non ex
illis fluctibus in portum, & ab terrenis ad coelestia & curam & animum meum revo-
carem?"

[149] *Epistolae*, 1:316.

[150] *Epistolae*, 1:317: "His ego de causis urbi salutem dixi: non amorem & charitatem Christianam deponens, sed contactum rerum turbulentarum reformidans."

[151] *Epistolae*, 1:317: "Sed quod dicebam modo, me ut absim ab urbe, non solum
voluntatis, verum etiam necessitatis vinculis constrictum esse...."

own will, but also of necessity, against whose divine power not even the gods themselves can strive, as the old saying goes.[152]

Sadoleto connects this *necessitas* not just to the *res turbulentae* that led to the Sack of Rome, but to the impact of the event itself. Although he has "suffered very great grief" over the misfortunes of Rome and of Roman friends, he acknowledges that the calamity "befell me not altogether unfortunately, since I left behind Roman matters by design and voluntarily, before that storm could drive me out from there."[153] After noting his own losses of possessions, drawing attention particularly to the loss of his books, he remarks that his body at least has remained unharmed. He portrays himself as one whose manner of life allows him to maintain inner calm despite external circumstances:

> I have been driven naked onto these shores, as if from a shipwreck, but still free and peaceful of mind, as is natural [for one] for whom quietness of mind and happiness of life have been stored up not in those external circumstances, nor in public esteem and regard, nor in riches and wealth, but in a certain other sure mode of living.[154]

Thus, in his new life in Carpentras, a kind of Christian Stoicism has allowed him to transcend his losses, which appear only to have sharpened his resolve to pursue the quiet life of study and of service to God in his diocese.

This new focus does not prevent Sadoleto from invoking the rhetoric of friendship or from trying to bolster his connectedness with Colocci and other friends in Rome. He notes that their remembering him fondly gives him great pleasure, "for there is nothing preferable to a man cultivating friendships with good faith ... than the like will

---

[152] *Epistolae*, 1:316: "Itaque facile patior, meum constitutum procul ab urbe manendi, vinculis iam ineluctabilibus constrictum esse, non solum voluntatis meae, verum etiam necessitatis: cuius numini non repugnare ne Deos quidem ipsos, vetere proverbio iactatum semper est."

[153] *Epistolae*, 1:315-16: "In quibus detrimentis, etsi maximum cepi ex urbis gravi casu, & vestrum omnium i<a>cturis, quos illa calamitas oppressit, dolorem: tamen id mihi accidit non incommode, quod consilio & voluntate reliqui res Romanas, antequam illa me istinc tempestas extruderet."

[154] *Epistolae*, 1:316: "Nudus in has oras, tanquam ex naufragio sum compulsus, at liber animi, & placatus tamen: utpote cui iam non in his rebus externis, non in honore & gratia populari, non in divitiis atque opibus, sed in alia quadam certa ratione vivendi, animi sit quies, & vitae beatitudo reposita."

of friends toward him."[155] He goes on to affirm the particular reasons for the bond of love between him and Colocci:

> Indeed, the reasons for this love are, moreover, many: the old friendship between us; also, the fellowship of the same studies, at the time when together we used to give assistance to the Greek scholar, [Scipio] Fortiguerra. From that time, indeed, I remember that neither my exceptional good will toward you, nor your affection for me, was ever missing. At that time, moreover, many things were often common to us—games, community life, walking—equal and almost the same in [choice of] friends, a sense of enjoyment out of the same circumstances.[156]

But this invocation of Ciceronian *amicitia*, based upon shared experience and choices, subtly undermines the protestations of connectedness: for no longer do the two share friends and activities as they had before. What now, after all, could remain of their earlier commonalities, other than the memory of them?

The keynote of the letter is discontinuity, with the Sack of Rome marking the end of an era. If Sadoleto remembers the community and pleasures of pre-Sack Roman humanism, he describes that world as having passed away: "The disaster that followed, and the bitter fortune of the republic, have ruined these times, and those charms of a pleasing and blessed life."[157] His years in Rome have become a memory that lives on with his friends. He asks for their continuing love and mutual friendship, but does so in a way that acknowledges that the friendship is now sustained over distance and founded not upon present experiences but instead upon recollection of past ones: "nearly all the joy of my mind depends upon your love toward me," and so he entreats them to "preserve the memory of me (being absent), by which good faith and by which constancy I, preserving the good faith of true friendship, assiduously show you...."[158]

Much of the appeal and significance of Rome for Renaissance

---

[155] *Epistolae*, 1:310: "Nihil enim est homini cum fide amicitias colenti, quo me ex genere hominum esse profiteor, pari amicorum erga se voluntate optatius."

[156] *Epistolae*, 1:314-15: "Sunt quidem & multae praeterea amoris causae; vetusta necessitudo inter nos: societas etiam eorundem studiorum, tum cum dabamus Graeco doctori Carteromacho simul operam. Quo quidem ex tempore recordor nec meam tibi insignem benevolentiam, nec tuum mihi studium unquam defuisse: tum autem multa saepe nobis communia, lusus, convictus, deambulatio: par prope atque idem in amicis delectus, ex eisdem rebus delectatio."

[157] *Epistolae*, 1:315: "Atque haec tempora, & has vitae iucundae ac beatae suavitates, insecuta clades & acerba fortuna reipublicae disiecit."

[158] *Epistolae*, 1:318: "Quod autem mihi vehementer cordi est, & de quo plurimum

humanists had always been based upon memory, the physical remnants of the city providing a context for its revival. Thus, in highlighting his attachment to the Eternal City, Sadoleto emphasizes the connection with the past that was so central to Roman humanism. He recalls his connectedness not only to present-day Rome, but also to the "hallowed shades of so many very distinguished and very brave men" who had inhabited the city in earlier times:

> In almost every step, when we were making our way through the quarters and streets of the city, we were setting foot in some monument of theirs and on some piece of history. Both the admiration of antiquity and the present majesty of the citizenry were bringing it about [that] I should love so much....[159]

But if the memory of antiquity had been combined with acknowledgment of Rome's newly restored greatness (*praesens civitatis maiestas*), now the latter had slipped away. When Sadoleto commemorates the Roman Academy, he does so with a sense of remoteness as temporal as it is spatial: he assures Colocci that he holds in his "innermost feelings" the memory not only of those who "are well and live on," but also "of those who, by destiny, have died, whose multitude is far greater."[160] He aims in his own writings, he says, to assure that their reputation endures into subsequent generations.

But in this letter Sadoleto is quite emphatic that the Roman culture that he recalls, no longer exists. Its demise has resulted in part from the departure of prominent individuals such as Lazzaro

laboro, ut salvum maneat mihi & praecipuum ornamentum praeteritae vitae, & futurae solatium: hoc est, ut vestra erga me voluntas incolumis permaneat, quando ex vestro amore erga me, vestroque iudicio, omnis prope mei animi laetitia pendet: id vos vehementer oratos & rogatos esse volo, ut mei absentis memoriam retineatis: quaque ego fide, quaque constantia, fidem verae amicitiae conservans vos in oculis atque in animo assidue gero; eandem vos mihi fidem benevolentiamque praestetis."

[159] *Epistolae*, 1:317: " Nulli unquam sua patria, solumque illud in quo quisque natus, & alitus, gratam incunabulorum memoriam secum perpetuo fert, tam charum fuit, tamque amabile, quam mihi urbs Roma, & sancti illi penates tot clarissimorum fortissimorumque hominum, quorum pene in passus singulos, cum per vicos & plateas urbis vadebamus, aliquod in monumentum, aliquamque in historiam pedem ponebamus. Cur autem tantum amarem, & vetustatis admiratio faciebat, & praesens civitatis maiestas...."

[160] *Epistolae*, 1:315: "Sed tamen illud intelligi a te volo, non vestrum solum, qui valetis & vivitis, (quorum quidem salus mihi ita iucunda est, ut mea sit vita propter vos mihi charior) sed eorum etiam, qui fato functi sunt, quorum maior longe est multitudo, memoriam cunctorum mihi in intimis sensibus inhaerere: quorum equidem omnium (si hoc ocium, quo nunc perfruor, Deus mihi fortunarit) nomen non patiar apud posteros ignorari."

Bonamico and Mario Maffei, but also from the deaths of many who had been active in the social world of Roman humanism: figures such as Tommaso "Fedra" Inghirami and Camillo Porzio, who had died much earlier, but also Andrea Navagero, Giovanni Francesco Forni, and Baldesar Castiglione, the last of whom had lived long enough after the Sack of Rome to write about it briefly in 1528.[161] As a whole, Sadoleto's description of the humanist sodalities of Colocci and Küritz offers a nostalgic recollection of a world that had slipped away. He could remember it fondly, as he did in perhaps the most famous and oft-cited passage in this letter:

> For me, recalling the leisure of a past time, and going over bygone events in my mind, when we many had been accustomed to gather together, and when our period of life was far more suited to every joy and cheerfulness of spirit, just think how many of those gatherings and banquets, which we were accustomed to hold among ourselves frequently, come to mind: when, either in your villa gardens, or in mine on the Quirinal, or in the Circus Maximus, or next to the temple of Hercules on the shore of the Tiber, and also at other times in other spots in the city, there used to be held assemblies of the most learned men, every single one of whom both his very own special virtue and the common proclamation of all was commending. There, after intimate dinners seasoned not so much by great delicacies as by the salt of

---

[161] *Epistolae*, 1:312-15. Mario Maffei, bishop of Aquino and a confidante of both Leo X and Clement VII, actually left Rome for Volterra well before the Sack. On Maffei, see John F. D'Amico, *Roman and German Humanism, 1450-1550* (Aldershot, 1995), essay VII: "The Raffaele Maffei Monument in Volterra: Small Town Patronage in the Renaissance." Tommaso Inghirami (d.1516), called "Fedra" after his role in a performance of Seneca's *Hippolytus* in 1486, produced both theatrical performances and public festivals in papal Rome. Along with Camillo Porzio, he orchestrated the pageantry surrounding the bestowal of honorary Roman citizenship upon Leo X's brother, Giuliano de' Medici, and their nephew, Lorenzo, in September of 1513. See Stinger, *Renaissance in Rome*, 97, 288; and Federico Ubaldini, *Vita di Mons. Angelo Colocci*, ed. Vittorio Fanelli (Vatican City, 1969), 71n. Andrea Navagero, who edited Latin authors for the Aldine Press and who later served as Venetian ambassador to the court of Charles V in Madrid, died in 1529 while on a mission to the court of Francis I in France. On Navagero's role as official historiographer of the Venetian Republic, see Gaetano Cozzi, "Cultura, politica e religione nella 'Pubblica Storiografia' Veneziana del Cinquecento," *Bollettino dell'Istituto di Storia della Società e dello Stato Veneziano* 5-6 (1963-64): 215-94. The Modenese humanist Giovanni Francesco Forni, a client of the Cardinal Ercole Gonzaga, died in Orvieto during Clement VII's exile there after the Sack of Rome. On Forni, see Ubaldini, *Vita di Mons. Angelo Colocci*, 73n. Baldesar Castiglione's letter to Alfonso de Valdés about the Sack appears in translation as an appendix to *Alfonso de Valdés and the Sack of Rome: Dialogue of Lactancio and an Archdeacon*, ed. and trans. John E. Longhurst (Albuquerque, 1952), 101-117.

wit, either poems used to be recited, or orations were delivered, with
the greatest pleasure of all of us who were listening, both since the
merit in those of the greatest ingenuity was obvious, and since those
things which were being presented were, moreover, full of festivity and
charm.[162]

But all that is a thing of the past. Now, precisely because of the
intensity of his love for Rome, he must stay away:

> I cannot convince myself that I might wish to see this city, beloved and
> dear to me..., disfigured by ruins, emptied of crowds, made destitute of
> many distinguished and illustrious men, ... [the city] tossed about even
> now, as well, by storms, exposed to tempests.[163]

Indeed, since he feels for Rome's fate and yet can do nothing (or at
least so he states) to help the city, he seeks "to avoid not only the
sight of such great sorrow, but also the mention itself."[164] Because of
his love for Rome, he insists, he must remain far away, in
Carpentras, where he can devote his life "not to the whim of any
human, but to the honor and worship of God Most High."[165]

With this letter, Sadoleto's change in orientation, which began
upon his departure from Rome in 1527, has reached a point of co-

---

[162] *Epistolae*, 1:310-11: "Ac mihi recordanti spatium praeteriti temporis, & vetera
animo repetenti, cum & plures convenire soliti eramus una, & erat aetas nostra ad
omnem alacritatem animique hilaritatem longe aptior: quoties venire in mentem
putas eorum coetuum conviviorumque, quae inter nos cr<e>bro habere solebamus:
cum aut in hortis t<u>is suburbanis, aut in meis Quirinalibus, aut in Circo maximo,
aut in Tyberis ripa ad Herculis, alias autem aliis in urbis locis conventus habebantur
doctissimorum hominum: quorum unumquemque & propria ipsius virtus, & communis cunctorum praedicatio commendabat. Ubi post familiares epulas, non tam cu-
pedia multa conditas, quam multis salibus, aut poemata recitabantur, aut orationes
pronuntiabantur, cum maxima omnium nostrum qui audiebamus voluptate: quod &
summorum ingeniorum in illis laus apparebat, & erant illa tamen quae proferebantur
plena festivitatis ac venustatis."

[163] *Epistolae*, 1:317: "Hanc igitur Urbem mihi dilectam & charam usque eo, ut
nihil in amore fieri possit ardentius, deformatam ruinis, exinanitam frequentia, plu-
rimis claris viris illustribusque orbatam, quorum in suavitate & benevolentia, mei
(quos pro republica capiebam) labores requiescebant, ut videre velim, animum in-
ducere non possum: iactatam praeterea etiam nunc procellis, obiectam tempesta-
tibus."

[164] *Epistolae*, 1:318: "Si quidem amantis est non solum appetere congressum eorum
quos amat, sed si quid illis accidat miseriae & calamitatis, cui ferre opem ipse non
possit, non modo aspectum tanti doloris, sed mentionem quoque ipsam devitare."

[165] *Epistolae*, 1:318: "Quamobrem immota haec quidem & in omnem partem sta-
bilis est animi mei sententia, tempus reliquum vitae quod superest, non in urbe
Roma, sed Carpentoracti: neque ad hominis ullius arbitrium, sed ad summi Dei
honorem atque cultum, mihi impendendum & consumendum esse...."

herent articulation. Whereas his initial letters from Carpentras to friends in Rome contained expressions of conflicting emotions and an uncertain sense of his obligations, here he has produced a consistent narrative that renders his decisions not only understandable, but actually laudable in every respect. No room remains for ambivalence about his responsibilities to his erstwhile patron, Clement VII. Instead of a recognition of conflicting obligations, he asserts with ostensible certainty that his primary duty is to serve God through his work and writings in Carpentras. His absence from Rome, he insists, stems not from any alienation from the city but instead, paradoxically, from his overwhelming love for it. And yet by reifying a static conception of "Rome," he has added to the spatial distance a temporal separation that his return to the physical locale nearly a decade later would not enable him to bridge.

Conclusion

Sadoleto's correspondence documents his gradual distancing from friends in Rome, from the city itself as he had conceived of it, and from his own former self. If letters represent the speech of absent friends, in this case they related the speech of a friend who believed his absence to be permanent. Although repeatedly asserting Sadoleto's attachment to Roman friends, in subtler ways the letters called attention to the distance separating him from them and from the humanistic culture in which they had all shared. What had been present relationships have been consigned to memories—a fact that no rhetorical acrobatics on his part can obscure.

Similarly, the letters have helped to articulate his separation from Rome. Lacking immediate experience of the city, even willfully averting his gaze from mental images of its present condition, he has clung to the memory of the Rome he had experienced, encapsulating it as a coherent unit that had ended in 1527. By telling its idealized story in the letter to Colocci, he has memorialized the "Roman Renaissance" (as we call it) not just for himself, but also for later historians, who have taken his sanguine assessment as transparent in meaning and accurate in detail. Thus, while the city began its slow recovery with the return of Pope Clement in October of 1528, for Sadoleto, "Rome" as he knew it had come to an end.

Finally, Sadoleto's letters provided him with a means of narrating his own "life" in a way that rendered his departure from Rome meaningful and that helped him to conceive of himself as having entered a new stage. The means of so doing, the dramatization of his inner struggles and the use of rhetorical commonplaces to gloss over potentially blameworthy actions, suggests "bad faith," in that he appears to have hidden behind tropes (e.g., the loss of books, the flight into scholarly *otium*, and the maintenance of friendship over distance), using a conventional conceptual vocabulary that facilitated personal expression, but that could also provide the means for evading responsibility for one's actions.

But if Sadoleto's writing of his life helped him to avoid taking responsibility in the short run, paradoxically, it helped ·prepare the way for his assumption of far greater responsibilities later on. While he was ensconced in Carpentras from 1527 to 1536, beyond attending to the needs of the diocese, Sadoleto wrote philosophical, educational, and theological treatises—works aimed at an audience not of courtiers, legates, and princes, but of the learned throughout Christendom.[166] When he at last returned to Rome in November of 1536 to serve on Paul III's "Commission of Nine," appointed to develop a reform agenda in anticipation of a general council of the Church, he did so not as a humanist who was a creature of the papal court, but as a long-resident bishop who perceived Christendom, and his own responsibilities to it, from a markedly different perspective. If his elevation to the cardinalate (December, 1536) moved Sadoleto closer than ever before to the center of power in the Church, he remained alienated from the curial culture in which he had once been immersed. Required to reside in Rome for most of the final decade of his life (he died in October of 1547), he could write to his relative and heir Paolo Sadoleto as late as June of 1546, "Against my will, I remain in this city [i.e., Rome], a place exceedingly alien to my designs for spending [my] life."[167]

---

[166] Sadoleto's published writings from the period 1527-1536 include three works of exegesis, two philosophical treatises, and an oft-reprinted dialogue on education, entitled *De pueris recte Instituendis*. On these works and their reception, see Douglas, 72-93.

[167] *Epistolae* 3:426-32 (lett. #430, dated 8 June 1546), at 430: "Nunc, ut de me ipso aliquid tibi scribam, ego invitus quidem in hac Urbe maneo, longe alieno loco a meis agendae vitae consiliis." He longs not specifically for Carpentras, but for any place where he can enjoy *solitudinem et silentium* (*Epistolae* 3:431): "Itaque nec Carpentoracte, nec Felicianum, neque hortos iam quosvis tam mihi propono, quam locum aliquod solum ubivis gentium, in quo mihi deponere omnes harum rerum & temporum curas & sollicitudines liceat."

142 CHAPTER FOUR

Sadoleto's letters to Roman friends written in the aftermath of the Sack of Rome make clear that his movement toward playing a leading role in the Catholic Reformation in fact began long before the reform commission of 1536, in a way that met his own immediate psychological needs as he adjusted to markedly changed circumstances. The ultimate curial humanist insider became an outsider, who was able to assess the city's culture and institutions, with which he no longer identified so closely, from a vantage point that rendered reform both more advisable and more feasible—a vantage point to which he had been driven by the events of 1527.

CHAPTER FIVE

THE ITALIAN HUMANISM OF PIERIO VALERIANO

Not until 11 May 1527, five days after the Sack of Rome, did news of
the event reach Florence, where Silvio Passerini, the Cardinal of
Cortona, had been governing the city since 1524 on behalf of the
teen-aged Ippolito and Alessandro de' Medici. He sought at once to
appease enemies of the regime, but without support from Rome he
found himself politically isolated. On 16 May, Passerini ceded control of the city to a new popular government. The following day, at
the insistence of Filippo Strozzi, who had negotiated the transition of
power, Passerini and his Medici charges left Florence. Exiting
through the Porta San Gallo, they traveled first to the Medici villa at
Poggio a Caiano, and thence to Pistoia and to Lucca. Their departure occasioned rejoicing among the many Florentines who had re-
sented Pope Clement's imposition of Passerini's rule upon them and
who had endured his administration with undisguised loathing.[1]

The expulsion of the Medici from Florence meant a severing of
the ties that had linked Florence and Rome with only brief interrup-
tion since Leo X's elevation to the papacy in 1513. In part the ties
were economic, as the papacy siphoned off Florentine money to help
finance its military objectives.[2] But the cultures of the two cities commingled as well, particularly in the first years of Clement's pontificate.[3] When Ippolito and Alessandro de' Medici went to Florence in
1524, their tutor Pierio Valeriano—a humanist who had been active
in the Roman sodalities of Küritz and Colocci—followed them.
When Alessandro and Ippolito were forced from Florence in 1527,
Valeriano accompanied them as far as Piacenza, where he took leave
of them for several months. At Clement VII's request, he subse-

---

[1] Cecil Roth, *The Last Florentine Republic* (London, 1925), 37-45; J. N. Stephens, *The Fall of the Florentine Republic, 1512-1530* (Oxford, 1983), 198-202.

[2] Melissa Meriam Bullard, *Filippo Strozzi and the Medici: Favor and Finance in Sixteenth-Century Florence and Rome* (Cambridge, 1980); eadem, "*Mercatores Florentini Romanam Curiam Sequentes* in the Early Sixteenth Century," *Journal of Medieval and Renaissance Studies* 6 (1976): 51-71.

[3] André Chastel, *The Sack of Rome, 1527*, trans. Beth Archer (Princeton, 1983), 151, goes so far as to speak of the "Tuscanization" of Rome under Clement VII.

quently rejoined his pupils in Parma. Then in January of 1529, Pope Clement fell gravely ill. False rumors of the pope's death prompted Ippolito and Alessandro to hasten to Rome, and Pierio followed once again in their domestic retinue.[4] This critical moment—Valeriano's first visit to Rome after it had been sacked—served as the setting for his famous dialogue, the *De litteratorum infelicitate*.[5] Evidently composed mostly in the 1530s, this important dialogue provided a forum for Valeriano to reaffirm his connection with humanist friends, to reëvaluate the cultural significance of Rome and, on a subtler level, to rewrite his own "life" so as to make sense of his move back to northern Italy in that decade.[6] While the dialogue redefined the *respublica litterarum* as less dependent upon the waning fortunes of post-Sack Rome, it similarly refashioned Valeriano's own professional identity. Previously a spokesman for *Romanitas* and for the papacy's program of cultural *renovatio*, he recast himself as advocate for the learned in all times and places.[7] In the dialogue, moreover, he emphasized the remoteness of the present culture from that of the early Cinquecento. In so doing he—like Alcionio, Corsi, and Sadoleto before him—gave conceptual closure to the Renaissance in Rome.

---

[4] Pastor, *History of the Popes*, 10: 39, gives details on the pope's illness. Ippolito and Alessandro de' Medici were present at least by the night of 10 January, when Clement conferred the cardinalate upon Ippolito.

[5] Pierio Valeriano, *De litteratorum infelicitate, libri duo* (Venice, 1[6]20), herein abbreviated as *DLI*. Valeriano includes himself in the retinue of the Medici nephews in *DLI*, 1.

[6] On the definition and significance of life-writing, see Thomas F. Mayer and D. R. Woolf, eds., *The Rhetorics of Life-Writing in Early Modern Europe: Forms of Biography from Cassandra Fedele to Louis XIV* (Ann Arbor, 1995).

[7] This interpretation does, of course, run directly counter to the hollow affirmation of culture as rising or falling with the health of Clement VII, asserted without explicit challenge toward the end of the dialogue. On the significance of the humanist dialogue as both the product and the idealized image of the sodality, the observations of De Caprio are instructive: "se il dialogo può presentarsi come la proiezione discorsiva della *sodalitas*, questa, a sua volta, si alimenta, si sviluppa, si trasforma sulla base di questa propria capacità proiettiva. Attraverso il dialogo l'istituto-cenacolo diffonde all'esterno un'immagine di sé che si pone come limite al quale tendere, strumento ideologico di lettura della *sodalitas* da parte dei protagonisti ed elemento di trasformazione della stessa tipologia aggregativa. Per questo la *sodalitas*, in sé, si rivela anche come una delle istituzioni quattrocentesche più produttive sul piano della capacità di delineare e di diffondere (e in qualche modo di realizzare, per autoconformazione ad esso) un proprio modello." Vincenzo De Caprio, "I cenacoli umanistici," in *Letteratura italiana*, vol. 1: *Il letterato e le istituzioni*, ed. Alberto Asor Rosa (Turin, 1982), 799-822, at 802. I am grateful to Professor Julia Haig Gaisser for bringing this important passage to my attention.

i. *Background and Career Advancement*

From early in his career, Pierio Valeriano benefited from connections that facilitated his rise to prominence within the republic of letters. Born in 1477 in the northeastern Italian town of Belluno, he studied Latin there in the public school of Faustino Giosippo Vicentino.[8] Valeriano's childhood—at least as he describes it in his autobiographical poem, *De calamitate vitae suae*—was blighted by poverty, particularly after his father's death left him, aged nine, to care for his mother and two younger sisters.[9] These responsibilities did not, however, keep him from leaving Belluno in 1493 for Venice, where he enjoyed the mentorship of his paternal uncle, the Conventual Franciscan Fra Urbano Valeriano.[10] Fra Urbano, who had traveled widely in the eastern Mediterranean with the grain merchant and future doge, Andrea Gritti, had also spent several years in Florence as tutor to Giovanni de' Medici before moving to Venice, where he taught school and became an intimate friend of Aldo Manuzio.[11] Doubtless in part through his uncle's agency, Pierio Valeriano be-

---

[8] Stefano Ticozzi, *Storia dei letterati e degli artisti del dipartimento della Piave*, vol. 1 (Belluno, 1813): 85-150, provides the standard "life" of Valeriano. On the biography of Valeriano, see also L. Alpago-Novello, "Spigolature vaticane di argomento bellunese. I. Un' opera inedita ed ignorata di Pierio Valeriano," *Archivio Veneto Tridentino* 9 (1926): 69-96, esp. 69-73; G. Bustico, "Pierio Valeriano, poeta bellunese del sec. XVI," *Atti della R. Accademia Roveretana degli Agiati* 11 (1905): 155-76; Julia Haig Gaisser, "Pierius Valerianus," in her "Catullus," in *Catalogus Translationum et Commentariorum*, vol. 7, ed. Virginia Brown (Washington, D.C., 1992), 255-59; V. Lettere, "Giovanni Pietro dalle Fosse," in *DBI* 32 (1986): 84-88; Giuliano Lucchetta, "Contributi per una biografia di Pierio Valeriano," *Italia medioevale e umanistica* 9 (1966): [461]-476; Guy de Tervarent, "Un Humaniste: Piero Valeriano," *Journal des Savants* (July-Sept., 1967): 162-71. Despite these studies, however, Vittorio Fanelli describes Valeriano as a "personaggio che meriterebbe di essere studiato più profondamente" (Federico Ubaldini, *Vita di Mons. Angelo Colocci*, ed. V. Fanelli (Vatican City, 1969), 9n). To date, there exists no adequate full-length biography.

[9] Ticozzi, *Storia dei letterati*, 85-88. *Joannes Pierius Valerianus vitae suae calamitas a se ipso deplorata*, etc. (1509). See also J.G. Meuschen, *Vitae summorum ... virorum*, vol. 1 (1735).

[10] Karl Giehlow, "Die Hieroglyphenkunde des Humanismus in der Allegorie der Renaissance," *Jahrbuch der Kunsthistorischen Sammlungen des Allerhöchsten Kaiserhauses* 32 (1915): 1-232, at 114. On Fra Urbano, see L. Gualdo Rosa, "Dalle Fosse (Bolzanio), Urbano," in *DBI* 32 (1986): 88-92.

[11] Valeriano, *DLI*, 100, gives an account of Urbano's travels, including two ascents of Mt. Etna. Manuzio commissioned and published Fra Urbano's *Institutiones graecae grammatices*, a Greek textbook for Latin readers that became quite popular. On Manuzio, see M. J. C. Lowry, *The World of Aldus Manutius: Business and Scholarship in Renaissance Venice* (Ithaca, 1979). Andrea Gritti became doge of Venice in 1523.

came acquainted with Giorgio Valla and Marcantonio Sabellico, who held, respectively, the first and second public lectureships in the humanities at the school of San Marco. He became particularly close to Sabellico, under whose direction he continued his studies, and who first called him "Pierius"—Latin for "of the muses"—a name which he assumed in 1500 in place of the more prosaic "Pietro."[12]

That same year, Pierio studied philosophy under Niccolò Leonico Tomeo in Padua, where he took part in a poetic sodality that included several of Aldo Manuzio's literary friends.[13] In 1504 Janus Lascaris, with whom Fra Urbano had studied Greek, came to Venice as the French ambassador, and Pierio worked with him as well. Soon he gained the patronage of three influential Venetian patricians: Marcantonio Contarini, Girolamo Donato, and Urbano's patron, Andrea Gritti, whose son Pierio tutored.[14]

These connections paid off handsomely when Valeriano left northern Italy in 1509 for the cultural magnet of the Rome of Julius II. There, he rapidly made influential friends, including Giles of Viterbo, who persuaded Pope Julius to endow Valeriano with his first sinecure, the parish of Santa Giustina di Limana.[15] Connections between humanists in Venice and Rome, as well as Venice's appointment of his patron Donato as an ambassador to the court of Julius II, doubtless contributed to Valeriano's rapid acceptance there.[16]

After the death of Donato in 1511, Valeriano seriously considered accepting an offer of employment from Jacopo Bannisio, a secretary and diplomat in the court of the Emperor Maximilian—an offer that

---

[12] Ticozzi, *Storia dei letterati*, 90-91. Alpago-Novello, "Spigolature vaticane," 69n-70n, notes that the surname "Bolzano," meanwhile, "fu arbitrariamente assunto da Pierio, e da lui attribuito anche allo zio, dopo l'estinzione della nobile famiglia bellunese Bolzania."

[13] Ticozzi, *Storia dei letterati*, 92-93. Lowry, *World of Aldus Manutius* (190-91, 197), has established from an early poem by Valeriano that "at least five of Aldus' closest associates belonged to some kind of poetic sodality in Padua during the early years of the sixteenth century...." Valeriano's sojourn in Padua—like that of Alcionio—was a natural step in the career of Venetian humanists.

[14] Ticozzi, *Storia dei letterati*, 92.

[15] Giehlow, "Die Hieroglyphenkunde," 115, documents Valeriano's association with Giles. On Giles's relationship with Julius II, see John W. O'Malley, *Giles of Viterbo on Church and Reform: A Study in Renaissance Thought* (Leiden, 1968).

[16] Pastor, *History of the Popes*, 2nd ed. (St. Louis, 1902), 6:316. Sabellico's participation in the Roman academy of Pomponio Leto several decades earlier may also have provided useful connections. Leto himself had been disgraced and had died in 1498, but many of his students and associates were still active in Rome in 1509, including Alessandro Farnese (the future Pope Paul III).

would have entailed, Valeriano says, leaving behind both Rome and his literary studies.[17] But when his uncle's old pupil Giovanni de' Medici was elevated to the papacy in 1513 as Leo X, Valeriano's fortunes at once improved. Pope Leo appointed him to the offices of papal notary and domestic prelate, and in 1517 awarded him another sinecure, making him archpriest of the Cathedral of Belluno, much to the exasperation of its local canons.[18] Thanks partly to the influence of Nikolaus von Schönberg, Leo X entrusted Valeriano with the guidance and education of his nephews, Ippolito and Alessandro de' Medici.[19] Finally, Valeriano was appointed secretary to Cardinal Giulio de' Medici (the future Pope Clement). Although the post required his spending much time in Florence, contacts with scholars in Rome—especially with Giles of Viterbo—remained important to him, and he maintained connections with both the Colocci and Küritz sodalities.[20] Meanwhile, he published several minor works and devoted much time to his magnum opus, the *Hieroglyphica*.[21] Shortly before Pope Leo's death in 1521, Valeriano became

---

[17] Ticozzi, *Storia dei letterati*, 98. Valeriano evidently sought patronage first from Donato, and then from Julius II, for a Latin poem on the "Triumph of the Martyrs." After both had died, Valeriano did not complete the work, which remained limited to the story of S. Gioatà, one of the protectors of Belluno, and was printed in Rome in 1512 as *Joathas rotatus* (Rome, 1512). See Alpago-Novello, "Spigolature vaticane," 81. Valeriano later credited Giles of Viterbo with having given him, throughout these first years in Rome, the support and courage without which he could not have remained there: see Pierio Valeriano, *Hieroglyphica, seu de Sacris AEgyptiorum Aliarumque Gentium Literis Commentarii...* (Lyons, 1602), dedicatory letter to chap. 17, to Giles of Viterbo (p.167). Around this time Valeriano also sought the patronage of Matthäus Lang, one of Maximilian's closest advisers, and he wrote a Latin "triumph" in honor of Lang's entry into Rome in 1512 to accept the cardinal's hat. *Epistola de Honoribus Illustrissimo ac Reverendissimo Gurcensi Caesareo Totius Italiae Vicario Urbem Ingredienti Habitis* (Rome, 1512), later reprinted at least three times. See Alpago-Novello, "Spigolature vaticane," 81; and Giehlow, "Die Hieroglyphenkunde," 116. On the rank of domestic prelate, see John F. D'Amico, *Renaissance Humanism in Papal Rome: Humanists and Churchmen on the Eve of the Reformation* (Baltimore, 1983), 42.

[18] Alpago-Novello, "Spigolature vaticane," 70n-71n; Alpago-Novello, "Nuove notizie intorno a Pierio Valeriano con documenti inediti," *Archivio storico di Belluno Feltre e Cadore* 6 (1934): 477-84, at 478.

[19] Alpago-Novello, "Spigolature vaticane," 71; Giehlow, "Die Hieroglyphenkunde," 116 and 116n. The letter to Schöenberg, written at a later date after Valeriano had become particularly closely allied with Ippolito, does not mention Alessandro.

[20] Valeriano, *Hieroglyphica*, dedicatory letter for chapter 17 (167-68), to Giles of Viterbo, provide further details on their interaction. See also Giles's response, which follows in the text (168). Phyllis Pray Bober, "The *Coryciana* and the Nymph Corycia," *Journal of the Warburg and Courtauld Institutes* 40 (1977): 223-39, at 228n, cites poems that Valeriano wrote in honor of Küritz's St. Anne altarpiece. See also Gaisser, "Rise and Fall."

Professor of Eloquence at the University of Rome, where he lectured on Catullus.[22]

Like many other curial humanists, Valeriano absented himself from Rome for much of Adrian's brief pontificate.[23] But when Giulio de' Medici was elevated as Pope Clement VII in 1523, he immediately recalled Valeriano to Rome, naming him apostolic protonotary and *cameriere segreto*, and reinstalling him in his position at the University of Rome.[24] The following year, Clement endowed him with two more sinecures, the parishes of Sospirolo and Castion, and elevated him to the position of canon of Belluno—appointments which sometimes required the pope to trample upon local prerogatives to provide for his client.[25] At Clement's behest, Valeriano once again directed the literary education of Alessandro and Ippolito de' Medici, traveling with them in 1524 to Florence, where he resided for the following three years.[26]

When the Medici were expelled from Florence in May of 1527, Valeriano initially followed Ippolito and Alessandro in their flight. After journeying on alone to Belluno, where he spent several months, at the request of Clement VII he rejoined his charges in Parma.[27]

---

[21] The first edition of the entire *Hieroglyphica* appeared in 1556.

[22] Julia Haig Gaisser, *Catullus and his Renaissance Readers* (Oxford, 1993), chap. 3: "*Praelectio*: Pierio Valeriano at the University of Rome" (109-145; notes, 331-55).

[23] Valeriano attacks Adrian as an enemy of the muses in *DLI*, 90: "Fuit et sub Hadriano <Sexto> par bonarum omnium litterarum infortunium. Nam cum is Leoni Decimo suffectus esset, ad quem utpote litteratum Principem magnus litteratorum numerus confluxerat, dum non minora de Hadriano sibi quisque pollicetur, ecce adest musarum, et eloquentiae, totiusque nitoris hostis acerrimus, qui litteratis omnibus, inimicitias minitaretur, quoniam ut ipse dictitabat, Terentiani essent, quos cum odisse, atque etiam persequi coepisset, voluntarium alii exilium, alias atque alias alii latebras quaerentes, tamdiu latuere, quo ad Dei beneficio altero Imperii anno decessit, qui si aliquanto diutius vixisset, Gottica illa tempora adversus bonas litteras videbatur suscitaturus."

[24] Alpago-Novello, "Spigolature vaticane," 71-72.

[25] Alpago-Novello, "Nuove notizie," 478, 480; Lucchetta, "Contributi," 462, dates his obtaining the sinecure of Castion to 16 January 1524, the date of the demise of the previous holder of the office. This corrects Alpago-Novello, who gives the date as 1523 (p.480). Valeriano was only able to take possession of the parish of Castion with the assistance of a papal bull and the payment of forty gold ducats to the original appointee.

[26] Alpago-Novello, "Spigolature vaticane," 72, cites this point without further evidence. Ticozzi, *Storia dei letterati*, 120. Rome continued to loom large in Valeriano's thinking in these years, as we can see in a letter to Giles of Viterbo in 1525, in which he recalled to Giles's mind the image of a Küritzian party: there, he says, Giles would find himself in the company of Sadoleto, Bembo, Sanazzaro, and other intimates. Valeriano, *Hieroglyphica*, 168.

[27] Giehlow, "Die Hieroglyphenkunde," 118-19; Guido Bustico, "Due umanisti

Then, in early January of 1529, Pope Clement, who had returned to Rome only three months before, fell gravely ill.[28] Upon hearing spurious reports that Clement had died, Ippolito and Alessandro hastened to Rome, and with them came Valeriano, who had not seen the city since before the Sack of 1527.[29] The grim spectacle that confronted them, a city depopulated and in ruins, provided a depressing counterpoint to earlier humanist images of Rome. Yet even in the midst of Rome's ruins, Valeriano's own career prospects seemingly improved: for on the night of 10 January, the ailing pontiff elevated Ippolito de' Medici to the cardinalate, a move transparently designed to perpetuate the family's prominence in the Roman curia, and one which also gave hope of continuing opportunities for humanists who were clients of the Medici. Soon thereafter, Valeriano wrote a short tract entitled *Pro sacerdotum barbis* ("Concerning the Beards of Priests"), which sought to vindicate Clement VII's decision to wear a beard as a sign of mourning after the Sack of Rome. Published in 1531 and dedicated to the newly minted Cardinal de' Medici, the tract provides a telling glimpse of the struggles of Clementine humanists to find some meaning and direction for their lives, and for Italian humanism, that could transcend the devastation and cultural lassitude of post-Sack Rome.[30]

ii. *The* Pro sacerdotum barbis *and the Sack of Rome*

In the dedicatory letter to Cardinal Ippolito de' Medici, Valeriano indicates the occasion of his writing. He speaks of certain unnamed powerful figures (*nonnulli haud postremae auctoritatis viri*) who have as-

veneti: Urbano Bolzanio e Pierio Valeriano [*sic*]," Civiltà moderna 4 (1932): 86-103, 344-79, at 370. Ticozzi, *Storia dei letterati*, 125, has Pierio (in an overworked topos which Ticozzi takes rather too literally) cultivating his garden far from the tumult of the cities.

28 Pastor, *History of the Popes*, 10:39.

29 *DLI*, 1. They were present in Rome at least by the night of 10 January, when Clement conferred the cardinalate upon Ippolito (Pastor, *History of the Popes*, 10:39).

30 Pierio Valeriano, *Pro sacerdotum barbis ad Clariss. Card. Hippolytum Medicen* (Rome, 1531) (hereafter, "*PSB*"), published "Cum Gratia & Privilegio Clementis VII." An English translation of the *Pro sacerdotum barbis* appeared two years later, bearing the title, *A treatise vvriten by Iohan Valerian, a greatte clerke of Italie, which is intitled in Latin Pro sacerdotum barbis; translated to Englysshe* [London, 1533]. The translation omits key passages in the Latin text. In *PSB*, B2, Valeriano sets the tract in 1529. On Clement's beard, see Chastel, *Sack of Rome*, 186-88.

sailed the ailing pope with criticism of the clerical wearing of beards, a position that they claim was taken by the Council of Carthage and subsequently renewed by Pope Alexander III.[31] In response to the criticisms, Valeriano deploys humanist critical skills to construct historical and philological arguments to support his point. Yet if the methods employed show continuity with earlier Roman humanism, the tract's elegiac tone and pessimistic predictions about Rome's future attest to a new, more sober perspective.

Like earlier humanist writings, the tract draws upon sources from antiquity as well as upon precedents in Christian history. Valeriano marshals classical Roman and Greek authors, ancient Egyptian lore, Mosaic law, and ancient Hebrew practice, to justify and dignify the wearing of beards. Alongside this evidence, he cites numerous barbate figures in the Christian tradition, such as John the Baptist, Christ Himself (at least as portrayed in art), the apostle James, St. Jerome, and most recently Popes Julius II and Clement VII.[32] In an extensive philological argument, Valeriano assails his opponents' use of sources, and he emphasizes that they have relied upon corrupt manuscripts that have deleted or added words in such a way as to reverse the meaning. For example, the sentence "*Clerici neque comam nutriant, neque barbam*" ("Clerics ought neither to grow out scalp hair nor to grow a beard"), which they have attributed to the Council of Carthage, actually shortens the text as presented in more reliable manuscripts, where the sentence ends with "radant" (i.e., "... nor should they shave the beard").[33] After highlighting his opponents' insufficiently critical use of sources, he laments more generally the copious errors that such corrupt codices continue to inspire daily.

When assessing the meaning of beards for clerics, and specifically for Romans, however, the tone of the tract shifts from triumphant to plaintive. True, beards affirm masculinity as opposed to feminine delicacy, a point to which Valeriano returns repeatedly;[34] but they

---

[31] Valeriano, *PSB*, A2.

[32] In a brief, dubious foray into medicine, he even argues that those with beards have healthier teeth than do the clean-shaven, since the beard helps to draw out foul humors. Valeriano, *PSB*, A4v: "Quod vero conferat ad valetudinem ex eo patet, quod dum ad sui nutricationem supervacaneum humorem exsugit, dentes diutius a putredine conservat, & ut firmiores gingivis insideant efficit, quod non aeque accidit iis, qui frequenter abraduntur." Such digressions, however, figure only marginally in the argument, which relies upon the mastery of evidence from the past.

[33] Valeriano, *PSB*, B3-B3v.

[34] e.g., Valeriano, *PSB*, D3v: "... Viri denique potius quam foeminae videamur."

serve too as signs of sadness, mourning, and a distressed mind.[35] And ought not priests be allowed to grieve? If no one thinks it proper to forbid a mother to weep at the funeral of her child, then surely these "dainty little critics" (*critici delicatuli*) of the Roman court ought not to forbid that we grieve at our very own funerals (*in nostrismet funeribus*)— that is, at the destruction of all Italy, the ruin and foul plundering of the city of Rome, the manifold vexation of the entire Christian name, and the disorder of the whole world![36]

Tellingly, the *Pro sacerdotum barbis* locates the causes of Rome's sufferings in the "feminine" delicacies of the Roman clergy, which had provoked the wrath of God and threatened to do so again. Because of the excesses, God "commanded that our goods be taken from us, that our rather sumptuous houses be either brought down or burned, and that the many delights of our too-wanton minds be plucked away from us."[37] The wearing of beards, then, signifies the effort to reform the "effeminacy" into which the clergy had slipped. But should reform not follow, and should Rome slide back into corruption, then God will become ever so much angrier, withdrawing His grace from the clergy, so that the rage of the entire world will turn against them. As a consequence, "both on account of our impiety and on account of the savageness and ferocity of foreigners, we shall be utterly annihilated."[38]

If the Roman clerics have brought God's punishment upon themselves, Valeriano does not wish to absolve foreign political powers from responsibility: "We have been deserted by so many princes of the Christian name," with whose counsel and authorization the Ro-

[35] Valeriano, *PSB*, D2v: "Fuerit barba tristitiae, luct[i]usque, & aZicti animi signum."

[36] Valeriano, *PSB*, D2v: "Et Aulae Romanae critici delicatuli in nostrismet funeribus. In Italiae totius eversione. In Romanae Urbis excidio, foedaque direptione. In totius Christiani nominis multiplici vexatione. In maximo undique imminentium periculorum metu, In universi demum orbis confusione nos moerere prohibeant."

[37] Valeriano, *PSB*, D4: "Quippe, ne Deum rursus adversus nos concitemus, quem ob huiusmodi delicias, &, quae hinc resultant, effaeminationes, ob luxum hoc genus, & mollitiem, ob huiusmodi cutis curationes, ustulationes, abrasus, volsionesque indignatum atrocissimas eas in Urbem Romam, quas adhuc perpetimur, calamitates immisisse, facile credendum. Ideo iussisse bona diripi, sumptuosiores aedes vel everti, vel incendi, multaque nimis lascivientium animorum oblectamenta summoveri."

[38] Valeriano, *PSB*, D4: "... Atque ita quod ipse idem avertat, universus hic concitati ad crudelitatem orbis totius furor in extremum ordinis nostri exitium convertatur, ac demum funditus, tam nostrorum impietate, quam Alienigenarum immanitate, truculentiaque deleamur." Similarly, on D2v, he anticipates flames bursting forth again from glowing coals beneath the ashes.

mans have been captured, despoiled of their goods, and worn out by "intolerable tributes."[39] While this passage refers transparently to Charles V and his troops, Valeriano claims that the entire world is eagerly opening its jaws to devour the remnants of Italy. To the north, in Germany, the people have fallen away from the traditional faith, casting out priests and profaning churches. To the east, Europe has been besieged and Italy threatened (i.e., by Turkish expansion). To the south, the Moors and Numidians menace Italian ships with daily incursions and piracy. And to the west, fighting amongst Christians has led to lakes of bloodshed. God must pacify this turmoil, or restore to his former health Pope Clement, "in whom is every hope of this concord."[40] Thus divine intervention, whether direct or through the agency of the ailing pontiff, stands as the only hope for Roman survival, let alone recovery.

Taken as a whole, the *Pro sacerdotum barbis* reflects upon the ideological incoherence of curial humanism in the aftermath of the Sack of Rome. In early 1529, before Pope Clement had embarked upon an alliance with Charles V, the future of Rome appeared bleak. Over the next decade, however, as Valeriano moved permanently to Belluno and reëstablished his career there, he reframed the image of Rome. In the *De litteratorum infelicitate*, probably written in large part over the course of the 1530s, his return to the Eternal City in 1529 provided a setting for rewriting his own relationship to the curial culture that he had subsequently chosen to leave behind, as well as for reconceiving the place of Renaissance Rome in the history of the republic of letters.

---

[39] Valeriano, *PSB*, D2v: "Nos a tot Christiani nominis principibus deserti, habitique indignissime sumus, quorum consilio permissuque in tam calamitosam obiecti praedam, capti ad unum omnes, quotquot Romae fuerunt, fortunis & bonis omnibus expoliati, intolerabilibus tributis exhausti, per summam acerbitatem, & iniuriam miserrima quaeque per<p>essi...." [*text* : perquessi]

[40] Valeriano, *PSB*, D3. The entire passage concerning the threats to Italy from all four sides is omitted from the English translation of 1533.

iii. *From "Roman" to "Italian" Humanism: The* De litteratorum
infelicitate *and its Cultural Significance*

The action of the *De litteratorum infelicitate* takes place soon after Valeriano's return to Rome in January of 1529. In its opening, he describes the chance gathering of several prominent Roman humanists
in the garden of the patrician Pietro Mellini, represented in the dialogue by the interlocutor *Melinus*.[41] By implication, this gathering
constitutes a reconvening of the Roman academies of the earlier
Cinquecento, and it includes as a participant the central figure
Angelo Colocci (*Colotius*).[42] Yet the ensuing dialogue is more oblique
in focus: for the interlocutor *Grana* recounts for the others an earlier
discussion, in which the Venetian patrician Gasparo Contarini
(*Contarenus*) had offered authoritative counsel to them all.

From its outset, the *De litteratorum infelicitate* explicitly addresses the
theme of Renaissance Rome's recent decline from a position of cultural greatness. Describing his earlier conversation with *Contarenus*,
Colotius, and *Pollio* on the "literature and the literati of every period,"
Grana notes that:

> Over the past eighty years, ... illustrious men have appeared who are
> found to rival antiquity, some in natural ability, others in erudition,
> and still others in eloquence. And when we arrived at the point of
> listing their names, other cities were discovered to have had barely one
> or two or at most three whom it seemed suitable to inscribe into this
> register; but we found the city of Rome, inasmuch as it is the common
> fatherland of the entire world, to be so fertile and abundant on account
> of its supply of literati—whether Rome itself showed forth its own or
> boasted that it had nourished foreigners in its bosom and had warmed
> them among its own—that, over a few years, there was a greater har-

---

[41] The other individuals that Valeriano selects as interlocutors, whose namesakes
in the dialogue are hereafter italicized, include Lorenzo Grana (*Grana*), Giovanni
Maria Cattaneo (*Cathaneus*), Tommaso Pighinuzzi da Pietrasanta (*Petrosantius*), Giovanni Antonio Buglio (*Pollio*), Pietro Corsi (*Cursius*), and the absent authority, Gasparo
Contarini (*Contarenus*). See Ubaldini, *Vita di Mons. Angelo Colocci*, esp. 38n-41n, for
details on all of these figures and their participation in the Colocci and Küritz
sodalities.

[42] Peter Burke, "The Renaissance Dialogue," *Renaissance Studies* 3 (1989): 1-12, at
7, notes the appropriateness of the dialogue form to Renaissance culture, which "was
still in many ways oral even at the level of the élites."

vest of literati just in Rome itself than in all the rest of Italy combined.[43]

But *Grana* describes the period of literary efflorescence in Rome as "now passing away."[44] More tellingly, he relates Contarini's disappointment upon visiting Rome as Venetian ambassador and discovering the decimation of the ranks of humanists:

> Good God, [Contarini is said to have exclaimed] when first I began to search everywhere for the philosophers, orators, poets, and professors of Greek and Latin literature whom I kept written down in my notebook, how great and how cruel a tragedy was forced upon my attention! I discovered that the learned men, whom I was hoping to see, pathetically lay dead in so great a number, and had been carried off by the cruelty of fate and afflicted with most-undeserved misfortunes. Some had been struck by pestilence, and others reduced to ruin in exile and poverty; some slaughtered by the sword, others destroyed by long-lasting tortures; and still others inflicted death upon themselves of their own accord—a thing which I judge to be the most dreadful of all calamities.[45]

This statement, with its focus on cultural decline in Rome, often has been taken to encapsulate the theme of the dialogue.[46] But such a reading misses the point, for the interlocutor *Pollio* immediately generalizes the argument beyond Rome:

---

[43] *DLI*, 5-6: "Tam clari octuagesimo abhinc anno viri extitere, qui certare cum antiquitate, alii ingenio, alii eruditione, alii eloquentia comperiuntur. Cumque deventum esset ad eorum nomenclaturam, urbes aliae vix unum, aut duos, aut tres ad summum habuisse deprendebantur, quos in hoc album referre congruum videretur, urbem autem Romam, utpote communem orbis totius patriam, ita litteratorum còpia fertilem, & abundantem intuebamur, sive ipsa suos ostentaret, sive peregrinos gremio susceptos aluisse, & inter suos fovisse gloriaretur; ut in ea ipsa demum per annos aliquot maior litteratorum proventus fuerit, quam in reliqua universa Italia."

[44] *DLI*, 5: "Ad haec quaesitum a declinatione Imperii Romani, quaenam aetas litteris magis Xorere visa fuerit, neque ulla comperta est, quae *tempori nunc elabenti* ante ferenda videretur." (emphasis added)

[45] *DLI*, 7-8: "Sed bone Deus, cum primum coepi Philosophos, Oratores, Poetas, Graecarum Latinarumque litterarum professores, quos in Commentario conscriptos habebam, perquirere, quanta, quamque crudelis tragoedia mihi oblata est, qui litteratos viros, quos me visurum sperabam, tanto numero comperiebam miserabiliter occubuisse, atrocissimaque fati acerbitate sublatos, indignissimisque affectos infortuniis, alios peste interceptos, alios in exilio, & inopia oppressos, hos ferro trucidatos, illos diuturnis cruciatibus absumptos; alios, quod aerumnarum omnium atrocissimum arbitror, ultro sibi mortem conscivisse."

[46] e.g., André Chastel, *The Sack of Rome, 1527*, trans. Beth Archer (Princeton, 1983), 123, and Charles Trinkaus, *Adversity's Noblemen: The Italian Humanists on Happiness* (New York, 1965; reprint of 1940 ed.), 137, both cite this particular passage.

it is far more miserable [he says] and worthy of tears that in our age, even throughout all Europe, scholarship has been so ravaged by the harshness of destiny that by now there is no territory, no city, no town in which, *over the past forty years*, some memorable calamity has not befallen this category of people. So, in our age, this storm has rained down upon every one of the most excellent men and, moreover, has deprived not only our regions, but also the entire world, of the luminaries of every branch of learning.[47]

If all good men "have been struck down with undeserved incidences of all afflictions," says *Pollio*, nonetheless the "arrows of adverse fortune are seen to overwhelm especially the literati."[48] In light of this pattern, he concludes reluctantly that "to be learned is the most wretched of all things."[49]

Thus, if Roman culture had enjoyed a position of leadership over the past eighty years, this culture—along with literary culture throughout Europe—already was showing signs of incipient decline for half of that period. The sufferings of contemporary scholars not only illustrate the current situation of the learned, but also serve by implication as *exempla* of the sorry condition of scholars in all times and places. The remainder of the dialogue consists mostly of around one-hundred and ten vignettes documenting the randomness and relentlessness with which fate has struck down humanists throughout the republic of letters within the memory of the interlocutors.[50] Both

---

[47] *DLI*, 8: "Longe igitur miserius, atque flebilius est per universam etiam Europam aetate nostra bonas litteras ita fatorum inclementia vexatas, ut nulla iam provincia sit, civitas nulla, nullum oppidum, in quo quadragesimo abhinc anno non aliqua insignis calamitas in hoc hominum genus incubuerit. Ita nostro saeculo tempestas haec in optimos quosque effusa est, atque adeo non nostras tantum regiones, sed & universum terrarum orbem omnifariae doctrinae luminibus orbavit." (emphasis added in translation)

[48] *DLI*: "Videtis enim, auditisque passim bonos omnes indignissimis aerumnarum omnium casibus afflictos, paucissimosque admodum enumerare possumus, qui felici usi, vel vita, vel senio, leniori mortis genere occubuerint, et, ut vera vobis fatear, quoniam haec iniquioris fortunae tela litteratos praecipue conficere videntur...."

[49] *DLI*, 8-9: "... quamvis ego horum hominum industriam, & virtutes unice amem, observemque, eorum tamen offensus damnis aerumnosissimum rerum omnium arbitror scire litteras."

[50] Dom. Egerton Brydges, Bar.ᵗᵒ, ed., Joannis Pierii Valeriani Bellunensis, *De litteratorum infelicitate, libri duo* (Geneva, 1821), provides in an appendix (115-18) a "Catalogue of the Unfortunate Literati" in order of appearance. Any such count can be misleading, in that Valeriano treats some figures in great detail while mentioning others only in passing. In his reckoning, Brydges appears to include only the names in the margins of the 1620 edition. Consequently, he omits from his list Lucas Tardolus and Petrus Alcyonius (Pietro Alcionio)—both of whom receive substantial attention—yet includes Fra Urbano Valeriano (under the name "Urbanus Bolzanius, *Bellunen-*

explicitly and implicitly, then, this morbid catalogue signals Valeriano's own move away from the focus on Rome that had marked his earlier writings.[51]

To be sure, Sack victims do figure prominently. Paolo Bombace, for example, was killed during the initial siege. Originally from Bologna, Bombace had publicly taught Latin and Greek literature at Naples until an influential patron, the Florentine cardinal Lorenzo Pucci, summoned him to Rome and showered favors upon him. But then, in the Sack of Rome, "when he was following his Maecenas, who was fleeing into the Castel Sant' Angelo, having been overwhelmed by a throng of cutthroats who were overtaking him, he was not able to escape savage slaughter."[52] Rather than use this story to document the uniqueness of the Sack of Rome, however, Valeriano places Bombace in the midst of a series of six individuals who suffered various forms of violent death.[53] He likens the tale of Bombace's demise specifically (*eandem fatorum inclementiam expertus & Paulus Bombasius*) to the immediately preceding story of Giovanni Muzzarelli, who had been found, along with his mule, dead in a well of deep water.[54] Right after the story of Bombace comes that of Donatus Polius, a lecturer in Leo X's Rome who was murdered in his sleep by a greedy servant unaware that his master was actually quite poor.[55] The irony of this purposeless death, like the seeming randomness of the death of Muzzarelli, places Bombace's story in a context that diminishes its effectiveness in communicating any message about the particular significance of the Sack of Rome.

---

sis"), whom the dialogue clearly describes as anything but "unfortunate."

[51] On Valeriano's earlier writings, see now Gennaro Savarese, *La cultura a Roma tra umanesimo ed ermetismo (1480-1540)* (Rome, 1993), esp. chap. 4; and Gaisser, *Catullus and his Renaissance Readers*, 109-145, 331-55.

[52] Valeriano, *DLI*, 22: "Eandem fatorum inclementiam expertus & Paulus Bombasius Bononiensis, qui Latinas, Graecasque litteras Neapoli summa cum laude publice professus, a magnae celebritatis Cardinali Pucio Romam accersitus, ab eoque in honore habitus a secretis fuit, liberaliterque tractatus iam locuples effectus erat, cum ecce repentina illa praedonum procella urbem Romam invasit, qua capta, cum is Maecenatem suum in arcem AEliam confugientem subsequeretur, superveniente sicariorum globo oppressus immanem caedem evitare non potuit."

[53] These six victims of violence are, in order of appearance, Hercules Stroza, Joannes Regius, Codrus Urceus, Mutius Arelius, Paulus Bombasius, and Donatus Polius.

[54] Valeriano, *DLI*, 22: "Vix pauculos nescio quot menses in eo vixerat otio, cum per multos dies a domesticis desideratus, in puteo demum quodam aquae profundissimae & ipse, & eius mula reperti sunt exanimati." Muzzarelli's name is Latinized as "Mutius Arelius."

[55] Valeriano, *DLI*, 22.

Valeriano also relates the stories of others, including Lucas Tardolus and Cristoforo Marcello, who died from torments that their Spanish captors inflicted upon them. While the occupying troops often applied tortures to extract ransom money or information about hidden treasure, on occasion they also indulged in gratuitous abuse. Tardolus, a prominent doctor, first witnessed the ransacking of his home for hidden valuables. When the search proved disappointing, however, the soldiers entertained themselves by attaching his arms, which were bound behind his back, to the pulley of a well rope, and then spinning him back and forth. Eventually either the rope snapped or the pulley broke, and the unfortunate Tardolus fell to the bottom of the well and drowned.[56] To avoid the blame for causing this purposeless death, says Valeriano, the soldiers actually claimed that Tardolus had thrown himself into the well to escape torture.[57]

The Spanish captors of Cristoforo Marcello, by contrast, were less concerned about keeping up appearances. Coming from a prominent Venetian noble family, Marcello was a man of exceptional probity and reputation, but he suffered "a fortune far removed from what his piety and dignity required."[58] After having been taken prisoner in the Sack of Rome, Marcello was unable to pay the exorbitant ransom sought by his captors, who proceeded to vent their frustrations upon him:

> It is said that after they realized that they had been disappointed of their hopes of the gold they had demanded, the Spaniards exposed this most-illustrious man naked to the open air, bound fast with a chain to the trunk of a certain tree, and they tore out his fingernails at the rate of one per day. And finally, amidst such very dreadful tortures, on top of hunger, sleeplessness, and the inclemency of the day and night air, he was put to death.[59]

[56] Valeriano, *DLI*, 56-57.

[57] Valeriano, *DLI*, 57: "quanquam Hispani, ut invidiam declinent, Lucam aiunt variis tormentorum generibus excruciatum, cum eis tolerandis impar esset, sponte se in puteum immisisse, atque ita morte voluntaria se ab Hispanorum crudelitate vindicasse."

[58] Valeriano, *DLI*, 10: "... ipse quoque longe alia fortuna, atque eius pietas, & dignitas postulabat...." On Marcello, who served as apostolic protonotary, wrote several important philosophical and religious works, and gave the opening oration for the fourth session of the fifth Lateran Council, see Nelson H. Minnich, "Concepts of Reform Proposed at the fifth Lateran Council," *Archivum Historiae Pontificiae* 7 (1969): 163-251, esp. 181-83.

[59] Valeriano, *DLI*, 10: "Aiunt enim Hispanos, posteaquam se auri, quod poposcerant, spe deiectos intellexerunt, clarissimum hunc virum catena religatum, nudum

In other vignettes, the Sack of Rome is shown as having ruined humanists in more subtle ways. Joannes Bonifacius's initial survival would make his subsequent demise all the more pathetic. Although captured and tortured by the Spanish invaders, he was able to make good his escape a few weeks later, when the plague began ravaging Rome, and he found passage on a small boat bound for southern Italy.[60] The boat, however, was contaminated with plague, and consequently was turned away from various ports until the passengers all died, either from disease or from hunger.[61]

Marco Fabio Calvo suffered less from active mistreatment, but in the end he fared little better. Since he was unable to pay the ransom that the Spanish soldiers demanded of him, they dragged him with them upon leaving the city, and he starved to death in a hospital for foreigners outside Rome.[62] Pietro Alcionio managed to escape into Castel Sant' Angelo, but was wounded in the process, and died within the space of a few months. Hieronymus Massainus, on the other hand, experienced long-term psychological trauma from a number of calamities, of which the Sack was only one. The cumulative effect of his misfortunes eventually caused him to die of grief.[63]

Valeriano further emphasizes the randomness and inevitability of humanists' sufferings in the Sack of Rome by noting the Imperialist soldiers' mistreatment of those to whom they ought to have been

---

sub Dio ad arboris cuiusdam truncum exposuisse, singulisque diebus digitos eius singulos exungulasse, eumque ita demum inter atrocissimos eos cruciatus, fame insuper, & vigilia, & diurni, nocturnique aeris inclementia necatum."

[60] Valeriano, *DLI*, 86: "... captus ab Hispanis, spoliatus, male tractatus, inedia, et cruciatibus omnibus affectus, cum teterrima illa pestis, quae statim depopulationem illam subsecuta est, urbem inuasisset, fuga is per occasionem arrepta, cymbam quandam ingressus est, ut in Lucaniam abnavigaret...." The use of "cymba"—the word commonly used for the boat Charon uses to ferry the dead across the river Styx—foreshadows the outcome of this episode.

[61] Valeriano, *DLI*, 86-87: "... accidit autem, ut bona Vectorum pars pestilentia ea' contacta, eodem navigio constiparetur, atque ita ei contagioni impar, delicatiore iuvenis corpore, tabe ea correptus est. Dum vero totam Italiae oram auxilium implorantes perlustrarent, a portibus et stationibus omnibus exclusi, neque quidem panis, neque aquae facta copia secundum littora Lucaniae oberrantes, et ipse, et plerique alii morbo ne, an fame teterrima contabescentes incertum: In eadem tamen omnes navi defecere."

[62] Valeriano, *DLI*, 81: "Nam cum intolerabilia, quae flagitabantur tributa, vir Codro & Iro pauperior solvendo non esset, neque tamen captivitate solveretur, rus Syllanum ab hostibus tractus, fame demum victus, vitam in xenodochio quodam cum morte miserrima commutavit."

[63] Valeriano, *DLI*, 71.

friendly. Three cases examined consecutively late in the dialogue—
those of Marcantonio Casanova, Georg Sauermann, and Johann
Küritz—illustrate this point.[64] The fortunes of Casanova, we are told,
rose and fell with those of the city of Rome.[65] In the Sack, even his
adherence to the Colonnese faction did not enable him to escape
unharmed.[66] Reduced to poverty, Casanova died from hunger and
disease on the streets of Rome, where he was unsuccessfully begging
for bread.[67] Sauermann fared none the better when he fell into the
hands of his German countrymen.[68] Following capture, he too was
despoiled of all his goods and cruelly treated. Infected with plague,
he spent his last days going door-to-door in a vain attempt to get
food.[69] Küritz's story is particularly poignant because of his centrality
in pre-Sack Roman humanistic culture.[70] After being captured and

---

[64] These three, along with Angelo Cesi, appear in sequence between the case of
Pomponio Leto and a discussion of the suppression of Pomponio's academy. Both
Casanova and Sauermann appear in Giovio's list of members of Küritz's academy.
See Ubaldini, *Vita di Angelo Colocci*, ed. Fanelli, appendix IV, 114-15.

[65] Valeriano, *DLI*, 86: "Quamdiu autem Roma floruit, ipse quoque rerum pene
omnium felicitate affluere visus est."

[66] Valeriano, *DLI*, 86: "Post Romae occasum, faedissimamque direptionem ipse
quamuis acerrimus Columnensis factionis sectator esset, pro qua potentissimorum
Principum inimicitias in se contraxerat, calamitoso tamen eo tempore, quo ea factio
Hispanis, Germanisque adscitis in omnia Romanorum bona acerbissimam domina-
tionem exercuit, nihil quicquam tale consequi potuit, ut a praeda, & captivitate incolumis evaderet." "Incolumis" may be a pun on "Columnensis" above, playing on
Casanova's lack of adequate Colonnese protection.

[67] Valeriano, *DLI*, 86: "Quin etiam in eam lapsus est egestatem, ut frustra panem
etiam emendicarit, quo non invento fame, tabeque, et omnium rerum incommodis
afflictus expiravit."

[68] Valeriano, *DLI*, 86, describes his captors as "Germanos suos Romae praeda-
tores," thus emphasizing his connection with them. Sauermann spent much of the
1520s in Rome and was active in humanist circles there. From 1520, he served
Charles V as Imperial procurator at the papal curia.

[69] Valeriano, *DLI*, 86: "Mendicabundus itaque, et morbo confectus, uno tectus
lineo, eoque lacero indumento, dum panem ostiatim frustra flagitat, in via media vi
pestis, et famis impotentia exanimatus concidisse repertus est."

[70] *DLI*, 87: "Ioannes vero Coricius cur non inter litteratos reponatur, qui litteratorum omnium tam studiosus fuit, ut in Romana aula ab Iulio ad Clementem
usque nemo unus eo lepidius, sincerius, et amicabilius sit amplexatus, et ut quae
privatim commoda quotidie in unumquenque conferebat, praetereamus, universae
etiam academiae, et omnibus, qui litterarum nomine censerentur, geniales hortos
suos ad Traianum consecraverat, conventumque insuper, et quoddam rei litterariae
certamen quotannis Divae Annae festo instituerat, longaque annorum serie celebra-
rat, quod tantum illi gratiae conciliavit, ut nemo unquam Principum aetate nostra
magis fuerit, quam unus Coritius litteratorum omnium carminibus celebratus, ve-
reque leporum omnium pater appellatus." This sympathetic portrait of the gatherings

forced to pay a large ransom, he was en route to his northern homeland to raise money to pay debts incurred in obtaining his release
when he fell mortally ill, his condition exacerbated by grief over lost
possessions and over the fate of Rome.[71]

Most of the prosopographical vignettes, however, are drawn from
throughout Italy and span a period of decades, their emphasis being
not upon the Sack of Rome and its consequences, but instead upon
the randomness of fortune. Indeed, Valeriano has his interlocutors
relate the stories in such a way as to deflect the reader from finding
any specific political or religious significance in recent events. For
example, he describes the demise of Giorgio Valla with ironic de-
tachment. While a lecturer in Venice, Valla became active in political concerns and "was such a very keen adherent of the Trivulzian
faction that he was barely able to restrain himself from cutting his
enemies to pieces publicly with invectives." Then, in 1496, he was
imprisoned because of suspected treasonous activity against Lodovico
"il Moro" Sforza of Milan. Although Valla soon was absolved and
restored to his professorial chair, this twist of good fortune did not
save him from a most curious end, which Valeriano describes in
language suggestive of Platonic dualism:

> Not much later, when he had been prepared very early in the morning
> to go to the auditorium where then he was lecturing upon Cicero's
> *Tusculan Disputations*, and where he was arguing daily most vehemently
> and most learnedly about the immortality of the soul, while in the
> meantime attending to his body, he expelled the waste remnants of
> food, and indeed simultaneously breathed out his soul in sudden
> death.[72]

contrasts with the one given by Giles of Viterbo in his response to Valeriano's dedicatory letter for chapter 17 of the *Hieroglyphica*. See Julia Haig Gaisser, "The Rise and
Fall of Goritz's Feasts," *Renaissance Quarterly* 48 (1995): 41-57, which provides a useful
account of the prejudices that Küritz (i.e., Goritz) and other transalpine humanists
encountered in Rome.

[71] *DLI*, 87-88.

[72] *DLI*, 27: "... dum Venetiis profitetur, Triultiae factionis sectator acerrimus, ita
ut, quin publice etiam adversarios maledictis proscinderet, minime sibi temperare
posset, hinc Ludovici Mediolanensis ducis inimicitiis vexatus, in ipsa, quam insti-
tuebat, civitate coniectus in carcerem, situ eo aliquandiu contabuit; cognita mox
causa, et absolutus, et cathedrae suae redditus, haud ita multo post cum mane summo paratus esset conferre se ad auditorium, ubi tunc Tusculanas Ciceronis quaes-
tiones praelegebat, deque animae immortalitate vehementissime, doctissimeque quotidie disserebat, dum interim corpori vacaturus excrementa cibi deiecit, animam
etiam morte subitaria exhalavit." On Giorgio Valla (1447-1500), who at the time of
his death held the chair of rhetoric at the Scuola di San Marco in Venice, see
Margaret L. King, *Venetian Humanism in an Age of Patrician Dominance* (Princeton, 1986),

While Valeriano concedes that Valla's means of leaving this world was fast and relatively carefree, he notes that the teacher's death "was certainly calamitous for us, his students, for whom he left behind so sad a longing for his erudition."[73]

Far grimmer is the account of the Veronese doctor Gabriele Zerbi.[74] The doctor's troubles began when the prominent Venetian grain merchant Andrea Gritti recommended his services to a highly-placed Turk named Scander who was suffering from dysentery. Zerbi succeeded in curing Scander, was highly rewarded, and was awaiting a Christian ship to carry him back home. But then came a strange reversal of fortune: while Scander was indulging his lust, he caught a worse disease than before, which rapidly killed him. Scander's sons, jealous of the riches their father had heaped upon Zerbi, spread lies that the doctor had poisoned the father, and they ordered Zerbi and *his* son detained. Thereafter, the well-intentioned doctor met an end that would lead the interlocutors to shudder and fall silent at the "monstrousness of barbarians": after watching his son sawed in half, Zerbi himself suffered the same fate.[75] As such lurid examples suggest, Valeriano indulges in what one might call "death-writing," the curious or graphic demises of his subjects frequently overshadowing the content of their lives. Rather than lauding his subjects as examples for imitation, he emphasizes the randomness of their fates, thereby rendering them exemplars of how humanists are ill-used by fortune.

This emphasis seems particularly forced in Valeriano's vignette on Leo X, whom he includes among the unfortunate literati. The sufferings of Leo that Valeriano enumerates are real enough: the deaths of many relatives, including that of his brother Giuliano, weighed upon him; his war with the King of France exhausted not only the public treasury but also his own resources and those of his friends;

439-40. Valla's great encyclopedic work, *De expetendis et fugiendis rebus opus*, was published posthumously (1501).

[73] *DLI*, 28: "At fuerit felix Valla, quia cruciatu nullo, nulliusque rei anxius e vita migravit, nobis certe eius discipulis calamitosa fuit hominis mors, quibus eruditionis suae tam triste desiderium reliquit."

[74] *DLI*, 39-40. On the life and works of Gabriele Zerbi (1445-1505), who held the chair in theoretical medicine at Padua from 1494 until his death, see L. R. Lind, *Studies in Pre-Vesalian Anatomy: Biography, Translations, Documents* (Philadelphia, 1975), 141-56.

[75] *DLI*, 40: "Exhorruerunt ad hanc barbarorum immanitatem omnium animi cunctique veluti stupore quodam attoniti conticuerant...."

and following his death he was defamed in print by members of rival
political factions to a degree unmatched in the cases of previous pontiffs.[76] Yet this portrait of Leo's care-worn life contrasts strikingly
with the pope's proverbial hedonism: his enjoyment of good food,
music, and especially the hunt.[77] Here, as throughout the dialogue,
Valeriano has fit his subject matter to the pattern of the narrative,
finding an overarching meaning in memories of humanists' misfortunes. Perhaps Valeriano has consciously sacrificed representational
accuracy in the interest of thematic consistency and literary coherence.[78] In light of current theories of memory, however, one can
surmise that at least some of the inaccuracies have resulted from
problems endemic to our ways of perceiving the past, with recalled
details being altered to fit new interpretive frameworks. Valeriano's
effort to create a coherent narrative thus may reflect not only stylistic
concerns but, more important, a desire to render meaningful his own
remembered past.[79]

Near its conclusion the dialogue creates some semblance of dis-
cord among its interlocutors, but only as a means of anticipating the
rapid and definitive resolution by the now-absent figure of *Contarenus*.
Reflecting upon the days' discussions, *Melinus* actually suggests that
those still living should envy the dead, since

> the collective condition of the learned—wherever you turn—has been
> so reduced that by now nothing at all joyful remains, but instead the
> entire world has been stirred up into arms, plundering, and outbreaks
> of violence to such an extent that by now there does not appear to be
> any place left, except for traitors and brigands.[80]

---

[76] Valeriano, *DLI*, 14.

[77] Roscoe, *Life and Pontificate of Leo the Tenth*, vol. 2, chapter 24 (374-97), gives a
sympathetic yet telling account of Leo's character and habits, including his love of
music, his amusement at court fools, and his predilection for hunting parties.

[78] For this interpretation, see Kenneth Gouwens, "Life-Writing and the Theme of
Cultural Decline in Valeriano's *De litteratorum infelicitate*," *The Sixteenth Century Journal*
27 (1996): 87-96.

[79] See the discussion of memory in chapter 1, 29-30.

[80] *DLI*, 95: "Multa quidem exempla litteratorum infelicia recitastis, sed obsecro
cur eos tantum calamitosos existimatis, quia vita cesserint fine haud satis auspicato,
cum longe miseriores plerique sint, propterea quod vivunt, quique fatum illud qua-
lecunque mortuis invident, eorumque potiorem sortem aestimant, quod cruciari iam
desierint, cum litteratorum conditio omnis, quoquo te verteris, eo redacta sit, ut nihil
iam laetabile usquam supersit, ita universus terrarum orbis ad arma, ad rapinas, ad
incendia concitatus est, ut locus iam non nisi perfidis, & latronibus superesse videatur."

Colotius seconds this judgment, but respectfully recalls the position that *Contarenus* had taken on the subject the previous day. Thus, Contarini is again the absent sage, cited second-hand, whose authoritative voice defines the present dialogue. In his view, we are told, "those deceased ones whom we have called 'unfortunate' are not only not 'unfortunate,' but are actually most-blessed."[81] *Infelicitas*, *Contarenus* had asserted, befalls all humans equally, learned and ignorant alike. Instead of mourning the fates of the men of letters, therefore, we should celebrate the fact that, through their writings, they open the way to immortality not so much for the patrons whom they honor as for themselves. Divine inspiration lends them strength in their trials. Their sufferings aside, as long as their upright lives and their writings are remembered, he had argued, they are quite fortunate after all.[82] This Stoic argument is allowed to stand as the final philosophical position of the *De litteratorum infelicitate*. *Colotius* adds his own lavish praise of Contarini, saying that *Grana* had asked to know Contarini's position not so that he might question it, but instead "so that we might enjoy fully his more abundant eloquence and sagacity."[83]

Political issues at last receive explicit attention in the final pages of the dialogue, where the subject turns to the Emperor Charles V. *Melinus* recalls *Pollio*'s mention that the pope had initiated plans to call the emperor into Italy (as in fact he did later in 1529). *Colotius* expresses concern over the pope's health, claiming that the death of Clement would have grave consequences for Italy. But again *Contarenus* has the last word:

> [Clement] has decided to summon Caesar into Italy so that he may openly discuss how great is the concord of the Christian republic, and so that he may show forth what would make for the greatest glory of that prince. And I, indeed, who was in earlier years an ambassador in

---

[81] *DLI*, 95: "COLOT. mecum sentis Meline, qui dictitare non desino nihil homine litterato, qui nunc vivat, infelicius. Nam extinctos hos, quos infelices appellitavimus [*sic*], non modo non infelices, sed etiam beatissimos heri Contarenus esse comprobavit...."

[82] *DLI*, 103–104. *Contarenus*, still quoted by *Colotius*, next proceeds to list many of the alleged "unfortunates" treated earlier in the dialogue, explaining how his argument applies to them.

[83] *DLI*, 108: "Haec sunt mi Petre, quae Contarenus suo illo erga litteratos et ingenio praestantes viros, ardore concitus, nobis nudiustertius disseruerat; ad quae Grana quaedam hodie repetiturus erat, non ut illam Contareni Sententiam sapientissime latam infirmare sibi proposuerit, sed ut affluentiori hominis facundia, prudentiaque perfrueremur."

the name of our republic [i.e., Venice] in the court of that very Caesar, have observed easily in Charles himself a certain great and outstanding goodness and a mind in him most alien to those things which his legions perpetrated in Italy with unrestrained daring.[84]

The pope's goal in calling Charles into Italy, we are told, is to enlist his help in turning allied forces against the enemies of the faith rather than against one another, and so (according to *Contarenus*) there is no need for concern.[85] No mention is made of the extraction of tribute money, an issue that had been specifically addressed in the *Pro sacerdotum barbis*. Gone, too, is the extreme pessimism of that tract. Instead, we are shown a Rome which, like the pope, is firmly established on the road of recovery. If the golden age of Italian letters has passed, so too has the grim nadir of Rome's fortunes in the two years following the Sack of 1527. Yet the tone of the dialogue is overwhelmingly elegiac and commemorative, and the promise of recovery in its closing pages appears hollow indeed in light of the evidence that precedes it.

The curious acrobatics in which Valeriano indulges to include Contarini as the authoritative (if absent) voice of the *De litteratorum infelicitate* cry out for explanation. In part, doubtless, he does so in order to court a patron whose power was based not in Rome, weakened politically and culturally by the Sack and its aftermath, but instead in northern Italy. But in the words he attributes to Contarini, Valeriano also helps to write his own way toward a coherent explanation of his withdrawal to his diocese of Belluno, the small town where he had spent his first years, and where he would reside for most of the rest of his career. The absent interlocutor *Contarenus*'s observations on *infelicitas* suggest a Stoic separation from the world rather than engagement. Valeriano's earlier career little prepares us to expect such an emphasis, and the contrast may reflect the diminished possibilities that confronted curial humanists in early 1529, when their politically weakened patron seemed on the verge of dying.

Previously, Valeriano had followed a pattern of employment and

---

[84] Valeriano, *DLI*, 110: "qui [i.e., Clemens] Caesarem in Italiam accersere decrevit, ut coram quanti sit Christianae Reipublicae concordia disputet, et quid ad summam eius Principis gloriam faciat, ostendat. Atque ego quidem, qui superioribus annis apud ipsum Caesarem Reipublicae nostrae nomine Legatus fui, facile perspexi in ipso Carolo summam, et egregiam quandam bonitatem, mentemque in eo alienissimam ab iis rebus, quas legiones eius ausu licentioso in Italia perpetrarunt."

[85] Valeriano, *DLI*, 110.

career advancement common to many Roman humanists of the early sixteenth century.[86] After his arrival in the Eternal City in 1509, he had financed his career by holding several clerical posts *in absentia*, and later by serving as tutor to the Medici nephews. For nearly two decades, he had divided his time between Florence and Rome, where he was able to maintain contact with curial humanist friends such as Mellini and Colocci. With the Sack of Rome, however, the pattern changed: although he remained an adherent of Pope Clement and especially of Ippolito until their respective deaths in 1534 and 1535, he spent little time in Rome. By 1537, he had become permanently re-established in his home diocese of Belluno.[87]

Significantly, in October of 1536, Cardinal Gasparo Contarini was nominated to be Bishop of Belluno, and following his official appointment in May of 1537, he began at once to reform the diocese.[88] That same year—perhaps not coincidentally—Valeriano at last decided to reside in his parish rather than holding it as a sinecure. Thereafter, if not before, Contarini served as a patron of sorts to Valeriano, ordaining him a priest and then making him *arciprete* of nearby Castion.[89] In the two decades remaining to him, Valeriano continued to be productive as a scholar and teacher, and he organized literary gatherings which in form, though not in magnitude, resembled the Roman academies of the early Cinquecento.[90] He did not, however, return to Rome, nor did his writings any longer make Rome central to the definition either of cultural efflorescence or of his own professional identity.[91] Just as *Contarenus* is absent from the

---

[86] On this pattern see D'Amico, *Renaissance Humanism*, part 1.

[87] Valeriano was in Belluno (to which he had returned in 1532) when he received word of the deaths of both Clement VII (25 Sept. 1534) and Ippolito (10 August 1535).

[88] Elisabeth G. Gleason, *Gasparo Contarini: Venice, Rome, and Reform* (Berkeley and Los Angeles, 1993), 135–36, details the controversy surrounding Contarini's appointment, which the Venetian Senate had delayed on technical grounds since the preceding autumn. Ironically, despite Contarini's extensive reform efforts in the diocese of Belluno, the bishop himself visited the diocese only once in the next five years. Gleason, 179-81, 266-68.

[89] Lucchetta, "Contributi," 468, and Alpago-Novello, "Spigolature Vaticane," 72, both provide details of Pierio's ordination by Contarini and his clerical residency. Perhaps significantly, the title page of at least one printed edition of the *DLI* includes, as an alternate title for the dialogue, "*Contarenus.*"

[90] Lucchetta, "Contributi," 468.

[91] The *Hieroglyphica*, which he at last completed in the 1550s, evidences the influence of the neoplatonic and hermetic interests of humanists he had known in Rome,

recorded discussion in Valeriano's dialogue, so too both patrons and scholars in Italian humanistic culture had become dispersed from an earlier concentration in Rome.

The *De litteratorum infelicitate*, set in 1529 but written in large part over the following decade, retrospectively foreshadows this change in intellectual orientation.[92] Beyond serving as a device for imposing order upon events to gain mastery over them—a function common to narratives of catastrophes both individual and collective—the dialogue allows Valeriano to script his own life, re-situating himself in the world of post-Sack Italian humanism. By presuming to give an authoritative account of that world, he asserts a degree of control over events, and he implicitly affirms his own role as part of an Italian humanistic culture that has survived recent disasters, if only in a much-attenuated form.[93] As a whole, then, despite its recounting of deaths, the *De litteratorum infelicitate* constitutes a form of life-writing, in which Valeriano used the power of the pen to create a script to lend meaning both to his own altered career path and to the fortunes of Italian humanistic culture over the course of his professional life.[94]

To Valeriano's credit, he appears to have been aware of the limited ability of writing to overcome shifts in real-world power relationships, as the dialogue's description of the fate of the prominent lawyer and elegant orator, Angelo Cesi, suggests. During the Imperialist occupation of Rome in 1527, soon after he had saved the lives of many citizens by guaranteeing payment to the Spanish soldiers, Cesi fell ill from his torments and fatigue and was forced to take to bed. Here the Spaniards accosted him with their weapons drawn, threatening him with death if he did not at once pay them the gold he had promised. His response suggests that, however eloquent he may have been, Valeriano's Cesi did not ultimately believe the pen to be mightier than the sword:

---

such as Giles of Viterbo, but it little reflected Valeriano's earlier role as a papal spokesman.

[92] Professor Julia Gaisser of Bryn Mawr College, who is currently preparing a critical edition and translation of Valeriano's *De litteratorum infelicitate*, concurs in viewing the dialogue as having been written over a period of years (and perhaps never polished to its author's satisfaction). Attribution of the dialogue to 1529 has been made only on the basis of literalistic readings of its contents.

[93] On the use of writing as a means of comprehending catastrophic events, see above, chapter 2, 64-71.

[94] On "life-writing," see Mayer and Woolf, eds., *Rhetorics of Life-Writing*.

They so thoroughly terrified him that he—a man not of great spirit, readier with the tongue than with the fist—was transfixed with terror to the point that he expired in the midst of their menacings, deprived of life because of bone-chilling fear.[95]

In the face of poignant problems, the learned could perhaps console themselves with philosophy, and with rhetoric; but the therapeutic value of writing was limited in its ability to influence (let alone control) the world outside the self. Thus, if Valeriano was scripting his own life, that act in itself served less to transform culture than to render coherent *for him* both that culture and his own place within it. Readers of the *De litteratorum infelicitate* have tended to overlook its author's oblique assertion of self. Whereas some have ripped Valeriano's carefully crafted vignettes from rhetorical context, interpreting them as reliable in detail and transparent in meaning, others have focused exclusively upon his invocations of the topoi of cultural decline and discontinuity.[96] In so doing, they have overlooked the dialogue's effort at meaning: its creation of a consistent identity over time for its author, and its construction of a coherent narrative of Italian (not Roman) humanistic culture. Both moves established—or at least imagined—a continuity that transcended the eclipsing of the High Renaissance in Rome.

---

[95] *DLI*, 88: "ecce adsunt Hispani latrones, qui morae impatientes promissum pro aliis auri pondus efflagitarent, strictisque mucronibus ad ita laborantem irrumpentes, interminati caedem, nisi pecunias actutum depromeret, ita hominem perterrefecerunt, ut non multi animi vir, lingua potius, quam manu promptus, eo terrore perculsus, inter eorum minas horribili prae metu exanimatus expirarit."

[96] Pastor, *History of the Popes*, 10:344-45. On 444, Pastor states, "Even so ardent a disciple of the culture of the Renaissance as Pierio Valeriano had now to admit that they had had no firm principles of life to offer, and that a revolution in morals had become a necessity." No such sentiment is found, however, in the *De litteratorum infelicitate*. Chastel, *Sack*, 123-24, issued later in French as *Le sac de Rome, 1527: du premier maniérisme à la contre-Réforme* (Paris, 1984), includes a curious description (173-74, French ed.) of the *De litteratorum infelicitate* as "un ouvrage vengeur," and an equally misleading statement that "Valeriano réagit comme un intellectuel qui n'a pas pris son parti des horreurs de la guerre et de la brutalité." Chastel offers these views without support. See now Vincenzo De Caprio, *La tradizione e il trauma: Idee del Rinascimento romano* (Manziana, 1991), 43-45, which deftly contrasts Valeriano's view of Rome as cultural center with that of Lapo da Castiglionchio a century earlier (1438).

CHAPTER SIX

TRAUMATIC MEMORY INTO HISTORY: THE CULTURAL SIGNIFICANCE OF HUMANISTS' NARRATIVES OF THE SACK OF ROME

In early 1528, after the troops who had sacked Rome left it for good, Pietro Alcionio speculated that "future generations for many centuries shall see nothing in Rome except that which is wretched and pitiable."[1] Yet within a decade, Pope Clement's successor, Paul III (Alessandro Farnese), was pursuing an ambitious program of reasserting political rights in the Papal States and of rebuilding the city of Rome.[2] Meanwhile, an infusion of new blood helped to restore vitality to Roman humanism. Thus the Venetian scholar Agostino Steuco, who came to Rome in 1536, used textual-critical methods to bolster the papacy's political claims, and he elegantly defended the Church's expenditures on sumptuous art and architecture as essential to inspiring reverence and piety.[3] Other humanists and artists drew upon examples from antiquity to dignify the Farnese pope, whom they likened to Alexander the Great. Even after the Council of Trent and the austere pontificate of Paul IV (1555-59), the intellectual ecology in Rome still favored the cultivation of an ideal of the Christian orator (*orator christianus*), the classically trained preacher who placed his rhetorical talents in the service of the *respublica Christiana*.[4]

Yet the surface continuities masked significant changes. Pope Paul

---

[1] BAV MS Vat. Lat. 3436, fol. 45r.

[2] Paolo Prodi, *Il sovrano pontefice. Un corpo e due anime: la monarchia papale nella prima età moderna* (Bologna, 1982); Christoph Frommel, *Der Römische Palastbau der Hochrenaissance*, 3 vols. (Tübingen, 1973).

[3] Ronald K. Delph, "Polishing the Papal Image in the Counter-Reformation: The Case of Agostino Steuco," *The Sixteenth Century Journal* 23 (1992): 35-47; *idem*, "From Venetian Visitor to Curial Humanist: The Development of Agostino Steuco's 'Counter'-Reformation Thought," *Renaissance Quarterly* 47 (1994): 102-139; and *idem*, "Valla Grammaticus, Agostino Steuco, and the Donation of Constantine," *Journal of the History of Ideas* 57 (1996): 55-77.

[4] Frederick J. McGinness, *Right Thinking and Sacred Oratory in Counter-Reformation Rome* (Princeton, 1995), provides an excellent and cogent account of post-Tridentine Roman humanist ideals and practice. McGinness proves conclusively that longstanding assumptions about the deleterious effect of the Council of Trent upon humanism have been wildly overstated.

III could not afford to dabble in international politics as had his predecessors, nor could he arrest Rome's decline in political inXuence relative to the northern European territorial states. While the Papal States provided revenue for the refurbishment of Rome, because of the Reformation, England and much of Germany no longer contributed to the papal coffers. As the schism worsened, a new siege mentality took hold in Rome. In this environment, as learned discourse increasingly centered on questions of Christian theology and righteousness, the surviving classicist element within Roman humanism—its conscious forging of links with the language and culture of ancient Rome—now threatened to diminish the Eternal City in the eyes of its critics. In the Counter-Reformation, the vindication of the culture of Catholic Rome required advocates of doctrinal orthodoxy—using Ciceronian eloquence, perhaps, but in carefully circumscribed contexts—who could bolster church authority not just with the grandeur of illustrative analogy but with the rigor of textual-critical proof.[5]

Of course, the Sack of Rome did not cause all these changes, either in European politics and culture or in the papacy's efforts at self-presentation; but it prompted even the staunchest papal advocates to reconsider Rome's significance, so that changes already underway came into sharper focus. Most immediately, the Sack circumscribed what curial humanists could convincingly claim on behalf of the papacy. In the remaining seven years of Clement's pontificate, assertions that the papacy would soon initiate a new age could only appear delusional. Those who anticipated an imminent golden age now looked hopefully to Charles V, and their expectations seemingly gained papal sanction in 1530 when Clement, once again allied with Charles, officially crowned him Holy Roman Emperor in Bologna.[6] Thereafter, even Giles of Viterbo, head of the Augustinian order and confidant of popes from Julius II to Clement VII, looked to the emperor as the leader who would help usher in the new age.[7]

---

[5] McGinness, *Right Thinking*, passim.

[6] Ottavia Niccoli, *Prophecy and People in Renaissance Italy*, trans. Lydia G. Cochrane (Princeton, 1990), 172-88, at 183, notes in particular Girolamo Balbi's prognostications of Charles's destiny.

[7] John W. O'Malley, S.J., *Giles of Viterbo on Church and Reform: A Study in Renaissance Thought* (Leiden, 1968), 110-11. The *Scechina*, which Giles began in 1530 at the request of Clement VII, is addressed to the emperor. Despite its pessimistic tone, O'Malley notes (111), the *Scechina* "tells Charles V that the times are ambiguous, and

The change of mood in Roman humanist writings pursuant to the Sack would provide a depressing backdrop for all subsequent efforts to polish the image of papal Rome.[8]

Prominent humanists elsewhere in Europe who supported Pope Clement identified themselves less immediately with Rome than did the curial humanists, and so they could better avoid confronting the unsettling implications of the Sack. In his *Dialogue Concerning Heresies* (1529), Thomas More recounted atrocities that the Imperial troops had committed in Rome, but he did so in order to make a broader point about the effect of heresy (in this case, Lutheranism) upon human character and behavior. He conveniently sidestepped the issue of why papal Rome in particular should have been victimized.[9] Erasmus preferred not to speculate at all upon the causes of the catastrophe. Even when writing to Pope Clement, he too took the subject as a springboard for invoking a broader issue, the importance of peace among Christians.[10]

Non-Roman humanists who were critical of Pope Clement, meanwhile, delighted in explaining the Sack as a divine punishment. Charles V's Latin secretary, Alfonso de Valdés, wrote a dialogue exculpating the emperor; instead he blamed the corruption of the Roman clergy and the ill counsel of Clement's advisors.[11] Pietro Are-

can resolve themselves either to the Church's utter ruin or to its great gain." O'Malley also writes (174) that "in the description of Clement's reform obligations his cooperation with the emperor receives more emphasis than was ever the case with his cousin, Leo X." See also the provocative essay by Massimo Firpo, *Il Sacco di Roma del 1527: Tra profezia, propaganda politica e riforma religiosa* (Cagliari, 1990), 60, which also treats the *Scechina*. Firpo ably sketches the prophetic overtones of the Sack and, more generally, addresses the meaning of the Sack by situating it in the context of contemporary prognostications and millennial expectations.

   8 The parallel story of the impact of the Sack upon the outlook of artists receives preliminary treatment in André Chastel, *The Sack of Rome, 1527*, trans. Beth Archer (Princeton, 1983). For an important and detailed case-study, see Michael Hirst, *Sebastiano del Piombo* (Oxford, 1981), esp. 108-119, which argues that a "mood of despairing quietism" (112) affected the artist's work in the years following the Sack of Rome. See too the observations of David Franklin, *Rosso in Italy: The Italian Career of Rosso Fiorentino* (New Haven, 1994), 155 and 157.

   9 Thomas More, *A Dialogue Concerning Heresies*, in *The Complete Works of St. Thomas More*, vol. 6, pts. 1 & 2, ed. Thomas M. C. Lawler, Germain Marc'Hadour, and Richard C. Marius (New Haven, 1981), esp. 1: 370-72.

   10 e.g., Chastel, *Sack*, 131.

   11 Alfonso de Valdés, *Diálogo de las cosas ocurridas en Roma*, translated by John E. Longhurst as *Alfonso de Valdés and the Sack of Rome: Dialogue of Lactancio and an Archdeacon* (Albuquerque, 1952). Longhurst's edition also includes translations of Charles V's letter to John III of Portugal (2 Aug. 1527), a letter drawn up by Valdés that contains the emperor's defense of his actions; and Castiglione's reply to Valdés (written after

tino, who had fled Rome in 1525 never to return, wrote the pope a missive so callous that it was said to have moved Clement to tears.[12] The pontiff's suffering, Aretino told him, served as fitting penance for the corruption of the priesthood that had brought on the catastrophe. He advised Clement to accept his fallen condition, forgive his enemies, turn to prayer, and take solace in the fact that God had placed him into the hands of Charles V.[13] But for those humanists who remained identified with the Roman court in 1527, making sense of the event that destroyed the culture that they had helped to shape necessarily proved more difficult.

Even had there been no Sack of Rome, those humanists who had devoted their energies to embellishing the papal image would have found themselves in a difficult position, for the niche that they had filled for over two decades in the intellectual environment of papal Rome was gradually disappearing in favor of another. To be sure, training in classical rhetoric and learning continued to be useful to a papacy and religious orders intent upon improving preaching and furthering Christian education. But that application of humanistic skills differed substantially from the wide-ranging revival of antiquity that had preceded it, in which humanists sought to re-create the classical world in their own age, drawing upon and imitating even the least edifying models from antiquity. Where now could there be room for the frivolity of Latin invective, let alone for satire? The broad scope of inquiry of Renaissance Roman culture, which encompassed for a while even the scurrilous Aretino, was giving way to the lavish yet more disciplined culture of the Counter-Reformation.[14]

But if the Sack did not cause these changes, it intensified them for the Roman humanists, who were forced to confront the contingency of their own positions even as they accommodated the diminished possibilities of Rome. Prior to 1527, immersion in the culture of papal Rome had facilitated Roman humanists' ready acceptance of collective "truths" which were reinforced both socially and intellectually. In private focused gatherings as in their official duties in the

---

August, 1528). Castiglione's letter, which combines venom with utter humorlessness, accuses Valdés of everything from sophistry to Lutheranism, Jewish ancestry, and even the envy and hatred of Christianity.

[12] Pietro Aretino, *Lettere: Il primo e il secondo libro*, ed. Francesco Flora (Milan, 1960), 17-19.

[13] *Ibid.*

[14] McGinness, *Right Thinking, passim.*

papal bureaucracy, they had minimized the import of criticisms that originated outside their self-validating interpretive community.[15] But the Sack of Rome fragmented that culture, and the humanists responded to the crisis in different ways. Remaining within Rome, Alcionio redefined *Romanitas* so as to disengage its fortunes (and his own fortunes as its self-appointed spokesman) from those of the papacy. Corsi sought with limited success to establish continuities with pre-Sack Roman humanism and formulated an attenuated curial humanism. Sadoleto, by contrast, treated the catastrophe as a watershed. While believing that corruption had brought it about, he redeemed the event by theologizing it as a necessary precondition for the reform of Rome and of the Church. Thus the crisis opened the way to a different and better future, not just for him—the fugitive from the court—but for that court as well.[16] Valeriano initially opined that corruption and weakness of the Roman clergy had brought on the catastrophe. In the years that followed, however, he eschewed such speculation in favor of lauding the virtue of all the literati who had suffered in a time that he perceived as having drawn decisively to a close.

Despite their differences, all four humanists examined in this study constructed narratives of the Sack that provided closure to a period of Renaissance Roman history that, at least for them, had definitively ended. The narratives passed over the tensions, pettiness, and feuding endemic to earlier Roman humanism in favor of the civility that had given shape to their collective identity. Reflecting upon the period before 1527, they recalled the images of it that they had shared

---

[15] On my appropriation of Goffman's term, "focused gatherings," and on the significance of interpretive communities, see Chapter One. On the self-validation endemic in early Cinquecento Roman culture, see the excellent and important study of Vincenzo De Caprio, *La tradizione e il trauma: Idee del Rinascimento romano* (Manziana, 1991), which came to my attention in time for supplementary consultation after the completion of this manuscript. De Caprio describes what he terms the "*falsa coscienza*" of the curial humanists (20-21), and he provides a suggestive analysis of how their ideology of the continuity of classical and papal Rome constrained their ability to perceive the critical impact of Christianity. Thus he refers, 20, to the "perdita del senso della grande novità introdotta nella storia umana dal cristianesimo su cui già aveva insistito Petrarca opponendo le età *antique* a quelle *nove*". Unlike the present study, De Caprio's *La tradizione* emphasizes the limiting and constricting effects of classical (and especially Ciceronian) discourse upon Renaissance humanists' thought and expression (e.g., 18).

[16] For this observation I am indebted to John Najemy, who notes the similarity of Sadoleto's narrative to the last chapter of Machiavelli's *Prince*: both interpret crisis as potentially opening the way to a different and better future.

in fashioning and deployed those images in narratives that invested them with meaning.[17] In this manner they came to "remember" a Renaissance in Rome that, for all its manifest glories, had never existed in quite such unalloyed splendor or stood in such sharp contrast to the present.

That humanists' remembering of Rome was itself a creative act should not surprise, given recent psychological findings on the malleability and tenuousness of memories.[18] Through their intensity of imagery and explicitness of detail, idealized accounts can become counter-narratives that rival or even displace recollections of what actually happened. Yet constructs of the past are not without their own historical significance. Later Roman humanists would indeed incline toward a more sober assessment of the city's mission in present history and a more modest appraisal of their own role in furthering that mission.[19] But if early Cinquecento Rome strikes modern historians as golden by contrast with the decades after 1527, it does so in part because its humanist spokesmen burnished its image so assiduously and embellished it so copiously. Too readily taking the humanists at their word, subsequent scholars have inclined to treat their nostalgic recollections of Renaissance Rome as accurate in detail and transparent in meaning. In later historians' accounts, as in the humanists' narratives, the Sack spurred the encapsulation of the decades that preceded it as a golden age: a world whose marvelous images obscured its seamier aspects, and whose remembered glories easily outshone the perceived realities of mid-Cinquecento Roman culture. To the extent that there persists an image of High Renais-

---

[17] This description could, in effect, be applied to any situation in which a toppled regime has left glowing rhetoric about itself. Thus, the lens of memory research helps us to appreciate the significance of Melissa Bullard's insights on Cinquecento Florentine idealizations of the "peace" under Lorenzo the Magnificent. See her *Lorenzo il Magnifico: Image and Anxiety, Politics and Finance* (Florence, 1994). In effect, Renaissance Rome arrived at a moment of nostalgic reflection later than did Renaissance Florence, where the crises of the 1490s had acute intellectual repercussions. Such reflection upon and encapsulation of an idealized past was arguably of wider significance throughout Italy in the period 1494-1530, the years of "crisis" and foreign invasions (see, for example, Castiglione's *Courtier*). Lilio Gregorio Giraldi's *Epistola* on the Sack of Rome includes a reflective, nostalgic catalogue of humanists, parallel in important ways to that in Sadoleto's famous letter of 1529 to Angelo Colocci. On Giraldi's *Epistola*, see Rosanna Alhaique Pettinelli, *Tra antico e moderno: Roma nel primo Rinascimento* (Rome, 1991), 51-62.

[18] On the forensic complexities of establishing the accuracy of memories, see the bibliography cited above in chapter 1.

[19] McGinness, *Right Thinking, passim.*

sance Rome as a distinct cultural period ending in 1527, an image that has dominated the historiography from Gregorovius and Pastor to Chastel and Stinger, that persistence is owed substantially to the extravagant claims and the vivid memories—not just to the actual accomplishments or the lived experiences—of the Roman humanists.

PLATES

Vat. Lat. 3436, Fol. 28ʳ. (Reproduced with permission of the Biblioteca Apostolica Vaticana.)

Vat. Lat. 3436, Fol. 39ᵛ. (Reproduced with permission of the Biblioteca Apostolica Vaticana.)

PIETRO ALCIONIO'S ORATIONS ON THE SACK OF ROME, TRANSCRIBED FROM AUTOGRAPH DRAFTS IN BIBLIOTECA APOSTOLICA VATICANA MS VAT. LAT. 3436

BAV MS Vat. Lat. 3436, fols. 23-34:

<23> Petri Alcyonii pro S.P.Q.R. oratio de republica reddenda atque e custodia liberando Clemente Septimo Pontifice Maximo ad Carolum Caesarem Designatum.

Cum primum ad nos allatum est, o Caesar, te graviter doluisse audito eo discriminum genere in quo post inducias cum Lanoio Neapolitani regni praeside factas versabamur, plurimum erecti sumus et animum ab omni propemodum solicitudine abstraximus. Intellectum est enim Clementi Pontifici Maximo, et omnibus qui Romae eramus, te ad ea sancienda quae praefectus tuus cui summam auctoritatem tribuisses in Italia nobiscum transegisset, eam quoque animi significationem adhibere voluisse quae constantiam et singularem fidei tuae laudem testaretur. Sed heu nos in omne tempus miseros! Praefecti tui, cum dissensionibus summisque discordiis conflictati Hispanorum ferociam et Germanorum furores aluissent, Carolum tandem Barbonium impulerunt ut contra Lanoii etiam auctoritatem generis utriusque milites ad sacerdotes delendos, ad Pontificem Maximum opprimendum, ad cives trucidandos, ad tecta inflammanda Romam duceret. Ille autem, qui paternum avitumque ulteriore in Gallia principatum amiserat, novum in Italia regnum animo concipiens omnia confundere ac nefario scelere foedare coepit. E citeriore igitur Gallia cum duabus Hispanorum legionibus movens, in Aemiliam irrupit castraque cum Cimbris et Theutonibus iunxit qui, proxima hieme in Italiam transgressi, in Aemilia consederant. Hanc quidem rerum omnium eversionem tam inopinatam, tam tetram et inhumanam Pontifex veritus, ad eos maximis itineribus Lanoium misit, qui cum iisdem ageret de officii sui ratione grandemque praeterea nomine suo atque etiam tuo pecuniam polliceretur, modo finibus Italiae excederent. Nihil Pontificis auctoritas Borbonium movit, nihil etiam Lanoii preces et **<23v>** precibus adiuncta ipsius voluntatis significatio, quam eandem ac tuam esse praedicabat. Qua in re mirabile et prodigio simile visum est te duces duos in Italia summae auctoritatis habere quorum uterque praesidio tui nominis niteretur, sed alter id ipsum salte<m> specie constantiae et studii pacis confirmaret ac tueretur, alter cupiditate rerum novarum, superbia immanitate et avaritia convelleret ac labefactaret. Pontifex autem quanquam novitate rei commovebatur, tamen non desistebat Borbonium admonere voluntatis tuae, existimationis, etiam fidei quam in induciis paulo ante pactis dedissent quibus nimirum cavebatur salvam omnino futuram Etruriam, salvam Romam, salvam Italiam; sed interim Urbis tectis, civium saluti deorumque immortalium templis ac sacris timens, eam Circi Neroniani in Vaticano partem quae infirmior videbatur celeriter munire et propugnatorum praesidio firmare instituit. Borbonius tamen celeritate incredibili exercitu per Etruriam ducto III nonas Maias in campo Vaticano[1] castra locat atque postridie, quem diem semper funestum et religiosum habebimus, ad munitiones aggressus quae tumultuario opere exstructae erant, eas transcendit atque inter primos ille in Urbem invadens occumbit, fuitque hoc perspicuum voluntatis Dei indicium, ut sceleratus dux eo tempore neglecti numinis spretaeque Pontificis auctoritatis poenas lueret. Non referam hic, o Caesar, ulla patriae funera quorum plane spectator fui, ne initio orationis meae ad eum te luctum vocem quem mox aptiore loco te editurum certo scio, cum illum debere intellegas Romanis quorum imperator es, quemque etiam persaepe alias edidisti cum audires opes reipublicae nostrae imminui idque veritus, ne impares futurae essent ad Turcarum potentiam frangendam et loc<u>pletissimum illorum imperium delendum. Legatus igitur missus a S.P.Q.R. (qualiscunque superstes est) hic adsum, qui te orem **<24>** et per omnia iura quae Christianum principem obstringere possunt obtester, ne patiare miseras reipublicae reliquias dissipari in ipsiusque Pontificis dignitatem amplius illudi. Praefecti enim tui omni duriti<a>[2] atque immanitate teterrimi rapinis templorum, caedibus civium, latrociniis cuiusque ordinis hominum haud contenti, Pontificem quoque ipsum in Mole Aelia inclusum cum XIII primoribus antistitum ad deditionem compulerunt quae ita facta est ut CCCCM aureorum nummorum ille se persoluturum receperit, quorum nonnullam partem cum

---

[1] See Cicero, *Att.* 13.33.4.
[2] *MS*: duritie

accepissent ita reliquam se accepturos affirma<ba>nt³ ut in custodia
ille cum primoribus antistitibus sit quoad arbitratu tuo de illo sta-
tuatur. Ergo et principem Christianum captivum et rempublicam
crudelissimo tuorum praefectorum dominatu devinctam habes.
Utraque plane res auditu tetra et visu foeda ac detestabilis est, et eo
quidem magis quod Pontifex is est qui privatus ad opes tuas in Italia
et Hispania stabiliendas magnum adiumentum aliquando attulit, et
ea est respublica cuius salutem tueri et libertatem augere maiores tui
semper consueverunt. Neque vero tu ingratus erga illum fuisti, aut in
hanc minus illustria ornamenta congessisti quam de maioribus tuis
aliquem congessisse accepimus. Laudem igitur tuorum beneficiorum
non nihil deturpatam et qui vivunt dictitabunt et posteri quoque ag-
noscent, nisi quae perculsa nunc et gravissimis tuorum latrociniis
prostrata iacere sentis sublevaveris et in pristinum statum ita omnia
restitueris ut lenitatem misericordiam fidem et integritatem magni-
tudinemque animi tui semper testentur. Et sane tantam imperii vim
tantamque ornamentorum omnium dignitatem propterea tibi datam
iudicamus ut eorum auctoritate, si quid tetrum impium nefarium et
crudele ab alienis in nos commissum esset, vindicares. Quanto autem
magis hoc ipsum praestare debes in tuorum insania reprimenda, au-
dacia **<24v>** coercenda, crudelitate ulciscenda et rapacitate punien-
da! Literis quidem proditum exstat Romanorum exercituum imperatores crudelissima de filiis etiam victoribus supplicia sumpsisse,
quod iniussu suo cum hostibus pugnassent. Legiones quoque victrices
a populo Romano totae hostibus traditae sunt quod signa contu-
lissent, spreta suorum ducum auctoritate. Rhegium quoque in prae-
sidium missa legio, interfectis per scelus principibus civitatis, urbem
opulenta<m> per decem annos tenuit, at in Forum Romanum
tan<d>em⁴ aliquando scelerati illi milites retracti securi percussi
sunt.⁵ Quid? quod e civibus Romanis non defuerunt qui aliquando
cogitarint de dando C. Caesare Transalpinis populis, quod nulla belli
occasione tam foederatas quam infestas ac feras gentes lacessisset. Et
hi quidem principes duces imperatores erant vel liberis civium suf-
fragiis vel magnis largitionibus creati. At tu imperator iis succedis qui
a Pontificibus Romanis hunc honorem consecuti sunt, nec legitimis
Augustorum ornamentis uti possunt nisi Pontifices quoque nostri ea-

---

³ *MS*: affirmant
⁴ *MS*: tantem
⁵ Cf. Livy, 31.31.6-7, and Orosius, 4.3.3-5, for antecedents.

dem ipsis et detulerint et rata fecerint. Adde religionem, cuius ratio ita mira sancta et pia semper fuit ut, qui captivi apud disparis Deorum cultus homines sunt redimi a nobis oporteat. Sed tu, o Caesar, patieris milites signa tua sequentes sociis tuis imo vero fidei patrocinio et sapientiae tuae credito populo arma intulisse, omneis sacerdotes oppressisse, Pontificem Maximum eundemque socium tuum omnibus contumeliis vexasse, et vexatum novo ac inaudito carceris genere in dies magis atque magis affligere? Omnia quidem in hoc tanto Urbis excidio cunctarumque rerum disperditione repagula iuris pudoris et officii perfracta, omnium bona praedam suam ab illis ductam, nullius rem tutam, nullius domum clausam, nullius vitam septam, nullius pudicitiam munitam contra talium insidiatorum cupiditatem ac teterrimorum paricidarum audaciam vidimus. Primum enim cruento ac funesto pestiferi illius ducis edicto quicunque aut nostri aut exteri generis armatus aut inermis inter Circum Vaticanum Aeliumque <25> Pontem occurrit cesus est. Saevitumque maxime hic et alibi tota Urbe in Hispanos et Germanos tuos, o Caesar, voluerunt, propterea quod diuturna illorum in Urbe commoratione fieri aiebant ut pecunia Pontifici suppeditaret bellumque duceretur. Atque sic crudeliter habiti ii potissimum fuerunt qui in augustissimum et religiosissimum illud D<ivi> Petri fanum confugerunt, existimantes omnino milites tuos placabiliores fore Christianis quam Goti Visgoti Vandali et reliqui eiusmodi barbari non satis Christiani olim Christianis fuerint. Hoc igitur templum ita foedarunt ut nullum genus crudelitatis latrocinii caedis omiserint. Sacerdotes quoque partim ad aras crudelissima morte mactarunt, partim divorum imagines complectentes iugularunt, partim semineces tractos pro templo canibus dilaniandos reliquerunt. Ex acervo dein cadaverum cum Transtiberinam regionem oppugnare instituissent paucorumque nostrorum defensorum virtute repulsi essent, tam magnus armatorum concursus est factus ut facile irruperint et perpetuam ad Septimianam quam portam vocamus stragem ediderint. Supererat Urbis illa pars, ubi nomen reipublicae vigebat et praecipua omnium nostrum sedes, arx regum ac nationum exterarum, lumen omnium gentium domiciliumque imperii et templa sanctissima et caput omnis amplitudinis fuerat, et ad quam nisi pontibus adiri non poterat. Sed fatalis nostrarum miseriarum vis eiusmodi fuit ut pontes superati, propugnacula diruta, munitiones disiectae, arma perrupta, praesidia oppressa, bellica tormenta diffracta et opera omnia natura et arte excitata facile eversa sint. Ex ponte Aurelio, qui nunc Xystius est, prima hostium irruptio fuit tanquam immanium ferarum in armenta irruentium. Hic variae voces variique clamores g<an>nitus lamentationes et ululatus strepitusque varii generis auditi sunt, ut aetas sexus fortuna civium erat patriae occasum cum sua pernicie exspectantium, et ut hostium natio aut cupiditas erat aut arma suppetebant ad pestem et exitium **<25v>** omnibus importandum. Nullus certus legatus, nullus certus dux aderat, nullius certi imperatoris auspiciis res gerebatur: unusquisque libidinem suam ducem habebat ad aras ad templa ad tecta urbis ad moenia subvertenda, ad civium vitam tollendam, ad fortunas diripiendas. Ideo nullus rapinis ante modus fuit quam omnia, et quidem longa felicitate et indulgentia fortunae cumulata, bona penitus ablata sint. Multiplex autem ratio inita est inquirendi in fortunas et diripiendi. Nonnulli enim, truculento militum ore minis verberibus atque etiam morte intentata deterriti, quae possidebant illis tradebant. Alii cum inopiam caussarentur multosque in famulatu haberent, suspicionem iisdem latronibus afferebant mendacii pro tempore conficti. Itaque pueri comprehendebantur exquisitisque tormentis lacerabantur, ut indicarent quo loci bona domini aut occultassent aut asportassent. Utinam hic, o Caesar, ea dicendi facultas suppeteret qua immanitatem rapacitatem et industriam istorum in praedando, non solum in animo tuo sed in oculis etiam conspectuque omnium exponerem, nimirum tantas esse sacerdotum civiumque Romanorum calamitates intel<le>geres quantas foeda aliquis crudelitate ac ferocia tyrannus excogitare posset, tum ut oculos pasceret, tum etiam ut animum exsaturaret.[6] Si igitur pueri abditas res ubi essent aut nescirent aut suspicari non possent, continuo in domini conspectu interficiebantur. Dein mira diligentia viscera et interiores aliae corporis partes explorabantur an illas per guttur demissas continerent, praesertim si dominum auro gemmis pretiosisque lapil<lis> abundare cognovissent. At domini, veriti ne idem crudelitatis genus subire cogerentur, statim et locum ubi sua deposuissent bona monstrabant et necessarios qui idem etiam fecissent prodebant, quibus tamen pro liberalitate **<26>** et gratificandi voluntate illud praemium eaque merces reddebatur ut, devincti <manibus> more servorum ut quadrupedes constricti et nulla tormentorum etiam acerrimorum vi praetermissa, grandem pro incolumitate corporis pecuniam et pollicerentur <et>[7] persolverent. Durum tetrumque ad-

---

[6] Cf. Cicero, *Ver.* 5.65: "supplicio pascere oculos animumque exsaturare."

[7] *Supplevi.*

modum, o Caesar, omnibus erat fortunas amisisse, ornamentis domesticis spoliatos omni pecunia exhaustos esse, mox pecunia etiam
multari ut pristinam recuperarent libertatem. Nulla vero imperandae
pecuniae certa ratio servabatur. Alii enim et quidem tenuis fortunae
homines tormentis cogebantur ad tam magnam pecuniae vim ex-
promendam ut multi locupletissimi vix satis unquam futuri essent ad
eam persolvendam, atque illam quidem si confestim repraesentare
non possent aut occidebantur aut in catenis habebantur aut tetrae
servituti addicebantur quoad eam dinumerarent. Alii quoque, si amicorum beneficentia adiuti se redemissent aut praedonum suorum misericordia, quod ex imperata pecunia aliquid condonatum esset,
liberi vagarentur, iterum capiebantur et tanquam novi captivi habebantur et, quod miserabilius mihi cogitanti videtur, tantae immanitatis tantaeque perfidiae eos non adhuc finem fecisse audio. Itaque
idem Christianus contra leges a tuis etiam maioribus vel conditas vel
ratas factas, o Caesar, bis ter quater decies aliquando capitur ven-
ditur servit verberatur torquetur vexatur excruciatur. Quid loquar de
infantibus qui magna ex parte in cunis vagientes occisi sunt? Qui
autem paulo adultiores erant, ut grandi pecunia a parentibus et quidem cernentibus redimerentur, novo quodam et prope alias insolito
tormenti genere afficiebantur: nam ignescenti adipe eodemque liqua-
to incessebantur et lancinabantur tanquam caro veru transfixa quae
dum torretur ut delicatioris gulae sit commendatur si liquescentem ac
stillantem imbiberit adipem. Nullum autem genus civium, nullius ordinis, nullius sexus, nullius aetatis homines expertes fuerunt latrocinii
fraudis crudelitatis istorum praedonum immaniumque <**26v**> latronum. Etenim maiores et minores Pontifices, atque in his plerique
summo loco nati et sanctitate vitae religionisque interpretatione insignes, eodem loco habiti sunt quo mancipia, quo paricidae, quo
sicarii, quo scelesti, et ab omni humanitatis sensu alieni; in hos eadem tormenta, eadem supplicia, eandem acerbitatem, eandem feritatem exerceri vidimus a qua victor Poenus aut Turca sine controversia abstinuisset. Praecipuum autem quoddam impuritatis genus
quod ad hos ipsos sacerdotes divexandos adhibitum esse constat, dignum est, o Caesar, quod nominatim a me referatur, ut illud pro
sapientia et iustitia, cuius laudem in te enitescere omnes fatemur,
acerbissime vindices. Joannes Copis Leodiensis praesul Anxuris ditis-
simus, cum in praedonem quendam aleae studiosum et pecuniae
egentem forte incidisset, post amissas opes, loco pecuniae ad ludum
persaepe depositus est. Atque ita praesul unus et idem popularisque

tuus, Caesar, non semel captivus sorti plerunque expositus multorum
avaritiam iniquitatem et crudelitatem experiri coactus est. Matronae
etiam illae a quibus reliquae omnis orbis feminae exempla pudicitiae
continentiae gravitatis et morum petebant, ut vivae ac mortuae tantarum virtutum laudem tuerentur, aliae in puteos se abiecerunt aut
in Tiberim praecipitarunt, aliae [ferro] aut[8] venenum hauserunt aut
alia morte voluntaria nefariam turpitudinem depulerunt, quanquam
nonnullae comunem pestem evaserunt cum in domum confugissent
clarissimi et amplissimi viri Pompei Columnae qui, ut ea ratione qua
posset luctibus et funeribus patriae subveniret, in urbem ab exsilio
redierat. Paucae quaedam aliorum Columnarum interventu ex impiis hostium manibus ereptae exsulatum in finitima municipia abie-
runt, ne iterum victoribus ludibrio essent. At sacrae illae virgines
quae veterum instar Vestalium perpetua corporis castimonia et erga
deos pietate in sui admirationem orbem terae converterant, si aetate
affectae erant ad deorum pulvinaria occidebantur, sin autem beneficio aetatis forma praestabant e sacris sedibus evellebantur, e com-
plexu sanctissimarum imaginum abstrahebantur ad incestum ad contumeliam ad maleficium ad poenas ad cruciatum ad carnificinam, ab
iis praesertim Germanis qui Luterum quendam, nostrae religionis
non minus licentiosum quam falsum interpretem, <27> in Germania sequebantur: hic enim omnia communia atque adeo voluptatem
et amoris fructus tralatitios esse censet et, praeter alia detestabilia
hominis consilia, reipublicae instituta quae ad Platonem auctorem
referuntur in magnam Germaniae partem induxit, ne posthac illa
respublica talis esse diceretur ut docti magis eam fingerent quam
nossent. Huius etiam generis Germani omni scelere imbuti, imo potius nullo deorum metu perterriti nullaque nefandae rei conscientia
exanimati nulloque religionis studio commoti, in omnia quae in templis sacerdotes reges Caesares denique ipsi religiosa et sacrosancta
voluerunt impii immanes tetri ac flagitiosi exstitere. Talium igitur
belluarum maleficio in tera iacent inflictae mutilatae et truncatae
Apostolorum statuae aliorumque divorum simulacra, quae talia erant
ut homines cum viderent aut ipsos se videre divos aut divorum effi-
gies non humana manu factas sed caelo delapsas arbitrarentur. Ubique etiam divorum membra pia religione multos annos adservata
calcantur et atteruntur. Pyxides arculae et alia loculorum genera au-

---

[8] After "ferro", the phrase to which it had been attached, "veneno sibi mortem
consciverunt", was deleted.

rea aut argentea in quibus eadem membra condebantur ablata sunt. Mortui etiam Pontifices Maximi et alii sacerdotes magnifice amicti qui in infinita prope altitudine humati erant, effossi sunt ut ornamenta illa detraherentur. Quid hac avaritia turpius? Quid foedius? Quid omnibus suppliciis dignius, Caesar? An tot Principes tot Reges tot etiam Caesares ex ultimis teris in Urbem se contulerunt haec sanctissima templa invisendi, haec Divorum membra venerandi caussa, ut Germani et Hispani quibus tu imperas sua crudelitate nefarioque scelere aliquando vanam illorum religionem fuisse docerent? An tot reges et liberi populi pretiosa veste, vasis aureis, aulaeis magnificentissimis, tensis pulcerrimis et donis aliis infinitis quae ad sacrorum apparatum pertinerent Romana delubra ornarunt ut milites qui perpetuis latrociniis vitam agere consueverant illa diriperent et universam praedam vel in saga et chlamydes, vel in calcaria et equorum ornamenta, vel etiam in vexilla quae sanguine Christianorum madida ferent converterent? An aurum argentum purpuram ebur, plurima vasa Myrrhina, incredibilem tabularum pictarum signorum toreumatum aeris copiam, plurimam stragulam, multam delicatam supellectilem, magnum numerum frumenti congestum putas ut omnia ab istis impor- <27v> tunis latronibus dissiparentur consumerentur et perderentur? An tot aedes propterea vel ab imis fundamentis magnifice exstructas, vel collapsas pulcrius renovatas aspiciebamus ut a militibus, in nomine tuo et specie stipendia tua merendi, comburerentur subverterentur et solo aequarentur? Gens plane dira et humani cruoris sitiens et aedificiorum disturbandorum avida, non solum omnia divina et humana violavit vexavit perturbavit evertit malaque omnia quae pro tempore inferre potuit intulit, sed plane effecit etiam ut deinceps infinita omni in genere suborirentur. Etenim cum templa porticus compita et viae hominibus semiambustis et iugulatis atque etiam equis ac multis iumentis constrata essent, in diesque maior etiam caedes fieret, tanta caeli gravitas et omnino intemperies consecuta est ut arbores sataque omnia propemodum exaruerint, pecudes occiderint, et cives multi, quos hostilis interficiendi satietas servarat, mortui sint. Accessit intoleranda vis aestus, qui ita corpora commovit varieque affecit ut infinita cotidie funera cernantur, quapropter ita animi superstitum efferati sunt, ut non modo lacrimis iustoque comploratu non prosequantur mortuos, sed ne efferant quidem aut sepeliant aut alio modo funeri operam dent. Itaque corpora, adhuc etiam strata eademque exanimata, visuntur in conspectu similem quoque mortem exspectantium mortuique aegrotos, aegroti firmos tum metu tum contagione morbi pestiferoque ardore conficiunt. Pestilentiamne hunc miserabilem rerum omnium occasum an fatalem calamitatem dixerim non satis constitutum habeo. Age vero, quid non atrox immite dirum de annona rerumque omnium penuria dici potest, Caesar, quam vulgata de scelere ist<o>rum⁹ fama peperit? Omnes propemodum e plebe qui caedibus et pestilentiae superfuerant caritate annonae, sterilitate agrorum, inopia frugum enecti tetraque fame confecti sunt. Multi etiam summae nobilitatis cives, cum ad alendam familiam impares se habere facultates cognoscerent, in balineis **<28>** interclusa anima obire satius putarunt quam vivere et filiis alimenta petentibus dare non posse. Qui autem in vasta desertaque Urbe nunc degunt victum petere constat e veterinis ac iumentis, si qua modo reperiuntur, et ex spurcissimis omnis generis animalibus atque etiam ex herbis radicibusque in pa<r>ietibus et in solitudine patentibusque Urbis locis iam enatis. Quod si forte quippiam frumenti aliunde advehitur, id totum non emptores sed raptores invenit illos ipsos immanissimos praedones qui etiam, ut ostendant omnem exsuisse humanitatem, civium nostrorum verbis cum illud petunt quasi convitiis irritati, horribiles et pertimescendos acuunt dentes ut in eos morsibus irruant. Itaque Urbs illa, o Caesar, quae tum propter loci opportunitatem, tum etiam propter civium naturam et institutum advenarum commercio gaudebat, calamitosorum profugio gloriabatur, peregrinorum celebritate florebat et regum splendore illustris et exterarum gentium adventu aliarum omnium facile princeps erat, suo populo caret ac fame premitur, inopia rei frumentariae nullum pristinae dignitatis et pulcritudinis vestigium retinet, rapinis foedata et incendiis deformata, squalore obsita, sordibus inquinata, humano cultu desolata est. Nec enim, o Caesar, illam praedonum et carnificum colluvionem quae nunc superba sua dominatione Urbem vexat unquam homines appellaverim, quandoquidem nihil aliud cogitant quam homines tollere, nomen Romanum funditus delere et plane efficere ut in suo proprioque cruore in dies magis atque magis Roma natare videatur. O homines, naturae et humanitatis hostes! O milites, ipsis feris tetriores rapaciores et humano generi infestiores! Cotidie Roma capitur, cotidie diripitur, cotidie disturbatur, co<ti>die caedibus cumulatur; dies noctisque passim omnia mulierum puerorumque vix spirantium et miseram animam ducentium qui rapiuntur atque

---

⁹ *MS*: istarum (amended from "istorum")

asportantur ploratibus circunsonant; ubique furiales voces nefariis latrociniis teterrimisque caedibus efferatae audiuntur. Pone, Caesar, ante oculos miseram quidem illorum et flebilem speciem, sed ad incitandum animum tuum necessarium: crudelissimum impetum in Urbem amicam et sociam, horribilem in singulas civium domos armatorum irruptionem, cum miseri illi prius vincula verbera <g>ladios secures sentirent quam vocem ullam enunciare possent: miserabilem igitur vastitatem et alte impressa vestigia inspiceres novae ac inauditae feritatis, inhumanae superbiae, foedissimae libidinis, teterrimae ferocitatis ad publica et privata monimenta demolienda et funesti cuiusdam deorum et hominum contemptus. Deforme item spectaculum semirutae et cotidie fumantis Urbis doleres, simulque pro eo Dei cultu et omni religionis studio quod debes locis illis sanctissimis ubi sanctissimae quoque religionis decus auctum est ad mortalium omnium pietatem et innocentiam lugeres, quod omnium seculorum posteritas intellectura esset qui <28v> in fide ac potestate tua sunt ausos fuisse statum omnium rerum ita calamitosum ita foedum ita luctuosum reddere. Itaque reges dynastae liberi populi omnis terae orbis exspectat, o Caesar, ut gravissimo istorum supplicio humanum genus edoceas ea sancta credere quae ab illis polluta et contaminata sunt. Clamat etiam ut a violatoribus divini humanique iuris gravia piacula exigas simulque nostras iniurias ulciscare, propterea quod eas alius omnino ulcisci non potest, nec multis de caussis, tum hac potissimum debet: nam cum Pontifex suis sociorumque armis Galliae citerioris florentissimas urbes cepisset atque regni Neapolitani multo maximam partem in ditionem suam redegisset, communis concordiae et pacis caussa arma deposuit et omnes quas Neapolitano in regno obtinebat urbes reddidit. Nonne igitur tua omnibus videri debeat iusta tantorum scelerum ultio, cum illa in amicum et socium tuum edita sint? Nonne iustitiae et fidei tuae gloriam confirmari eo in loco maxime tibi optabile sit, ubi contra iustitiam et fidem omnia ita foede commissa sunt ut his foedius nihil unquam Sol viderit? Nonne Caroli nomen, Italiae semper faustum, Romae autem salutare, tale quoque tuum fuisse confestim probabis? Nonne laudem integritatis sapientiae pietatis et religionis Austr<i>ae familiae domesticam augebis? Nonne decus gravitatis pudoris abstinentiae et aliarum virtutum quarum pleraque documenta iam dedisti propagabis? Nonne beneficium denique illud Clementis insigne medio belli ardore in te collatum remunerabere? Quaeris hoc beneficii genus quale sit, quo vel maxime hostis tuorum praefectorum Clemens te ornatum voluerit, imperium tibi conservasse cum illud facile abrogare potuisset, nulloque exsecrationum genere te insectatum esse, quod quidem ut faceret non solum iustam verum etiam necessariam propemodum habebat caussam, idque superiorum Pontificum exemplo qui arma cum Caesa<r>ibus contulerunt? Omnes enim hi fere **<29>** legiones exercitus classes socios reges duces imperatores omnemque armorum apparatum leviorem infirmioremque semper putarunt ad hostium suorum opes labefactandas abrogato imperio, tum etiam interdictis et exsecrationibus, quas pro iure sacerdotii et rerum humanarum fastigio quod tenebant infligere poterant. Atque nullus unquam, o Caesar, fuit qui, cum hoc armorum genere petitus esset, non ad extremum maiora tropaea, clariora victoriae insignia, illustriores triumphos de se Pontificibus dederit, quam si vi et armis victus in potestatem hostis redactus esset. Diversum Clementis Pontificis iudicium fuit in dissensione sua tecum et cum tuis ducibus, suscepto bello. Nec enim sua auctoritate unquam factum voluit ut exercitus in Hispania contra te a Gallis ducerentur, nec a Britanis classes ad maritimam Germaniae oram depopulandam mitterentur, nec Oceanum Belgicum et Germanicum tuis infestum redderent, nec ex Icio armati Belgarum fines ingressi populos infirme animatos et novarum rerum exspectatione suspensos ad defectionem solicitarent. Arma tantummodo praefectis tuis in [in] Gallia citeriore intulit ut servile iugum e Transpadanarum civitatum cervicibus deiiceret quod illi ipsi praefecti, tanquam crudelissimi et importunissimi tyranni, imposuerant. Quae autem in regno Neapolitano mota sunt arma eo spectare videbantur ut Lanoium vel ad pacem componendam vel ad inducias paciscendas compellerent. Bellum confectum Pontifex dicebat pactis induciis, arma utrinque posita credebat quia ipse posuerat, cum tamen belli fluctus in pestem capitis sui, in exitium urbis, in perniciem bonorum omnium senserit redundare. Nam dux latronum Borbonius, tuo nomine adhuc armatus, illum quietum inermem nihilque tua vel tuorum arma amplius extimescentem oppressit. At nimirum tanta calamitatum moles in nos minime decubuisset si hostili animo in te fuisset, si imperii tui dedititios a te abalienasset, si reges Christianos in te concitasset, si liberos populos et provincias armasset, si summo honore te spoliasset, si denique publice te devovisset **<29v>** dirisque detestationibus exsecratum e Christianorum communione exterminasset. Haec quidem omnia pro amplitudine sua maximoque honore praestare potuisset si, ut commemoravi, talis in te fuisset qualem miserrimus luctuosissimusque rei eventus docuit quemvis alium Pontificem futurum fuisse. Ergo beneficium acceptum te agnoscere et colere oportet ut gratus omnique ope divina et humana dignus videare. Optatissimum enim omnibus erit pulcerrimumque et gloriosissimum tibi, primum e labe ignominiaque Germanos vindicare qui ante, quanquam genere a nobis disiuncti erant, animo tamen et voluntate non dissidebant? At nunc genere animo et voluntate non modo a nobis disiuncti, verum etiam ereptores nostrarum fortunarum, expugnatores pudicitiae, hostes sacrorum et paricidae bonorum omnium fuerunt. Quanta cum omnium nostrum voluptate, o Caesar, superioribus annis audivimus te sanxisse ut Germania sui similis esset, hoc est ut eam in interpretanda Christi religione sententiam sequeretur quam Romae maiores nostri et illorum in Germania probassent! Providisti enim quantum auctoritate et consilio tuo fieri poterat, ne mali contagio quod a furcifero illo Lutero ortum habebat latius serperet atque per alias imperii tui provincias pervaderet, simulque cavisti ut provincia nobilissima quae tuo ortu ac educatione gloriatur fide et observantia erga te esset singulari mandataque tua omni in genere faceret imperioque etiam tuo studiosius quam aliorum Caesarum temporibus facere solitam accepimus pareret. Et eo quidem magis quod nullum verum officii studium nullaque ad obsequium propensio et coniunctio esse potest si religionis intercedat disiunctio. Verum tantum abfuit ut quae sapientissime a te decreta sunt quicquam nobis profuerint, ut ipsi maxime Germani incredibili rabie signa infesta in nos intulerint et, cum amicitia societateque tecum iungi et religionis vinculis adstringi diceremus, ipsi responderint se in bello Christi religionem nullam agnoscere et bona tua se direpturos, crudelitatem quoque in te ipsum, <o> Caesar, adhibituros **<30>** fuisse, si in urbe adesses, et eo quidem magis quod nullo multos iam menses stipendio a te affecti essent. Propterea affirmabant id sibi licere quod semper licuisset praedonibus sicariis paricidis carnificibus perditissimisque latronibus. Vides, o Caesar, perniciosam audaciam, praecipitem furorem, turpissimam rapacitatem, impurissimos mores eius gentis quam gloriae tuae studiosam, honoris cupidam semper te habere existimasti, quamque nobiscum et praeclarissimis vitae officiis et omni religionis parte coniunctam reddere studuisti. Non dissimilis perversitas Hispanorum et atrocitas fuit, si quis mores et verba observasset, atque eo magis in illos animadvertendum iudicabis quod nihil tale ab iisdem exspectabamus. Horum enim cum Ferdinandus, avus tuus maternus, diu rex fuerit, qui multis erga rempublicam piorum officiorum gradibus ad

Religiosi nomen ascenderat, semper etiam pro Christianae religionis dignitate tuenda illos in armis habuit. Itaque magnam Africae partem illorum opera suo imperio adiecit, insulas multas Turcis ademit, fines quoque Hispaniae non solum adversus Gallos tutatus est, verum etiam finitimas plerasque urbes in potestatem suam redegit. Omnino nullius populi copiae magis expeditae nulliusque principis auxilia magis parata fuerunt ad bella quae Alexander, Iulius et Leo administrarunt quam illius sapientissimi regis. Sed fortissimi hi milites ad id reservati, ad id unum delecti videri possunt ut eos occiderent qui socii bellorum gerendorum aliquando fuissent, quique pro communi salute ac dignitate tuenda infinita pericula subiissent. Imo potius ad id comparati esse voluerunt, ut spolia ex iis detraherent qui eos veste commeatu pecunia semper iuvissent, tecta etiam illorum subverterent diuturno quorum hospitio usi essent, denique sanguinem eorum haurirent qui ipsos egestate perditos aluissent, nudos fovissent, abiectos extulissent, inglorios ornassent aeternaque bellicae virtutis memoria insignes reddidisse<n>t. **<30v>** Hi praecipui fuerunt, Caesar, duces nostrarum rapinarum, hi milites nefarii belli, hi auctores casus nostri tam funesti, tam gravis, tam repentini, tam miserabilis. Hi etiam summam operam navarunt ut Urbs, antiquissimum religionis domicilium tutissimumque illud omnium gentium profugium, tolleretur et corrueret martiique illi Romanorum sp<i>ritus et animi nec constarent nec vigerent. Qua quidem in re non intellegere visi sunt facilius (ut ita dicam) solem e mundo excidere posse quam mortales Roma carere et rempublicam nostram perpetuam ibi sedem non habere ubi fundamenta iacta sunt sanguine divorum quos martyras vocant compacta, et perampla religionis moles sanctitate innocentia virtute pietate Christianorum ex cunctis orbis terae partibus confluentium superstructa est. Quid? quod ut aeternum statum haec obtineant incredibiles iam omnium regum et populorum apparatus fiunt omniumque bonorum conatus eo spectant ut tanquam e materia semicinefacta redivivus ignis effulgeat qui novo quasi lumine omnia illustret. Siquidem multorum literis, fama denique ipsa ad te allatum esse arbitror, Caesar, Venetos maximam ornasse ac instruxisse classem qua Ionium et omne Superum infestum reddant et regni Neapolitani urbes quas superiore bello amiserant recuperent Apuliamque et Calabriam vastent. Mari Infero Auria non minus Gallicae Venetaeque classi imperat quam toti mari quod inter Hispaniam et Italiam profunditur, atque ideo sic difficilis tuorum navigatio est ut nemo tanto periculo se obiicere audeat. Praetereo illa

quae praetermittenda non sunt, reges Galliae et Britaniae tera mar-
ique omnia quae ad bello gravissimo te implicandum pertinent moliri. Ambo enim infinitam auri vim omnemque suam regiam gazam
effundere statuerunt in hoc bellum quod sacrum appellant, quia templorum sacrilegia vindicanda et sacerdotum trucidationes[10] etiam
tuorum trucidatione ac sanguine expiand<a>e[11] sunt. Maximas
quoque copias omni ex parte comparant ut Pontificem in libertatem
vindicent, carcere extrahant et honestis, ut ita dicam, vinculis sol-
vant. Atque etiam in **<31>** id potissimum incumbunt, ut importuna
illa monstra adhuc etiam per urbem divagantia totumque Latium
debacchantia universa opprimantur tollantur conficiantur et delean-
tur. Et eo quidem magis quod compertum habent satius esse sacerdotes inter feras aetatem agere quam in illa tanta immanitate versari.
Bestiae enim pastae feritatem deponunt, rapiendi vim remittunt,
alieno abstinent, ferinos illos spiritus comprimunt, placidae et quietae
degunt; denique interdum se bestias esse obliviscuntur. Pestes illae ac
furiae, quanquam epulis ac tempestivis conviviis saginatae, tamen
semper esuriunt, semper in alienas fortunas invadunt, semper commoda aliorum oppugnant et saluti insidiantur; nunquam insitam
omnia perturbandi, omnes occidendi cupiditatem abiiciunt; ad extremum semper fraudulento, semper maximo furore ac scelere ad
nefarium latrocinium inflammatos se praestant. Fac igitur hoc
beneficium miserias tantas levandi, tum etiam conservandi Pontificis
et reddendae reipublicae tuum potius sit quam aliorum, o Caesar; fac
ut sanctitas et religio quam praetefers suum decus nanciscatur ex
laude huius sanctissimi ac religiosissimi facti. Quid enim sanctius et
religiosius hac re unquam existimabitur? Quid divinius illustrius humano denique generi commodius praestare poteris, quam afflictam
eversam et perditam rempublicam sublevare, in pristinoque statu ad
commune mortalium beneficium collocare? Fuit enim his auspiciis
nostra constituta respublica ut munera illius unusquisque Christianus
obire posset, nullaque ratio nationis generis aut ullius rei haberetur
nisi virtutis, cuius omnino qui compos esset eiusdem reipublicae particeps, eiusdem temperator, eiusdem quoque princeps esse posset.
Quam ob rem ut amissa illius dignitas recipiatur tamque honesta
praeclara et laudabilia instituta perpetua conserventur, nemo Christiani generis futurus est qui libentissime pecuniam arma equos classes

---

[10] *MS*: illegible letters (possibly cancelled) follow "trucidationes".
[11] *MS*: expiande

omne genus opis et praesidii non conferat. Haec ideo etiam com-
memorare operae pretium duxi, ut ad hanc memorabilem pulcer-
rimamque **<31v>** gloriam excitem restituendae libertatis cum omnibus reipublicae ornamentis Pontifici, si non hominis at saltem
personae caussa. Pontifices enim Maximi, ut homines, possunt errare
decipi falli et omnino haud secus offendere quam hominum conditio
postulat; ut personam Christi sustinent, nihil plane est quod a nobis
non debeatur, quandoquidem in terris nihil illis est admirabilius, nihil augustius, nihil sanctius, nihil divinius, nihil etiam omni religione
munitius. Quin etiam suorum erratorum si qua committunt vindicem
duntaxat habent Deum, non homines, cum in Pontificibus quiddam
semper insit maius homine. Propterea suae caussae iudicem et cog-
nitorem, non qui minor se ipsis est sed qui maior, et habere et de-
poscere debent. Veteres igitur Pontifices sibi Caesares adsciverunt,
quo tanti sui numinis tantaeque maiestatis non modo propugnatores
essent, verum etiam advocati et adstipulatores. Quicumque autem
Caesares illis adfuerunt atque sacerdotum caussam complexi sunt
primum quid officii sui ratio exigeret praestiterunt, mox hominibus
gratos se senserunt, postremo deos etiam ipsos propicios habuerunt.
Nullus autem post Caesarum memoriam magis hoc praestare debet
quam tu, quia nullus etiam maiora Deo beneficia debet. Vix enim
xiix annos natus regnum Neapolitanum Siciliam Sardiniam His-
pania<m> iure haereditario obtinuisti. Absens Caesar es designatus
idque praeteritis competitoribus tam multis tam gratiosis tam po-
tentibus, quem honorem etiam si tu maxime optare videbare, tamen
vixdum sperare audebas. Victoriae complures eaeque incredibiles tibi
contigerunt, tum quod maximae tum etiam quod incruentae et sine
tuorum luctu fuerint. Legati quoque tui nunquam cum hostibus tuis
signa contulerunt quin illos vicerint, victos fuderint, fusos et pro-
fligatos castris exsuerint.[13] Regem Galliae, tuum hostem et hostilis
animi haeredem **<32>** quem semper illius maiores contra maiores
tuos habuerunt, acie victum ad pedesque stratum habuisti. Demum
tot victorias et triumpos reportasti quot bella gessisti. Verum hae
victoriae, hi triumphi (dant animum ad libere loquendum ultimae
miseriae) sanguine Christianorum parti, Christianis etiam quantum
grati aliquando videri poterunt tibi aestimandum reliquerim. Quod si
foeditatem avaritiam et immanitatem illorum prodigiorum compres-

---

[12] e.g., Livy 5.19.8, 3.68.13, 2.31.1, 3.67.5, 41.12.6, 39.21.3, 37.52.4, 32.6.7,
8.33.19, 40.48.7.

seris et viceris, illa nimirum victoria tibi aeterna, nomini tuo gloriosa, omnibus iucunda, omnibus probata, omnibus celeberrima fuerit. Addo etiam illud, Deum hoc tam felici tamque admirabili rerum eventu qualem commemoravi periculum facere voluisse tuae lenitatis grataeque voluntatis et beneficae naturae. Omnium autem eiusmodi virtutum argumenta dabis maxima si furias illas et faces ex Urbis possessione detraxeris, si horribilem armorum fremitum quo omne Latium commotum est dispuleris, si Pontificem liberaveris, si rempublicam reddideris. Neque vero exitiosae illae pestes senserunt, cum bellum inexpiabile nobiscum susceperunt, quo scelere se devinxerint;[13] nunquam nostrae excisionis inflammationis eversionis depopulationis vastitatis te vindicem aut ultorem timuerunt; efferatum suum furorem alere se posse diuturna licentia ac impunitate iudicarunt. Hac igitur ipsa re quam a te, o Caesar, petimus te docere par est illos multum et opinione sua falsos, et te verum populi Romani esse imperatorem qui illum armorum tempestate oppressum excitaveris levaveris extuleris. Quanquam autem idem populus his tam infinitis malis nunc obrutus quo tempore sit omnino emersurus non satis intellegere videatur, tamen Caesaris nomen cum Pontificio iunctum ita illius memoriae insidet ac in medullis haeret ut magnopere susten<ea>tur,[14] et ad celebritatem famae utriusque plausus clamores testimonia indicia sui amoris eximiaeque observantiae det. Utriusque nomen mortalibus perpetuum, orbi terae faustum et for- **<32v>** tunatum, in caelo illustre et felix augurantur, utriusque etiam auspiciis veterem splendorem amissamque maiestatem se recuperaturum sperat. Quantum postremo dignitatis nomini utriusque affertur, tantum gloriae aeternaeque laudi suae accedere sentit. Quid? quod laetitiam tuam privatam nonnihil etiam ad se pertinere existimat, idque hoc in primis tempore quo filio es auctus. Etenim, o Caesar, ad rei tam iucundae tamque optatae nuncium nemo nostrum fuit quin testatus sit salvam esse Germaniae dignitatem, felicem regum Hispaniae successionem, potentissimum populum Romanum cuius imperatori patri imperator filius succederet, atque etiam crediderit deos immortaleis incredibilem tibi potestatem et fortunam dedisse qua novum beneficium nova etiam remuneratione illustrares, quae quidem singularem animi tui magnitudinem, summam boni-

---

[13] Cicero, *Post reditum (De haruspicum responsis)*, 2.4: "cum his ... paene huius imperii pestibus bellum mihi inexpiabile dico esse susceptum."

[14] *MS*: sustentur

tatem et perpetuam tuae virtutis laudem ad infinitam omnium seculorum posteritatem propagare posset. Quae cum ita sint, o Caesar,
tuum iam animum revoca ad miserias illius Populi contemplandas et
levandas, pro quo armatus in aciem contra hostes illius descendere
debes, nedum acrem te vindicem ostendere illius carnificinae et bonorum direptionis, tectorum excisionis praediorumque depopulationis. A templis quoque ac delubr<i>s pestiferam illam et nefariam
sacerdotum necandorum atrocitatem depelle. Repraesenta maiestatem tui populi, salutem Italiae, Pontificis Maximi libertatem sempi-
terna turpitudine illorum insidiatorum et carnificum qui, non solum
intemperantia et scelere, sed etiam consuetudine et studio in omni
flagitio stupro ac caede versantur. Poenas ab excursoribus illis, tam
diris et spurcis hominibus, omnino expete quibus nostrorum mor-
tuorum manes expies; nostras etiam calamitates funestas iisdem
effice. Crede, o Caesar, crede optimum et sanctissimum illum Carolum qui primus ab Leone Tertio Pontifice Maximo Caesar appellatus est, et veteres tuos Germanos, tanta fortitudine tanta religione
tanta pietate homines quanta omnes norunt, tecum ita locuturos
fuisse si sepultae illorum reliquiae sensus humanos recipere et huiusmodi rerum intellegentia uti possent: "Ideo, o Caesar, Langobardis et
aliis Pontificum hostibus terror, ideo spes subsidiumque Christianorum fuimus ut nulla **<33>** importuna prodigia sacerdotes violarent,
nemo item esset quem egestas, aeris alieni magnitudo, levitas impro-
bitas crudelitas ulli duci latronum constrictum addiceret. Afflictam et
oppressam Christi rempublicam cuius princeps in terris vicarius illius
est in veterem dignitatem suumque decus semper vindicavimus. Signa nostra victricesque aquilas ad Euphratem, ad Tigrin, ad Nilum
ipsumque Oceanum intulimus. Romanosque imperatores nos esse
probavimus, non solum tam illustribus faustisque signis, verum etiam
victoriis triumphis tropaeis, atque adeo omnibus praeclarae virtutis
insignibus Christi nomen gentibus iis quibus invisum erat ut salutare
agnoscerent perfecimus. Illius numen propicium bonis omnibus esse
ostendimus, illius religionem ut veram unicam piam sanctissimam
Transmarinos recipere coëgimus, in Italia quietae gentes nostrorum
armorum beneficio quae per provincias vagabantur fuerunt. Propterea stupor et amentia quaedam ac oblivio bonorum morum et ex-
quisitarum literarum quae hominum animis irrepserat excussa est.
Inde multa eluxerunt quae vitam iuvare potuerint: salubria instituta,
templorum instaurationes, pietatis exempla, ingenuarum artium studia, liberalium officiorum cognitio ad illaque obeunda propensio.

Tantorum quidem meritorum magnitudo tibi, o Caesar, in salute Pontificis augenda est nec permittendum ut in illius exitio occidat, immortalitati tantarum laudum consulendum, gentilitia tantarum virtutum gloria magis atque magis illustranda. Meminimus enim, meminimus, cum Augustorum ornamenta a Pontificibus accepimus, nos pollicitos diligentem eorum ipsorum advocationem perpetuumque reipublicae patrocinium. Talis quoque tu esse debes, quanquam nondum Augustus appellatus, ut dignus ea appellatione iudicere." His omnino verbis tecum ageret divus ille Carolus, et reliqui maiores tui tantis beneficiis a Pontificibus ornati a te deprecarentur hominem, qui suffectus esset iis qui custodes salutis suae, **\<33v\>** fautores honoris fuissent. Auctoritate etiam contenderent, gratia eniterentur, precibus quoque si opus esset obtestarentur, lacrimis et misericordia permoverent animum tuum ut salvum Pontificem, ornatum omnium antistitum ordinem, florentem rempublicam velles, pestiferosque illos praedones qui ignibus et ferro vastitatem Urbi intulerunt feris discerpendos obiiceres, fortunam miseram et luctuosissimam bonorum omnium qui Urbem communem patriam iudicant respiceres, fontem unde incredibiles redundant dolores in sacerdotes exhaurires. Haec quidem omnia, o Caesar, a te tum ipsa caussa impetrare debet, tum est tui animi atque virtutis declarare tibi, cum me audis, ante oculos propositum esse primum Lanoium regni Neapolitani Praesidem inducias nomine tuo cum Pontifice paciscentem, concordiam et pacem a nobis petentem eundemque praesidem festum ludorum diem celeberrimum et sanctissimum Romae nobiscum agentem. Quo tempore ipse Lanoius, exercitus tui imperator, et caeteri duces copias omneis tuas nihil contra nos molituras esse spoponderunt receperunt et polliciti sunt, cum tamen non multo post ab ipso Borbonio, duce item tuo, perculsi oppressi et eversi simus. Dein ob oculos etiam tuos obversentur omnes reges, omnes populi promissa a te repetentes, fidem tuam exigentes, virtutem innocentiam probitatem et integritatem tuam implorantes. Tum etiam illud cogita: sic te Caesarem designatum ut a Pontifice libero, non captivo, Augustus appelleris. Nec vero tu alium Pontificem auctorem tantae tuae felicitatis exspectare debes quam hunc qui in fide ac potestate tua est, ne id tibi eveniat quod avo tuo paterno evenisse doluimus qui, cum modo hunc modo illum Pontificem suspectum haberet, summum Imperii honorem a nullo Pontifice sibi ratum factum habuit. Accedat etiam illud, ut hodie decernas concordiam nostram tecum fuisse pactionem induciarum non legem servitutis, atque etiam amicitiam et societatem quam reges ac dynastae tuis cum praefectis iungunt non calamitati sed ornamento illis <34> futuram. Postremo illud fixum in animo tuo teneto: in hac ipsa caussa te ostensurum auxilia classes exercitus, arma omnis generis tua quae toties ad communem omnium Christianorum dignitatem defendendam nobis pollicitus es ita parata esse ut bellum geratur pro conservanda religione, principe religionis conservato, non oppresso et libertate omnique dignitate privato, a qua certe re tantum ipse, Caesar, abhorrere debes quantum virtuti fidei sapientiae humanitati et clementiae tuae convenit et populo Romano atque adeo Christianis omnibus, quorum imperator es, expedit. DIXI.

BAV MS Vat. Lat. 3436, fols. 35-40:

<35> Inter maximos dolores quos in huius Urbis disturbatione miserabilique tua fortuna capio, ille non mediocris est, o Clemens, quod complures ex hostili Caesarianorum exercitu cerno, qui tam insigni temeritate ac impudentia sunt ut ad conspectum tuum cotidie se conferre audeant, tum beneficia impetrare et commoda denique omnia a te sperare quae vel socii a sociis vel milites a suo imperatore sperare solent, cum tamen ii praecipue sint qui sacris initiati religionis dignitatem convellerint et ad te sacrorum principem opprimendum armati Urbem invaserint. Atque ex illorum numero duo isti barbari quos vides adsunt, sacerdotes domestici Barbonii Caesarianorum latronum ducis, qui a te petunt ut integra tua gratia Barbonii cadaver in Iäcobi aede situm effodiant Mediolanumque transferant. Neque vero primum intellegere visi sunt quam magnum flagitium commiserint, cum homini pila ex aeneo tormento displosa percusso adsederint atque non multo post mortuum in tuum publicae domus sacellum intulerint et mox ad Iäcobi sepelierint, cum impius sceleratusque dux omni humano officio indignus esset. Atque ibi omnino relinquendus videretur ubi conciderat, ut ab avibus et nocturnis canibus discerperetur teraeque ea pars quae cadentem exceperat sepienda esset, tanquam vicus aut campus aliquis sceleratus et plane eiusmodi locus ut ne perpetua quidem expiatione pristinae naturae restitui posse videretur. Sed cum tanta illius auctoritas apud sui simileis latrones esset ut vivus, quae praecipiti audacia concupisceret, facile obtineret, neminem mirari oportet si semineci quoque et extincto ea omnia officia sui praestanda ille senserit quae piis et optimis viris deberentur. Accedebat etiam crudelis militum qui operam illi in bello navarant importunitas. Hi enim adhuc armati et praeda ac victoria feroces, tan-

tum terroris multis nostri ordinis hominibus incutiebant ut nihil paulo liberius vel agere **<35v>** vel dicere auderent, id quod nunc ipse
etiam fecissem, nisi arrogantissimis istorum sacerdotum postulatis
provocatus tandem aliquando statuissem omne vitae periculum ne-
glegere ut nostri ordinis auctoritatem, sacrorum cultum, religionis
decus et ipsius Dei numen defenderem. Principio igitur censeo, o
Clemens, ut ius tuum et simul nostrum persequare, hoc est ut nulla
ratione voluntati istorum sacrificulorum respondeas; imo vero quam
primum iubeas eo advolandum ubi Barbonii cadaver situm est ut
illud quidem effodiatur, non ut Mediolanum transvehatur, id quod
isti petunt, sed per Urbem unco impacto tractum in Tiberim proiiciatur. Hic enim fluvius aptior est ad recipiendum tantis vitiis conta-
minatum hominem quandoquidem, etsi humano cruore magnopere
est infectus, tamen cum perenni cursu deferatur tanta<m> foeditatem amittere potest; verum Mediolanensis tera, si sacra fuerit, profana reddetur recepto omnium sacrorum hoste; sin profana, nec
mundi pars habebitur nec elementi nomine amplius indicabitur.
Enimvero constat ad salutem civium et incolumitatem urbium vitamque hominum et beatam et quietam a sacrosanctis Pontificibus conditas esse leges. Nulla<m> autem ad id ipsum aptiorem esse putarunt quam eam quae timorem iniicit ablatae sepulturae et iustarum
exequiarum. Cum enim homo unus animalium omnium rerum prae-
sentium sensum cum futurarum spe ac providentia connectat, non
potest de ea re non magnopere esse solicitus quae vitam recte aut
turpiter actam testificari possit. Tota autem huiusce rei vis sepulturae
honore aut turpitudine continetur, cuius quidem sepulcri sanctitas tanta est ut ipsum etiam locum in quo habetur sanctum quoque
efficiat, nec ulla vi moveri aut auferi possit atque, uti cetera
extingu<an>tur, sic sepulcra fiunt sanctiora vetustate. Itaque pru-
dentissimi illi Caesares, quorum multa exstant ad salutem mortalium
tum sapienter dicta tum recte excogitata, in primis sanxerunt licere
alio transferri cadaver ex auctoritate praesidis provinciae, si vis
fluminis reliquias detegeret aut si alia iusta et necessaria esset caussa.
Auctoritatem igitur transferendi cadaveris in praeside esse voluerunt,
quoniam si sepultura affectus **<36>**[1] esset mortuus idque praesidis

---

[1] In top margin, not incorporated into text: "nemo fuit dignior, qui e rege, et ex
illo rege nasceret<ur>. Lex a Tyranno constituta, et in Tyrannidos <mi>nisterint"
also in top margin: "educat exercitum citra Rubiconem tetra et pestifera belua <..>
teria"

imprudentia aut gratia, ius etiam penes eundem esset, mutata sententia, illius eruendi et operimento terae, quasi matris, quo obducebatur
nudandi. Quid? Quod, Clemens, non solum te inscio verum etiam
invito in possessionem tuam latronis illius corpus illatum est. At constat certiore etiam iustioreque caussa corpus tale effodi debere, cum
locus ille religiosus adhuc factus non sit, quippe qui ex voluntate
domini tantummodo religione obligari queat. Dicent omnino nunc
(quod alias quoque dicere audivi) Borbonium numquam contendisse
aut elaborasse ut vastitas tanta Urbis consequeretur, nec ut sacerdotes tam nefarie affligerentur, et ipse, Clemens, tam impie ac miserabiliter opprimerere, ideo pacis conditiones tulisse. Praeclara defensio facinoris Borbonii! Neque rectum neque fas est credere, o
Clemens, illum sacrorum hostem et religionum omnium praedonem,
transgressum Appeninum cum tanta latronum multitudine, aliud
quaesisse nisi id quod evenit, hoc est extremum reipublicae fatum
atque etiam ut cum omnibus fortunis crudelissimo hosti esses praedae. Quae autem latae sunt pacis conditiones propterea latae videri
possunt, ut, interposita in consultando mora, tuis minus rebus consuleres; tum etiam ut, aliqua primum lenitatis specie quaesita, nihil
tam atrox et crudele esset quod ad internicionem nostram non aggrederetur—non ut salus urbis integra permaneret ac dignitas tua
inviolata constaret—et eo quidem magis, quod iam sentiebat exercitum tuum sui exercitus extremum agmen carpere, itaque non multo post affuturum. Nonne igitur spe praesentis pacis perpetuam pacem te amittere volebat? Nonne specie concordiae immortalium
discordiarum semina iacere studebat? Cur, si pacem optabat, tuos de
pace legatos cum ultra Appeninum erat tam contumaciter repudia-
vit? Cur delatam pecuniam in stipendium non tuorum militum sed
suorum, quod vix credibile videatur, contempsit? Cur ad Lanoii preces surdum, ad auctoritatem tuam et voluntatem barbarum et super-
bum se praebuit? Dux nimirum ille semper hoc quaesivit, ut quemadmodum ipse patria <36v> careret et Galliam diuturna armorum tempestate pressisset, ita tu, o Clemens, patria libertate atque
adeo vita careres; tum Urbem caperet, captam diriperet, direptam
excideret universamque Italiam perniciosissimo et luctuosissimo bello
everteret. Horum quidem delictorum conscientia cuiusvis animum
perculisset praeter Barbonii, qui sic usu latrocinandi obcalluerat ut
parem audaciam et pertinaciam ad omne nefandum scelus molien-
dum afferre soleret. Talis autem vobis, o detestabiles sacerdotes, sepulturae honore afficiendus videtur in ullo Italiae templo, qui,

pen<e> exercitu ex omni genere barbarorum conflato, Italiae atque
adeo huius religiosissimae Urbis templa sacrilegiis violavit, caedibus
foedavit et maximis ruinis deformavit? In Varensi quidem conventu
decretum legimus e templis eiiciendos qui pias in delubra erogationes
aut intervertunt aut intercipiunt. De vivis id genus sceleris obeuntibus
intellegendum sapientissimus quisque arbitratur, in quibus sane adhuc spiritus viget, voluntas etiam expiandi animi et poenitentiae
agendae esse potest. At Borbonius cum viveret non solum auctor fuit
ut eiusmodi erogationes non fierent, sed etiam factas compilavit nec
moriens ullum ea de re animi soliciti signum dedit. Et tu, o Clemens,
patieris illum extinctum in aedem ullam recipi, qui tam exsecrabili
feritate omnem sacrorum honorem convellerit et de gradu suo vel
ipsam sanctissimam religionem deiecerit? At quae est caussa cur
maiores nostri tanta asperitate et severitate sibi agendum statuerint in
eos qui pias sanctasque erogationes interciperent? Nempe quod tanquam interfectores pauperum ac tenuiorum iudicarentur. Pauperes
enim et calamitosos qui contemnit, si Christianus est, et contemnen-
dus et pro nihilo putandus videtur; quod si **<37>** interfector illorum
et percussor est, carnificem homini vivo adhibere oportet ad facinus
vindicandum, in occisum vero et a carnifice necatum omnino sunt
canes incitandi qui corpus lacerent, viscera distrahant et omneis partes crudelissime discerpant. Utere igitur beneficio daeorum immortalium, o Clemens, qui, etsi rebus omnibus eversis captivus afflictaque fortuna es, tamen integram tibi potestatem adhuc relictam
volunt de rebus sacris statuendi, idque iure sacerdotii quo praeditus
agnosceris. Utere etiam legibus quas superiores Pontifices tulerunt et,
in publicis Christianorum conventibus confirmatas, servandas omnino edixerunt. His nimirum cavetur neminem etiam pie mortuum
condendum intra templum, sed vel in atrio vel in porticu vel in exe-
dra; in summa autem templi parte ad aram maximam nullum omnino locum qui ad sepeliendum pateat relinquendum, ne augustus ille
rei divinae quae ibi fieri solet honos contaminetur et sacrorum religio
polluatur. O audaciam non ferendam! O temeritatem singularem!
Vos, impuri sacrificuli, Borbonium collocastis ad ipsam Iácobi principem aram quam omni ratione subversam voluit, ad loculos ubi
crustulum illud sacrosanctum adservatur, in quo Christus inest, quod
non semel in teram deiectum et calcatum vidimus ad conspectum
divorum quorum cerimonias sacra et religionem tanta turpitudine
violavit. Loricam etiam galeam ocreas prope statuistis ut clarior testa-
tiorque illius spurcissimae beluae ferocia esset, qua fretus amicum

Pontificem perculerit et tam impie armatus ad cuiusque ordinis antistites et sacerdotes confodiendos, ad sanctissima Urbis templa spolianda et demolienda venerit. At vero non defuerunt ex superioribus Pontificibus quorum et pietas insignis et eximia sapientia celebratur, qui usum sepeliendorum in templis cadaverum probarint, quoniam sperabant qui e nostri generis hominibus ibi humati essent gratiores Deo fore, cum praesertim sperarent commendatione divorum martyrum, qui prope iacerent, nihil ad salutem suam pertinere quod illi a Deo facile impetrare non possent. At qui iam erunt divi martyres qui impiae atque illius funestae pestis manes Deo com- <37v> mendent? An illi quorum ossa et corporis reliquias in fanorum direptione dissipavit? An sacerdotes et alii viri sanctissimi quos vexavit verberavit necavit excarnificavit, non ut cultum Christi et constantem illius religionis defensionem excuteret, id quod veteres Romae Caesares faciebant, sed ut vestem sacram, calices, acerras et alia ad rem divinam peragendam necessaria instrumenta ex sacellis prompta auferret et quicquid auri ac argenti multos annos adservatum esset extorqueret. "E praecipua," inquiunt, "Galliae nobilitate Barbonius fuit: illustres maiorum imagines, decus rerum praeclare gestarum, regum etiam splendorem in familia sua afferre potest; ideo ratio maior habenda est illius, nec eodem severitatis genere in eum agendum videtur quo in privatos homines et ulla domestica amplitudine insignes." Nemo quidem inficiatur natales hominis tam illustreis fuisse ut soli dignitatem Gallicae nobilitatis sustinere potuerint. Sed nonne domesticam tantorum ornamentorum gloriam et generis claritatem obscuravit, coniuratione inita primum de interficiendo Francisco rege Galliae, mox consilio suscepto de Pontefice maximo opprimendo? Quam ob rem hostis iudicatus proscriptus et proditoris nomine per universam Galliam notatus, et principatus illius publicatus est et bona voci praeconis subiecta sunt. A nobis autem nihil aliud in eum decretum est, nisi quod decerni solet in eos qui omnia dixerint et fecerint quibus et vera religio polluta et Pontificium numen laesum existimari possit; et, si haec recentiora decreta quibus concissis civibus satis alicui videri non possint ad hominem invisum reddendum omni seculorum posteritati, hic animo secum reputet funesta hominis latrocinia in Gallia citeriore, Aemilia, Etruria. Quid postremo hanc Urbis vastitatem, has caedes, haec incendia, has rapinas, has scelerum impunitates, fugas trepi[ta]dationes orbitates civium referam quae ex illo fonte manarunt? Nonne haec satis digna semper iudicabuntur ut nomen illius hominum interitu obruatur et posteritatis oblivione penitus extinguatur? Arcebantur olim a templis qui rem sua persona minus dignam effecissent; e templis quoque non solum exturbabantur sed etiam e societate Christianorum exterminabantur qui perperam de religione sentientem hominem defendissent aut excepissent aut officio complexi essent. At locum veniae et clementiae in tanta legum asperitate etiam relictum maiores nostri voluerunt, nam ita perperam sentientem hominem semel atque iterum vere pietatis admonendum censuerunt; si bene monenti non obtemperasset, publico incendio poenas dabat <38> suae contumaciae et obstinati in falsa religionis interpretatione tuenda animi. Et ii qui religionis veritatem convellebant libris commentationibus disputationibus utebantur ad nostrum statum labefactandum. Quid de illis sancitum existimas, o Clemens, qui barbari et barbarorum armis stipati aliquando nos invasissent, infesta signa intulissent, fortunas sacerdotum dissipassent, sanguinem expetiissent, ipsum etiam Pontificem afflixissent oppressissent et propemodum e medio sustulissent? Nihil, inquam, aliud sancitum scias nisi quod sanciri debet contra Sarracenos, contra Poenos, contra Mauros, contra Turcas et alias gentes Christianis infestas: horum certe nomen exsecrari solemus, congressum evitare, vivos insectari, semimortuos aut canibus dilaniandos exponere, aut in viis comburere aut in mare proiicere. Certum autem definitumque ius religionis, vetustas exemplorum, auctoritas sacrarum literarum, perpetua monimentorum gloria huiusce rei fidem facit. Neque vero in hoc solum divina maiorum nostrorum apparet sapientia, verum etiam in decernendo ut, si forte religionis falsus interpres ab amico rei ignaro humatus esset, ille veniam impetrare non posset nisi vel manibus suis cadaver effodisset, effossum ut rem exsecrandam et detestabilem reliquissent. Addunt etiam locum in quo ille humatus primum fuisset perpetuo fore profanum, nec ulla ratione religiosum effici posse. Et certe prudenter ac recte hoc crimen tam atrociter vindicandum putarunt, ne ordinis nostri dignitatem et tam eximium religionis decus ulla perditorum hominum impuritas de statu suo dimoveret. Quod si veteres illi constantissimi et longe omnium innocentissimi viri impares se sensissent ad sustinendam tantarum rerum auctoritatem, memores eius quae propria sacerdotum esse debet libertatis, illam ipsam morte honesta potius quam <38v> infami ac turpissima servitute finiebant. Neque vero insolens hoc erit factum, o Clemens, si Borbonium hostem nullo sepulturae genere prosequendum mandaveris. Fabulas hic non consectabor de Polynece quem Creontis iussu omnes insepultum relinquere debebant ut hostem regis, cuius tamen imperium Antigone soror haud verita illum sepeliit; idcirco viva sub

tera condita est. Nonne Sulla victor sitas C. Marii apud Anienem
reliquias dissipari iussit? "Non exemplis," inquiunt, "illorum est nobiscum agendum qui religionis christianae expertes fuerint; huius
enim auctoritate ac praeceptione formamur ad omnem patientiam,
ad omnem lenitatem animi omnemque ad veniam dandam facilitate
ac propensione, nec Pontificum acerbitas ultra mortem debet progre-
di." Sexcenta, o Clemens, leguntur exempla, publicis Pontificum mo-
nimentis consignata quae ad refellendam istorum sententiam maxime
pertinent. Paucis tamen contentus docebo eos ignorare verum illius
gloriae iter, in quo suscipiendo Christianus sacerdos admirabiliter
illustrari possit. Foedericus iunior Caesar Germanus, iniecto in os
pulvillo a Manfredo filio eodemque spurio necatus, inhumatus relic-
tus aut, quod non nulli scribunt, parum religiose sepultus est, idque
ex auctoritate Innocentii Quarti Pontificis Maximi propterea quod
impiis armis aequaleis omneis Pontifices vexarat atque etiam, illis
contemptis, ad sacerdotia elegerat quos eligi non oportebat et electos
pontificio ritu consecrabat, tum etiam iis ornamentis donabat quae
ineundo sacerdotio legitima esse videbantur. Quid commemorem
Ecelinum Transpadanum tyrannum, qui in castris eiusdem Foederici
eam disciplinam perceperat ut esset perpetuus sacerdotum hostis,
fanorum expilator, Pontificiae maiestatis illusor, communis quietis
perturbator, civitatum Italiae carnifex, religionis et Dei contemptor?
At postquam e suis alios vidit iugulari, alios trucidari, alios dilacerari
et semineces ac humi iacentes saepe repetito vulnere confodi, ipse
sinistro crure tragula traiecto et telo in caput impacto Soncini proiec-
tus, sepultura caruit, ut homo aeternis suppliciis devotus, et diris ab
Alexandro Quarto imprecationibus petitus et quocunque exsecrationum genere agitatus. Non dissimilis etiam acerbitas fuit Clementis
Quarti in Conradinum, cuius dominatione non solum crudeli ac superba sed etiam ignominiosa ac flagitiosa premebatur Campania
Samnium Apulia. Hunc enim acie victum Carolus Rex Neäpolitanus
securi percussit, mox ipsius Clementis imperio parens ad ferarum
pastum exposuit. **<39>** Ita quoque Martinus Quintus Brachium
Amiternina acie superatum ac interfectum in agrumque Romanum
delatum primum noluit ad sepulturam dari deorum, ne videretur
imbutus tanta crudelitate quantam Brachii facinus postulabat.
pag<ina> 238 ad Pont<ificem>[2] Illum ad primum ab Urbe lapidem

---

[2] By inserting this marginal phrase, Alcionio seems to mark a point where he plans
to lift passages or ideas from another source. If he did so, I have no evidence of it.

humari in tera permisit quae nulla religione nec religaretur nec teneretur. Vide, o Clemens, quanta sacerdotii tui amplitudo, quanta Pontificiae personae quam sustines potestas sit, quantum etiam numen tu sine controversia ut illa obtineas. Nemo tum ausus est quicquam moliri quod contra horum Pontificum voluntatem actum videri posset, iustaque ultio suscepta videbatur in eos qui in Italia bella excitarant diuturna et pestifera quique efferatam crudelitatem intolerabili insaniae genere exercuerant. Veteres enim et splendidas familias ex urbibus partim eiecerant, partim delerant, infantes alios ab gremio matrum raptos atque adeo in co<n>spectu parentum erutis oculis vigilia atque inedia enecarant, alios interfecerunt.[3] Matronas nobiles et pudicas virgines eo traxerant quo libido et singularis quaedam omnia foedandi cupiditas impulerat. Augustissima templa combusserant, aurum argentum gemmas, fabrefacta vasa et omnem supellectilem qua in sacrorum cerimoniis festisque diebus arae Divorum magnifice exornari solebant abstulerant, aras sanguine sacerdotum funestarant, funestatas diruerant. At vero quid miremur si Pontifices Roman<i>[4], qui ideo Maximi appellantur quod maximam obtineant potestatem, tam invictos constantes graves et severos contra hostes suos certamque de religione[m] sententiam pervertentes et verum Deorum cultum contamin<antes> se praebuerint, cum sacerdotes transmarini iidemque privati Michaëlo Caesari Byzantio, qui tamen religionem nostram magnifico et pio cultu prosecutus fuerat,[5] monimentum in sacro loco statui prohibuerint, quod in conventu Lugdunensi auctoritatem Latinorum secutus esset in religionis interpretatione? Nec quisquam e satrapis bene sentientibus extincti Caesaris propinquus aut familiaris istorum Graeculorum decreto ausus est intercedere usque eo cerimoniarum, sacrorum, perversae atque impiae religionis, et omnino rerum divinarum patrocinium inter transmarinos provincialeis insigni erat auctoritate et gratia. <39v> Reliquum est, o Clemens, ut te admoneam te nulla ratione me iudicare debere tam iratum caussae Borbonii esse ob privatas quas accepi iniurias (id quod isti sacrificuli aiunt), quoniam existimav<i>

---

[3] *Sic.*

[4] *MS*: Romanos

[5] At bottom of 39r, originally inserted to this point (but insertion marks are deleted): "Magnum igitur nomen, magna species, magna dignitas, magna maiestas Pontificis. Non capiunt, o sacrificuli, angustiae pectoris vestri, non recipit levitas ista, non egestas animi, non infirmitas ingenii, non insolentia rerum secundarum intellegit quid efficere et possit et debeat quem Christus in teris suum constituit vicarium."

fortunas quas hostes compilarunt, domestica ornamenta quae eripuerunt et tot gravia, pene mortifera quae inflixerunt vulnera, cu<m> te publicamque domum defenderem, nihil me unquam movere posse, quotienscunque animum refero (id quod semper facio), ad publicas et miserabiles civium clades et gravissimum ac luctuosissimum totius Urbis exitium, quod infinitis lacrimis ex hac mole prospeximus. Publica igitur caussa meum in vos odium accendit, sanguis tot sacerdotum ita impie proefusus me severum implacabilem inexorabilem in vos reddit. Honos etiam numinis Dei violati hanc constantiam in me excitat. Illa denique sanctorum martyrum ossa ac sepultae reliquiae, quas Borbonius effodit et dissipavit, faciunt ut ipsi Pontifici auctor sim talionem quoque Borbonio reddendam, hoc est illum effodiendum, discerpendum et more veterum Romanorum in Tiberim proiiciendum. At si me non audiendum, Clemens, statuis, auctoritatem saltem eorum Pontificum intueare quos commemoravi; illorum enim auctoritate fretus tua quoque uti poteris auctoritate nec de iure tuo decedere. Imo vero debes et hoc ipso et aliis pulcerrimis iustitiae gravitat[at]is magnitudinis animi et constantiae exemplis Romani Pontificatus potestatem sancire. Ita enim probabis quae sermonibus prudentissimorum hominum de Pontificatu tuo divulgata sunt: illum hactenus fuisse libertati Italiae calamitosum, Urbis saluti funestum, dignitati religionis luctuosum et universae Dei ecclesiae tetrum ac pestiferum, eorum caussam Fortunam sustinere, quae quidem non eadem te principem quae privatum complexa est. Omnes praeterea boni te indignum existimabunt in cuius nomen voces afflictorum civium amplius erumpant, si—decet enim te more veterum Pontificum tam liberas voces audire, et quidem tuorum familiarum— si tuarum legum idem non auctor fueris ac eversor, si malos suasores insano quorum arbitrio et perversis consiliis Pontificatum gessisti repudiaveris, si rem frumentariam ita curaveris ut nec tu nec tui illam ad lucrum et praedam intellegantur revocare, languescentem ac prope demortuam illustrium ac doctorum virorum memoriam a silentio et iniquissima fati conditione adserueris, si praemia vigiliis ac laboribus eorum qui duce virtute emergere student decreveris, si ad sacerdotia viros tum probos tum eruditos legeris, si denique maiores illos tuos, quibus omnis plane aeternitas debetur, tibi non modo sequendos sed etiam aemulandos proposueris. Illi enim, quanquam patriae suae cives privati oriebantur, tamen ita vivebant ut nec magnificentia iustitia et excelsi animi splendore ab regibus, nec integritate pudore et religionis <40> laude ab ipsis etiam Pontificibus superarentur. Miserabilis haec tua fortuna vindicem et acrem omnino adsertorem Deum habebit qui, ut mea fert opinio, carcere orbitate rerum carissimarum tantisque malis te conflictari voluit ut certo scires liberalitatem ac innocentiam fidissimam tui custodiam futuram fuisse, non arma. Illarum enim virtutum praesidio nullos saltem barbaros (ut de aliis sileam), hostes habuisses, et si quando habuisses illis tandem venerationi fuisses. Armorum fiducia immanissimos barbaros lacessisti, quibus tandem praedae ac ludibrio fuisti. Quare miseram tuam ex atrocibus periculis erumnosaque vita factam prudentiam, o Clemens, gloriosam tibi et humano generi salutarem deinceps fore speramus, propterea quod, omnibus consiliis tuis ad hanc summam vel pietatis vel beneficentiae revocatis, miserias nostras levabis et simul quae tum ad Urbem sine legibus, sine iudiciis, sine iure, sine fide relictam incendiis maiorib<usque> ruinis restituendam, tum ad ius sacerdotii tui tuendum pertinent illustri omnium gratia feliciter curabis. DIXI.

BAV MS Vat. Lat. 3436, fols. 41v-45v:

[Editor's note: there exists an earlier transcription of this oration, which appears as an appendix in the second edition only of Aida Consorti, *Il Cardinale Pompeo Colonna: su documenti editi e inediti* (Rome: S. Consorti, 1909), 190-98. Consorti's transcription, similarly taken only from Vat. Lat. MS 3436, fols. 41v-45v, is severely flawed (e.g., on occasion skipping entire lines). The edition that follows therefore omits any comparative analysis with Consorti's text.]

<41v> Petrus Alcyonius Uberto Strozae salutem.
Iudicium eorum semper probavi, mi Stroza, qui arbitrantur ad te maxime pertinere quicquid de Pompeio Columna aut scribitur aut dicitur. Nam cum in dies ab eo maioribus honoribus afficiare, nimirum par est te ita studiosum illius esse ut spectata fides eximiaque virtus et perpetua grati animi tui laus videtur postulare. Meam igitur orationem de patria servata ad te mitto, in qua quidem laudes tanti principis ita complexus videor ut et veritati servierim et nullam cuipiam iniuriam fecerim. Quod sane praescriptionis ac moderationis genus retinere difficillimum iudico, in primisque temporibus iis, quibus nonnulli eam licentiam sibi permitti volunt alicuius laudandi ut alios vituperatos relinquant. Leges autem si non auctoris caussa, saltem argumenti, quod quidem tam admirabile ac divinum est ut

cuique scriptori magnam componendi facultatem praebere possit. Neque vero lectorem solum te velim sed etiam testem earum laudum quas in hoc principe ita feliciter es admiratus ut dignus habitus sis qui omnium familiarium illius esses amplissimus et clarissimus. Vale.

<42> Petri Alcyonii oratio pro S. P. Q. R. ad Pompeium Columnam de urbe servata

Maxime optabat S. P. Q. R. ut tibi pro patria servata urbanisque rebus compositis tum, o Pompei, gratias agerem cum statuam decretam poneret, cuius quidem honorem multo illustriorem fore sperabat, si eodem tempore orationem eam adiungeret quae laetitiam suam et grati animi voluntatem declararet. Sed cum hi principes civitatis intellegerent tam salutaris beneficii tui magnitudinem non una tantum oratione celebrari oportere, nunc maxime testari voluerunt quantum omnes tibi deberemus, eo tamen animo ut, si quid praetermissum esset quod ad maiorem nominis tui gloriam pertineret, id totum aliis deinceps orationibus exponeretur. Et eo quidem magis quod compertum habet huiusce rei tam prudenter tamque studiose administratae laudem ita insignem et memorabilem esse ut praeferri sine dubio omnibus possit quas post hominum memoriam contigisse accepimus. Qui enim aliâs ad discordias civileis domesticasque dissensiones sedandas animum contulerunt, hi nullo ferme negotio se omnia transigere posse sperarunt, quandoquidem sibi rem esse videbant vel cum civibus qui, privata potentia freti, privatas iniurias ulcisci volebant, vel cum nostri[1] generis dynastis qui opes suas libenter ad comprimendas ambitiosorum Pontificum insanias conferebant. Sed in tanti belli incendio salute patriae extinguendo et urbe servanda difficultateis, quae infinitae ex ferocia perfidia et immanitate tot barbarorum suboriebantur, omneis vicisti idque ultro occurrens, arbitratus sapientiae auctoritatis consilii diligentiae et virtutis tuae **<42v>** gloriam tum gratam, tum etiam aeternam fore, si quae ab aliis deposita et plane deplorata erant, ipse restitueres, cum praesertim eiusmodi in re non unius generis difficultates te sensisse constet, sed universas quae, ut quietior rerum status desperari posset[2] concurrere solent. Ferocissimi primum Cimbri et Theutones, inter quos multi Iudaei et Syri, iam inde ab illis Antonianis Ituraeis quibus M. Tullius subsellia occupari conquerebatur originem forsitan du-

---

[1] May be lightly deleted. Original word choice, "Italici," is clearly deleted.
[2] *Sic.*

centes; caeteri fere omnes Lutherani. Itaque alii Christianae religionis omnino eversores, alii eorum oppugnatores erant qui non perinde ut ipsi de illa sentiebant. Mox fortissimi Hispani, et his quidem permisti qui fictae religionis sunt, Marani vulgo appellati, qui omnes bellicae virtutis laudem perpetuis victoriis auxerant. Horum etiam duces tum Germani, tum Hispani atque etiam Itali, in occidendo rapiendo et latrocinandi artificio nihil tantae Germanorum aut Hispanorum barbariei cedentes. Adde mutuas suspiciones ob linguarum varietatem, adde nullam vitae aut victus usum propter diversam morum rationem, adde nullam commertii diuturni spem ob praedandi cupiditatem et dominandi consuetudinem. Tu vero alios minis et armorum terrore fregisti, alios muneribus epulis et largitionibus benevolos tibi reddidisti, alios obsequio et patientia quae mater est felicitatis, mitigasti ita ut, ab Urbe non omnino incensa armatis abductis, cives mortis periculo soluti sint et ipse Pontifex Maximus custodia liberatus incolumi maiestate fuerit. Et certe summa haec tua ad benemerendum de salute patriae alacritas <**43**> atque etiam insignis ac memorabilis in sacerdotibus conservandis industria, et industriae adiuncta felicitas, et memoria perfuncti periculi et praedicatione amplissimi beneficii et laude officii praesentis et testimonio praeteriti temporis in dies magis atque magis efflorescet domesticaque vestrae familiae ornamenta ita amplificabit ut, quae alii gesserunt pro dignitate et gloria reipublicae, vel certiora a te confirmata habebuntur vel admirabiliora tam illustrium patriae commodorum accessione exsistent. Multum quidem antea optimo illi Pontifici Martino Quinto eidemque in omni virtute principi, debebamus ob praestantissima illius in rempublicam merita, sed iustae nunc et necessariae sunt caussae cur multo plus tibi et debeamus et debere gaudeamus. Ille enim labantem ac prope cadentem rempublicam fulxit et sustinuit, tu collapsam et prostratam excitasti ac erexisti. Ille in turbulenta republica pontificiam auctoritatem in suum decus asseruit, tu afflicta et funditus deleta republica pontificiam auctoritatem a propinquo interitu vindicasti, vindicatam honore auxisti, laude ornasti. Ille liberos antistites, liberiores omnis generis sacerdotes conservavit, tu captivos in libertatem adseruisti, discruciatos recreasti, et spiritu anima omnique propemodum humano sensu carenteis ad vitam revocasti. Ille, quamvis trans Alpeis inter barbaros versaretur, tamen hospes et amicus ad eos se contulerat. Propterea nullum genus armorum sibi intentari verebatur; non supplicia, non tetrum carcerem, non cruciatus, non tormenta, non denique mortem extimescebat. Tu inter barbaros agens qui barbaro animo, hostili impetu Urbem invasera<n>t diripuerant inflammarant omniaque in nihilum redegerant, <43v> eorum iram placasti rabiemque lenisti; et omnes ad nutum voluntatemque tuam convertisti et auctoritati tuae parere coegisti; denique perfecisti ut, qui servitute nostra contenti non viderentur sed nullum ludum iucundiorem putarent quam cruorem caedes et ante oculos trucidationem civium, hi Urbe excesserint et nos libertate recepta quietos omnino reliquerint. Ad extremum ille Transalpinis e provinciis sacerdotes in Italiam reduxit in Urbeque opulentissima pulcerrima et omni copiarum genere florentissima imperium constituit, ut tanquam gubernator navis in puppi sederet. Tu, perculsis sacerdotibus a Cimbris Theutonibus Iudaeis Epirotis Macedonibus Graeculis Afris Hispanis Gallis (duce Gallo hoste latrone et paricida patriae suae ut alienae eversor esset), Urbe excisa disturbata et ferarum nationum armis inhumanaque crudelitate oppressa nullaque parte reipublicae salva, gubernatore excusso, ipsam Urbem suis civibus reddidisti, amplissimum orbis terae consilium de integro instituisti atque ut ab omnis generis mortalibus, qui in nullam spem reditus dissipari videbantur, tuto frequentari posset auctor fuisti, tum quae ex procella atrocique tempestate diffractae navis partes colligi poterant collegisti pristinumque gubernatorem et moderatorem eidem imposuisti. Merito igitur et pater patriae et Italiae servator et orbis terae liberator vocaris; etenim opera et consilio tuo salus et incolumitas ea quae humana ope afferri potuit patriae est allata, atque ne Italia vastaretur communique fortunae iniuria perculsa agnosceretur perfectum est, et orbem terae, sublatis his barbaris e Roma, quod illius caput est, pacatiorem et tranquilliorem redditum videmus.[3] Atque haec tria cognomina nec apud Graecos in sua patria aut <44> regione nec apud veteres Romanos ulli contigisse legimus. Propterea quicunque deorum immortalium benignitate et excelsi divinique animi tui virtute post tantas patriae ruinas adhuc vivimus, mirabiliter laetamur ad praeclarissima fortunae et animi tui ornamenta hoc etiam immortale ex sapientia ac virtute partorum cognominum decus accessisse, quod quidem eo splendidius et gloriosius iudicabitur, quo calamitatibus reipublicae levandis aptius et reddendae omnium nostrum libertati opportunius fuit. Docuistique nimirum, ea re ita magnifice et praeclare gesta verum esse quod

---

[3] *Sic.*

plerique[4] rerum scriptores literis prodiderunt, Romae omnia mala, omneis pestes, omneis miserias, omneis labes, omneis ruinas timendas esse a barbaris, verum illam fatali quodam eventu restitui ac renovari non posse nisi ab Romanis. Tu quidem Romanus talis beneficii auctor praedicabere, et quidem ab exsilio reversus, qualis celebrari meruit Camillus ille, Romani nominis lumen et rite secundus ab Romulo Urbis conditor appellatus, ut omnino eadem te laus liberatae ac restitutae patriae sequeretur, qua illum floruisse constat. Ambo enim antea exsules iidemque magnanimi et beneficae voluntatis pleni ad omneque rectum officium nati, salutem et vitam iis dedistis qui vobis ereptam volebant, atque huius honestissimi facti admirabilis gloria cum per se grata est, tum etiam gratior propter celeritatem. Siquidem conatus qui ad benemerendum de humano genere suscipiuntur rariorem quandam voluptatem afferre et summam laetitiae vim animis in nostris ingenerare solent, si ut salutares et optabiles sunt, ita repentini inopinati et celeritate sua admirabiles exstiterint. **<44v>** Quid? quod tantae rei atrocitas nihilo minorem postulabat celeritatem, cum media in Urbe castra locarentur, stationes et excubiae militares haberentur, signa in templis figerentur, conciones in delubra classico et Martio tubarum sono convocarentur, edicta tum lingua et sono vocis, tum re ipsa etiam barbara et contumeliosa semper auribus nostris obstreperent, caedes optimorum civium cotidie atque impetus in illorum fortunas fierent, omnisque gladiorum impunitas esset, et voces horrificae in sacerdotes illorumque mores et vitam, atque adeo in ipsius captivi Pontificis instituta omnesque actiones emitterentur. Quid? quod tantam immanitatem magnopere interdum efferare videbantur minis etiam teterrimis et gravissimis, cum modo se eundem Pontificem in extremas orbis terae partes ut pestiferum quoddam et spurcissimum monstrum deportaturos, modo illum ut publicae infelicitatis auctorem in Tiberim e Mole Aelia ubi custodiebatur deturbaturos, modo crudeli alia ratione interfecturos iactarent, quandoquidem belli lege et iure victoriae ipse et reliqua omnia in Urbe capta sui iuris, suae potestatis, suae libidinis, suae etiam tyrannidis essent. Ne multis! Haec omnia et ignominiam quoque, ac dedecus tale antistitum ordini inuri non posthac videbimus, quale superiora secula nec viderunt nec fieri posse unquam cogitarunt, ut a Cimbris istis qui, eversa Urbe, postquam e

---

[4] Following "plerique", "Romanarum" appears lightly deleted in the MS.

Narnia redierant quo pestilentiae evitandae caussa secesserant, cotidie obsides quos Pontifici imperarant in catenis habiti ad eum locum
adducerentur ubi, instar furiae, posita sunt ligna quibus fures et
gravioris delicti sontes laqueo suspenduntur, idque ut ut terrore mortis incusso, et pecuniam quantam vellent[5] et dominatum eorum lu-
crorum quae sibi opportuna iudicarent a nobis extorquerent. Quam
ob rem ille dies quo in patriam rediisti instar felicitatis nostrae et
immortalitatis tuae videri potest, cum, etsi proprios tuarum rerum
dolores habebas, tamen civitatis miserias a te ipso alienas non putasti,
simulque de reipublicae incolumitate solicitus populique Romani fortunis iam eversis semper cogitans, ea curasti quae efficerent ut in
possessionem libertatis propriam Romani generis et nominis pedem
ponere inciperemus, et non modo certum reipublicae statum sed bonum etiam, beatum et florentem efficerent. Dixi beatum et florentem, o Pompei, non ignarus tantam vim huius teterrimi <45> et
calamitosissimi belli tantumque ardorem animorum et armorum
fuisse ut omnia foede prostrata sint, atque etiam nihil nos et multorum seculorum posteros in Urbe visuros nisi erumnosum funestum
detestabile luctuosum et miserabile. Sed tamen id nunc beatum et
florens appellaverim quod pro temporum ratione non omnino malum est, imo potius quod vitam et spiritum nos quoquo modo aut
ducere aut recipere sinit. Itaque praeclarissima et sapientissima illa
vox tua saepe numero audita est: funera patriae quoquo modo nunc
suscitanda et excitanda, quia ipsius Urbis nomen satis esse potest ad
sui restitutionem et salutem. At te cive, et quidem ita nobili ut Romanae nobilitatis princeps sis, sperare possumus illam aliquando nonnullam eorum ornamentorum partem recuperaturam quae vim maximam habere videntur ad summam dignitatem et perpetuam gloriam. Iam vero nemo est tam rerum ignarus, tam rudis in republica,
tam nihil unquam nec de sua nec de communi salute cogitans, tam
denique humanorum officiorum iniustus ratiocinator qui integra veritate adseverare non queat bis te de Clemente Pontifice ita benemeritum, ut tempora illius ferebant: semel cum privato summam potestatem detulisti, iterum cum eandem pene amissam restituisti. Ob
eamque rem patria novum hunc honorem (sic enim pontificatus
maximus Romae est confirmatus) quo illum affecisti ita gratum
habuit ut non modo omnium generum aetatum ordinum omnes viri

---

[5] *Sic.*

ac mulieres omnis fortunae et loci, sed moenia etiam ipsa visa sunt[6]
et tecta Urbis ac templa laetari. Et quo admirabilius omnibus videri
debet, nihil aliud te eidem Pontifici nunc respondere **<45v>** sensimus, cum tibi ob collatum beneficium ageret gratias, quam id quod
alias cum in pontificatu adipiscendo homini studebas, respondisti: te
hoc solum ab eo et petere et exspectare ut princeps bonus esset, ut in
pacem constituendam inter reges Christianos incumberet, ut se vicarium Christi meminisset. Dignus nimirum hoc solo nomine immorta-
lis famae celebritate et admirandus simul videbere, quod ad antiqua
et plurima in eundem merita cumulum hunc amplissimum adtuleris,
idque nec offensione ulla nec suspicione commemorata sed, ut mag-
nanimum[um] decet, sola gratificandi voluntate adductus soloque
bene merendi proposito fretus, omnia quae ad incolumitatem et pristinam fortunam dignitatemque illius restituendam pertinebant egisti,
tum etiam omnem nocendi facultatem occasionem iuvandi existimasti, et tempus quod ad maleficium et contumeliam aptum erat ad
beneficium honorem et gratiam arripuisti. Quod sane clementiae et
humanitatis genus ei non dissimile est quo in M. Marcello conservan-
do C. Caesar aliquando usus legitur. Et fortasse maius illustriusque
habebitur quod ille, commemoratis offensionibus et suspicionibus, M.
Marcellum Senatui reipublicaeque concessit; tu autem, nulla offensionum aut iniuriarum aut suspicionum mentione facta, praeterita
tempora ex omni memoria aeque evulsa esse voluisti ac illorum sensum nullum unquam habuisses. Et certe par erat ut, qui Caesar Pompeium armis, caeteros omneis armis lenitate ac misericordia vicisset,
ab aliquo tandem Pompeio Romano vinceretur si non armis aut misericordia aut humanitate et clementia, saltem ratione utendae mise-
ricordiae placabilitatis et clementiae. Hoc igitur factum tum beneficio
gratum, tum fama gloriosum erit, cum praesertim audaciam atque
importunitatem illorum etiam fregeris qui armis in Urbem redierunt,
e qua legibus excesserant. **<end of extant folio>**

---

[6] *Sic.*

LETTERS FROM JACOPO SADOLETO TO CLEMENT VII
(1527-28)
TRANSCRIBED FROM THE AUTOGRAPH
MANUSCRIPTS IN THE ARCHIVIO SEGRETO
VATICANO

ASV MS Arm. XLV, 42, fols. 41-42v: original autograph letter;
Sadoleto to Pope Clement, 1 September 1527.

<41> Pater Sanctissime. Etsi omni argumento scribendi ad Sancti-
tatem Vestram careo—propterea quod, neque dolori meo quem ex
incommodis Reipublicae et Vestrae Sanctitatis maximum accepi verba, neque meae erga illam voluntati et observantiae litterae ullae
satisfaciunt—tamen cum haberem certum nuncium qui in Italiam et
Romam esset profecturus, quod antehac mihi scribere cupienti non
contigit, statui mei officii esse aliquid litterarum dare ad Sanctitatem
vestram non tam leniendi doloris sui causa, quam mei declarandi,
quamquam ut dixi, hoc quidem fieri per me nullo modo potest, tantus enim est et fuit ut quod post meum ex Urbe discessum produxi
vitae id mihi omni morte deterius fuisse videatur. Sed ego quae a
prudentia et religione Sanctitatis Vestrae, quam utranque in ea semper cognovi, maximam proficisci potuerunt ad infestos adversosque
casus constanter et moderate tolerandos omnemque spem et fidem in
Deum iaciendam ea arbitror satis fuisse in tantarum concursu calamitatum adhibita. Novi enim pacem animi Vestrae Sanctitatis novi
erga Deum egregiam fidem. Quae autem mihi ad scribendum apta
esse videantur, ea brevi complectar. Sic enim statuo tantam acerbitatem poenae non Sanctitati Vestrae sed temporibus fuisse divinitus
illatam. Cum enim Sanctitas Vestra omni virtute et bonitate praedita
esset, in ea tempora tamen inciderat quae, corruptissimis moribus
sine ullis bonis legibus, iram Dei omnino ad vindicandum provo-
cabant. Quae cum Vestra Sanctitas vellet et conaretur corrigere
(cuius ego voluntatis optimus sum testis), tamen vincente eius mentem sanctissimam et hominum perfidia et vitiorum mole, ab optimo
et saluberrimo consilio non tam depulsa fuit quam retardata. At ego

semper et sensi et prospexi clarius etiam aliquanto quam ea quae oculis cernuntur, aut mutandum ordinem disciplinae publicae, aut ad extremum interitum praecipitandum esse. Accidit alterum id quod minime vellem, nec quicquam mihi acerbius potuit contingere. Sed si est Dei iracundiae et severitati nostris suppliciis satisfactum atque haec poenarum asperitas aditum ad bonos mores et sanctiores leges patefactura est, fortasse nobiscum non erit pessime actum. Illa enim bona profecto quae virtutis et integritatis et in verum Deum perfectae pietatis sunt longe his sunt anteferenda quae, ubi laboraris, coacervaris. cum invidia plerunque et infamia possederis, facillime tamen extorquentur e manibus saepiusque illis sunt noxia qui possident, quam qui eis carent aut qui privati sunt. Quae ego ad homines impios contemptores omnis humani divinique iuris transisse non omnino moleste fero. Transiit enim ad eos una cum eis illa infanda avaritia qua nomen sacerdotii sanctissimum tantopere laborabat. Transiit corruptrix animorum <41v> et corporum luxuria quae ferme divitiarum et opulentiae socia est, quodque imprimis necesse est, ira Dei et celestis ultio in eam quoque partem transgressa est. Itaque nuncio Sanctitati Vestrae celeriter sceleratos homines, quos nec ab impietate Deus nec a crudelitate humanitas nec a violatione foederum fides ipsa potuit deterrere. daturos poenas immanitatis suae. Utinam illi ad poenitentiam revertantur et misericordiam Dei promereantur! Sed quoniam hoc nobis qui Christi Dei imitatione et praeceptis ad precandum pro inimicis nostris parati sumus. magis optandum est quam sperandum, quae Dei sunt Deo erunt curae. Quod vero ad nos quoque ipsos attinet. quando melior multo vitae conditio nobis est parata, quae nullis armis eripi potest, sic dirigamus actus cogitatusque nostros ut verum sacerdotii splendorem veramque magnitudinem nostrae potestatis in ipso vero Summoque Deo statuamus. Quo cum, si erimus coniuncti, non inimici homines nos afflixisse, sed nos illos ad interitum dedisse videbimur, cuius optimi instituti atque consilii Sanctitas Vestra ut dignitate cunctorum princeps sic in experiundo et agendo prima esse debet. Sicut tamen et fuit semper et magis etiam si per difficultatem temporum licuisset, ut esset conata est. Ego qui summum illum amorem incredibilemque charitatem qua Sanctitatem Vestram iam diu complexus sum, et conservo in animo integram inviolatamque et perpetuo sum servaturus, quanquam in hoc Dei servitio et famulatu affixus meaeque sponsae copulatus, constitutum habeo et deliberatum in hoc munere finire vitam cui eam dicavi. Tamen, si Sanctitas Vestra extra Italiam ad aliquas longinquas regiones se contulerit aut deducta fuerit, non deero nec amori nec observantiae erga illam meae particulamque totius temporis quod Deo et Dei rebus per me devotum et consecratum est, in Sanctitatis Vestrae obsequium conferens, non arbitrabor me abesse ab eius cultu quem posthac solum colere iam decrevi. Valeat quotidie melius atque felicius Sanctitas Vestra, cui et me et harum latorem Gregorium Physicum, hominem probum et fidelem eundemque bonorum morum et bonarum partium, quanto animi studio possum diligenter enixeque commendo. ut eius liberalitate aliquod commodum consequatur cui, cum mandaverim non<n>ulla etiam meis verbis Sanctitati Vestrae exponenda, atque ut preces quasdam pro me porrigat. Oro atque rogo Sanctitatem Vestram ut suam mihi, supplici et fideli suo, solitam benignitatem exhibere dignetur, cuius sanctissimos pedes <**42**> corde et animo absens infinito cum amore quodam et debita reverentia prostratus osculor. Dominus Deus Sanctitati Vestrae omnia bona prosperaque concedat. Carpentoracti prima Septembris. M.D.XXVII.

Devotissimus et humillimus servus Iacobus Sadoletus epi. ...

ASV MS Lettere di Principi, t.4, fol. 311 (mechanical numeration), autograph draft:

Pater Sanctissime mihi patrone unice et vere pater: Hoc recente nuncio liberationis Sanctitatis Vestrae quae mea letitia et gratulatio sit exponere satis non possum. Est enim ea quam incredibilis quidam amor meus erga Sanctitatem Vestram postulat, etsi nondum mente conquiesco, quod facturus sum ubi intellexero quo in statu sint res et Vestrae Sanctitatis libertas veraque dignitas. Itaque ego, ille qui ante hunc diem semper precatus sum toto corde Dominum Deum ut erueret Vestram Sanctitatem de impiorum manu, nunc convertor ad illam orationem: Dirige eum, Domine, secundum clementiam Tuam in viam salutis aeternae. Nunc enim nunc tempus est ut iter tutum et salutare capiatur, quod si erit rite captum, non solum amissa recuperabuntur sed maior quam ante dignitas et maior gloria acquiretur. Sed quod spectat ad prudentiam, Sanctitas Vestra est prudentissima; quod ad bonitatem, eadem est optima. Unum opto et desidero et precor, ut eorum consilia audiantur qui maxime ad tranquillitatis et gravitatis et pietatis studia apti sunt. Ego in hoc Dei Summi servitio

assiduus sum, neque in omnibus meis precibus praetermitto locum
pro Vestra Sanctitate orandi et deprecandi, ad quam haec pauca
nunc scripsi, repentino nuncii discessu, uberiora scri<bere> non
valens. Scribam autem et saepe et longius cum cognovero certum
quo et quo modo scribendum mihi sit, idque non ingratum Vestrae
Sanctitati intellexero, cuius ego <scilicet>[1] salutem et honorem
habeo mea ipsius etiam cariorem. Valeat Sanctitatis Vestrae felicis-
sime cuime devotissime commendo. Carpin. xxx decembris
M.D.XXVIII. Sanctitatis Vestrae s..mirum pedum.

Lettere di Principi, t.5, fols. 169-70v:
<169> Cupienti mihi iandudum ad Vestram Sanctitatem scribere,
longus et difficilis morbus fuit impedimento quo tamen relevari iam
videor; is porro me ab hoc scribendi officio mihi iucundissimo deti-
nuit. Etenim si cum praesens eram coramque Sanctitatis Vestrae singulari illa humanitate et sapientia perfruebar, nihil habebam iucundi-
us quod vel optare auderem, restat ut absens quoquo modo possum
idem contendam et cum Sanctitate Vestra litteris quasi colloquar:
cuius nomen et memoriam assidue in animo meo infixam gero ut
eam inde nulla unquam dies nulla neque rerum possit neque temporum perturbatio delere. Quid autem scribam, quid? Opinor id quod
maxime est in promptu, nihil esse mea erga Sanctitatem Vestram
observantia nihil incredibili benivolentia ardentius quae usque adeo
valet in me et potest ut ego ipse, qui rerum mearum proprios affectus
a me metipso abdicare iam institueram unamque et eam solam curam susceperam, quo pacto Deum Omnipotentem meis peccatis propitium facerem, ex Vestrae tamen Sanctitatis et adversis rebus maximo dolore perturbatus et melioribus ad aliquam animi aequitatem
restitutus sim, Deum et Dominum Nostrum assidue deprecans ut
Sanctitatis Vestrae omnia acta consiliaque secundet. Quod utinam
videam tempus illud quo, compositis et placatis rebus omnibus, aliam
intelligam Vestrae Sanctitatis virtute et sapientia iniri viam aliam
suscipi rationem redintegrandae in veterem dignitatem dei religionis
et ecclesiasticae auctoritatis quam antehac inita aut suscepta est:
quod ipsum tamen ab eadem Sanctitate Vestra iam tractari audio.
Atqui facilis est totius rei et explicata ratio: si enim quae obtentu dei
et religionis aguntur conceduntur ut ea non ad alios fines detorta sed

---

[1] *MS*: illegible.

ad eum ipsum Deum et Dei veritatem fuerint relata, eiecta omni suspitione invidiosi quaestus, splendor sanctissimi sacerdotii omnibus gentibus venerabilis elucebit, cuius rei et rationis caput fuerit ecclesiis et ecclesiasticis beneficiis idoneos homines praeficere. Atque hoc quod ego ita opto precorque, cum considero Vestrae Sanctitatis bonitatem sapientiam integritatem facillimum mihi factu videtur esse. Cum autem mores et tempora intueor, vereor ne sit aliquanto quo velim et quam reipublicae expediat difficilius. Sed tamen hoc meum optatum et votum suo iudicio comprobavit Deus qui, cum tanta et tam gravi imposita mulcta, suos sacerdotes edocuit. Ubi veneratio absit et sanctae ac religiosae vitae opinio, caeteras opes parvi momenti ad stabilitatem fortunae et conservationem salutis ac dignitatis existere aperte declaravit, alios se mores alia vitae instituta a genere nostro ordineque requirere. Nam quo plus valent res quam verba, hoc acrior vox Dei illa <169v> existimanda est, quae est factis declarata non verbis. Atque illud quoque pro infinito amore meo erga Sanctitatem Vestram mihi accideret optatissimum, si hanc Ipsa precipue gloriam hanc apud Deum gratiam sibi compararet, ut correctrix temporum lapsorum perditorumque restitutrix antiquae virtutis et religionis existeret, habuisset prior aetas pontifices qui statum et magnitudinem suam ex opibus ex divitiis ex auro et gaza regia, ex imperiis, ex provinciis, ex perniciosis bellis atque victoriis, ex omnium rerum copia et affluentia, denique ex quotidiano delicatissimae vitae cultu fructuque aestimassent, novi saeculi auctor esset Clemens novorum temporum, novorum institutorum, novorum morum, sed quorum tamen novitas ad sanctam illam et piam antiquitatem imitatione proxime accederet. Tunc ego exultarem gaudio et triumpharem laetitia, illum Summum Pontificem intuens quem ego mitto nunc venerationem atque observantiam quae maxima est (de ardore meae erga eum benivolentiae loquor quem, ego inquam, amplius cunctis hominibus quos unquam noverim amavi amoque), in tantae possessione gloriae esse constitutum. Sed ego forsitan scribo ista audacius, in quo tamen amore efferor non temeritate. In eo plane ero audax qui affirmabo et repetam Sanctitati Vestrae etiam atque etiam, gnarus optime et prudens eorum quae loquor, minime esse habendam his saeculi principibus fidem, in quibus nulla est salus, quorum ab omni spe atque expectatione si ipsa se se dissolverit, et in Deo animique sui virtute atque constantia omnem vitae spem omnia praesidia constituerit, vae illa etiam apud eos melius obtinebit statum et gravitatem auctoritatis suae. Sed de his satis. Ego, pater sanctissime et mi patrone desideratissime, post multas et graves angustias ac difficultates rerum omnium quae me et meam familiam omnem vexaverunt quos istorum temporum procella quae caeteros pessundedit etiam afflixit, iam e morbo convalescens referre incipio aspectum et cogitationem ad mea illa pristina studia optimarum artium recolenda in quibus, si beneficio Magni Dei tantum profecero quantum cogito optoque, manabit ad posteritatem profecto aliquod illustre testimonium mei in Sanctitatem Vestram et amoris et iudicii, vicissim eandem deprecans, ut suam illam benignissimi animi erga me propensionem conservet, quam tanti facio ut nihil sit maius quod audeam postulare. Quod si aliorum etiam mihi apud Sanctitatem Vestram non interclusa commendatio est, et quod dicam ex vero animi mei sensu non ex ulla cupiditate videbor dicere, cuperem maxime, pater sanctissime, idque honoris Sanctitatis Vestrae et publici commodi causa ut ad Sanctitatis Vestrae latus et aurem assiduus Baro Burgii adesset qui, quanquam est in officio et munere necessario constitutus, tamen eximiam illius viri virtutem ac prudentiam coniunctam pari <170> fide et integritate optandum erat his temporibus praesertim, in omnibus consiliis de republica capiundis Sanctitati Vestrae proximam versari: de quo homine, quid ego multa dicam, cum is Vestrae quoque Sanctitati optimae cognitus et in magnis rebus obeundis ab illa probatus sit? Binum autem meum quem ego institui et erudii ad illas actiones exercendas in quibus ego tot annos versatus sum omni studio animi eidem Vestrae Sanctitati commendo, a qua, si adhibebitur ad eius generis scripta et epistolas ad quas vehementer aptus est, sentiet ex eo Vestra Sanctitas non mediocre commodum, sedes apostolica non parvum ornamentum qui, cum inops egensque sit, fide tamen et virtute ornatus meae Disciplinae alumnus. Habeo gravem iustamque causam pro eo Vestram Sanctitatem deprecandi ut eius benignitate ac beneficentia is aliquod tot suorum laborum praemium et vitae subsidium possit consequi, in quo sum reputaturus me ipsum a Sanctitate Vestra augeri et beneficio affici. sit felix in dies magis magisque Sanctitas Vestra cuius sanctissimis pedibus me osculatis cum charitate devotioneque commendo. Carpentoracti. xv. Kal. Maii. M.D.XXVIII

Devotissimus Servus Iacobus Sadoletus
<170v> Sanctissimo ac Beatissimo Domino Nostro Papae.

BIBLIOGRAPHY

Manuscript Sources

Bologna. Archivio Isolani. MS F 6 1.
Florence. Biblioteca Riccardiana. MS 2022.
Paris. Bibliothèque Nationale. MS Ital. 2033.
Perugia. Biblioteca Comunale Augustea. MS G 99.
Rome. Biblioteca Corsiniana. MS 33 E 26.
Rome. Biblioteca Corsiniana. MS 45 D 4.
Vatican City. Archivio Segreto Vaticano. Armaria XLV, t.42.
Vatican City. Archivio Segreto Vaticano. Lettere di Principi, t.4 and t.5.
Vatican City. Biblioteca Apostolica Vaticana. MS Vat. Lat. 2835.
Vatican City. Biblioteca Apostolica Vaticana. MS Vat. Lat. 3353.
Vatican City. Biblioteca Apostolica Vaticana. MS Vat. Lat. 3436.
Vatican City. Biblioteca Apostolica Vaticana. MS Vat. Lat. 5225, t. IV.
Vatican City. Biblioteca Apostolica Vaticana. MS Vat. Lat. 5383.
Vatican City. Biblioteca Apostolica Vaticana. MS Vat. Lat. 5892.
Vatican City. Biblioteca Apostolica Vaticana. MS Vat. Lat. 8122.

Printed Primary Sources

Anon. *Pasquinate romane del Cinquecento.* Ed. Valerio Marucci, Antonio Marzo, and Angelo Romano. 2 vols. Rome: Salerno, 1983.
Alcionio, Pietro. ["Declamatio in literas Caesaris."] "Oratio habita in Senatu Romano praelectis literis a Carolo V. post Urbis direptionem scriptis." In: Christophus Godofredus Hoffmannus, *Nova Scriptorum ac Monumentorum Partim Rarissimorum, Partim Ineditorum Collectio....* Vol. 1: 550-88. Leipzig: Sumptibus Haered. Lanckisianorum, 1731.
———. *Medices legatus: de exsilio.* Venice: Aldus and Andrea Asulanus, 1522.
Aretino, Pietro. *Lettere: Il primo e il secondo libro.* Ed. Francesco Flora. Milan: Mondadori, 1960.
Aristotle. *De generatione et interitu....* Trans. Pietro Alcionio. Venice: Bernardus dei Vitali, 1521.
Berni, Francesco. *Opere burlesche di M. Francesco Berni, con annotazioni e con un saggio delle sue lettere piacevoli.* Milan: Classici Italiani, 1806.
Corsi, Pietro. *Petri Cursii civis Ro<mae> Defensio pro Italia ad Erasmvm Roterodamvm.* Rome: Antonius Bladus de Asula, 1535.
———. *[Romae urbis excidium.] Ad humani generis servatorem in urbis Romae excidio P. Cursii civis Rom. deploratio.* Ed. in Léon Dorez. "Le poème de Pietro Corsi sur le sac de Rome." *Mélanges d'Archéologie et d'Histoire de l'Ecole Française de Rome* 16 (1896): 420-436.
Erasmus, Desiderius. "The Ciceronian: A Dialogue on the Ideal Latin Style." Trans. Betty I. Knott. Vol. 28 in: *The Collected Works of Erasmus.* Ed. A.H.T. Levi et al. Toronto and Buffalo: University of Toronto Press, 1986.
———. *The Correspondence of Erasmus: Letters 446 to 593, 1516 to 1517,* vol. 5 in: *The Collected Works of Erasmus.* Trans. R.A.B. Mynors and D.F.S. Thomson. Ed. Peter G. Bietenholz et al. Toronto: University of Toronto Press, 1977.
———. *Opus Epistolarum Des. Erasmi Roterodami.* Ed. P.S. Allen. 12 vols. Oxford: Clarendon, 1906-58.

Giovio, Paolo. *[Elogia virorum illustrium] Gli elogi degli uomini illustri (Letterati—Artisti—Uomini d'Arme)*. Ed. Renzo Meregazzi. Vol. 8 in: *Pauli Iovii Opera*. Ed. Societas Historicae Novocomensis. Rome: Istituto Poligrafico dello Stato, Libreria dello Stato, 1972.

Giovio, Paolo. *[Elogia virorum illustrium] An Italian Portrait Gallery*. Trans. Florence Alden Gragg. Boston: Chapman & Grimes, 1935.

Giraldi, Lilio Gregorio. *[Dialogi duo] De poetis nostrorum temporum*. Ed. Karl Wotke. Berlin: Weidmann, 1894.

Gruterus, Ianus, comp. *Delitiae CC. Italorum poetarum, huius superiorisque aevi illustrium*, collectore Ranutio Ghero. 2 vols. [Frankfurt], 1608.

Guicciardini, Francesco. *Storia d'Italia*. Ed. Silvana Seidel Menchi. 3 vols. Turin, 1971.

Guicciardini, Luigi. *The Sack of Rome*. Trans. and ed. James H. McGregor. New York: Italica, 1993.

Lettere di Principi 1. Venice: Ziletti, 1570.

Lettere di Principi 2. Venice: Ziletti, 1581.

Longueil, Christophe. *C. Longolii Lucubrationes... Epistolarum libri IIII*. Lyon, 1542.

More, Thomas. *A Dialogue Concerning Heresies*. In *The Complete Works of St. Thomas More*, vol. 6, pts. 1 & 2, ed. Thomas M. C. Lawler, Germain Marc'Hadour, and Richard C. Marius. New Haven: Yale University Press, 1981.

Palladio, Blosio, ed. *Coryciana*. Rome: L. de Henricius and L. Perusinus, 1524.

Sadoleto, Jacopo. *Epistolarum libri sexdecim. Eiusdem ad Paulum Sadoletum Epistolarum liber unus. Vita Eiusdem autoris per Antonium florebellum*. Lyon: [Gryphius], 1560.

———. *Epistolae quotquot extant proprio nomine scriptae nunc primum duplo auctioores in lucem editae*. Ed. Vincenzo Costanzi. 5 vols. Rome: G. Salomonius, 1760-67.

———. *Jacobi Sadoleti Cardinalis et Episcopi Carpentoractensis viri disertissimi, Opera quae exstant omnia*. 4 vols. in 2. Verona: Tumermani, 1737-38.

Sanuto, Marino. *I diarii di Marino Sanuto*. 58 vols. Venice: Visentini, 1879-1903.

Sepúlveda, J.G. *Libri Aristotelis, quos vulgo latini, parvos naturales appellant; Errata P. Alcyonii in interpretatione Aristotelis, a Ioanne Genesio Sepulveda Cordubensi collecta*. [Bologna, 1522].

[Valdés, Alfonso de.] *Alfonso de Valdés and the Sack of Rome: Dialogue of Lactancio and an Archdeacon*. Ed. and trans. John E. Longhurst. Albuquerque: University of New Mexico, 1952.

Valeriano, Pierio. *De litteratorum infelicitate, libri duo*. Ed. Dom. Egerton Brydges, Bar.^to. Geneva, 1821.

———. *Epistola de Honoribus Illustrissimo ac Reverendissimo Gurcensi Caesareo Totius Italiae Vicario Urbem ingredienti Habitis*. Rome: Jo. Mazzocchius, 1512.

———. *La infelicità dei letterati, di Pierio Valeriano, ed Appendice di Cornelio Tollio. Traduzione dal latino*. Milan: Tipogr. Malatesta di C. Tinelli, 1829.

———. *Joannis Pierii Valeriani ... De litteratorum infelicitate, libri duo*. Venice: Jacobus Sarzina, 1[6]20.

———. *Ioannis Pierii Valeriani Bellvnensis, Hieroglyphica, sev de Sacris AEgyptiorvm Aliarvmque Gentivm Literis Commentarii....* Lyon: Paulus Frelon, 1602.

———. *Pierii Valeriani Amorum Libri V*. Venice: Gabriel Giolito di Ferrara, 1549.

———. *Pro Sacerdotum barbis ad Clariss. Card. Hippolytum Medicen*. Rome: Calvo, 1531.

———. *A treatise vvriten by Iohan Valerian, a greatte clerke of Italie, which is intitled in Latin Pro sacerdotum barbis; translated to Englysshe*. [London: in aedibus Tho. Bertheleti, 1533].

Secondary Sources

Alpago-Novello, Luigi. "Nuove notizie intorno a Pierio Valeriano con documenti inediti." *Archivio storico di Belluno Feltre e Cadore* 6 (1934): 477-84.

——. "Spigolature vaticane di argomento bellunese. I. Un' opera inedita ed ignorata di Pierio Valeriano." *Archivio Veneto Tridentino* 9 (1926): 69-96.

Asor Rosa, Alberto, ed. *Letteratura italiana—Storia e geografia.* Vol. 2: "L'età moderna." Turin: Einaudi, 1987.

Asor Rosa, Alberto et al., ed. *Il Sacco di Roma del 1527 e l'immaginario collettivo.* Rome: Istituto Nazionale di Studi Romani, 1986.

Avesani, Rino. "Bonamico, Lazzaro." *DBI* (1969) 11:533-40.

Ballistreri, G. "Bini (Bino), Giovanni Francesco." *DBI* 10 (1968): 510-13.

Bandura, Albert. "Self-Efficacy Conception of Anxiety." *Anxiety Research* 1 (1988): 77-98.

——. "Self-Efficacy Mechanism in Human Agency." *American Psychologist* 37:2 (Feb. 1982): 122-47.

Baron, Hans. "Cicero and the Roman Civic Spirit in the Middle Ages and Early Renaissance." *Bulletin of the John Rylands Library* 22 (1938): 72-97.

——. *The Crisis of the Early Italian Renaissance.* Rev. ed. Princeton: Princeton University Press, 1966.

——. "Leonardo Bruni: 'Professional Rhetorician' or 'Civic Humanist'?" *Past and Present* 36 (1967): 21-37.

Bartlett, Frederick C. *Remembering: A Study in Experimental and Social Psychology.* Cambridge: Cambridge University Press, 1932.

Bayle, Pierre. *Dictionaire historique et critique, par Mr. P.B. Cinquième edition, revue, corrigée et augmentée....* First edition published in 1696. 4 Vols. Amsterdam: P. Brunel, 1740.

Biagioli, Mario. "Galileo's System of Patronage." *History of Science* 28 (1990): 1-62.

Bietenholz, Peter G. and Thomas B. Deutscher, eds. *Contemporaries of Erasmus: A Biographical Register of the Renaissance and Reformation.* 3 vols. Toronto and Buffalo: University of Toronto Press, 1985-87.

Billanovich, Guiseppe. *Petrarca letterato.* Rome: Edizioni di storia e letteratura, 1947.

Blasio, Maria Grazia. *Cum gratia et privilegio. Programmi editoriali e politica pontificia, Roma 1487-1527.* Rome: Associazione Roma nel Rinascimento, 1988.

Bober, Phyllis Pray. "The *Coryciana* and the Nymph Corycia." *Journal of the Warburg and Courtauld Institutes* 40 (1977): 223-39.

Bonito, Virginia Anne. "The St Anne altar in Sant' Agostino in Rome: a new discovery." *The Burlington Magazine* 122 (1980): 805-812.

——. "The Saint Anne altar in Sant' Agostino: restoration and interpretation." *The Burlington Magazine* 124 (1982): 268-76.

Bouwsma, William J. "Review Article: Renaissance Humanism: Foundations, Forms and Legacy." *Church History* 59 (1990): 65-70.

——. "The Two Faces of Humanism: Stoicism and Augustinianism in Renaissance Thought." In: *Itinerarium Italicum.* Ed. Heiko A. Oberman and Thomas A. Brady, Jr. Leiden: Brill, 1975. 3-60.

Bruschi, Arnaldo. *Bramante architetto.* Bari: Laterza, 1969.

Bullard, Melissa Miriam. *Filippo Strozzi and the Medici: Favor and Finance in Sixteenth-Century Florence and Rome.* Cambridge and New York: Cambridge University Press, 1980.

——. *Lorenzo il Magnifico: Image and Anxiety, Politics and Finance.* Florence: Olschki, 1994.

——. "*Mercatores Florentini Romanam Curiam Sequentes* in the Early Sixteenth Century." *Journal of Medieval and Renaissance Studies* 6 (1976): 51-71.

Burke, Peter. "The Renaissance Dialogue." *Renaissance Studies* 3 (1989): 1-12.

Bustico, Guido. "Due umanisti veneti: Urbano Bolzanio e Pierio Valerianio." [sic] *Civiltà moderna* 4 (1932): 86-103, 344-79.

——. "Pierio Valeriano, poeta bellunese del sec. XVI." *Atti della R. Accademia roveretana degli Agiati* 11 (1905): 155-76.

Campana, Augusto. "The Origin of the Word 'Humanist.'" *Journal of the Warburg and Courtauld Institutes* 9 (1946): 60-73.

Chastel, André. *Le sac de Rome, 1527: du premier maniérisme à la contre-Réforme*. Paris: Gallimard, 1984.

——. *The Sack of Rome, 1527*. Trans. Beth Archer. Princeton: Princeton University Press, 1983.

Clough, Cecil H. "The Cult of Antiquity: Letters and Letter Collections." In: *Cultural Aspects of the Italian Renaissance: Essays in Honour of Paul Oskar Kristeller*. Ed. Cecil H. Clough. New York: A. F. Zambelli, 1976. 33-67.

Cochrane, Eric. *Italy, 1530-1630*. Ed. Julius Kirshner. New York: Longman, 1988.

Coffin, David R. *The Villa in the Life of Renaissance Rome*. Princeton: Princeton University Press, 1979.

Consorti, Aida. *Il Cardinale Pompeo Colonna: su documenti editi e inediti*. 2nd ed. Rome: S. Consorti, 1909.

Cozzi, Gaetano. "Cultura, politica e religione nella 'Pubblica Storiografia' Veneziana del Cinquecento." *Bollettino dell'Istituto di Storia della Società e dello Stato Veneziano* 5-6 (1963-64): 215-94.

Cummings, Anthony M. *The Politicized Muse: Music for Medici Festivals, 1512-1537*. Princeton: Princeton University Press, 1992.

D'Amico, John F. *Renaissance Humanism in Papal Rome: Humanists and Churchmen on the Eve of the Reformation*. Baltimore: Johns Hopkins University Press, 1983.

——. *Roman and German Humanism, 1450-1550*. Ed. Paul F. Grendler. Aldershot: Variorum, 1993.

D'Ascia, Luca. *Erasmo e l'Umanesimo romano*. Florence: Olschki, 1991.

De Caprio, Vincenzo. "L'area umanistica romana (1513-1527)." *Studi romani* 29 (1981): 321-35.

——. "I cenacoli umanistici." In *Letteratura italiana*. Vol. 1: *Il letterato e le istituzioni*. Ed. Alberto Asor Rosa. Turin: Einaudi, 1982. 799-822.

——. "'Hor qui mi fa mestier lingua di ferro.' Note sull'immaginario poetico." In: *Il Sacco di Roma del 1527 e l'immaginario collettivo*. Ed. Alberto Asor Rosa et al. Rome: Istituto Nazionale di Studi Romani, 1986. 19-41.

——. "Intellettuali e mercato del lavoro nella Roma medicea." *Studi romani* 29 (1981): 26-46.

——. *La tradizione e il trauma. Idee del Rinascimento romano*. Manziana: Vecchiarelli, 1991.

De Nolhac, Pierre. *La bibliothèque de Fulvio Orsini: contributions à l'histoire des collections d'Italie et à l'étude de la Renaissance*. Paris: Vieweg, 1887.

——. *Les correspondants d'Alde Manuce*. [Extract from *Studi e documenti di storia e diritto* 8 (1887): 247-99; and 9 (1888): 203-48.] Turin: Bottega d'Erasmo, 1967.

Debenedetti, Santorre. "Le ansie d'un bibliofilo durante il Sacco di Roma." In: *Mélanges offerts à M. Émile Picot*. Paris: Librairie Damascène Morgand, 1913. 1:511-14.

Delph, Ronald K. "From Venetian Visitor to Curial Humanist: The Development of Agostino Steuco's 'Counter'-Reformation Thought." *Renaissance Quarterly* 47 (1994): 102-139.

——. "Polishing the Papal Image in the Counter-Reformation: The Case of Agostino Steuco." *Sixteenth Century Journal* 23 (1992): 35-47.

——. "Valla Grammaticus, Agostino Steuco, and the Donation of Constantine." *Journal of the History of Ideas* 57 (1996): 55-77.

Delumeau, Jean. *Vie économique et sociale de Rome dans la seconde moitié du XVIe siècle*. 2 vols. Paris: Boccard, 1957-59.

Desmarais, Regnier. "Dissertation Sur le Traité de Cicéron de Gloria et sur Alcyonius." In: *Les Deux Livres de la Divination de Cicéron....* Trans. *idem*. New ed. Paris: Barbou, "L'an III. de la République Française." 467-80.

Dorez, Léon, ed. "Le sac de Rome (1527). Relation inédite de Jean Cave, Orléanais." *Mélanges d'archéologie et d'histoire de l'Ecole Française de Rome* 16 (1896): 355-419.

Douglas, Richard M. *Jacopo Sadoleto, 1477-1547: Humanist and Reformer.* Cambridge, Mass.: Harvard University Press, 1959.

Durling, Robert M. "The Ascent of Mt. Ventoux and the Crisis of Allegory." *Italian Quarterly* 18:69 (1974): 7-28.

———. "Petrarch's 'Giovene donna sotto un verde Lauro.'" *MLN* 86 (1971): 1-20.

Erickson, Milton H. "The Confusion Technique in Hypnosis." *American Journal of Clinical Hypnosis* 6 (1964): 183-207.

Erikson, Kai T. *In the Wake of the Flood.* London: Allen and Unwin, 1979.

———. "Loss of Communality at Buffalo Creek." *American Journal of Psychiatry* 133 (1976): 302-304.

Ferguson, Wallace K. *The Renaissance in Historical Thought: Five Centuries of Interpretation.* New York: Houghton Mifflin, 1948.

Festinger, Leon, Henry W. Riecken, and Stanley Schachter. *When Prophecy Fails.* Minneapolis: University of Minnesota Press, 1956.

Field, Arthur. *The Origins of the Platonic Academy of Florence.* Princeton: Princeton University Press, 1988.

Findlen, Paula. "Humanism, Politics and Pornography in Renaissance Italy." In: *The Invention of Pornography: Obscenity and the Origins of Modernity, 1500-1800.* Ed. Lynn Hunt. New York: Zone, 1993. 49-108, 345-58.

———. *Possessing Nature: Museums, Collecting and Scientific Culture in Early Modern Italy.* Berkeley and Los Angeles: University of California Press, 1994.

Firpo, Massimo. *Il Sacco di Roma del 1527. Tra profezia, propaganda politica e riforma religiosa.* Cagliari: CUEC, 1990.

Fish, Stanley. *Is there a Text in this Class?: The Authority of Interpretive Communities.* Cambridge, Mass.: Harvard University Press, 1980.

Floriani, Piero. "La 'questione della lingua' e il Dialogo di P. Valeriano." *Giornale storico della letteratura italiana* 155 (1978): 321-45.

Franklin, David. *Rosso in Italy: The Italian Career of Rosso Fiorentino.* New Haven and London: Yale University Press, 1994.

Freccero, John. "The Fig Tree and the Laurel: Petrarch's Poetics." *Diacritics* 5 (1975): 34-40.

Frenz, Thomas. *Die Kanzlei der Päpste der Hochrenaissance (1471-1527).* Tübingen: Max Niemeyer, 1986.

Frommel, Christoph Luitpold. *Der Römische Palastbau der Hochrenaissance.* 3 vols. Tübingen: Wasmuth, 1973.

Gaisser, Julia Haig. "The Catullan Lectures of Pierius Valerianus." In: *Acta Conventus Neo-Latini Guelpherbytani.* Ed. Stella P. Revard et al. Binghamton: Medieval & Renaissance Texts & Studies, 1988. 45-53.

———. "Pierius Valerianus." In *eadem*, "Catullus." In *Catalogus Translationum et Commentariorum, Medieval and Renaissance Latin Translations and Commentaries.* Vol. 7. Ed. Virginia Brown. Washington, D.C.: Catholic University of America Press, 1992. 255-59.

———. *Catullus and his Renaissance Readers.* Oxford: Clarendon Press, 1993.

———. "The Rise and Fall of Goritz's Feasts." *Renaissance Quarterly* 48 (1995): 41-57.

Garin, Eugenio. *Italian Humanism: Philosophy and the Civic Life in the Renaissance.* Trans. Peter Munz. New York: Harper, 1965.

Giehlow, Karl. "Die Hieroglyphenkunde des Humanismus in der Allegorie der Renaissance." *Jahrbuch der Kunsthistorischen Sammlungen des Allerhöchsten Kaiserhauses* 32 (1915): 1-232.

Gilbert, Felix. *Machiavelli and Guicciardini: Politics and History in Sixteenth-Century Florence.* Princeton: Princeton University Press, 1965.

———. *The Pope, His Banker, and Venice.* Cambridge, Mass.: Harvard University Press, 1980.

Giustiniani, Vito R. "Homo, Humanus, and the Meanings of 'Humanism.'" *Journal of the History of Ideas* 46 (1985): 167-95.

Gleason, Elisabeth G. *Gasparo Contarini: Venice, Rome, and Reform*. Berkeley and Los
Angeles: University of California Press, 1993.
—. "Who Was the First Counter-Reformation Pope?," *Catholic Historical Review* 81
(1995): 173-84.
Gnoli, Domenico. "Un giudizio di Lesa Romanità sotto Leone X." *Nuova antologia*
115 (1891): 251-76, 691-716; and 116 (1891): 34-63.
—. *La Roma di Leon X*. Ed. Aldo Gnoli. Milan: Hoepli, 1938.
Gouwens, Kenneth. "Ciceronianism and Collective Identity: Defining the Bounda-
ries of the Roman Academy, 1525." *The Journal of Medieval and Renaissance Studies*
23 (1992-93): 173-95.
—. "Discourses of Vulnerability: Pietro Alcionio's Orations on the Sack of Rome,"
Renaissance Quarterly 50 (1997): 38-77.
—. "Life–Writing and the Theme of Cultural Decline in Valeriano's *De litteratorum
infelicitate*," *The Sixteenth Century Journal* 27 (1996): 87-96.
Grafton, Anthony. *Defenders of the Text: The Traditions of Scholarship in an Age of Science,
1450-1800*. Cambridge, Mass.: Harvard University Press, 1991.
Grafton, Anthony, ed. *Rome Reborn: The Vatican Library and Renaissance Culture*. New
Haven: Yale University Press, 1993.
Gray, Hanna H. "Renaissance Humanism: The Pursuit of Eloquence." *Journal of the
History of Ideas* 24 (1963): 497-514.
Gregorovius, Ferdinand. *History of the City of Rome in the Middle Ages*. Trans. Annie
Hamilton. 8 vols. in 13. London: Bell, 1894-1902.
Grendler, Paul F. *Schooling in Renaissance Italy: Literacy and Learning, 1300-1600*. Balti-
more and London: Johns Hopkins University Press, 1989.
Guillén, Claudio. "Notes toward the Study of the Renaissance Letter." In: *Renais-
sance Genres: Essays on Theory, History, and Interpretation*. Ed. Barbara Kiefer Lewalski.
Cambridge, Mass.: Harvard University Press, 1986. 70-101.
Hallman, Barbara McClung. *Italian Cardinals, Reform, and the Church as Property*.
Berkeley and Los Angeles: University of California Press, 1985.
Hankins, James. *Plato in the Italian Renaissance*. 2 vols. Leiden: E. J. Brill, 1990.
Hay, Denys. *The Church in Italy in the Fifteenth Century*. Cambridge: Cambridge Univer-
sity Press, 1977.
Hill, Christopher. *The Experience of Defeat: Milton and Some Contemporaries*. Harmonds-
worth: Penguin, 1984.
Hirst, Michael. *Sebastiano del Piombo*. Oxford: Clarendon, 1981.
Hook, Judith. "Clement VII, the Colonna and Charles V: A study of the political
instability of Italy in the second and third decades of the sixteenth century." *Euro-
pean Studies Review* 2 (1972): 281-99.
——. "The Destruction of the New 'Italia': Venice and the Papacy in Collision."
Italian Studies 28 (1973): 10-30.
——. "Habsburg Imperialism and Italian Particularism: The Case of Charles V and
Siena." *European Studies Review* 9 (1979): 283-312.
——. *The Sack of Rome, 1527*. London: Macmillan, 1972.
Jacks, Philip. *The Antiquarian and the Myth of Antiquity: The Origins of Rome in Renaissance
Thought* (Cambridge: Cambridge University Press, 1993.
——. "The *Simulachrum* of Fabio Calvo: A View of Roman Architecture all'*antica* in
1527." *Art Bulletin* 72 (1990): 453-81.
Jacobs, Frederika Herman. "Studies in the Patronage and Iconography of Pope Paul
III (1534-1549)." Ph.D. diss., University of Virginia, 1979.
Jardine, Lisa. *Erasmus, Man of Letters: The Construction of Charisma in Print*. Princeton:
Princeton University Press, 1993.
Jedin, Hubert. "Giovanni Gozzadini, ein Konziliarist am Hofe Julius II." *Römische
Quartalschrift* 47 (1939): 193-267.
King, Margaret L. *Venetian Humanism in an Age of Patrician Dominance*. Princeton:
Princeton University Press, 1986.

Kristeller, Paul Oskar. *Iter Italicum: A Finding List of Uncatalogued or Incompletely Catalogued Humanistic Manuscripts of the Renaissance in Italian and Other Libraries.* 6 vols. to date. Leiden: E. J. Brill, 1963.

——. *Renaissance Thought: The Classic, Scholastic, and Humanist Strains.* New York: Harper, 1961.

Kuhn, Thomas. *The Structure of Scientific Revolutions.* 2nd ed. Chicago: University of Chicago Press, 1970.

Lancellotti, G. F. *Poesie italiane e latini di mons. A. Colocci.* Jesi, 1772.

Le Clerc, Jean. *Bibliotheque Choisie, Pour Servir de Suite a la Bibliotheque Universelle.* Amsterdam: Henri Schelte, 1707 or 1708.

Lettere, V. "Giovanni Pietro dalle Fosse." *DBI* 32 (1986): 84-88.

Levine, Lawrence W. *Highbrow/Lowbrow: The Emergence of Cultural Hierarchy in America.* Cambridge, Mass.: Harvard University Press, 1988.

Lifton, Robert J. *Death in Life: Survivors of Hiroshima.* New York: Basic, 1967.

Lind, L. R. *Studies in Pre-Vesalian Anatomy: Biography, Translations, Documents.* Philadelphia: The American Philosophical Society, 1975.

Loftus, Elizabeth. *The Myth of Repressed Memory: False Memories and Allegations of Sexual Abuse.* New York: St. Martin's, 1994.

Losada, Angel. *Juan Gines de Sepulveda: A Traves de su "Epistolario" y Nuevos Documentos.* Madrid: Instituto de Derecho Internacional "Francisco de Vitoria," 1973.

Lowry, M.J.C. "The 'New Academy' of Aldus Manutius: A Renaissance Dream." *Bulletin of the John Rylands University Library of Manchester* 58 (1975/76): 378-420.

——. *The World of Aldus Manutius: Business and Scholarship in Renaissance Venice.* Ithaca: Cornell University, 1979.

Lucchetta, Giuliano. "Contributi per una biografia di Pierio Valeriano." *Italia medioevale e umanistica* 9 (1966): 461-76.

MacDougall, Elisabeth B. "The Sleeping Nymph: Origins of a Humanist Fountain Type." *Art Bulletin* 57 (1975): 357-65.

Maragoni, Gian Piero. *Sadoleto e il Laocoonte: Di un modo di descrivere l'arte.* Parma: Zara, 1986.

Marsh, David. *The Quattrocento Dialogue: Classical Tradition and Humanist Innovation.* Cambridge, Mass.: Harvard University Press, 1980.

Martines, Lauro. *The Social World of the Florentine Humanists, 1390-1460.* Princeton: Princeton University Press, 1963.

Mayer, Thomas F., and D. R. Woolf, eds. *The Rhetorics of Life-Writing in Early Modern Europe: Forms of Biography from Cassandra Fedele to Louis XIV.* Ann Arbor: University of Michigan Press, 1995.

Mazzuchelli, G.M. *Gli scrittori d'Italia I, i.* Brescia, 1753.

McGinness, Frederick J. *Right Thinking and Sacred Oratory in Counter-Reformation Rome.* Princeton: Princeton University Press, 1995.

McManamon, John M., S.J. *Funeral Oratory and the Cultural Ideals of Italian Humanism.* Chapel Hill: University of North Carolina Press, 1989.

——. "The Ideal Renaissance Pope: Funeral Oratory from the Papal Court." *Archivum Historiae Pontificiae* 14 (1976): 9-70.

Minnich, Nelson H., S.J. "Concepts of Reform Proposed at the Fifth Lateran Council." *Archivum historiae pontificiae* 7 (1969): 163-251.

Mitchell, Bonner. *Rome in the High Renaissance: The Age of Leo X.* Norman: University of Oklahoma Press, 1973.

Mitchell, R.J. *The Laurels and the Tiara: Pope Pius II, 1405-1464.* Garden City: Doubleday, 1962.

Mommsen, Theodor E. "Petrarch's Conception of the 'Dark Ages.'" *Speculum* 17 (1942): 226-42.

Monaco, Michele. *La situazione della reverenda Camera Apostolica nell'anno 1525.* Rome, Biblioteca d'arte editrice, 1960.

Najemy, John M. *Between Friends: Discourses of Power and Desire in the Machiavelli-Vettori Letters of 1513-1515*. Princeton: Princeton University Press, 1993.

Neisser, Ulric, and Robyn Fivush, Eds. *The Remembering Self: Construction and Accuracy in the Self-Narrative*. Cambridge: Cambridge University Press, 1994.

Niccoli, Ottavia. *Prophecy and People in Renaissance Italy*. Trans. Lydia G. Cochrane. Princeton: Princeton University Press, 1990.

Niceron, Jean Pierre. *Mémoires pour servir à l'histoire des hommes illustres dans la République des lettres avec un catalogue raisonné de leurs ouvrages*. Paris: Briasson, 1729-45.

Novick, Peter. *That Noble Dream: The "Objectivity Question" and the American Historical Profession*. Cambridge: Cambridge University Press, 1988.

O'Malley, John W., S.J. *Giles of Viterbo on Church and Reform: A Study in Renaissance Thought*. Leiden: Brill, 1968.

——. *Praise and Blame in Renaissance Rome: Rhetoric, Doctrine, and Reform in the Sacred Orators of the Papal Court, c.1450-1521*. Durham: Duke University Press, 1979.

Ong, Walter, S.J. *Fighting for Life: Contest, Sexuality, and Consciousness*. Ithaca: Cornell University Press, 1981.

——. "Latin Language Study as a Renaissance Puberty Rite." In: *idem, Rhetoric, Romance, and Technology: Studies in the Interaction of Expression and Culture*. Ithaca: Cornell University Press, 1971. 113-41.

Paparelli, Gioacchino. *Enea Silvio Piccolomini: L'Umanesimo sul soglio di Pietro*. 2nd ed. Ravenna: Longo, 1978.

Partner, Peter. *The Pope's Men: The Papal Civil Service in the Renaissance*. Oxford: Clarendon Press, 1990.

——. *Renaissance Rome, 1500-1559: A Portrait of a Society*. Berkeley and Los Angeles: University of California Press, 1976.

Partridge, Loren and Randolph Starn. *A Renaissance Likeness: Art and Culture in Raphael's Julius II*. Berkeley and Los Angeles: University of California Press, 1980.

Pastor, Ludwig von. *The History of the Popes from the Close of the Middle Ages. Drawn from the Secret Archives of the Vatican and Other Original Sources*. Ed. and trans. F. I. Antrobus et al. 40 vols. Third edition. London: Kegan Paul, 1901-1933.

Pecchiai, Pio. *Roma nel Cinquecento*. Bologna: Capelli, 1948.

Petrucci, F. "Pietro Corsi." In: *DBI* 29 (1983): 579-81.

Pettinelli, Rosanna Alhaique. *Tra antico e moderno: Roma nel primo Rinascimento*. Rome: Bulzoni, 1991.

Pitts, Vincent J. *The Man Who Sacked Rome: Charles de Bourbon, Constable of France (1490-1527)*. New York: Peter Lang, 1993.

Prodi, Paolo. *Il sovrano pontefice. Un corpo e due anime: la monarchia papale nella prima età moderna*. Bologna: Mulino, 1982.

Prosperi, Adriano. *Tra evangelismo e controriforma: G. M. Giberti (1495-1543)*. Rome: Edizioni di storia e letteratura, 1969.

Rabil, Albert, Jr., ed. *Renaissance Humanism: Foundations, Forms, and Legacy*. 3 vols. Philadelphia: University of Pennsylvania Press, 1988.

Raphael, Beverley. *When Disaster Strikes: How Individuals and Communities Cope with Catastrophe*. New York: Basic, 1986.

Reeves, Marjorie, ed. *Prophetic Rome in the High Renaissance Period*. Oxford: Clarendon Press, 1992.

Reiss, Sheryl E. "Cardinal Giulio de' Medici as a Patron of Art, 1513-1523." 3 vols. Ph.D. diss., Princeton University, 1992.

Renazzi, Filippo Maria. *Storia dell' Università degli Studi di Roma*. 4 vols. Rome: Pagliarini, 1803-06.

Reynolds, Anne. "Cardinal Oliviero Carafa and the Early Cinquecento Tradition of the Feast of Pasquino." *Roma Humanistica: Journal of Neo-Latin Studies* 34A (1985): 178-208.

——. "The Classical Continuum in Roman Humanism: The Festival of Pasquino, the *Robigalia*, and Satire." *Bibliothèque d'Humanisme et Renaissance* 49 (1987): 289-307.

———. *Renaissance Humanism at the Court of Clement VII. Francesco Berni's* Dialogue Against Poets *in Context. Studies, with an edition and translation by Anne Reynolds.* New York and London: Garland, 1997.

Rill, G., and G. Scichilone. "Burgio, Giovanni Antonio Buglio barone di." *DBI* 15 (1972): 413-17.

Robin, Diana. *Filelfo in Milan: Writings, 1451-1477.* Princeton: Princeton University Press, 1991.

Rocke, Michael. *Forbidden Friendships: Homosexuality and Male Culture in Renaissance Florence.* Oxford: Oxford University Press, 1996.

Romei, Danilo. "*Pas vobis, brigate:* una frottola ritrovata di Pietro Aretino." *Rassegna della letteratura italiana* 90 (1986): 429-73.

Rosa, Mario. "Pietro Alcionio." In: *DBI* 2 (1960): 77-80.

Roscoe, William. *The Life and Pontificate of Leo the Tenth.* Seventh ed. Rev. by Thomas Roscoe. 2 vols. London: Bell, 1878.

Ross, James Bruce. "Venetian Schools and Teachers, Fourteenth to Early Sixteenth Century: A Survey and a Study of Giovanni Battista Egnazio." *Renaissance Quarterly* 29 (1976): 521-66.

Roth, Cecil. *The Last Florentine Republic.* London: Methuen, 1925.

Rowland, Ingrid D. "Abacus and Humanism." *Renaissance Quarterly* 48 (1995): 695-727.

———. "Raphael, Angelo Colocci, and the Genesis of the Architectural Orders." *Art Bulletin* 76 (1994): 81-104.

———. "'Render unto Caesar the Things Which are Caesar's': Humanism and the Arts in the Patronage of Agostino Chigi." *Renaissance Quarterly* 39 (1986): 673-730.

———. "Some Panegyrics to Agostino Chigi." *Journal of the Warburg and Courtauld Institutes* 47 (1984): 194-99.

———. "A Summer Outing in 1510: Religion and Economics in the Papal War with Ferrara." *Viator* 18 (1987): 347-59.

Samuels, Richard S. "Benedetto Varchi, the *Accademia degli Infiammati,* and the Origins of the Italian Academic Movement." *Renaissance Quarterly* 29 (1976): 599-634.

Savarese, Gennaro. *La cultura a Roma tra Umanesimo ed Ermetismo (1480-1540).* Rome: De Rubeis, 1993.

Schevill, Ferdinand. *Medieval and Renaissance Florence.* 2 vols. First edition published in 1936. New York: Harper, 1963.

Seidel Menchi, Silvana. "Alcuni attegiamenti della cultura italiana di fronte a Erasmo (1520-1536). In: *Eresia e riforma nell'Italia del Cinquecento. Miscellanea I.* Ed. Luigi Firpo and Giorgio Spini. Florence: Sansoni, 1974. 71-133.

———. *Erasmo in Italia, 1520-1580.* Turin: Bollati Boringhieri, 1987.

Seigel, Jerrold E. "'Civic Humanism' or Ciceronian Rhetoric? The Culture of Petrarch and Bruni." *Past and Present* 34 (1966): 3-48.

———. *Rhetoric and Philosophy in Renaissance Humanism: The Union of Eloquence and Wisdom, Petrach to Valla.* Princeton: Princeton University Press, 1968.

Shapin, Steven. *A Social History of Truth: Civility and Science in Seventeenth-Century England.* Chicago: University of Chicago Press, 1994.

Shaw, Christine. *Julius II: The Warrior Pope.* Oxford: Blackwell, 1993.

Shearman, John. "The Vatican Stanze: Functions and Decoration." In: George Holmes, ed. *Art and Politics in Renaissance Italy: British Academy Lectures.* Oxford: The British Academy, 1993. 185-240.

Simar, Théophile. *Christophe de Longueil, humaniste (1488-1522).* Louvain: Peeters, 1911.

Spiegel, David. "Hypnosis in the Treatment of Victims of Sexual Abuse." *Psychiatric Clinics of North America* 12 (1989): 295-305.

Spiegel, David, Thurman Hunt, and Harvey E. Dondershine. "Dissociation and Hypnotizability in Posttraumatic Stress Disorder." *American Journal of Psychiatry* 145 (1988): 301-305.

Starn, Randolph. *Contrary Commonwealth: The Theme of Exile in Medieval and Renaissance Italy.* Berkeley and Los Angeles: University of California, 1982.

——. "Historians and 'Crisis.'" *Past and Present* 52 (1971): 3-22.

——. "Who's Afraid of the Renaissance?" In: *The Past and Future of Medieval Studies.* Ed. John Van Engen. Notre Dame: University of Notre Dame Press, 1994. 129-147.

Stephens, J. N. *The Fall of the Florentine Republic, 1512-1530.* Oxford: Clarendon, 1983.

Stinger, Charles L. *The Renaissance in Rome.* Bloomington: Indiana University Press, 1985.

Tafuri, Manfredo. "*Roma coda mundi.* Il Sacco del 1527: fratture e continuità." *Ricerca del Rinascimento. Principi, città, architetti.* Turin: Einaudi, 1992. 223-53.

Tervarent, Guy de. "Un Humaniste: Piero Valeriano." *Journal des Savants* (July-Sept., 1967): 162-71.

Terr, Lenore. *Unchained Memories: True Stories of Traumatic Memories, Lost and Found.* New York: Basic, 1994.

Ticozzi, Stefano. *Storia dei letterati e degli artisti del dipartimento della Piave.* 2 vols., Belluno: F.A. Tissi, 1813.

Tiraboschi, Girolamo. *Storia della letteratura italiana.* 8 vols. in 12. Milan: Società Tipografica de' Classici Italiani, 1822-26.

Toulmin, Stephen. *Cosmopolis: The Hidden Agenda of Modernity.* Chicago: University of Chicago Press, 1990.

——. *Human Understanding.* Vol. 1. Princeton: Princeton University Press, 1972.

Trinkaus, Charles. *Adversity's Noblemen: The Italian Humanists on Happiness.* Reprint of 1940 edition with additional material. New York: Octagon, 1965.

——. "*In Our Image and Likeness: Humanity and Divinity in Italian Humanist Thought.*" 2 vols. Chicago and London: University of Chicago Press, 1970.

——. *The Poet as Philosopher: Petrarch and the Formation of Renaissance Consciousness.* New Haven: Yale University Press, 1979.

Tucker, G. Hugo. "Exile Exiled: Petrus Alcyonius (1487-1527?) in a Travelling-Chest." *Journal of the Institute of Romance Studies* 2 (1993): 83-103.

Ubaldini, Federico. *Vita di Mons. Angelo Colocci: Edizione del testo originale italiano (Barb. Lat. 4882).* Ed. Vittorio Fanelli. Vatican City: Studi e testi, 1969.

Valentini, Roberto. "Erasmo di Rotterdam e Pietro Corsi: a proposito di una polemica fraintesa." *Rendiconti della Reale Accademia Nazionale dei Lincei.* Classe di scienze morali, storiche e filologiche. Ser. 6. Vol. 12 (1936): 896-922.

Varillas, [Antoine]. *Les anecdotes de Florence, ou L'histoire secrete de la maison de Medicis.* La Haye: A. Leers, 1687.

Waley, Daniel. *The Papal State in the Thirteenth Century.* London: MacMillan, 1961.

Watzlawick, Paul. *How Real is Real? Confusion, Disinformation, Communication.* New York: Random, 1976.

Wind, Edgar. *Pagan Mysteries in the Renaissance.* Rev. ed. New York: Norton, 1968.

Witt, Ronald G. Medieval *Ars Dictaminis* and the Beginnings of Humanism: A New Construction of the Problem." *Renaissance Quarterly* 35 (1982): 1-35.

Yates, Frances A. *Astraea: The Imperial Theme in the Sixteenth Century.* London: Routledge & Kegan Paul, 1975.

[Zeno, A.] "Articolo I." *Giornale de' letterati d'Italia* 1:3. Venice: G. G. Hertz, 1710: 1-42.

Zimmermann, T. C. Price. *Paolo Giovio: The Historian and the Crisis of Sixteenth-Century Italy.* Princeton: Princeton University Press, 1995.

INDEX

BRILL'S STUDIES
IN
INTELLECTUAL HISTORY

1. POPKIN, R.H. *Isaac la Peyrère (1596-1676).* His Life, Work and Influence. 1987. ISBN 90 04 08157 7
2. THOMSON, A. *Barbary and Enlightenment.* European Attitudes towards the Maghreb in the 18th Century. 1987. ISBN 90 04 08273 5
3. DUHEM, P. *Prémices Philosophiques.* With an Introduction in English by S.L. Jaki. 1987. ISBN 90 04 08117 8
4. OUDEMANS, TH.C.W. & A.P.M.H. LARDINOIS. *Tragic Ambiguity.* Anthropology, Philosophy and Sophocles' *Antigone.* 1987. ISBN 90 04 08417 7
5. FRIEDMAN, J.B. (ed.). *John de Foxton's Liber Cosmographiae (1408).* An Edition and Codicological Study. 1988. ISBN 90 04 08528 9
6. AKKERMAN, F. & A. J. VANDERJAGT (eds.). *Rodolphus Agricola Phrisius, 1444-1485.* Proceedings of the International Conference at the University of Groningen, 28-30 October 1985. 1988. ISBN 90 04 08599 8
7. CRAIG, W.L. *The Problem of Divine Foreknowledge and Future Contingents from Aristotle to Suarez.* 1988. ISBN 90 04 08516 5
8. STROLL, M. *The Jewish Pope.* Ideology and Politics in the Papal Schism of 1130. 1987. ISBN 90 04 08590 4
9. STANESCO, M. *Jeux d'errance du chevalier médiéval.* Aspects ludiques de la fonction guerrière dans la littérature du Moyen Age flamboyant. 1988. ISBN 90 04 08684 6
10. KATZ, D. *Sabbath and Sectarianism in Seventeenth-Century England.* 1988. ISBN 90 04 08754 0
11. LERMOND, L. *The Form of Man.* Human Essence in Spinoza's *Ethic.* 1988. ISBN 90 04 08829 6
12. JONG, M. DE. *In Samuel's Image.* Child Oblation in the Early Medieval West. 1996. ISBN 90 04 10483 6
13. PYENSON, L. *Empire of Reason.* Exact Sciences in Indonesia, 1840-1940. 1989. ISBN 90 04 08984 5
14. CURLEY, E. & P.-F. MOREAU (eds.). *Spinoza. Issues and Directions.* The Proceedings of the Chicago Spinoza Conference. 1990. ISBN 90 04 09334 6
15. KAPLAN, Y., H. MÉCHOULAN & R.H. POPKIN (eds.). *Menasseh Ben Israel and His World.* 1989. ISBN 90 04 09114 9
16. BOS, A.P. *Cosmic and Meta-Cosmic Theology in Aristotle's Lost Dialogues.* 1989. ISBN 90 04 09155 6
17. KATZ, D.S. & J.I. ISRAEL (eds.). *Sceptics, Millenarians and Jews.* 1990. ISBN 90 04 09160 2
18. DALES, R.C. *Medieval Discussions of the Eternity of the World.* 1990. ISBN 90 04 09215 3
19. CRAIG, W.L. *Divine Foreknowledge and Human Freedom.* The Coherence of Theism: Omniscience. 1991. ISBN 90 04 09250 1
20. OTTEN, W. *The Anthropology of Johannes Scottus Eriugena.* 1991. ISBN 90 04 09302 8
21. ÅKERMAN, S. *Queen Christina of Sweden and Her Circle.* The Transformation of a Seventeenth-Century Philosophical Libertine. 1991. ISBN 90 04 09310 9
22. POPKIN, R.H. *The Third Force in Seventeenth-Century Thought.* 1992. ISBN 90 04 09324 9
23. DALES, R.C & O. ARGERAMI (eds.). *Medieval Latin Texts on the Eternity of the World.* 1990. ISBN 90 04 09376 1
24. STROLL, M. *Symbols as Power.* The Papacy Following the Investiture Contest. 1991. ISBN 90 04 09374 5
25. FARAGO, C.J. *Leonardo da Vinci's 'Paragone'.* A Critical Interpretation with a New Edition of the Text in the *Codex Urbinas.* 1992. ISBN 90 04 09415 6

26. JONES, R. *Learning Arabic in Renaissance Europe*. Forthcoming. ISBN 90 04 09451 2
27. DRIJVERS, J.W. *Helena Augusta*. The Mother of Constantine the Great and the Legend of Her Finding of the True Cross. 1992. ISBN 90 04 09435 0
28. BOUCHER, W.I. *Spinoza in English*. A Bibliography from the Seventeenth-Century to the Present. 1991. ISBN 90 04 09499 7
29. McINTOSH, C. *The Rose Cross and the Age of Reason*. Eighteenth-Century Rosicrucianism in Central Europe and its Relationship to the Enlightenment. 1992. ISBN 90 04 09502 0
30. CRAVEN, K. *Jonathan Swift and the Millennium of Madness*. The Information Age in Swift's *A Tale of a Tub*. 1992. ISBN 90 04 09524 1
31. BERKVENS-STEVELINCK, C., H. BOTS, P.G. HOFTIJZER & O.S. LANKHORST (eds.). *Le Magasin de l'Univers*. *The Dutch Republic as the Centre of the European Book Trade*. Papers Presented at the International Colloquium, held at Wassenaar, 5-7 July 1990. 1992. ISBN 90 04 09493 8
32. GRIFFIN, JR., M.I.J. *Latitudinarianism in the Seventeenth-Century Church of England*. Annotated by R.H. Popkin. Edited by L. Freedman. 1992. ISBN 90 04 09653 1
33. WES, M.A. *Classics in Russia 1700-1855*. Between two Bronze Horsemen. 1992. ISBN 90 04 09664 7
34. BULHOF, I.N. *The Language of Science*. A Study in the Relationship between Literature and Science in the Perspective of a Hermeneutical Ontology. With a Case Study in Darwin's *The Origin of Species*. 1992. ISBN 90 04 09644 2
35. LAURSEN, J.C. *The Politics of Skepticism in the Ancients, Montaigne, Hume and Kant*. 1992. ISBN 90 04 09459 8
36. COHEN, E. *The Crossroads of Justice*. Law and Culture in Late Medieval France. 1993. ISBN 90 04 09569 1
37. POPKIN, R.H. & A.J. VANDERJAGT (eds.). *Scepticism and Irreligion in the Seventeenth and Eighteenth Centuries*. 1993. ISBN 90 04 09596 9
38. MAZZOCCO, A. *Linguistic Theories in Dante and the Humanists*. Studies of Language and Intellectual History in Late Medieval and Early Renaissance Italy. 1993. ISBN 90 04 09702 3
39. KROOK, D. *John Sergeant and His Circle*. A Study of Three Seventeenth-Century English Aristotelians. Edited with an Introduction by B.C. Southgate. 1993. ISBN 90 04 09756 2
40. AKKERMAN, F., G.C. HUISMAN & A.J. VANDERJAGT (eds.). *Wessel Gansfort (1419-1489) and Northern Humanism*. 1993. ISBN 90 04 09857 7
41. COLISH, M.L. *Peter Lombard*. 2 volumes. 1994. ISBN 90 04 09859 3 (Vol. 1), ISBN 90 04 09860 7 (Vol. 2), ISBN 90 04 09861 5 (Set)
42. VAN STRIEN, C.D. *British Travellers in Holland During the Stuart Period*. Edward Browne and John Locke as Tourists in the United Provinces. 1993. ISBN 90 04 09482 2
43. MACK, P. *Renaissance Argument*. Valla and Agricola in the Traditions of Rhetoric and Dialectic. 1993. ISBN 90 04 09879 8
44. DA COSTA, U. *Examination of Pharisaic Traditions*. Supplemented by SEMUEL DA SILVA'S *Treatise on the Immortality of the Soul*. Tratado da immortalidade da alma. Translation, Notes and Introduction by H.P. Salomon & I.S.D. Sassoon. 1993. ISBN 90 04 09923 9
45. MANNS, J.W. *Reid and His French Disciples*. Aesthetics and Metaphysics. 1994. ISBN 90 04 09942 5
46. SPRUNGER, K.L. *Trumpets from the Tower*. English Puritan Printing in the Netherlands, 1600-1640. 1994. ISBN 90 04 09935 2
47. RUSSELL, G.A. (ed.). *The 'Arabick' Interest of the Natural Philosophers in Seventeenth-Century England*. 1994. ISBN 90 04 09888 7
48. SPRUIT, L. Species intelligibilis: *From Perception to Knowledge*. Volume I: Classical Roots and Medieval Discussions. 1994. ISBN 90 04 09883 6
49. SPRUIT, L. Species intelligibilis: *From Perception to Knowledge*. Volume II: Renaissance Controversies, Later Scholasticism, and the Elimination of the Intelligible Species in Modern Philosophy. 1995. ISBN 90 04 10396 1
50. HYATTE, R. *The Arts of Friendship*. The Idealization of Friendship in Medieval and Early Renaissance Literature. 1994. ISBN 90 04 10018 0
51. CARRÉ, J. (ed.). *The Crisis of Courtesy*. Studies in the Conduct-Book in Britain, 1600-1900. 1994. ISBN 90 04 10005 9

52. BURMAN, T.E. *Religious Polemic and the Intellectual History of the Mozarabs, 1050-1200.* 1994. ISBN 90 04 09910 7
53. HORLICK, A.S. *Patricians, Professors, and Public Schools.* The Origins of Modern Educational Thought in America. 1994. ISBN 90 04 10054 7
54. MacDONALD, A.A., M. LYNCH & I.B. COWAN (eds.). *The Renaissance in Scotland.* Studies in Literature, Religion, History and Culture Offered to John Durkan. 1994. ISBN 90 04 10097 0
55. VON MARTELS, Z. (ed.). *Travel Fact and Travel Fiction.* Studies on Fiction, Literary Tradition, Scholarly Discovery and Observation in Travel Writing. 1994. ISBN 90 04 10112 8
56. PRANGER, M.B. *Bernard of Clairvaux and the Shape of Monastic Thought.* Broken Dreams. 1994. ISBN 90 04 10055 5
57. VAN DEUSEN, N. *Theology and Music at the Early University.* The Case of Robert Grosseteste and Anonymous IV. 1994. ISBN 90 04 10059 8
58. WARNEKE, S. *Images of the Educational Traveller in Early Modern England.* 1994. ISBN 90 04 10126 8
59. BIETENHOLZ, P.G. *Historia and Fabula.* Myths and Legends in Historical Thought from Antiquity to the Modern Age. 1994. ISBN 90 04 10063 6
60. LAURSEN, J.C. (ed.). *New Essays on the Political Thought of the Huguenots of the Refuge.* 1995. ISBN 90 04 09986 7
61. DRIJVERS, J.W. & A.A. MacDONALD (eds.). *Centres of Learning.* Learning and Location in Pre-Modern Europe and the Near East. 1995. ISBN 90 04 10193 4
62. JAUMANN, H. *Critica.* Untersuchungen zur Geschichte der Literaturkritik zwischen Quintilian und Thomasius. 1995. ISBN 90 04 10276 0
63. HEYD, M. *"Be Sober and Reasonable."* The Critique of Enthusiasm in the Seventeenth and Early Eighteenth Centuries. 1995. ISBN 90 04 10118 7
64. OKENFUSS, M.J. *The Rise and Fall of Latin Humanism in Early-Modern Russia.* Pagan Authors, Ukrainians, and the Resiliency of Muscovy. 1995. ISBN 90 04 10331 7
65. DALES, R.C. *The Problem of the Rational Soul in the Thirteenth Century.* 1995. ISBN 90 04 10296 5
66. VAN RULER, J.A. *The Crisis of Causality.* Voetius and Descartes on God, Nature and Change. 1995. ISBN 90 04 10371 6
67. SHEHADI, F. *Philosophies of Music in Medieval Islam.* 1995. ISBN 90 04 10128 4
68. GROSS-DIAZ, T. *The Psalms Commentary of Gilbert of Poitiers.* From *Lectio Divina* to the Lecture Room. 1996. ISBN 90 04 10211 6
69. VAN BUNGE, W. & W. KLEVER (eds.). *Disguised and Overt Spinozism around 1700.* Papers Presented at the International Colloquium, held at Rotterdam, 5-8 October, 1994. 1996. ISBN 90 04 10307 4
70. FLORIDI, L. *Scepticism and the Foundation of Epistemology.* A Study in the Metalogical Fallacies. 1996. ISBN 90 04 10533 6
71. FOUKE, D. *The Enthusiastical Concerns of Dr. Henry More.* Religious Meaning and the Psychology of Delusion. 1997. ISBN 90 04 10600 6
72. RAMELOW, T. *Gott, Freiheit, Weltenwahl.* Der Ursprung des Begriffes der besten aller möglichen Welten in der Metaphysik der Willensfreiheit zwischen Antonio Perez S.J. (1599-1649) und G.W. Leibniz (1646-1716). 1997. ISBN 90 04 10641 3
73. STONE, H.S. *Vico's Cultural History.* The Production and Transmission of Ideas in Naples, 1685-1750. 1997. ISBN 90 04 10650 2
74. STROLL, M. *The Medieval Abbey of Farfa.* Target of Papal and Imperial Ambitions. 1997. ISBN 90 04 10704 5
75. HYATTE, R. *The Prophet of Islam in Old French:* The Romance of Muhammad *(1258) and* The Book of Muhammad's Ladder *(1264).* English Translations, With an Introduction. 1997. ISBN 90 04 10709 2
76. JESTICE, P.G. *Wayward Monks and the Religious Revolution of the Eleventh Century.* 1997. ISBN 90 04 10722 3
77. VAN DER POEL, M. *Cornelius Agrippa, The Humanist Theologian and His Declamations.* 1997. ISBN 90 04 10756 8
78. SYLLA, E. & M. McVAUGH (eds.). *Texts and Contexts in Ancient and Medieval Science.* Studies on the Occasion of John E. Murdoch's Seventieth Birthday. 1997. ISBN 90 04 10823 8

79. BINKLEY, P. (ed.). *Pre-Modern Encyclopaedic Texts.* Proceedings of the Second COMERS Congress, Groningen, 1-4 July 1996. 1997. ISBN 90 04 10830 0
80. KLAVER, J.M.I. *Geology and Religious Sentiment.* The Effect of Geological Discoveries on English Society and Literature between 1829 and 1859. 1997. ISBN 90 04 10882 3
81. INGLIS, J. *Spheres of Philosophical Inquiry and the Historiography of Medieval Philosophy.* 1998. ISBN 90 04 10843 2
82. McCALLA, A. *A Romantic Historiosophy.* The Philosophy of History of Pierre-Simon Ballanche. 1998. ISBN 90 04 10967 6
83. VEENSTRA, J.R. *Magic and Divination at the Courts of Burgundy and France.* Text and Context of Laurens Pignon's *Contre les devineurs* (1411). 1998. ISBN 90 04 10925 0
84. WESTERMAN, P.C. *The Disintegration of Natural Law Theory.* Aquinas to Finnis. 1998. ISBN 90 04 10999 4
85. GOUWENS, K. *Remembering the Renaissance.* Humanist Narratives of the Sack of Rome. 1998. ISBN 90 04 10969 2
86. SCHOTT, H. & J. ZINGUER (Hrsg.). *Paracelsus und seine internationale Rezeption in der frühen Neuzeit.* Beiträge zur Geschichte des Paracelsismus. 1998. ISBN 90 04 10974 9